international
review of
social history

Special Issue 27

Free and Unfree Labor in Atlantic and Indian Ocean Port Cities (1700–1850)

Edited by Pepijn Brandon, Niklas Frykman, and Pernille Røge

Published by the Press Syndicate of the University of Cambridge
The Pitt Building, Trumpington Street, Cambridge, CB2 1RP
1 Liberty Plaza, Floor 20, New York, NY 10006, USA
10 Stamford Road, Oakleigh, Melbourne 3166, Australia

© Internationaal Instituut voor Sociale Geschiedenis

*A catalogue record for this book is available
from the British Library*

Library of Congress Cataloguing-in-Publication Data applied for

ISBN 9781108708562 (paperback)

Printed in the UK by Bell & Bain Ltd, Glasgow, UK.

CONTENTS

Free and Unfree Labor in Atlantic and Indian Ocean Port Cities (1700–1850)

Edited by
Pepijn Brandon, Niklas Frykman, and Pernille Røge

IRSH 64 (2019), pp. 1–18 doi:10.1017/S0020859018000688

Free and Unfree Labor in Atlantic and Indian Ocean Port Cities (Seventeenth–Nineteenth Centuries)

PEPIJN BRANDON*

International Institute of Social History
Cruquiusweg 31, 1019 AT Amsterdam, The Netherlands
Vrije Universiteit
De Boelelaan 1105, 1081 HV Amsterdam, The Netherlands

E-mail: pepijn.brandon@iisg.nl and p.brandon@vu.nl

NIKLAS FRYKMAN

Department of History, University of Pittsburgh
3903 Posvar Hall, Pittsburgh, PA 15260, USA

E-mail: nef13@pitt.edu

PERNILLE RØGE

Department of History, University of Pittsburgh
3901A Posvar Hall, Pittsburgh, PA 15260, USA

E-mail: per20@pitt.edu

ABSTRACT: Colonial and postcolonial port cities in the Atlantic and Indian Ocean regions functioned as crucial hubs in the commodity flows that accompanied the emergence and expansion of global capitalism. They did so by bringing together laboring populations of many different backgrounds and statuses – legally free or semi-free wage laborers, soldiers, sailors, and the self-employed, indentured servants, convicts, and slaves. Focusing on the period from the seventeenth to the mid-nineteenth centuries, a crucial moment in the establishment of the world market, the transformation of colonial states, and the reorganization of labor and labor migration on a transoceanic scale, the contributions in this special issue address the consequences of

---

* Pepijn Brandon's contribution to this Introduction, as well as his editorial work for this Special Issue, was financed under his NWO Veni project 275-53-015.

the presence of these "motley crews" on and around the docks and the neighborhoods that stretched behind them. The introduction places the articles within the
context of the development of the field of Global Labor History more generally. It
argues that the dense daily interaction that took place in port cities makes them an
ideal vantage point from which to investigate the consequences of the "simultaneity"
of different labor relations for questions such as the organization of the work process
under developing capitalism, the emergence of new forms of social control, the impact
of forced and free migration on class formation, and the role of social diversity in
shaping different forms of group and class solidarity. The introduction also discusses
the significance of the articles presented in this special issue for three prevailing but
problematic dichotomies in labor historiography: the sharp borders drawn between
so-called free and unfree labor, between the Atlantic and the Indian oceans, and
the pre-modern and modern eras.

This special issue examines the variegated combinations of workers that formed
the laboring population of colonial and postcolonial port cities in the Atlantic
and Indian Ocean world from the seventeenth to the nineteenth centuries. The
central question guiding each of the nine articles presented here is how the presence of a multiplicity of labor relations in a relatively confined geographical
area influenced the nature of work, social control, conflict, and solidarity.
Drawing on research on a large number of port cities across the Americas
and Southern Asia (see Figure 1), the articles focus on the spaces and conditions
under which legally free or semi-free wage laborers, soldiers, sailors, the self-
employed, indentured servants, convicts, and slaves met on the waterfront.
Port cities were not, of course, unique in bringing together such motley groups
of workers. For example, ships, prisons, and households historically contained,
in a single place, workers with vastly different backgrounds and statuses.[1]
However, port cities formed a specific location in the accelerating integration
of the world market – as connectors between different regions of production,
trade, and consumption, as stopping points in transcontinental labor migration,
and as strategic posts in establishing and securing colonial and postcolonial
states. They were mixed labor zones par excellence. For this reason, Peter
Linebaugh and Marcus Rediker assigned them a privileged place in their recon-
ceptualization of early modern class formation and transnational social

---

1. Ships: Emma Christopher, *Slave Ship Sailors and their Captive Cargoes, 1730–1807*
(Cambridge, 2006); Marcus Rediker, *Outlaws of the Atlantic: Sailors, Pirates, and Motley
Crews in the Age of Sail* (Boston, MA, 2014); Matthias van Rossum, "A 'Moorish World'
Within the Company: The VOC, Maritime Logistics and Subaltern Networks of Asian
Sailors", *Itinerario*, 36:3 (2012), pp. 39–60. Prisons: Christian De Vito and Alex Lichtenstein
(eds), *Global Convict Labour* (Leiden, 2015). Households: Marco H.D. van Leeuwen and
Ineke Maas, "Endogamy and Social Class in History: An Overview", *International Review of
Social History*, 50:S13 (2005), pp. 1–23, as well as other contributions in that Special Issue.

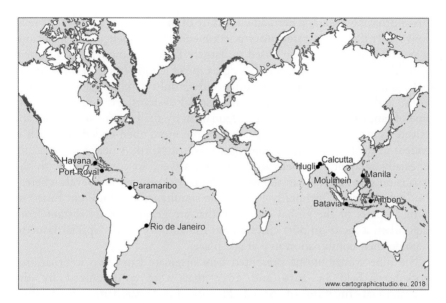

Figure 1. Port cities that are the focus of the nine contributions to this Special Issue.

struggle.[2] Likewise, ports and their associated industries have figured prominently in comparative labor histories of the nineteenth and twentieth centuries.[3]

Colonial and postcolonial port cities are the central focus of this special issue because of their ability to bring out a central theme in labor history more broadly. In her recent overview of the evolution of work in the last millennium, Andrea Komlosy argues that "the combination of labor relations at an individual point of time" is a key aspect of the long-term evolution of societies.[4] This observation is broadly shared by researchers working in the field of Global Labor History. To give just one example, the centrality of what Komlosy calls "simultaneity" forms the basis of the long-running "Global Collaboratory on the History of Labour Relations", which categorizes and quantifies the different forms of labor that coexisted in countries across the world in selected years between 1500 and today.[5] Simultaneity in

2. Peter Linebaugh and Marcus Rediker, *The Many-Headed Hydra: Slaves, Sailors, Commoners, and the Hidden History of the Revolutionary Atlantic* (Boston, MA, 2000).
3. Sam Davies *et al.* (eds), *Dock Workers: International Explorations in Comparative Labour History 1790–1970*, 2 vols (Aldershot, 2000); Raquel Varela, Hugh Murphy, and Marcel van der Linden (eds), *Shipbuilding and Ship Repair Workers Around the World: Case Studies 1950–2010* (Amsterdam, 2017), available at http://www.oapen.org/search?identifier=625526, last accessed 15 February 2019.
4. Andrea Komlosy, *Work: The Last 1,000 years* (London, 2018), p. 223.
5. Karin Hofmeester *et al.*, "The Global Collaboratory on the History of Labour Relations, 1500–2000: Background, Set-Up, Taxonomy, and Applications", working paper, 2016, available

this approach is seen as a permanent feature of the development of labor relations rather than a mere transitory phenomenon.[6] It challenges linear notions of working-class formation based on largely European models.[7] Traditional labor history tended to focus on a single type of laborer (most of the time the male, wage-earning proletarian), often did so only within a national framework, and theoretically assumed that social systems are defined by one type of labor relation (for example, feudalism by the labor of serfs, and capitalism by wage labor).[8] The influence of the more open-ended approach is evident in the recent wave of "new histories" of North American capitalism, especially in their treatment of plantation slavery in connection with the expansion of wage labor in the world's industrial centers. However, whereas the "new histories" primarily look at the simultaneity of different forms of labor in parts of the global economy that are geographically distant from each other, a focus on port cities allows the authors of this Special Issue to examine their combination in a single place.[9]

The nine contributions presented here originate from two international workshops held in 2016 and 2017 that were co-organized by the International Institute of Social History in Amsterdam, the Collège d'Études Mondiales in Paris, and the University of Pittsburgh.[10] Taking as the point of departure the interaction of multifarious groups of laborers along the quays and docks and in the bustling neighborhoods that stretched

at: http://hdl.handle.net/10622/4OGRAD; last accessed 6 November 2018. For publications arising from this project, see https://collab.iisg.nl/web/labourrelations; last accessed 9 August 2018.

6. Komlosy, "Introduction", *Work*; Marcel van der Linden, *Workers of the World: Essays Toward a Global Labor History* (Leiden and Boston, MA, 2008).

7. Marcel van der Linden and Jan Lucassen, *Prolegomena for a Global Labour History* (Amsterdam, 1999). Some important strands of historiography that started from the problem of simultaneity predated the challenge to the old paradigm mounted by Global Labor History, for example the long line of debates in Latin America on capitalist development in underdeveloped countries and the "articulation of modes of production". Other similar challenges emerged more or less in the same period. These include Dipesh Chakrabarty, *Rethinking Working-Class History: Bengal 1890–1940* (Princeton, NJ, 1989), and Linebaugh and Rediker, *Hydra*.

8. For the differences between the two approaches, see the recent exchange in this journal between Peter Ackers and Marcel van der Linden. Peter Ackers, "Workers of the World? A British Liberal-Pluralist Critique of Marcel van der Linden's Global Labour History", *International Review of Social History*, 62:2 (2017), pp. 253–269; Marcel van der Linden, "Ghostbusting or *Real* Pluralism? A Brief Response to Peter Ackers", *International Review of Social History*, 62:2 (2017), pp. 271–278.

9. Sven Beckert, *Empire of Cotton: A Global History* (New York, 2014); Jürgen Kocka and Marcel van der Linden (eds), *Capitalism: The Reemergence of a Historical Concept* (London, 2016); Sven Beckert and Christine Desan (eds), *American Capitalism: New Histories* (New York, 2018).

10. The workshops took place on 6–7 May 2016 and on 5–6 May 2017 at the University of Pittsburgh. We would like to thank all the participants, commentators, and visitors for their valuable input, as well as our fellow organizers Marcus Rediker and Françoise Vergès.

behind them, participants reflected on the following questions. How did the interaction of laborers under different labor relations affect the economy of port cities and the rise of global capitalism? How did the employment of these laborers at the same site affect the development of new forms of social control, the racialization of hierarchies, and changes in gender relations? How did the influx of large numbers of laborers of different statuses change patterns of forced and voluntary labor migration, including opportunities for desertion, marronage, and jumping ship? How did the interactions of different groups of laborers in port cities affect the development of working-class cultures, forms of solidarity, and theories and practices of resistance?

The topic, geographical demarcation, and temporal framework were chosen to challenge three prevailing but problematic dichotomies in labor historiography: the sharp borders drawn between so-called free and unfree labor, between the Atlantic and the Indian oceans, and the pre-modern and modern eras.

This introduction situates the interaction between different types of laborers in the social environment of the port city, in the different imperial and oceanic settings, and in wider systemic shifts that occurred in the eighteenth and nineteenth centuries, such as the abolition of slavery in the Americas, the strengthening of colonial states, and changes in transoceanic circuits of indentured and convict labor. In his afterword, Marcus Rediker will draw out what the contributions to this Special Issue reveal about the nature of the "motley crew" – the multi-status, multi-ethnic, and in all imaginable ways diverse working class that was thrust together to create and channel the commodity flows that made capitalism global.

PORT CITIES, LABOR, AND COMMODITY CHAINS

The integration of the Atlantic and Indian Oceans into increasingly capitalist circuits of international trade was already well underway before the period under study in this Special Issue. From the late fifteenth century, Portuguese and Spanish ships turned seas and oceans into global highways whose maritime infrastructure connected an expanding web of ports and their respective hinterlands. By the late sixteenth century, the Spanish treasure fleet and the Manila galleons had merged Atlantic, Indian, and Pacific Ocean economies into an incipient single trading system to secure for European markets the Chinese goods that American silver allowed them to procure. Other European powers further integrated existing and novel subsystems across the globe when they joined the Spanish and Portuguese in the following century, linking together over vast distances peoples, polities, economies, and ecosystems. The complex processes they unleashed transformed the world beyond recognition, tilting the global balance of power towards the Western Eurasian periphery. While global and world historians have explored these broader transformative currents from a bird's-eye view, regional specialists have long concentrated on important subsystems connected to the rise of the global economy. Whole fields have been built up around particularly the Atlantic and Indian Ocean regions, which continue to generate important research and debates.[11] The recent emphasis on the porousness of borders, imperial entanglements, and connected histories is simultaneously bringing scholars of separate ocean worlds into dialogue.[12] New multi-sited studies of labor within, beyond, and across empires complement this trend, highlighting through a combination of global, regional, and local scales the processes that structured the lives of laboring people.[13]

Port cities have rightfully come to play a prominent role in this literature. Yet, despite a flurry of important studies on everything from the peculiarities of gender and sexuality on the libertine waterfront to the unstable formation of national, imperial, and cosmopolitan identities in the maritime borderlands, the majority of work remains focused on the commodities that came from the hinterland, passed through port and onto ship, and from there were transported across the oceans and on to other destinations.[14] During the past few decades, historians have uncovered in granular detail the credit arrangements and familial, diasporic, and religious networks that made this trade possible, the legal and fiscal frameworks that supported it, and the public-private military infrastructures that protected it.[15] But while a rich

---

11. Classic meta narratives include Fernand Braudel, *Civilization and Capitalism, 15th–18th Century*, 3 vols (London, 1981–1984); Immanuel Wallerstein, *The Modern World-System*, 4 vols (Berkeley, CA, 2011). For the Indian Ocean, the classic studies include Kirti N. Chaudhuri, *Asia before Europe: Economy and Civilisation in the Indian Ocean from the Rise of Islam to 1750* (Cambridge, 1985), and Ashin Das Gupta, *The World of the Indian Ocean Merchant 1500–1800: Collected Essays* (New Delhi and New York, 2001). For the Atlantic, see Eric Williams, *Capitalism and Slavery* (Chapel Hill, NC, 1944).

12. See the forum edited by Amélia Polónia, Ana Sofia Ribeiro, and Daniel Lange on "Connected Oceans: New Pathways in Maritime History", *International Journal of Maritime History*, 29:1 (2017), and David Armitage, Alison Bashford, and Sujit Sivasundaram (eds), *Oceanic Histories* (Cambridge, 2018).

13. For some recent examples of such multi-sited labor histories, see Lisa Lowe, *The Intimacies of Four Continents* (Durham, NC and London, 2015); Molly A. Warsh, *American Baroque: Pearls and the Nature of Empire, 1492–1700* (Chapel Hill, NC, 2018).

14. For a sampling of recent work, see Brad Beavan, Karl Bell, and Robert James (eds), *Port Towns and Urban Cultures: International Histories of the Waterfront, c.1700–2000* (London, 2016); and Jessica Choppin Roney, "Distinguishing Port Cities, 1500–1800", *Early American Studies: An Interdisciplinary Journal*, 15:4 (2017). For a recent collection focused especially on port city merchant networks, see Adrian Jarvis and Robert Lee (eds), *Trade, Migration and Urban Networks in Port Cities, c.1640–1940* (Liverpool, 2008).

15. See, for example, Francesca Trivellato, *The Familiarity of Strangers: The Sephardic Diaspora, Livorno, and Cross-Cultural Trade in the Early Modern Period* (New Haven, CT, 2009); Sanjay Subrahmanyam (ed.), *Merchant Networks in the Early Modern World, 1450–1800* (Aldershot, 1996); David Hancock, *Citizens of the World: London Merchants and the Integration of the British Atlantic Community, 1735–1785* (Cambridge, 1995); Sebouh Aslanian, *From the*

and varied literature has grown up around port city merchants engaged in international commerce, the physical labor that actually moved commodities across the global marketplace has received far less attention.[16]

As the articles collected in this volume demonstrate, the concentration of vast numbers of specialized workers in port cities, and their complex combination at key nodal points in a globe-spanning network of commodity chains, is not a new phenomenon. Indeed, they show clearly just how much physical labor was required to make the early modern market work. This basic observation clashes even with prominent strands of Marxist historiography, otherwise quite attuned to the role of labor in history, which have tended to treat the market as a sphere where commodities circulated as if by magic and without the blood and sweat of human toil.[17] Envisioning commodity circulation in such a way not only excludes the labor that was directly implicated in the transportation of goods. It also hides the varied and vast amount of labor that built, maintained, and protected the infrastructure that made such movements possible, including roads, canals, streets, warehouses, stables, wells, aqueducts, barracks, prisons, fortresses, shipyards, docks, seawalls, and breakers.

This volume concentrates primarily on colonial and postcolonial port cities in the Americas, the greater Indian Ocean world, and the western Pacific rim. Depending on whether they were initially the products of European colonization, such as Paramaribo in Dutch Suriname or Rio de Janeiro in Portuguese Brazil, or instead indigenous cities conquered and integrated by expanding maritime empires, such as Manila in the Spanish Philippines or Calcutta in British India, the infrastructure supporting their integration into global economic networks either had to be built from scratch or expanded dramatically.

Indian Ocean to the Mediterranean: The Global Trade Networks of Armenian Merchants from New Julfa (Berkeley, CA, 2011).

16. Merchant seamen and dockers are partial exceptions to this picture, as are the many workers directly involved in shifting goods from ship to shore and beyond in the current era of containerization and the logistics revolution. Marcus Rediker, *Between the Devil and the Deep Blue Sea: Merchant Seamen, Pirates and the Anglo-American Maritime World, 1700–1750* (Cambridge, 1987); Sam Davies *et al.*, *Dock Workers*; Edna Bonacich and Jake B. Wilson, *Getting the Goods: Ports, Labor, and the Logistics Revolution* (Ithaca, NY, 2008); Stefano Bellucci *et al.*, "Introduction: Labour in Transport: Histories from the Global South (Africa, Asia, and Latin America), c.1750 to 1950", *International Review of Social History*, 59:S22 (2014), pp. 1–10; Peter Cole and Jennifer Hart, "Trade, Transport, and Services", in Karin Hofmeester and Marcel van der Linden (eds), *Handbook Global History of Work* (Berlin and Boston, MA, 2018), pp. 278–295, especially pp. 278–282.

17. See, as an example, Wallerstein, *The Modern World-System*. Robert Brenner's critique of Wallerstein likewise ignores the productive labor of transportation workers: Robert Brenner, "The Origins of Capitalist Development: A Critique of Neo-Smithian Marxism", *New Left Review*, I/104 (1977), pp. 25–92. Peter Linebaugh articulates a similar point about the labor that makes the market in "All the Atlantic Mountains Shook", *Labour/Le Travail*, 10 (1982), pp. 87–121.

During the early modern period, this infrastructure was concentrated mostly at the port and in the city itself. Commodities usually arrived either by coastal and riverine transport, or by ocean-going ships from a more extensive "maritime hinterland" that included both distant ports and nearby productive "hinterseas", such as fishing grounds, oyster beds, or the wreck sites that Kevin Dawson explores in his contribution to this Special Issue.[18]

By the nineteenth century, some ports that had previously been oriented predominantly toward the sea and each other began to extend their influence deep into landlocked interiors. This created new waves of labor migration, first sending out soldiers, settlers, and slaves to conquer and work the land, followed by thousands of laborers to build the roads, canals, and railroads that physically integrated and drained the new hinterlands of agricultural commodities and funneled them towards the rising industrial cities of the metropole.[19] On the back of these transformations, some ports, for example New York in the United States or Rio de Janeiro in Brazil, managed to remake themselves into new centers of imperial power. In the process, they spawned yet another round of labor-intensive infrastructure construction as their populations grew into the hundreds of thousands and their urban landscapes were transformed to rival established seats of power in the old world.[20]

MIGRATION, GENDER, AND PORT DEMOGRAPHY

The demographic specificities of port cities in the colonial and postcolonial world had a large impact on how groups of workers interacted. Historically, port cities everywhere have been characterized by "a disproportionate dependency for population growth on in-migration and the specific configuration of migrant streams".[21] But an important difference in the way that colonial port cities met their labor requirements when compared to their metropolitan counterparts was the preponderance within this in-migration stream of coerced workers, including slaves, indentured servants, debt

---

18. Mary Draper, "Timbering and Turtling: The Maritime Hinterlands of Early Modern British Caribbean Cities", *Early American Studies*, 15:4 (2017), pp. 769–800.
19. This process has received particular attention in the historiography of North American nineteenth-century capitalism. See, for example, Seth Rockman, *Scraping By: Wage Labor, Survival, and Slavery in Early Baltimore* (Baltimore, MD, 2009); Peter Way, *Common Labor: Workers and the Digging of North American Canals, 1780–1860* (Cambridge, 1993). For nineteenth-century Havana and its hinterland, see Evelyn Jennings's contribution to this Special Issue.
20. On New York, see Brian Phillips Murphy, *Building the Empire State: Political Economy in the Early Republic* (Philadelphia, PA, 2015). On Rio, see Martine Jean's contribution to this Special Issue.
21. Robert Lee and Richard Lawton, "Port Development and the Demographic Dynamics of European Urbanization", in *idem* (eds), *Population and Society in Western European Port-Cities, c.1650–1939* (Liverpool, 2002), pp. 1–36, 11.

peons, prisoners of war, convicts, and conscripted military personnel.[22] Although particular sectors within these port city economies continued to experience both acute and chronic labor shortages well into the nineteenth century, as the mad scramble for labor in both Evelyn Jennings's and Martine Jean's articles in this Special Issue illustrate, more well-established port cities – fed by continuous in-migration from their own rural hinterland and far-distant regions overseas – tended to develop sizeable wage labor, informal, and criminal sectors that operated alongside highly coercive labor relations. In addition, port cities also received large numbers of transitory migrants, such as sailors and soldiers, who often worked as day laborers or carried out specific tasks for local employers.[23] Taken together, this made for an unusual degree of diversity and flexibility in the combination of port city labor relations.

Their distinct migratory patterns also influenced the demography of port city laboring populations in another significant way: more than is often acknowledged, resident port city workforces were predominantly female. In addition to the regular coming and going of migratory male seafaring labor, depending on a city's size and location, the seasonal arrival and departure of fleets could mushroom or collapse a town's population overnight, suddenly adding or subtracting several thousand mostly young and single men to and from a population that often did not exceed 20,000. This not only gave many colonial port cities constantly fluctuating population levels and a huge number of temporary residents, it also increased dramatically the proportion and economic importance of women among the permanent and semi-permanent population.[24] Common images of brawny longshoremen, careless sailors, or bean-counting clerks thus obscure the far more typical female port city worker. As both Titas Chakraborty's and Melina Teubner's contributions to this Special Issue highlight, women's indispensable labor assured the reproduction of those predominantly male workers who were more directly involved in the movement of goods and the building of the infrastructure that supported it.

Port cities have frequently been described as enclaves of potential and contested freedom. For example, Douglas Catterall and Jodi Campbell have

---

22. See the contributions of Matthias van Rossum, Clare Anderson, and Evelyn Jennings to this Special Issue.
23. Karwan Fatah-Black, "Slaves and Sailors on Suriname's Rivers", *Itinerario*, 36:3 (2012), pp. 61–82. The idea that, from the point of view of the city workforce, sailors, soldiers, and company employees should be viewed as temporary migrants connects to the typology of migration as developed in Jan Lucassen and Leo Lucassen, "Theorizing Cross-Cultural Migrations: The Case of Eurasia since 1500", *Social Science History*, 41:3 (2017), pp. 445–475.
24. Christine Stansell, *City of Women: Sex and Class in New York, 1789–1860* (Champaign, IL, 1987); Elaine Forman Crane, *Ebb Tide in New England: Women, Seaports, and Social Change, 1630–1800* (Boston, MA, 1998); Douglas Catterall and Jodi Campbell (eds), *Women in Port: Gendering Communities, Economies, and Social Networks in Atlantic Port Cities, 1500–1800* (Leiden and Boston, MA, 2012).

suggested that female port city workers were often able to carve out independent survival and career trajectories that would have been far more difficult to accomplish in either the ossified social order of a metropolitan port or in the violent environment of the colonial hinterlands.[25] Similarly, those whose racial or ethnic heritage might identify them as bound laborers in the hinterland often found in the fluidity of social relations that prevailed on the waterfront the ability to disappear and obfuscate their personal history.[26] Moreover, the difficulty of maintaining effective social control and surveillance among the broad diversity of workers who toiled side by side, and lived together along the waterfront, combined with the easy availability of news and rumors from similar communities overseas, often allowed for the emergence of counter-hegemonic, cosmopolitan, anti-racist working-class cultures that in moments of crisis could make port cities the centers of revolutionary mobilization.[27] Such militancy never went unchallenged, however. As the history of eighteenth-century barrels, nineteenth-century militarized docklands, and twentieth-century container ships demonstrates, authorities may have found it difficult to break working-class power on the waterfront, but they often managed to gain the upper hand – at least temporarily – by developing new technologies, new ways of eroding inter-group solidarity, and new mechanisms for social control.[28]

FREE AND UNFREE LABOR

The distinction between free and unfree laborers is perhaps the most generic way in which to capture the dividing line between the groups of workers encountered in port cities. It has long been central to the historiography

---

25. Douglas Catterall and Jodi Campbell, "Introduction: Mother Courage and Her Sisters: Women's Worlds in the Premodern Atlantic," in *idem* (eds), *Women in Port*, pp. 1–36, 9–24.
26. On desertion and port cities, see Matthias van Rossum and Jeanette Kamp (eds), *Desertion in the Early Modern World: A Comparative History* (London, 2016); and Titas Chakraborty, Matthias van Rossum, and Marcus Rediker (eds), *A Global History of Runaways: Labor, Mobility, and Capitalism, 1650–1850* (Berkeley, CA, forthcoming). On marronage, see Linda Rupert, "Marronage, Manumission and Maritime Trade in the Early Modern Caribbean", *Slavery & Abolition*, 30:3 (2009), pp. 361–382.
27. The classic statement is Linebaugh and Rediker, *Hydra*. See also Julius Scott, *The Common Wind: Afro-American Currents in the Age of the Haitian Revolution* (London, 2018). Even today, port city workers are among the most militant sectors of the global labor movement: Jake Alimahomed-Wilson and Immanuel Ness (eds), *Choke Points: Logistics Workers Disrupting the Global Supply Chain* (London, 2018).
28. On working-class struggle and eighteenth- and early nineteenth-century transportation technologies, see Peter Linebaugh, *The London Hanged: Crime and Civil Society in the Eighteenth Century* (Cambridge, 1992), pp. 153–183, 371–441; on containerization and the logistics revolution, see Deborah Cowen, *The Deadly Life of Logistics: Mapping Violence in Global Trade* (Minneapolis, MN, 2014).

on the "making of the working class". But it is also a highly problematic one, as a large body of literature demonstrates.[29] For example, to consider wage labor as free labor does not make much sense for one of the emblematic groups of wage laborers in port cities: sailors. Even when working under contract and for a wage, which was not always the case, the conditions of their employment often imposed severe limits on their freedom of movement, stipulated corporal punishment for even minor offenses, and mostly entailed long-term contracts that they could exit before their time was due only through desertion or death.[30] Important differences between such "bound" wage laborers and those working in absolute dependency certainly existed. Nevertheless, it makes much more sense to understand the growing differentiation between them as taking place within a wide spectrum of coerced labor relations, than through a clear juxtaposition.[31] Similar conclusions have been drawn by Paul Craven and Douglas Hay, who have looked at the evolution of penal codes for slave labor and contractual employment in the British Empire. Complicating the notion of a clear evolutionary path from unfree to free labor, they argue that "penal sanctions not only persisted but increased in much English and colonial master and servant law in the eighteenth century, and enforcement rates increased significantly in Britain in the nineteenth century, and massively in many colonies".[32] Again, in their recent special issue in this journal, Clare Anderson, Ulbe Bosma, and Christian De Vito outlined how, in the course of the nineteenth century, convict labor increased on a massive scale. In colonial contexts, this type of labor directly complemented indentured labor as a new, state-organized source of

29. Ira Berlin and Herbert G. Gutman, "Natives and Immigrants, Free Men and Slaves: Urban Workingmen in the Antebellum American South", *The American Historical Review*, 88:5 (1983), pp. 1175–1200; Tom Brass and Marcel van der Linden (eds), *Free and Unfree Labour: The Debate Continues* (Bern, 1997); Robert J. Steinfeld, *Coercion, Contract, and Free Labor in the Nineteenth Century* (Cambridge, 2001); Alessandro Stanziani, "Introduction: Labour Institutions in a Global Perspective, from the Seventeenth to the Twentieth Century", *International Review of Social History*, 54:3 (2009), pp. 351–358; Alessandro Stanziani, *Labor on the Fringes of Empire: Voice, Exit and the Law* (Cham, 2018); Komlosy, *Work*.
30. Rediker, *Between the Devil*; Van Rossum and Kamp (eds), *Desertion in the Early Modern World*. The same can be said for soldiers, another omnipresent group of waged workers. Erik-Jan Zürcher (ed.), *Fighting for a Living: A Comparative History of Military Labour, 1500-2000* (Amsterdam, 2014), available at http://www.oapen.org/search?identifier=468734, last accessed 15 February 2019.
31. Marcel van der Linden, "Dissecting Coerced Labor", in *idem* and Magaly Rodríguez García (eds), *On Coerced Labor: Work and Compulsion after Chattel Slavery* (Leiden and Boston, MA, 2016), pp. 293–322.
32. Paul Craven and Douglas Hay, "Introduction", in *idem* (eds), *Masters, Servants, and Magistrates in Britain and the Empire, 1562-1955* (Chapel Hill, NC and London, 2004), pp. 1–58, 27.

coerced labor to replace slavery.[33] Meanwhile, coercion continued to play an important role in the working lives of sailors and soldiers, especially but not exclusively those recruited among colonial subject populations.[34]

Putting interaction between workers of different statuses center stage shows that the boundaries between free and unfree laborers were porous not only in legal terms, but also in daily practice. This is even so at the individual level. In their own lives, many workers experienced a variety of gradations of coerced labor relations. Recently arrived slaves from Africa in an Atlantic or Indian Ocean port might have experienced personal independence, or slavery of different types, before being captured by Europeans. Meanwhile, artisans working along the waterfront might previously have been slaves, indentured servants, or soldiers, or might even have fulfilled several of these roles at the same time.[35] Collective experiences also blurred group distinctions. Whether diving for treasure in the Caribbean (Dawson), building roads and prisons in nineteenth-century Havana and Rio de Janeiro (Jennings and Jean), loading and unloading goods for the Dutch East India Company in Batavia in the seventeenth century (Van Rossum), or performing the work of war and conquest (Thomas), mixed groups of workers often performed more or less the same tasks in close proximity, if not jointly. Furthermore, the image that emerges from the articles gathered here is one of laborers of different statuses intermingling in many settings outside of their workplaces. They encountered each other when socializing in spaces such as bars and brothels (Chakraborty), around street stalls selling food (Teubner), or at public festivities and riots (Brandon). On and off the job, they depended on each other for care, provisions, protection, or news. None of the contributions idealize these daily encounters and dependencies. Sometimes they were extremely unequal, competitive, hostile, and exploitative. But not always. Even though the comparative lack of sources on ordinary people in non-conflictual situations means that the importance of mutual trust and everyday solidarities across sectional interests is underrepresented in the archives, cooperation and common resistance, sometimes across seemingly impregnable barriers, are a crucial part of the history of port city class formation.[36]

33. Christian De Vito, Clare Anderson, and Ulbe Bosma, "Transportation, Deportation and Exile: Perspectives from the Colonies in the Nineteenth and Twentieth Centuries", *International Review of Social History*, 63:S26 (2018), pp. 1–24.

34. Alessandro Stanziani, *Sailors, Slaves, and Immigrants: Bondage in the Indian Ocean World, 1750–1914* (New York, 2014), pp. 33–68.

35. Marcel van der Linden, "The Promise and Challenges of Global Labor History", *International Labor and Working-Class History*, 82 (2012), pp. 57–76, 63–65.

36. Nineteenth-century slave narratives are one set of sources in which the individual impact of such solidarities can be quite clearly observed. See, for example, Frederick Douglass, "Narrative of the Life of Frederick Douglass, an American Slave, Written by Himself (1845)", in William L. Andrews and Henry Louis Gates Jr. (eds), *The Civitas Anthology of African American*

While neither freedom, nor unfreedom, nor the distinction between them, were absolute, there were of course stark differences in levels of coercion experienced by various groups of workers. Often, the fear of being pushed downward on the scale of coercion created competition and hatred between groups that could be exploited by those in power. Indeed, all the evidence collected in the articles presented here suggests that ruling classes were frequently highly conscious of the specific mixture of backgrounds and statuses that went into the port city populations under their control. Seeking the in-migration of specific types of laborers functioned primarily as a condition for economic expansion, but it was also a useful political instrument. In her study of the West African slaving port of Benguela, Mariana Candido describes how this dynamic worked not only between so-called free and unfree laborers, but also among different groups that entered colonial society as coerced laborers. From the seventeenth century onward, Portuguese rulers increasingly shipped European convicts from Portugal and Brazil to different colonies to replenish their local white populations. As Candido describes,

> though considered criminals elsewhere, they became the face of the Portuguese colonial state and were employed in the military forces and official colonial positions. Whites were saved from hard labor, showing the importance of skin color in defining roles in the Portuguese empire. Governors constantly requested more people, especially convicts from Brazil, although they also complained about their highly disruptive behavior.[37]

Spatial segregation, if necessary, enforced by military means, and the creation of strict rules and taboos about interaction across boundaries of status, gender, or ethnicity became important instruments of control.[38]

THE ATLANTIC AND INDIAN OCEANS, SEVENTEENTH TO NINETEENTH CENTURIES

Looking at combinations of labor relations in port cities in the Atlantic and Indian Oceans between the seventeenth and nineteenth centuries brings out notable connections, similarities, and parallels that the historiographical division between the two basins tends to obscure. Certainly, major differences existed, and it is important to recognize that they did. It is clear that before the mid-eighteenth century early modern European powers were far less able

Slave Narratives (Washington, DC, 1999), pp. 105–194, 139–140. For another example of interracial solidarity on the waterfront, see Michael D. Thompson, *Working on the Dock of the Bay: Labor and Enterprise in an Antebellum Southern Port* (Charleston, SC, 2015).

37. Mariana P. Candido, *An African Slaving Port and the Atlantic World: Benguela and its Hinterland* (Cambridge, 2013), p. 92.

38. Remco Raben, "Batavia and Colombo: The Ethnic and Spatial Order of Two Colonial Cities, 1600–1800" (Ph.D. dissertation, Leiden University, 1996). See in particular the contributions by Brandon and Jennings in this Special Issue.

to impose themselves in the broader Indian Ocean region than in the Americas. Large Eurasian states, such as the Ottoman and Mughal empires and Ming and Qing China, were formidable powers capable of confining first the Portuguese, and then the Spanish, Dutch, English, French, Danish, and Swedish, to the edges of their territories. Only from the mid-eighteenth century onward, and with accelerated force from the nineteenth century, were Europeans – whose technological, military, and fiscal tools of domination had been sharpened through inter-European rivalry – able to turn the tables on Eurasian empires, and that only at a moment when the internal struggles of the latter weakened their ability to resist European military aggression. In contrast, the devastation wrought by Conquistadors in the Caribbean islands and against the Aztec and Inca empires triggered a demographic crisis that allowed Europeans to take control of islands, littorals, and vast land masses at a much earlier stage.[39]

The failure of European states and companies to build a plantation sector in the New World based on indigenous labor and indentured Europeans prompted them to carry over twelve million African captives across the Atlantic between 1500 and 1900, approximately the same number of Africans as were forced into Asia as slaves between 800 and 1900.[40] African slavery and the racial hierarchies that accompanied it consequently shaped labor relations in the Atlantic basin more pervasively than in the Indian Ocean. As a result, until well into the nineteenth century, Abolitionism, a movement that runs throughout many of the contributions in this Special Issue, remained much more focused on the plantation complex in the Atlantic than on the extensive but more dispersed use of slave labor in the Indian Ocean.[41]

Yet, one can easily overstate the contrasts between the Indian and Atlantic Oceans. Enslaved Africans were traded into both the Indian and Atlantic Oceans; both basins saw the enslavement of indigenous populations and the modification of pre-existing forms of coerced labor; and both regions witnessed different combinations of plantation slavery with household slavery, indentured servitude, wage labor, and penal labor. In this Special Issue, Van Rossum's contribution in particular brings out the large variety of coerced labor relations at different locations in the seventeenth- and

---

39. John Darwin, *After Tamerlane: The Rise and Fall of Global Empires, 1400–2000* (London, 2007), chs 1–3.

40. Robert O. Collins, "The African Slave Trade to Asia and the Indian Ocean Islands", *African and Asian Studies*, 5:3–4 (2006), pp. 325–346.

41. On the Dutch slave trade in the Indian Ocean, see Markus Vink, "'The World's Oldest Trade': Dutch Slavery and Slave Trade in the Indian Ocean in the Seventeenth Century", *Journal of World History*, 14:2 (2003), pp. 131–177; Linda Mbeki and Matthias van Rossum, "Private Slave Trade in the Dutch Indian Ocean World: A Study into the Networks and Backgrounds of the Slavers and the Enslaved in South Asia and South Africa", *Slavery & Abolition*, 38:1 (2017), pp. 95–116. For other European powers, see Richard B. Allen, *European Slave Trading in the Indian Ocean, 1500–1850* (Athens, OH, 2014).

eighteenth-century VOC empire, challenging the notion that European companies across the board resorted to "milder" forms of exploitation in the context of the Indian Ocean world.

The centrality of race in defining different groups of workers thrown together in colonial port cities is a particularly strong theme in Atlantic history. Yet, this process is often studied separately from the development of ethnic categorizations as a tool of colonial administration in other parts of the world. Reading Brandon's and Thomas's articles side by side offers a way to discern more nuanced parallels and differences in the processes of racialization that played out in both oceans, though not necessarily at the same time or in the same form, nor perhaps to the same degree. Brandon's article pays close attention to racialization and social control in eighteenth-century Paramaribo. His contribution highlights the fact that despite the preponderance of African slavery, race as a category of separation always operated in combination with other markers of difference. It also shows racialization to have been a contested process, sometimes reinforcing competition between groups of laborers with diverging economic interests, but at other times clashing with everyday solidarities. A good example of the latter is the story of a German immigrant in Paramaribo, Christiaan Crewitz, who had first carved out a living for himself by "catching tortoises with the Indians", before being arrested for illegally serving beer and soup to black slaves at his tavern.

Similarly drawing attention to the importance of overlapping forms of categorization, Thomas shows the obsession of British officials with the composition of the military forces sent by the British East India Company to conquer Manila in the Seven Years' War. In doing so, they not only attached importance to the balance between European and Asian soldiers, but also to a large variety of differences within these broad groups (including Catholic Swiss, Irish, and Scottish troops, as well as French deserters, "sepoys", "Coffreys", "Topasses", "Chinese coolies", and "lascars"). Significant differences were introduced in the payment systems and the enforcement of discipline between these groups, even if they performed the same type of military labor. Nevertheless, Thomas describes instances in which laborers merged into a motley crew that not only captured Manila, but also plundered, protested, and deserted together. While ethnic categorization and racialization offered colonial and postcolonial governments in the Indian and Atlantic Ocean worlds an impressive tool of social control between the seventeenth and nineteenth centuries, solidarity and camaraderie among workers continued to find ways to challenge it, even if only intermittently.

Interesting parallels also existed with respect to the roles performed by women in both ocean basins. Chakraborty's and Teubner's contributions both address the issue of economic opportunities for women in the reproductive trades. In her article on women in household and caregiving occupations in East India Company ports in eighteenth-century Bengal,

Chakraborty reveals how women who attained their freedom after years of enslavement as household workers sometimes managed to gain economic independence through their ongoing contribution to these industries. Such economic autonomy resonates with Teubner's attention to the upward mobility of female street-food vendors who worked in Rio de Janeiro between the 1830s and 1870s. Her article mentions the example of an enslaved woman from Africa, Emília Soares do Patrocinio, who sold vegetables at different stands at the city market. That such female labor was not confined to petty trades is shown by the fact that the same Emília Soares do Patrocinio was able to acquire considerable wealth and become the owner of enslaved workers herself, leaving to her heirs several properties, twenty slaves, jewelry, and money. As the transition from slavery to slave ownership in the latter example suggests, upward mobility for individuals did not necessarily imply the negation of wider oppressive structures. The multi-layered inequalities that shaped reproductive labor are brought out in the horrible story related by Chakraborty of the rape of the two slave girls Sabina and Biviana, nine and five years old respectively, by EIC sailors Michael Cameron and John Massey.

Abolitionism, one of the major forces that transformed the world in the nineteenth century, is another important backdrop against which to explore changes in labor relations in the Indian Ocean and the Atlantic Ocean jointly rather than separately. The campaign to abolish slavery was spearheaded by the British, but only after the burning of Cap Français and the violent interaction among slaves, sailors, free Africans, and *petits blancs* in revolutionary Saint-Domingue had ended slavery in Haiti. The ending of the legal slave trade pushed European states and capitalist interests in one region after another to find alternative sources of labor. In doing so, they altered interoceanic migration flows considerably.[42] While East African slaves were systematically channeled into the Atlantic to work on plantations, at least from the 1770s, plantation owners and states also began to tap into alternative pools of Asian labor. As Jennings's contribution shows, between the 1840s and 1870s, Chinese workers were forced into the Atlantic to work as contract laborers, under deeply exploitative conditions, to help the Spanish build the railroads that connected Havana to Cuban sugar plantations in the hinterland. This happened on the heels of decades of failed experiments with different forms of labor relations to build up Cuba's infrastructure. Other interlinked migratory patterns also allowed Abolitionism to thicken

---

42. On the abolition of slavery in a global context, see Seymour Drescher, *Abolition: A History of Slavery and Antislavery* (Cambridge, 2009). On the transition to a multiplicity of labor regimes on the heels of abolition, see, for instance, Laurence Brown, "The Three Faces of Post-Emancipation Migration in Martinique, 1848–1865", *The Journal of Caribbean History*, 36:2 (2002), pp. 310–335. On the Cap Français uprising, see Jeremy Popkin, *You Are All Free: The Haitian Revolution and the Abolition of Slavery* (New York, 2010).

connections between the Atlantic and Indian oceans. Clare Anderson's contribution to this volume reflects how penal labor, long exploited in the Atlantic in conjunction with plantation slavery, expanded in the Indian Ocean in the nineteenth century. Her contribution highlights the fact that penal labor was marketed as a form of "enlightened labour relations" in India to "seek advantage in global markets that were increasingly sensitive to the expropriation of slave labour."

CONCLUSIONS

Combinations between the different kinds of labor implicated in capitalist development are still primarily examined across long distances, through the working of anonymous markets, global commodity chains, or a spatial division of labor between core and peripheral regions within the world economy.[43] So far, interconnectedness in Global Labor History has therefore mostly taken the form of "teleconnections" – the kind of dependencies between workers in different parts of the world that arise as a result of the consumption of distantly produced goods. Such connections, while potentially having an enormous impact on people's lives, can largely exist without leaving a trace in the participants' consciousness.[44] Situations in which combination took place in close proximity – through joint work in a single environment, workplace, or even work process – have not received comparable attention. Colonial and postcolonial port cities form an ideal case study to look at this particular form of "simultaneity" of different types of labor relations. Sometimes through microhistory, sometimes through long-term comparative history, the contributions gathered in this special issue show that central hubs in the developing world market were built by highly diverse laboring populations that interacted in close proximity. This also allows the authors to address the key questions that lay at the foundation of this project in new ways. There is now an enormous body of literature that shows why and how the emergence of global capitalism did not promote a single and universal shift from "unfree" to "free" labor. Nevertheless, there were significant differences over time and place in the composition of such mixed labor systems, as well as in the intensity of interaction that they entailed, and port cities prove to be a good vantage point from which to

---

43. Beckert, *Empire of Cotton*; Ed Baptist, *The Half Has Never Been Told: Slavery and the Making of American Capitalism* (New York, 2014). Chris Evans, "El Cobre: Cuban Ore and the Globalization of Swansea Copper, 1830–70", *Welsh History Review/Cylchgrawn Hanes Cymru*, 27:1 (2014), pp. 112–131; Dale W. Tomich, "World of Capital, Worlds of Labor: A Global Perspective", in *idem*, *Through the Prism of Slavery: Labor, Capital, and World Economy* (Lanham, 2004), pp. 32–55.
44. Van der Linden, "Promise and Challenges", p. 68.

examine such varieties and changes. In general, the articles show that it was precisely the relative freedom of movement and the easy availability of contact provided by port cities that also made them battlegrounds for the increase in social control and the refinement of apparatuses of repression. Migration was an essential determinant of class formation in port cities, continuously changing the composition of the labor force in terms of background, gender, and social status, while at the same time underlying the wild circulation of experiences, ideas, and forms of resistance. New connections and solidarities could and did emerge in the process, as did new animosities that rulers hardly ever failed to exploit.

Most of the articles in this special issue start their explorations from a single place. However, what these case studies aptly demonstrate is that the "simultaneity" in different types of labor relations that fueled the integration of world markets was often conditioned by inter-oceanic processes, which in individual port cities received a variety of expressions depending on the ways in which specific local, regional, and global forces combined at a given time and place. The impact of Abolitionism on the composition of port city working classes is a case in point, showing highly diverse outcomes, though nowhere simply leading to a transition from coerced to free labor. To wholly capture the scope of such processes, it would be necessary to expand the frame even beyond the Atlantic and Indian oceans to see how continental societies and empires evolved in the same period. But we also need to keep in view the insights that this series of single case studies offer us. While most of the time long-term global transformations remain like the rumbling of the waves in the distance, the nine contributions here speak directly to the ways in which managing the social composition of the port city remained a social experiment that often far exceeded the capacities of the authorities. A key factor in this – one that port city authorities and metropolitan states tried to counter but never could completely predict or control – was the self-activity of the various groups of port city workers. The balance of forces between the state, individual employers, and laborers that contributed to the specific mixture of free and unfree laborers employed in the port was never static. Partly, it was determined by the social struggles between all the different groups that made up port city societies. Partly, it was a product of the seismic shifts in global connections that undergirded the rise of capitalism, to which the labor of port city workers so significantly contributed.

IRSH 64 (2019), pp. 19–42 doi:10.1017/S0020859019000014
© 2019 Internationaal Instituut voor Sociale Geschiedenis

Labouring Transformations of Amphibious Monsters: Exploring Early Modern Globalization, Diversity, and Shifting Clusters of Labour Relations in the Context of the Dutch East India Company (1600–1800)*

MATTHIAS VAN ROSSUM

International Institute of Social History
Cruquiusweg 31, 1019 AT Amsterdam, The Netherlands

E-mail: mvr@iisg.nl

ABSTRACT: Early modern globalization depended on labour-intensive production and transport of global commodities. Throughout the Dutch Empire of the seventeenth and eighteenth centuries labour was mobilized through a variety of different labour relations (especially casual, contract, slave, and corvée labour). The mobilization of these workers often entailed movements over short, but more often long, distances. Port cities were crucial nodal points connecting various sites of production and circuits of distribution. Furthermore, these ports were themselves also important working environments (ranging from transport and storage, to production and security). As a result, workers from various regional, social, and cultural backgrounds worked in the same environments and were confronted with each other – as well as with the legal and disciplining regimes of early modern urban and corporate authorities. This article studies the development of labour relations in the port work of the Dutch Asian empire, looking at the mobilization and control of labour for dock work (loading and unloading of ships) and transport in its urban surroundings. It will analyse and compare the development of the need for labour, the employment of different sets of labour relations, and the mechanisms of control that developed from it. As the largest trading company active in Asia (up to the 1750s), the case of the Dutch East India Company (VOC) is crucial in understanding the impact of early imperial and capitalist development in changing global social and labour relations.

In 1734, the "indigo maker Christiaan Frederik Canselaar was sent to Ambon accompanied by four Javanese" for the purpose of disseminating

* This article draws on research conducted as part of the "Between Local Debts and Global Markets: Explaining Slavery in South and Southeast Asia, 1600–1800" project (Matthias van Rossum, NWO Veni Grant, 2016–2019) and the "Resilient Diversity: The Governance of Racial and Religious Plurality in the Dutch Empire, 1600–1800" project (Cátia Antunes, Ulbe Bosma, Karwan Fatah-Black, and Matthias van Rossum, NWO Vrije Competitie Grant, 2017–2021).

the production of indigo, one of the global commodities crucial to early
modern globalization and European expansion.[1] The Javanese were contracted for five *rijksdaalder* per month.[2] The population of Ambon was
mobilized for labour by other means. Reporting to the authorities in the
Dutch Republic, the *Generale Missiven* noted that "the population of [the
island] Amblau was exempted from service on Buru on condition that they
keep to their promise to plant indigo themselves".[3] The *dienst* (service)
referred to here was the coerced corvée labour that local subjects had to perform for the Dutch East India Company (VOC), which was now exchanged
for the production of indigo. This interest in the management of cash-crop
production by the VOC was no coincidence. The report continues with
explicit rationales, pointing out that "the ground of [the neighbouring island]
Hitu does not seem very promising for indigo cultivation", while at the same
the "cultivation of coffee was not encouraged because Java was already delivering enough".[4]

The historical perspective on early modern world trade and European
expansion has been strongly influenced by the notion of *itinerario*, which
can be translated as a guide for travelling or for finding one's route, and is
derived from the Latin verb *itineror*, to travel. The landmark account of
the richness of late-sixteenth-century Asia, published under this title by
Jan Huygen van Linschoten in 1596, had already systematically described
ports, commodities, and trading opportunities.[5] The influence of this perspective is still felt in the process of early globalization, which is to a large
extent understood as trade-driven maritime European expansion, captured
with concepts such as *merchant empires* and *merchant capitalism*.[6] The
VOC is an interesting and crucial example of this, with an extensive historiography describing it as a trading company or a merchant warrior.[7] The con-
ceptualization of the VOC as a *merchant* has been strengthened by the

1. W.P. Coolhaas *et al.*, *Generale Missiven van Gouverneurs-Generaal en Raden aan Heren
XVII der Verenigde Oostindische Compagnie*, 14 vols (The Hague, 1960–2007), IX, p. 548.
2. Or 12.5 guilders, roughly an average monthly salary for a Company servant.
3. "De bevolking van Amblau is vrijgesteld van de dienst op Buru mits men zich aan zijn belofte
zelf indigo aan te planten houdt." *Generale Missiven*, IX, p. 548.
4. *Ibid.*
5. Jan Huyghen van Linschoten, *Itinerario, voyage ofte schipvaert van Jan Huygen van
Linschoten, naer Oost ofte Portugaels Indien, 1579–1592* (Amsterdam, 1596).
6. For example, N. Steensgaard, *The Asian Trade Revolution of the Seventeenth Century*
(Chicago, IL, 1973); J.D. Tracy (ed.), *The Rise of Merchant Empires: Long-Distance Trade in
the Early Modern World, 1350–1750* (Cambridge, 1990), pp. 102–152.
7. G.D. Winius and M.P.M. Vink, *The Merchant-Warrior Pacified: The VOC (The Dutch East
India Company) and its Changing Political Economy in India* (Oxford, 1995); F.S. Gaastra,
Geschiedenis van de VOC. Opkomst, Bloei en Ondergang (Zutphen, 2009).

dominant perspective of *departure* (and return). For long, many studies focused on the ships setting sail to Asia from the Dutch Republic, the sailors departing, and the trading goods brought back.[8]

Only more recently have the importance of the Asian or "overseas" sides of the organization of the VOC, its social, economic, and political dimensions, received more attention. Several studies opened up "Asian" perspectives on the Dutch East India Company, rather than solely the perspective of "intercontinental" connections, pointing out that the trade within Asia was crucial to the Company.[9] With regard to the VOC's workforce, it has been stressed that the VOC employed most of its personnel in Asia, and that roughly half of the workforce was Asian.[10] The VOC actually employed most of its ships *in* intra-Asiatic shipping and manned those ships with multicultural European and Asian crews.[11] Despite this shift, the perspective of the merchant has remained strong, even dominant. Els Jacobs, for example, admits that "European trading companies possessed the power and means to enforce the essential native cooperation through violence", but nevertheless

---

8. This argument has been preluded in M. van Rossum, *Werkers van de wereld. Globalisering, arbeid en interculturele ontmoetingen tussen Aziatische en Europese zeelieden in dienst van de VOC, 1600–1800* (Hilversum, 2014), and some of its implications have been explored in *idem*, "Sampans, hout en slaven. De overzeese infrastructuur voor scheepsbouw en -onderhoud van de Verenigde Oost-Indische Compagnie in Zuid- en Zuidoost-Azië", *Tijdschrift voor Zeegeschiedenis*, 36:2 (2017), pp. 3–21 [translated into English as "Building Maritime Empire: Shipbuilding and Networks of Coercion under the Verenigde Oost-Indische Compagnie (VOC) in South and Southeast Asia", *International Journal of Maritime History* (submitted). For examples of this, see J.K. Beers and C. Bakker, *Westfriezen naar de Oost. De kamers der VOC te Hoorn en Enkhuizen en hun recruteringsgebied, 1700–1800* (Schagen, 1990); J.R. Bruijn, F.S. Gaastra, and I. Schöffer, *Dutch-Asiatic Shipping in the 17th and 18th Centuries* (The Hague, 1979–1987); J.R. Bruijn and F.S. Gaastra (eds), *Ships, Sailors and Spices: East India Companies and Their Shipping in the 16th, 17th and 18th Centuries* (Amsterdam, 1993); D. van den Heuvel, "*Bij uijtlandigheijt van haar man*". *Echtgenotes van VOC-zeelieden, aangemonsterd voor de kamer Enkhuizen (1700–1750)* (Amsterdam, 2005); W.M. Jansen and P.A. de Wilde, "Het probleem van de schaarste aan zeevarenden in de achttiende eeuw" (MA thesis, University of Leiden, 1970); H. Ketting, *Leven, werk en rebellie aan boord van Oost-Indiëvaarders (1595–1650)* (Amsterdam, 2002); J. Parmentier, *Uitgevaren voor de Kamer Zeeland* (Zutphen, 2006); K.L. van Schouwenburg, "Het personeel op de schepen van de Kamer Delft der VOC in de eerste helft der 18e eeuw", *Tijdschrift voor Zeegeschiedenis*, 7 (1988), pp. 76–93; K.L. van Schouwenburg, "Het personeel op de schepen van de Kamer Delft der VOC in de tweede helft der 18e eeuw", *Tijdschrift voor Zeegeschiedenis*, 8 (1989), pp. 179–218.

9. Gaastra, *Geschiedenis van de VOC*; E. Jacobs, *Koopman in Azië* (Zutphen, 2000); J.R. Bruijn, "De personeelsbehoefte van de VOC overzee en aan boord, bezien in Aziatisch en Nederlands perspectief", *Bijdragen en Mededelingen betreffende de Geschiedenis der Nederlanden*, 91:2 (1976), pp. 218–248.

10. Jan Lucassen, "A Multinational and its Labor Force: The Dutch East India Company, 1595–1795", *International Labor and Working-Class History*, 66:2 (2004), pp. 12–39.

11. Van Rossum, *Werkers van de wereld*.

argues that a survey "of all settlements makes quite clear that the Company in Asia really operated as a merchant".[12] This article argues there is a need to break with such perspectives, and it aims to explore the implications of doing so.

In recent decades, research has made it increasingly clear that the VOC cannot be characterized solely as a merchant organization, and that the functions of the Company extended to those of continuous warfare, government responsibilities, and even interfering in and organizing agricultural production. Recent studies remind us that the Company acted with different degrees of sovereignty and took on a pivotal role in regulating regimes of slavery, administering the slave trade and enforcing corvée duties.[13] The VOC operated not only at sea and in ports; it was a more amphibious monster, acting not only as "merchant", but also taking on multiple roles as "ruler", "soldier", and "producer".

This article explores the way the Dutch East India Company operated in employing and developing labour regimes in both production and transport work throughout its Asian empire. It does so as a case study to understand early global capitalism through the lens of the mobilization and control of labour employed for the production and transportation of several key global trading commodities of this period, including indigo, but also cinnamon, pepper, sugar, and coffee. It will analyse and compare the development of the need for labour, the employment of different sets of labour relations, and the mechanisms of control and regulation of diversity that developed from this in different parts of the empire of the VOC. The implications of this exercise range wider than merely providing a different account of the VOC but hold important clues for advancing global historical debates on shifts in labour relations, as well as on the nature and impact of early empire. It indicates that the reach of early modern (merchant) capital extended well beyond maritime trade and port economies, but also aimed to control and shape the South and South East Asian countryside, significantly impacting shifts in labour regimes and social relations in regions that were drawn into the spheres of direct and indirect influence of early empires.

---

12. Jacobs, *Koopman in Azië*, "De rondreis langs alle vestigingen maakt goed duidelijk dat de Compagnie in Azië werkelijk als een koopman opereerde".
13. G. Knaap, "De 'core business' van de VOC: Markt, macht en mentaliteit vanuit overzees perspectief", inaugural lecture, University of Utrecht, 10 November 2014; M. van Rossum, *Kleurrijke tragiek. De geschiedenis van slavernij in Azië onder de VOC* (Hilversum, 2015); Linda Mbeki and Matthias van Rossum, "Private Slave Trade in the Dutch Indian Ocean World: A Study into the Networks and Backgrounds of the Slavers and the Enslaved in South Asia and South Africa", *Slavery & Abolition*, 38:1 (2017), pp. 95–116; Jan Breman, *Mobilizing Labour for the Global Coffee Market: Profits from an Unfree Work Regime in Colonial Java* (Amsterdam, 2015), available at: https://www.oapen.org/search?identifier=597440; last accessed 15 February 2019.

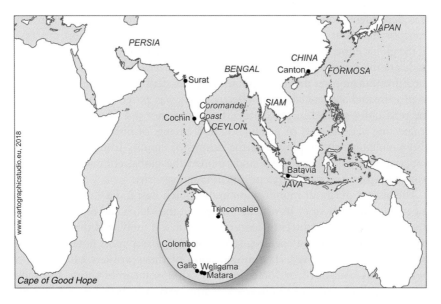

Figure 1. Selected places in the Dutch East India Company Empire that are mentioned in this article in relation to forced labour relations or transformations in labour relations.

EXPLORING GLOBALIZATION, CAPITALISM, AND IMPACT

As the largest company active in Asia (up to the 1750s), the case of the VOC is key to understanding the impact of early imperial and capitalist development in changing global social and labour relations. The proponents of the perspective of early modern globalization and capitalist expansion as being characterized predominantly as *trade* or *merchant* phenomena have raised doubts concerning the links, or causal effects, of colonialism. Jan de Vries, for example, challenges "the argument that intercontinental trade, through its differential impact on the location of commercial life, forced changes in political institutions that were favourable to long-term economic growth" in Europe. De Vries concludes: "When all is said and done, we are presented with two simultaneous developments – the establishment and development of a global maritime trading system under western European direction and the divergent growth of the western European economies – and are asked to believe that a causal link exists connecting the first to the second".[14]

The case of the Dutch East India Company is an important reminder that such links remain insufficiently explored up to this day and should also be investigated in the reverse direction. Given that early modern globalization

14. J. de Vries, "The Limits of Globalization in the Early Modern World", *The Economic History Review*, 63:3 (2010), pp. 710–733, 712.

was dependent not only on the highly labour-intensive modes of maritime transportation but also on labour-intensive, often rural production processes of the global commodities involved, the best places to study the effects of global trade are the spheres of production and transport *outside* Europe. Throughout the European empires that underpinned early modern global trade, the pressure to procure and allocate labour in effective ways was extremely high. Therefore, the port cities studied in this Special Issue were not just crucial nodal points connecting various sites of production and circuits of distribution, they were also simultaneously employed as the centres of empire, from which coercive imperial activities radiated that underpinned the global commodity chains – from transport and storage, to production and security.

The history of labour mobilization in the Dutch East India Company empire is part of this larger story in which, throughout the Dutch and other empires of the seventeenth and eighteenth centuries, labour was mobilized through a variety of different, but often coercive, labour regimes, based most notably on contracts, slavery, and corvée. The mobilization of these workers often entailed more or less controlled or forced mobility over sometimes short, and more often long, distances. As a result, workers from various regional, social, and cultural backgrounds came to work in the same environments in these ports and their hinterlands. There they were confronted with each other within the framework of legal and disciplining regimes of early modern imperial state-corporate and private authorities. In the case of the European companies in Asia, all this occurred in the context of a highly developed world, with strong states in South, South-East and especially East Asia, and by complex economic systems marked by markets, monetization, and a high diversity of labour relations, ranging from casual wage, contract, slave, and corvée labour.

The labour regimes of ports and hinterlands – the regimes of waterfronts, cities, and rural places of agricultural production – were not separated, but deeply connected. Entanglements between the systems of labour mobilization came about not only through the flows of commodities and the chains of imperial command, but especially through the *exchange*, *interaction*, and *overlap* of labour systems employed and refined by global organizations such as the Dutch East India Company. The active engagement and experimenting of the VOC with the refinement and transplantation of labour regimes indicates that we should consider the deeper impact of the transformations set in motion by the socio-economic and political regimes behind the early modern trade connections. Whereas the study of globalization has been largely *connection-centred*, cultural historical studies such as that by McCants remind us that such early connections may have been restricted to "small luxuries" but nevertheless led to "mass consumption".[15] Taking on

---

15. A. McCants, "Exotic Goods, Popular Consumption, and the Standard of Living: Thinking about Globalization in the Early Modern World", *Journal of World History*, 18:4 (2007), pp. 433–462.

board these insights into the field of social and labour history means we should consider much more systematically how the production, transport, and control of such "small" luxuries actually demanded massive mobilization of labour globally. The labour-intensive character of early global contacts affected a multiplicity of aspects of people's lives – work, migration, social and political relations, policing, and more – and fuelled experiments with labour regimes – in maritime hubs and in agricultural hinterlands. The impact and transformative effects of this remain to be scrutinized much more systematically in *global labour history* as a field.

A consideration of the role of the changes set in motion by globally integrating commodity chains under war capitalism, like that of Sven Beckert in his study of global capitalism through the history of cotton, is a crucial step forward. Emphasizing the role of conquest and coercion in early modern capitalism, Beckert also argues, however, that the expansion of merchant capital, especially in Asia, occurred "largely without exploding older social structures" until the late eighteenth century.[16] This might indeed be the case for commodities like cotton, in which strong networks of producers and merchants were able to maintain rather high degrees of control, but it seems to have played out differently for other key global commodities. We should reconsider, therefore, whether the characterization of war capitalism accounts sufficiently for the nature and scope of social and labour transformations already set in motion by early modern imperial and capitalist expansion. The expansion of world trade resulting from European expansion in the quest for global commodities in Asia, such as nutmeg, cinnamon, and pepper, but also indigo, sugar, and coffee, seemed to have important *transformative* effects.

This insight is important especially in the light of recent historiographical turns in global labour history, which have indicated that many forms of labour relations, ranging from free to unfree, existed and continued to exist throughout history. Early modern (and later) global and capitalist expansions were intimately linked to unfreedom and coercive labour relations.[17] Since the search for linear shifts from unfree to free labour relations has been abandoned, it is increasingly recognized that multiple labour relations not only existed *alongside* each other, but also *in relation to* each other. This implies we should start to think about transformations in labour regimes from the notion of *clusters of labour relations*. Rather than the occurrence and development of single labour relations, it is the specific cluster (or "combinations") of labour relations as they occur in a specific historical context that

16. S. Beckert, *Empire of Cotton: A New History of Global Capitalism* (London, 2014), pp. 3–55, 22.
17. A. Stanziani, *After Oriental Despotism: Eurasian Growth in a Global Perspective* (London, 2014); Beckert, *Empire of Cotton*; M. van der Linden and M. Rodríguez García (eds), *On Coerced Labor* (Leiden, 2016).

should be understood and explained. This holds equally true for historical transitions in labour regimes – these entail not merely the shift from one labour relation to another, but also shifts of specific combinations or clusters of a set of labour relations to another cluster of labour relations.[18]

The case study of labour relations under the VOC indicates the importance of revising our understanding through such an approach. The VOC employed contract labour, slave labour, corvée labour, and casual wage labour, and actively attempted to manage and transplant labour regimes across different regions. This provides an interesting insight into how the labour-intensive character of early modern globalization motivated the drivers of the early capitalist expansion that supported it (corporations, states) to develop practices for the mobilization of labour that had *a deep and lasting impact* on a multitude of local societies across the globe. This impact was not limited to the organization and management of labour, and the histories of slavery and coercion, but also – through regimes of control and differentiation – extended into wider spheres of social and cultural relations.

CONQUEST, CORVÉE, AND TRADE – THE DUTCH OVERSEAS MONSTER AT WORK

As the largest company operating in Asia from the beginning of the seventeenth century until the mid-eighteenth century, the Dutch East India Company provides an interesting and important case.[19] The Company's activities were not limited to that of trade, but extended to include diplomatic relations, and more importantly to warfare and government responsibilities such as taxes, administration, and justice. Roughly a quarter to a third of the VOC workforce were military personnel.[20] In 1760, according to a survey of the political positioning of the VOC by Knaap, the VOC had sovereignty in six regions (Batavia, Java's north-east coast, Banda, Ambon, Ceylon, and the Cape of Good Hope), suzerainty (indirect rule) in twelve regions, and extra-territorial rights in five places (Japan, China, Bengal, Surat, and Persia).[21]

---

18. M. van Rossum, "Redirecting Global Labor History?", in C. Antunes and K. Fatah-Black (eds), *Explorations in History and Globalization* (London, 2016), pp. 47–62, 52; Matthias van Rossum *et al.*, "Moving the 'Free and Unfree Labour' Debate Forward", *ISHA Newsletter*, 5:1 (2016), pp. 15–18, 16.

19. Van Rossum, *Werkers van de wereld*, pp. 70–74.

20. Knaap, "'Core business'", p. 17; M. van Rossum, "'Working for the Devil': Desertion in the Eurasian Empire of the VOC", in M. van Rossum and J. Kamp (eds), *Desertion in the Early Modern World: A Comparative History* (London, 2016), pp. 127–160, 133.

21. Knaap, "'Core business'", pp. 18–19. In some places categorized under suzerainty, the VOC had stretches of land, such as the Malabar coast, where it owned and leased out lands in the conquest of Paponetty.

This was part of a system in which the VOC had gained access to global commodities through balancing trade, monopoly claims, and warfare. At the beginning of the seventeenth century, the VOC had secured control over the islands that produced cloves (Ambon, 1605), mace, and nutmeg (Banda, 1621) through a series of conquests. After the conquest and destruction of Jacatra (1619), the Company built the settlement of Batavia as its main headquarters. From here it pursued the trade in that other important spice, pepper. The VOC would never completely possess the areas producing pepper (Sumatra, Malabar), but, over the course of the seventeenth and eighteenth centuries, it would increase its influence by building up a strong political presence through conquest (Cochin, 1663) or establishing suzerainty. Increasingly, the Company was able to enforce contracts for the delivery of pepper for prices below market value. The VOC continued its conquests more to the north of the Indonesian archipelago, where it conquered the important trading hub of Malacca (1641), and especially Formosa (1622–1663), a crucial link in the trade with China, but also interesting as a site for the production of sugar.

Having established the core of its power, the VOC turned its eyes to the Indian Ocean, where it gained control over coastal Ceylon, the only major area producing cinnamon, in a series of conquests (Galle, 1641; Colombo and Jafnapatnam, 1654–1658). As the Coromandel coast was crucial for obtaining high-quality textiles, which were important trading goods in South East Asia and elsewhere, the VOC established a series of forts and trading offices there, as well as control over several cities. The VOC obtained permission to build a fort in Bengal (Houghly) as a way to secure its position in the trade in saltpetre, opium, and silk. The Cape of Good Hope (1652) had become an important resupply station for shipping between Europe and Asia, and with the expansion of European settlement in the hinterland over time it developed into an agricultural production area. In the meantime, the city of Batavia and its surroundings (*ommelanden*) developed into one of the major production areas for sugar, which was exported largely to Japan and the Western-Indian Ocean region. In the eighteenth century, coffee and tea would become crucial trading commodities for the European markets. Tea was obtained mainly through direct trade in Canton, but coffee was produced in Java.

Two observations are important for our understanding of early modern globalization. First, although their rapid expansion over the seventeenth and eighteenth centuries may have been an important factor in the acceleration of connections, it was not only European markets driving the demand for the global commodities pursued by companies like the VOC. The trade *within* Asia was extremely important for the VOC, and was not negligible, even compared to the bulk trade in spices, coffee, and other goods to Europe. Especially sugar (Figure 2) and textiles, but also pepper and other commodities such as opium, were important trading goods for Asian

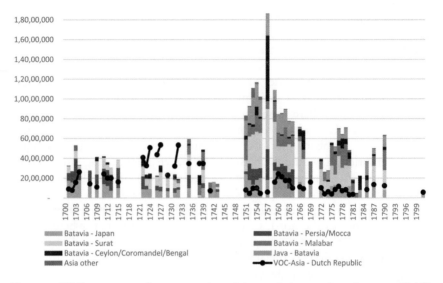

Figure 2. VOC transport of sugar on intra-Asian and intercontinental routes (lbs).[22] *Boekhouder-Generaal Batavia (BGB), available at: http://bgb.huygens.knaw.nl; last accessed 5 November 2018.*

markets. It is important, therefore, to assess the volume of trade not only along the Europe-Asia axis of global connections, but also through long-distance connections in a truly global sense. Asia was not only a production site, it was also a crucial market for several of the global commodities the VOC traded in. Any assessment of the impact of global trade must therefore account for the activities in Asia's long-distance trade.[23]

Second, the VOC was heavily involved in the production of many of its key commodities, directly and indirectly stimulating coercive production regimes. The production of cloves on Ambon, for example, was undertaken by the local inhabitants, but controlled by the VOC through monopoly claims. The population was obliged to sell the entire harvest of cloves to the Company for a fixed price. The VOC prohibited the production of cloves elsewhere and organized annual *hongi-tochten* (extirpation expeditions) for inspection and extermination.[24] The thousands of Ambon workers (mainly

22. To avoid double counting resulting from transshipment, the data for the route Batavia-Malabar excludes Malabar-Ceylon, and the data for Batavia-Ceylon/Coromandel/Bengal excludes Ceylon Republic and Bengal Republic.
23. Cf. De Vries, "The Limits of Globalization in the Early Modern World", p. 720; J. de Vries, "Connecting Europe and Asia: A Quantitative Analysis of the Cape-Route Trade, 1497–1795", in Dennis O. Flynn, Arturo Giráldez, and Richard von Glahn (eds), *Global Connections and Monetary History, 1470–1800* (Aldershot, 2003), pp. 46–49, 56–61. See, for this critique, Van Rossum, *Werkers van de wereld*, introduction and ch. 1.
24. G.J. Knaap, *Kruidnagelen en Christenen: de Verenigde Oost-Indische Compagnie en de bevolking van Ambon 1656–1696* (Leiden, 2004); Jacobs, *Koopman in Azië*.

rowers) recruited for these *hongi-tochten* were mobilized through *corvée* labour services. A similar monopoly system was employed for the Banda Islands, but here production was organized around small plantations (*perken*). The land was owned by the VOC and leased out to European (and later mestizo) owners, who worked with enslaved labourers. The VOC actively sought Europeans, who would be able to "govern slaves", and also actively sustained the enslaved population, providing slaves for cost price from Timor and elsewhere.[25]

On Ceylon, the VOC profited from a system of corvée labour for the production of cinnamon and various other kinds of work. Different groups of inhabitants were obliged to perform different kinds of labour. The production of cinnamon was organized through the obligation that *chialias* (caste groups) harvest and deliver cinnamon for the Company. Other groups were obliged to provide military labour (*lascarins*) or general services, such as transport (*koelies*).[26] These were significant obligations. In 1657, for example, it was reported that the "chaleas from the Seven Corlas [Districts] had delivered approximately 670 *bhaer* cinnamon of 480 pounds [321,600 pounds in total] to the warehouses of Negombo".[27] The pressures of corvée labour led time and again to resistance from the local population, with recurrent revolts in the periods 1736–1737, 1744–1747, 1757–1762, and 1783–90.[28] On 28 April 1730, several heads of the districts around Colombo and Negombo petitioned the VOC concerning the introduction of (obligated) pepper production, because "the people were burdened with many other Companies services", such as "the planting of Cardamom", the "planting and maintenance of the coffee trees", and the "harvesting and transport of cinnamon".[29]

Whereas cinnamon production would rise to over 700,000 pounds per annum (Figure 3), Ceylonese coffee production did not develop quickly under the VOC, with the harvest not exceeding 67,000 pounds in 1740.[30] Resistance to new crops seems to have played an important part in this. In a revolt among cinnamon peelers in 1736, a group of 1,000 protesters attacked the Company's cow barn, refinery, and warehouses and caused damage "to the Company's coffee-garden".[31] Not much later, it was decided no

---

25. For example, H.T. Colenbrander, *Jan Pietersz Coen: bescheiden omtrent zijn bedrijf in Indië*, 7 vols (The Hague, 1919–1953), I, pp. 374, 708.

26. See, for example, the instructions for the captain of the cinnamon peelers, "Instructie voor de kapitein van de kaneelschillers", 21 June 1661, in L. Hovy, *Ceylonees Plakkaatboek: Plakkaten en andere wetten uitgevaardigd door het Nederlandse bestuur op Ceylon, 1638–1796*, 2 vols (Hilversum, 1991), I, no. 64.

27. *Generale Missiven*, III, p. 169.

28. Hovy, *Ceylonees Plakkaatboek*, LXIII.

29. Nationaal Archief [hereafter, NA], Archive of the VOC [VOC], archive number 1.04.02, inventory number 8952, fos 791–793 [scan 819–821].

30. *Generale Missiven*, X, p. 442.

31. *Generale Missiven*, IX, p. 732.

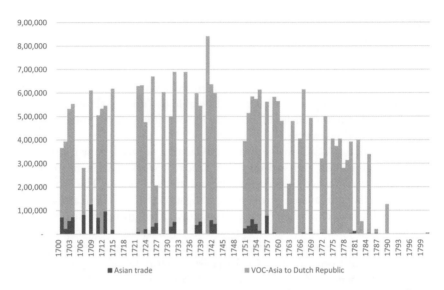

Figure 3. VOC transport of cinnamon on intra-Asian and intercontinental routes (lbs).[32]
BGB, available at: http://bgb.huygens.knaw.nl; last accessed 5 November 2018.

longer to encourage "coffee cultivation" on Ceylon and to try to promote "in the kindest manner" the production of pepper instead by obligating community heads to deliver specific amounts to the Company.[33] The production of coffee on Java was more successful, with harvests reaching almost six million pounds as early as the mid-1730s, peaking at almost eleven million pounds in the 1790s (Figure 4).[34] Introduced on Java in the first decade of the eighteenth century, the production of coffee was brought under the monopoly system in 1723, making it illegal to sell coffee produced on Java to anyone other than the VOC, and it became an obligated corvée service in the following years. The VOC's role in coffee production was significant – the residents and regents in these parts of Java fell directly under VOC rule.[35]

The active role of the VOC in the production of its trade commodities becomes clear also from the continuous search to improve and develop the cultivation of different "cash crops" (*cultures*) in its empire, with the VOC experimenting with coffee and pepper on Ceylon, and with indigo and silk

32. Data are based on all cinnamon cargoes recorded in the *Boekhouder-Generaal Batavia*, expressed in pounds and *balen*; the weight of a *baal* is estimated at 55 pounds. The Asian trade includes all cargo shipments on Asian routes, except the Ceylon-Batavia route (which was mainly for transshipment to the Dutch Republic); the intercontinental trade is included through all cargo shipments to the Dutch Republic.

33. *Generale Missiven*, X, pp. 207, 442.

34. Breman, *Mobilizing Labour*, p. 83.

35. *Ibid.*, pp. 75–77, 21.

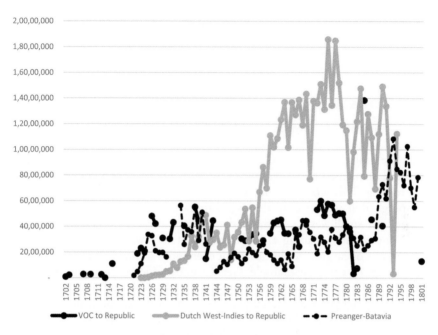

Figure 4. Coffee transport from Dutch East Indies and Dutch West Indies to the Dutch Republic, including deliveries of obligated coffee production in Batavia (lbs).
BGB, available at: http://bgb.huygens.knaw.nl; last accessed 5 November 2018.

on Java, for instance. Corvée labour played an important role in this search. In this context, the population of the island of Amblau were "exempted from service on Buru on condition that they kept their promise to plant indigo".[36] For those inhabitants who went to the neighbouring island of Buru to work in the indigo culture, the Company paid "one stuiver and a pound of rice daily, being the same as what the *quaartslieden* [corvée labourers] receive in that province".[37]

In some cases, mainly textile, sugar, and pepper, there were also exceptions to the direct role of the VOC in the production regimes of the main global commodities. In the case of pepper, the VOC tried to increase its influence by putting political pressure on local rulers in places like Bantam and Palembang. In the case of sugar, the VOC actively governed the Batavian *ommelanden* where its production took place. For both products, coerced labour played an important role. Slaves seem to have been employed in the native pepper fields on Sumatra, but also in the sugar fields, sugar mills, and refineries owned by mainly Chinese and European entrepreneurs in

36. *Generale Missiven*, IX, p. 548.
37. *Ibid.*, p. 628.

the Batavian *ommelanden*. As roughly one third of the population of Batavia and the *ommelanden* consisted of slaves, the VOC actively regulated the institution of slavery as well as the slave trade.[38]

GLOBAL TRADE AND THE DEMAND FOR LABOUR

It was not only the production of early modern global commodities that required large numbers of workers. The transport of the many trade goods from the hinterlands to ports and on to ships was also highly labour intensive, and demanded large amounts of physical labour – carrying, lifting, towing, rowing. This work was not without skill but required organization and planning. Skill was vital in dealing with cargoes during transfers, loading chests into small vessels without damaging the cargo, for example. Even more importantly, loading a ship in the right way was crucial not only for the amount of cargo it could carry, but even more so for the sailing capacities of the ship. In 1717, for example, Gerrit van der Zijden, the equipage master of Batavia, responded to the accusation that two ships had not been loaded well, explaining that had the saltpetre and iron nails not been placed in this manner the ships "would have been barely able to cross the sea".[39]

An illustrative example of the massive work entailed is provided by historian Lodewijk Wagenaar in his study of the port city of Galle. He describes the laborious task of loading (and unloading) vessels through the examples of two ships, *De Drie Papegaaien* and *Leimuiden*, destined for a return voyage to the Dutch Republic. The ships would transport almost 1,200 chests (*kisten*) of Javanese coffee and 132 chests of Ceylon coffee, each weighing 250 pounds. Another 160,000 pounds of cinnamon was brought on board, distributed over some 1,000 bales. Some 30,000 pounds of tin and over 100,000 pounds of coral stone were packed in bags or chests. The South Indian cloth was bound together in 1,000 packages and the cloth from Surat in some 120 packages, each weighing some 145 pounds. The most important part of the cargo was 336 tons of Malabar and Ceylon pepper, transported in thousands of jute bags. The cargo was distributed over an estimated total of 14,000 bags, bales, packages, and chests.

To an important extent, the geography of hinterlands and ports shaped the work and the demand for labour. Throughout the early modern period, the large seagoing ships needed to be anchored just offshore. This meant that the handling of cargoes was divided into several stages (from warehouse to dock, to small vessel, to ship) and cargoes needed to be rowed or sailed in small vessels from docks, through rivers or even across the surf. In some places, like Batavia and Siam, the VOC located warehouses on islands. In other

---

38. Van Rossum, *Kleurrijke Tragiek.*
39. NA, Collectie Brugmans, 1.10.13, inv. 168, no. 3.

places, warehouses remained in the city, near loading docks, like the *moelje* in Galle. This meant that here "the chests needed to be brought downstairs from the first floor of the large storehouse, through the gate and on to the pier, then into one of the small vessels used for loading and unloading, and into the bay to the seagoing ships, in order finally to be stowed in the ships' hold".[40]

The volume of the trade flows thus becomes not only an indicator of the thickness of global connections, but also (and especially) of the massive labour demands in the environments of production and transportation. In the second half of the seventeenth century, the VOC shipped around four million pounds of pepper and half a million pounds of nutmeg and cinnamon to the Dutch Republic annually.[41] In the eighteenth century, the VOC exported products in even larger quantities, for example large amounts of pepper (some six to ten million pounds), sugar (from four to almost twelve million pounds around the middle of the century), and coffee (from four to six million pounds, to over ten million pounds towards the end of the century) (Figures 2–5).

The workforce employed by the VOC grew along with the expansion of empire and trade. The number of workers directly employed by the Company increased from approximately 15,000 in 1625 to around 42,000 in the late 1680s, peaking at 57,000 in the mid-eighteenth century.[42] Most of them were either contract labourers, especially European and Asian sailors, soldiers, and artisans, or slaves, bought or hired to work in the service of the Company. These estimates exclude the layer of workers drawn into Company service in other ways, especially populations living in Company-subjected territories, who were obliged to perform corvée services. Good surveys of the populations and obligated corvée labour in the VOC empire are lacking, but some sense of scale can be derived from illustrative examples. In the coastal districts of Ceylon, for example, the VOC ruled over an estimated population of almost 280,000 by the late seventeenth century.[43] The population under Company authority on the Ambonese islands in the 1690s has been estimated at almost 64,000, all of whom could potentially be drafted for a total of more than two million days of work.[44]

---

40. L. Wagenaar, *Galle, VOC-vestiging in Ceylon. Beschrijving van een koloniale samenleving aan de vooravond van de Singalese opstand tegen het Nederlandse gezag, 1760* (Amsterdam, 1994), pp. 125–126.
41. Jacobs, *Koopman in Azië*, p. 51.
42. Lucassen, "A Multinational and its Labor Force", pp. 12–39, 15; revised in Van Rossum, "'Working for the Devil'", p. 133.
43. P. de Zwart, "Labour Relations in Ceylon in the Late Seventeenth Century", paper supplement to "Ceylon 1650" database, part of the Global Collaboratory on the History of Labour Relations 1500–2000 (International Institute of Social History).
44. Knaap, *Kruidnagelen*, pp. 139, 199. Knaap indicates that a small part of this was drafted yearly for the *hongi* and court services (*hofdiensten*).

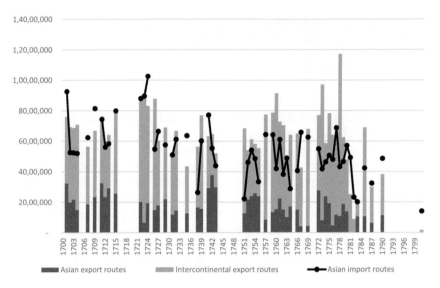

Figure 5. VOC transport of pepper on intra-Asian and intercontinental routes (lbs).[45]
BGB: *http://bgb.huygens.knaw.nl; last accessed 5 November 2018.*

MOBILIZING LABOUR, MANAGING DIVERSITY

The VOC empire revolved around the organization and control of production and transportation in ports and hinterlands. These environments were not isolated, but strongly related. The circulation of goods or the mobility of people, of course, brought about material connections between ports and their urban and rural hinterlands. Much stronger ties came about, however, through the structures of labour mobilization and control, which were organized for production and transport by the VOC in similar and interrelated ways. The ways in which labour was mobilized in specific settings was not merely a function of geography, production relations, or the location of working environments within the larger socio-political (VOC) system. The VOC actively organized the mobilization of labour around the adaptation, creation, and nurturing of the binding mechanisms engrained in contract, slavery, and corvée; in physical and administrative boundaries; and in legal and socio-ethnic divisions. Although the mechanisms of different patterns

45. Data are based on the total pepper cargoes in the *Boekhouder-Generaal Batavia* provided in pounds. With a total of 644,356,437 pounds of pepper accounted for, this excludes 28,270 bags of pepper, 3,384 *pikol* of pepper, and 2,361 *bahar* of pepper. The Asian import routes are included as all cargo shipments on Asian routes to one of the transshipment harbours for Asian and intercontinental destinations (Batavia, Ceylon, and the Cape of Good Hope); Asian export routes are included through all other cargo shipments on Asian routes (either directly from pepper-production areas, or from the transshipment harbours); the intercontinental export routes are included through all cargo shipments to the Dutch Republic.

of labour exploitation, control, and coercion could, at times, result in very similar workers' experiences, their effectiveness lay especially in their differentiating effects, increasingly segmenting and tying down workforces.

The case of transport labour in ports and their hinterlands in different parts of the VOC empire is illustrative. In the metropole of Batavia, ships were loaded and unloaded by contract workers (both Europeans and Asians), slaves (Asians), and casual wage workers (Asians). The port of Batavia was a bewildering world of work places, mostly accessible by small rowing and sailing vessels, lying along rivers and canals in Batavia or on nearby islands in the Bay of Batavia. The storehouses were located along the city walls, near canals. The ships wharf was located on the island Onrust and the equipage wharf was located along Batavia's Ciliwung river. Several crucial work sites were located on other islands, such as Edam (rope factory) and Kuyper (ships' repair works). The ocean-going ships of the VOC needed to be anchored some hundred metres offshore as they could not enter the river. The ocean-going ships were loaded and unloaded by small vessels, which could be sailed or rowed from the river to the ships, and back, but needed to be rowed or towed upriver into Batavia.[46]

As Batavia was the main place of arrival for incoming new European personnel, there was always an important reservoir of contract workers, especially sailors, who could be employed in loading and unloading vessels. Being at the end of long intercontinental voyages, however, crews were severely weakened. Ill sailors were immediately placed in the hospital, while soldiers would later be stationed in the military quarters on land rather than remain on board the anchored vessels. In port work, newly arrived sailors were employed alongside Company workers and local workers. They were very visible, not so much owing to their skills as to their behaviour (and inexperience with the climate). Local Chinese port workers distinguished between "orang lama" – old people – and "orang beharu" – new people – who would still have a fairly white skin and would get terribly sunburnt while loading and unloading the ships in Batavia.[47]

From the early seventeenth century onwards, port work in Batavia was done by Company sailors, slaves, and casual local Chinese wage labourers. In 1632, it was decided to employ more slaves and sailors in order to cut back on the cost of hiring Chinese workers.[48] By the mid-seventeenth century, however, the loading and unloading of vessels was still done by Chinese workers alongside the European sailors and soldiers stationed on

---

46. Van Rossum, *Werkers van de wereld*, pp. 153–163.

47. Johann Jacob Merklein, *Reise nach Java, Vorder- und Hinter-Indien, China und Japan, 1644–1653* (The Hague, 1930); Van Rossum, *Werkers van de wereld*, pp. 250–251.

48. J.A. van der Chijs, *Nederlandsch-Indisch Plakaatboek, 1602–1811*, 17 vols (Batavia and The Hague, 1885–1900), I, p. 269.

the ships before they arrived in Batavia.[49] With the increasing employment of
Indian sailors from the second half of the seventeenth century, however, vital
aspects of Batavia port work would become the domain of Indian sailors. In
contrast to the local Chinese casual wage workers, these Indian sailors served
on multi-annual labour contracts similar to those of European sailors and
soldiers. By the mid-eighteenth century, almost 490 "Moorish" (Indian) sailors were registered as employed in Batavia, of whom 272 on the equipage
wharf, 105 in rowing and towing vessels upriver ("aan de ploeserscagie"),
and thirty-two on one of the flat cargo vessels used in port work ("aan de
haijbok").[50] The Indian sailors employed in Batavian port work were settled
in separate quarters near the *ploesercasie* (boathouse), just under the castle
and along the river.[51]

In the 1780s, over one hundred Indian sailors were still employed in port
work in Batavia, but in the second half of the eighteenth century increasing
numbers of Chinese casual wage workers were again hired to complement
the labour force of Indian, European, and slave workers. In 1765, Batavia's
opperequipagemeester (head equipage master) argued for the need to "be
assisted with Chinese or [other] natives", resulting from the "frequent ill-
nesses of the few available sailors".[52] Hiring new workers among the local
Batavian Chinese community immediately led to complaints about the rising
costs of the Chinese hospital, confronted with increasing numbers of injured
Chinese port workers going there for treatment and recovery.[53] In the late
1780s, in the face of difficulties in bringing in Indian sailors from South
Asia as well as in recruiting local workers, the VOC began employing
Javanese sailors, hired as contract labourers, on the local small vessels used
for port work. Owing to high desertion rates among local Javanese workers,
the VOC once again resorted to (more expensive) Chinese and Indian
sailors.[54]

Almost from the start, the VOC also relied extensively on the employment
of slave labour for the loading and unloading of vessels as well as for the
transportation of goods within the city. In the early seventeenth century,
unloading the rice brought from ships using small vessels to the storehouses
on the east side of Batavia was the work of slaves.[55] The slave labour
employed for the port work comprised slaves owned by the Company,

---

49. Merklein, *Reise nach Java*, p. 10f. He mentions: "Zu solcher Arbeit [das Schiff auszuladen]
werden fürnehmlich die Chinenser (derer so wol in, als ausser der Stadt Batavien eine überaus
grosse Menge, in der Holländer Schutz, und Tribut wohnet) um einen gewissen Lohn; und
dann auch die Europeische Schiffleute und Soldaten gebraucht".
50. NA, VOC, 5199.
51. On this, see Van Rossum, *Werkers van de wereld*, pp. 153–164.
52. Van der Chijs, *Nederlandsch-Indisch Plakaatboek*, VIII, pp. 53, 128, 416.
53. *Ibid.*, pp. 580–581.
54. NA, Collectie Brugmans, 171, f. 99.
55. *Generale Missiven*, I, p. 422.

but also slaves hired from private slave owners. With this category of "hired slaves", the boundaries between workers become extremely fluid. The city of Batavia held a very active "coolie" (labour) market of workers performing casual labour, mainly for general work such as (local) transportation of goods or other manual tasks. The word "coolie" here referred to the performance of actual casual wage labour – coolies being hired per day, half day, or even per hour. These casual wage labourers could be both free and enslaved workers, ranging from Mardijkers (local free Asian Christians) or other free inhabitants of Batavia, to slaves being hired out directly by their masters or being sent to hire themselves out to earn "coolie money" (*koelie-geld*) for their masters. The mobility of these diverse groups of workers was a direct stimulus for the implementation of two types of pass systems directed at both free and enslaved populations. A formal system was imposed by the Company upon Asian sailors and soldiers who left the service of the Company in order to distinguish them from others, especially unfree and Company workers. An informal system was upheld by slave masters, providing written notes to the enslaved when they were sent for work that entailed crossing military posts, or entering or exiting neighbourhoods or parts of the city. Guards would act upon such notices, or the absence of such notices, by permitting slaves to cross or by incarcerating them and sending them back.[56]

Corvée labour played no role in the loading and unloading of vessels in Batavia, but it was crucial for the functioning of the port. Large numbers of corvée labourers were regularly requested from local rulers in order to clear the bed of the sandy Ciliwung river. In 1699, for example, the VOC sent a message to the resident of Cheribon noting that "the Princes here have accepted to provide 500 [subjects] to the Company for some time for the clearing of the sandbanks that have grown before the mouth of the river of this city". They announced "that a vessel will be sent off today or tomorrow to summon these men" and warned that they should not delay or wait until "current tasks" had been finished.[57]

ADMINISTRATING EXTRACTION, REGULATING MOBILITY

Along the coast of north-east Java, the VOC increasingly came to rely on a mix of corvée and casual wage labour. In Java, the VOC did not demand or

---

56. Van Rossum, *Kleurrijke tragiek*; Hendrik E. Niemeijer, *Batavia. Een koloniale samenleving in de 17de eeuw* (Amsterdam, 2005), p. 200. Illustrative is the example of Ontong of Palembang, locked in a trunk for two days and nights at the Moorish Guard in the Chinese campong after being suspected of being absent from house without leave. NA, VOC, 9467, case 15.
57. ANRI, file 2519, fos 245–246.

administer the corvée labour directly but demanded it from local rulers. At least from the early eighteenth century onwards, the VOC would strike agreements with these rulers on the number of workers to be sent to work for the Company and the compensation to be paid by the VOC to the ruler. In some cases, the ruler would pay modest compensation to workers. Luc Nagtegaal argued that this "forced labour came to be used with increasing frequency" and that "this was not because of any lack of a free labour market", but because it served as an efficient and extremely cheap way of supplying labour.[58] Indeed, wage labourers could be recruited along the Javanese coast, which was an area with fairly well developed labour markets from early on.[59] The Company nevertheless pursued a policy increasing the burden and spread of corvée labour systems in Java.[60]

The obligated corvée labourers were employed in the loading of Company ships, which transported especially timber and rice from the Javanese coast. They were also responsible for the transportation of wood from inland areas, along the rivers to the beaches. An agreement with local rulers around Tagal in 1732 obliged the residents of Tagal to "collect the wood rafts from Wallerij, and bring them to the corner of Brebes, where once they arrived there the people of Brebes were to unload the wood rafts and bring them ashore". Furthermore, "when any Company ship was in need of being unloaded or loaded, this was to be done also by the joint Tagal residents".[61] The daily number of forced corvée workers from Tagal would rise from forty in the 1700s, to sixty in the late 1710s, seventy in the early 1720s, and eighty in the 1730s. In addition, the regents of Pekalongan and Batang would each send some sixty workers daily to Tagal. Similar arrangements were in place along the coast. Nagtegaal states that "in Demak, the inhabitants of eleven villages shared the responsibility for hauling the logs that were floated downstream onto the riverbanks. When a Company ship arrived, these *batur tugu* or 'log workers' would drag the logs into the sea."[62] He argued that there was a division between the employment of corvée labour in regions with stronger rulers, such as Surabaya, Tagal, and Demak, and regions with weaker rulers such as Semarang, where the VOC more generally chose to employ wage labour. These casual wage workers engaged in loading and unloading ships in Semarang would be recruited every morning near the

58. Luc Nagtegaal, *Riding the Dutch Tiger: The Dutch East Indies Company and the Northeast Coast of Java, 1680–1743* (Leiden, 1996), pp. 204–206.
59. See, for example, on wage labour: U. Bosma, "Database 1650-1900" and "Methodological Paper" (June 2011), The Global Collaboratory on the History of Labour Relations, 1500–2000, available at: http://hdl.handle.net/10622/LCALNW; last accessed 3 November 2018. On sailors: Van Rossum, *Werkers van de wereld*.
60. Breman, *Mobilizing Labour*.
61. NA, VOC, 7822, 531.
62. Nagtegaal, *Riding the Dutch Tiger*, pp. 204–206.

alun-alun (the communal square). Only "at certain peaks, such as when rice had to be loaded on the ships, forced labour was used".[63] Later in the eighteenth century, the VOC sent Chinese wage workers, recruited in the larger Javanese port cities along with their vessels sailing along the Javanese coast, to work as *sjouwers* (carriers) and assist in the loading and unloading of the vessels.[64]

In Galle, much of the work in loading and unloading ships was done by the sailors employed by the Company. As return voyages were more heavily manned than intra-Asiatic voyages, sailors must have been more readily available in Galle, which was the second most important port from which return voyages to the Dutch Republic departed. Sailors were, therefore, employed on board the vessels, taking on board the goods and stowing them in the hold. Sailors were also employed on the small vessels sailing between the sea-going vessels and the pier, as well as on the pier itself, for the transport of the goods into the small vessels.[65]

The number of Company workers available was not sufficient, however, for the enormous amounts of goods that needed to be transported from land to shore, and on land, in relatively short periods of time. The VOC therefore employed slaves, who "were used for the loading and unloading of the ships" and were "employed for the work on the fortifications when there was no other work".[66] The VOC also employed the local population subjected to obligated labour services. In and around Galle, the obligated labour of the "Mooren" – members of South Asian or Muslim communities – was used for "the loading and unloading of the return and other vessels". On 30 September 1751, it was noted in Galle that of a "total of 513 heads" there were 213 "*dienstbare*" [serving] individuals, of whom 72 were "heads who were living in the city of Galle".[67] The Moors were not the only group obligated to work in the loading and unloading of ships in Ceylonese VOC settlements. In 1751, the registration of 138 "Christians, heathen Chittijs, as well as Paruas, and freed slaves, both of the Honourable Company as private" referred to the employment of "these people in a fashion similar to the Moors" in the loading of vessels and "other services needed by the Company".[68]

63. *Ibid.*
64. Van Rossum, *Werkers van de wereld.*
65. Wagenaar, *Galle*, pp. 123–124.
66. *Generale Missiven*, IV, p. 453.
67. Sri Lanka National Archives [hereafter, SLNA], 1/2758, no. 18.
68. SLNA, 1/2758, no. 20. Dutch original: "Christen en heijden Chittijs mitsgaders Paruassen en vrijgelaten slaven, zowel van d"E: Comp: als particuliere"; "ten eijnde zijlieden als de Mooren bij de afladinge en ontlossing der retour en andre scheepen, mitsgaders verder nodige "s Comp: diensten te konnen werden g"emploijeert".

In other parts of Ceylon, obligated corvée labour was also employed in loading and unloading goods. Early in February 1760, the transport of chalk near Weligama was delayed because many of the fishermen who were obliged to load the chalk and man the vessels as part of their corvée duties had run away to another district. In March 1760, the obligated corvée labour of fishermen from Matara of the Karawa caste were employed in the transport of wood with rafts.[69] As late as 1788, it was reported that the "koelies" employed at the works of the forts of Trincomalee as part of their obligated labour services were used partly in the warehouses and in loading and unloading vessels.[70] In the second half of the eighteenth century, large numbers of "koelies" were sent from different districts to Colombo and Galle as part of their corvée service every year.[71] Following the mobility involved in corvée duties and in response to corvée workers avoiding their duties by "roaming around the country", the Company issued regulations proclaiming that "all chitties, Moors or paruas, without distinction and nobody excluded, are obliged to carry a pass signed by the supervisor of their residency", and that they "were obliged to be able to provide this pass to anyone legitimated to ask for it". These passes indicated the place and the number under which the person was administrated on the *oeliammersrolle* (the corvée duty roll), ensuring the effectiveness of the corvée labour system.[72]

CONCLUSIONS

The impact of early globalization went well beyond that of market integration or cultural exchange. The case of the VOC provides a clear picture of the drastic effects of labour mobilization on the production and transport of the global commodities involved. Systems of coerced labour were at the core of the Dutch East India Company empire. The VOC interfered in the production of its main trading commodities in different, but at times far-reaching, ways, nurturing more or less directly systems of slave and corvée labour for the production of cloves, mace, nutmeg, cinnamon, and coffee, and playing more indirect roles in coercive labour relations in the production of sugar and pepper. Coercive labour regimes were not restricted to

---

69. Wagenaar, *Galle*, pp. 166–171.
70. See the reports of overseers and engineers in SLNA 1/3164.
71. SLNA 1/443.
72. Hovy, *Ceylonees Plakkaatboek*, p. 324. Original: "dat na deezen all chittys, Mooren of paruassen, zonder onderscheyt en niemand uytgezondert, gehouden [zullen zyn] een briefje door den gebieder harer woonplaats selfs voor de eerste maal en vervolgens (dat verjaard zijnde) door iemand anders onderteekent [bij zich] te dragen, en telkens als haar dat gevergt word door degene die daartoe gewettigt zijn te vertoonen, waarbij zal blijken moeten dat zij [weezent]lijk op de oeliammersrolle aldaar en onder wat nommer zij op dezelve bekent staan".

agricultural production sites. Slaves were employed on board small vessels transporting cargo between port and ships, or hinterland and port, in Batavia as well as Galle. These slaves were either owned or hired by the Company or merchants loading its ships. Just as important were the corvée labour systems that were appropriated and intensified by the Dutch in different parts of the Dutch-Asian empire. This type of bonded labour, which is often associated with local systems of agricultural production, was just as easily redirected by the VOC for transportation and port work (Ceylon, Java).

Port work was typically the place where labour regimes employed on land and at sea collided and/or functioned alongside each other. Indeed, throughout the early modern period, much of the work "on water" was done by the sailors of the oceangoing ships that were loaded and unloaded. Other groups of local workers, however, seem to have been crucial in all parts of the processes involved, both for the work on land as well as on the water, right up to the transferring of goods onto the oceangoing ships. The labour relations under which these local workers were employed often reflected the practices in use locally, which were strongly shaped by larger processes of imperial expansion.

Ports especially were places were sailors – mainly working on long-term, strict labour contracts – could be employed alongside casual wage workers as well as coerced workers. Systems of labour exploitation on the waterfronts of the Dutch early modern empire were extremely flexible. Casual wage labour was used for port work and related transportation in economic (and imperial) cores, as well as peripheries. Although urban and more rural markets for casual wage labour were widespread (Batavia; north-east Java), coerced labour was crucial also in urban contexts, partly undermining workers' bargaining position. In Batavia, Chinese casual wage labourers were replaced (to some extent successfully) with Indian sailors (contract workers), European sailors, and Asian slaves. On the north-east coast of Java, intensifying systems of corvée labour were preferred to the use of casual wage labour.

This global history of production and transportation furthermore indicates that the waterfronts and hinterlands of the ports of the early modern Dutch Empire witnessed a complex interplay between systems of organizing work through labour contracts, casual wage labour markets, enslavement, and corvée labour obligations. Sailors employed on contract labour were employed everywhere – most of them worked on the ships being loaded or unloaded; in some cases, these sailors were not employed onboard ships, but solely for port work. In addition to (specialized, contracted) sailors, large numbers of other, local workers were employed in the loading and unloading of ships and the related transportation work on land and water. Among this large body of workers, coercive labour relations were at the core. Corvée, slave, and (in some cases) casual wage labour were employed alongside each other.

This overview of labour relations in the production and transport stages of the commodity chains of key global commodities of the VOC gives us a picture of a so-called "trading company" that operated more as a coercive state and creative agriculturalist than as a joint-stock merchant enterprise. The Dutch East India Company was an amphibious monster that not only worked from sea to land, but increasingly worked from land to sea. The results hint, firstly, at the need to rethink existing notions of the making of the modern world, the development of capitalism, of "free" labour markets, and of wage labour. It indicates the importance of further scrutinizing how coercive and casual labour systems existed or functioned in "clusters" – *alongside* and *in relation to each other* – and how these transformed not linearly and singularly but transitioned from one specific constellation of clusters of labour relations to another. And, secondly, it seems to stress the importance of further questioning early modern global changes with an open understanding of the concepts of imperialism and capitalism, and with new interest in the early transformations set in motion by merchant capital not only on the imperial maritime frontiers, but also in the South and South East Asian and wider global countryside.

IRSH 64 (2019), pp. 43–70 doi:10.1017/S0020859019000026
© 2019 Internationaal Instituut voor Sociale Geschiedenis

History Below the Waterline: Enslaved Salvage Divers Harvesting Seaports' Hinter-Seas in the Early Modern Atlantic

KEVIN DAWSON

University of California, Merced
5200 North Lake Rd., Merced, CA 95343, USA

E-mail: kdawson4@ucmerced.edu

ABSTRACT: This article considers how enslaved salvage divers cooperated and conspired with slaveholders and white employers to salvage shipwrecks and often smuggle recovered goods into homeports, permitting them to exchange their expertise for semi-independent lives of privileged exploitation. Knowing harsh treatment could preclude diving, white salvagers cultivated reciprocal relationships with divers, promoting arduousness by avoiding coercive discipline while nurturing a sense of mutual obligation arising from collective responsibilities and material rewards. Enslaved salvagers were, in several important ways, treated like free, wage-earning men. They were well fed, receiving daily allowances of fresh meat. Most resided in seaports, were hired out, and received equal shares of recovered goods, allowing many to purchase their freedom and that of family members. Divers produced spectacular amounts of wealth for their mother countries, owners, and colonial governments, especially in the maritime colonies of Bermuda, the Bahamas, and Cayman Islands. Their expertise was not confined to maritime colonies. Even as plantation slavery was taking root during the mid-seventeenth century, salvage divers provided an important source of income for planter-merchants.

INTRODUCTION

The African-honed expertise that enslaved underwater divers carried throughout the Atlantic world allowed them to quickly recover several tons of gold, silver, and other items from shipwrecks, especially old Spanish treasure hulks. Possessing proficiencies held by few in the world, divers exchanged their unique ability to rapidly produce capital for semi-independent lives of privileged exploitation. Most were hired from their owners and treated like free, highly skilled, craftsmen, receiving both wages and equal shares of salvage, enabling some to purchase their freedom and that of family members. Even as terrestrial bondage compelled captives to spend the majority of their day toiling for slaveholders, aquanauts dove less than two hours per day and performed no other substantial work while salvaging. Divers were not motivated by coercive discipline. Instead, white salvagers cultivated a sense of mutual obligation arising from collective responsibilities, material rewards, and other circumstances, convincing divers to cooperate and conspire with them to salvage and smuggle recovered goods into homeports.[1]

By considering seaports' relationships with coastal seas "History Below the Waterline" integrates the ocean into Atlantic history and African immersionary traditions into maritime history. This article follows salvage divers deployed from seaports throughout the Atlantic world to nearby and far-off shipwrecks that served as hinter-seas of economic production. Scholars typically situate seaports between hinterlands and overseas markets, assuming colonial economies pivoted on rural production. This article shifts our intellectual focus seaward to consider how salvage divers harvested others' misfortune from the seafloor to produce capital that helped finance terrestrial production throughout the British Empire.

SEAS OF POSSIBILITIES

Scholars have documented how coastal waters served as hinter-seas of economic production for those daring enough to ply them while fishing for fined fish, shellfish, and whales. Thousands of ships sank in the western Atlantic, providing opportunities for salvagers who, in early modern vernacular, "fished" upon wrecks. The shallow, coral-toothed shipping lanes encompassing Caribbean and Bahamian islands were well-traveled, tricky, and dangerous to navigate, making them fertile hinter-seas.[2]

Most shipwrecks occurred in coastal and inter-island waters, after a vessel struck a reef, coming to rest in waters thirty to seventy feet deep and often relatively close to port. Diving deeper than about twenty-five feet presents increasingly greater challenges. For instance, as one descends, mounting

1. For water as a cultural space, see Epeli Hau'ofa, "Our Sea of Islands", in *idem*, *We Are the Ocean: Selected Works* (Honolulu, 2008), pp. 27–40; W. Jeffrey Bolster, "Putting the Ocean in Atlantic History: Maritime Communities and Marine Ecology in the Northwest Atlantic, 1500–1800", *American Historical Review*, 113:1 (2008), pp. 19–47; Kevin Dawson, *Undercurrents of Power: Aquatic Culture in the African Diaspora* (Philadelphia, PA, 2018); Karin Amimoto Ingersoll, *Waves of Knowing: A Seascape Epistemology* (Durham, NC, 2016).
2. For example, see Michael J. Jarvis, *In the Eye of All Trade: Bermuda, Bermudians, and the Maritime Atlantic World, 1680–1783* (Chapel Hill, NC, 2010), especially p. 211; Hau'ofa, "Our Sea of Islands"; W. Jeffrey Bolster, *The Mortal Sea: Fishing the Atlantic in the Age of Sail* (Cambridge, MA, 2012); Daniel Vickers, *Farmers & Fishermen: Two Centuries of Work in Essex County, Massachusetts, 1630–1850* (Chapel Hill, NC, 1994); Andrew Lipman, *The Saltwater Frontier: Indians and the Contest for the American Coast* (New Haven, CT, 2015). I owe special thanks to Niklas Frykman, who suggested using "hinter-seas".

water pressure increasingly hurts the divers' ears. At sixty feet, the air in the divers' lungs is compressed, creating negative buoyancy, causing their bodies to sink rather than float.[3]

Aquanauts were adept at what is now called freediving, or diving with only the air in one's lungs. Freedivers spent years honing their minds and bodies to meet underwater challenges, a process beginning during youth. Medical research suggests the physiology of enslaved freedivers adapted to repeated prolonged submersion, water pressure, and oxygen apnea by, among other things, slowing their metabolism, enabling them to more efficiently consume oxygen, and sharpening underwater vision up to twice the normal range.[4] Pieter de Marees, a Dutch merchant-adventurer who traveled to Africa's Gold Coast and ostensibly the Caribbean during the 1590s, seemingly reported on this, saying Africans "can see underwater".[5]

Freedivers learn to pressurize their ears and breathe effectively. Many inhale and exhale deeply several times to expand their lung capacity and oxygenate their blood before taking one deep breath. During descents, they must equalize their middle and inner ear with surrounding water pressure by letting air into the Eustachian tubes, otherwise their eardrums can rupture, which can cause disorientation and drowning.[6]

Composure precluded the release of oxygen-depleting adrenalin as freedivers coped with variables in water pressure, temperature, and visibility. Surge (the underwater effects of oceanic forces pushing water into shallows) thrust divers shoreward then pulled them seaward, while prevailing currents, wind patterns, and far-off storms produced stratified flows that moved in diverse directions at different depths, creating a perplexity of forces. Divers calculated these forces by feeling the movement of their body and observing the motions of boats, fish, and submarine vegetation.[7] They similarly remained calm when entering wrecks and encountering sharks, with one observer noting that "Each [Key Wester] vessel has a diver, who will go into the cabin of a ship, or to the bottom of the sea, if not over six fathoms [thirty-six feet] deep". Divers seemingly understood that most shark species did not pose

3. Kevin Dawson, "Enslaved Swimmers and Divers in the Atlantic World", *Journal of American History*, 92:4 (2006), pp. 1346–1350.
4. *Idem, Undercurrents of Power*, p. 67. On training skilled slaves, see Richard Follett, *The Sugar Masters: Planters and Slaves in Louisiana's Cane World, 1820–1860* (Baton Rouge, LA, 2009), pp. 5, 118–150, 124–130, especially 126; Dawson, "Enslaved Swimmers", pp. 1327–1355.
5. Pieter de Marees, *Description and Historical Account of the Gold Kingdom of Guinea*, trans. Albert van Dantzig and Adam Jones (New York, 1987 [1602]), p. 186. De Marees seemingly visited South America, read extensively about the region, and was tuned into Dutch, Portuguese, and French discussions. Email correspondence with Adam Jones, 3 December 2011, and Ernst van den Boogaart, 5 December 2011.
6. Dawson, *Undercurrents of Power*, pp. 68–69.
7. Author's observations during decades of freediving and spearfishing.

a risk to humans, prompting one traveler to write that Bahamians "appear to have little dread of sharks".[8]

Making one dive every five to ten minutes, salvagers worked from morning until about noon, when winds made conditions rough. Most could hold their breath for about two or three minutes, a rare few four minutes. One Bahamian boasted, in 1824, that he "has among his slaves divers who can go to depths of *sixty feet* & remain under water from *two* to *three* minutes".[9]

Spanish policies precipitated numerous shipwrecks. Spain forced Amerindians and enslaved Africans to mine precious metals, amassing these commodities, along with Asian goods, in Havana. Annual treasure fleets departed for Europe during late summer and fall, sailing through the shallow reef-encrusted Bahamas and Florida Straits during hurricane season, causing many shipwrecks (Figure 1).[10]

Wreck locations were written upon the lips of merchants, fishermen, and sailors, who saw masts protruding from the depths or dark hulks silhouetted against white sands beneath clear Caribbean waters. Verbal accounts of shipwreck survivors, sometimes passed down through the years, disclosed the location of others. These whisperings inspired treasure hunters to cruise rumored waters, dragging grappling hooks across the seafloor, and sending down divers to investigate when something was snared or promising objects spotted.

Salvagers immediately worked recent wrecks, before oceanic forces broke them apart and scattered them. Older hulks were typically salvaged from spring through fall, when seas were calm and underwater visibility good, making operations safer and easier. Wills, estate inventories, runaway slave advertisements, auction notices, and other documents indicate that most English seaports, from Barbados to Virginia, were home to a few divers who were owned by slaveholding mariners and waterside planters. At any given time, perhaps 500 experts regularly worked as salvage divers. Divers were usually owned by several different slaveholders who brought them together to form teams of two to six aquanauts and a few enslaved apprentices.[11]

8. Kenneth Scott (ed.), "The City of Wreckers: Two Key West Letters of 1838", *Florida Historical Quarterly*, 25:2 (1946), p. 195; Edward Sullivan, *Rambles and Scrambles in North and South America* (London, 1852), p. 284.

9. Johann David Schoepff, *Travels in the Confederation 1783–1784*, 2 vols (Philadelphia, PA, 1911), I, pp. 284–285; John Hope, "Description of Bermuda", 1722, CO 37/10, fol. 218, Bermuda Archives. Dive times based on William Hubert Miller, *Nassau, Bahamas, 1823–4: The Diary of a Physician from the United States Visiting the Island of Providence* (Nassau, 1960), p. 34; interview with Tanya Streeter, 16 May 2014; author's observations.

10. Dawson, *Undercurrents of Power*, p. 73; Arturo Giráldez, *The Age of Trade: The Manila Galleons and the Dawn of the Global Economy* (New York, 2015).

11. For wrecks mentioned without detailing salvage operations, see *The South Carolina and American General Gazette*, 18 and 27 May 1774; *The Virginia Gazette*, 15 and 25 November

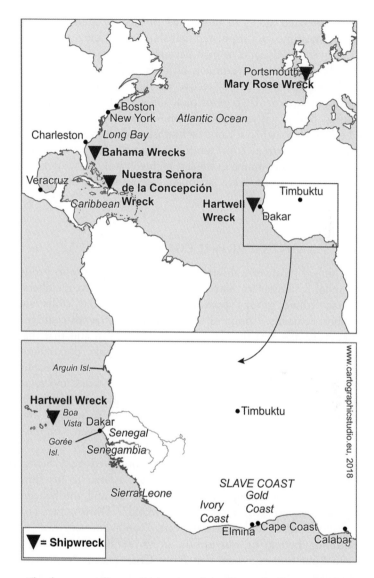

Figure 1. The above maps illustrate the location of the shipwrecks discussed in this article: the *Mary Rose*, the *Nuestra Señora de la Concepción*, "Bahama Wrecks", and the *Hartwell*. Also shown is Arguin Island, which is reportedly where the *Mary Rose* salvage divers were from.

1775; Charlesworth Ross, *From an Antiguan's Notebook* (Bridgetown, 1962), pp. 12–14; Jas. A Thome and J. Horace Kimball, *Emancipation in the West Indies: A Six Months' Tour in Antigua, Barbadoes, and Jamaica, in the Year 1837* (New York, 1838), p. 324; Robert H. Schomburgk, *The History of Barbados* (London, 1848), pp. 181, 323–325; Kenneth Morgan (ed.), *The Bright-Meyler Papers: A Bristol-West India Connection, 1732–1837* (Oxford, 2007), p. 327.

Salvagers operated along an ill-defined border separating legal activities from piracy. Maritime laws stipulated that shipwrecks remained their owners' property, requiring *salvagers* to gain permission to work them or turn over salvage to shipowners or government officials, usually receiving twenty-five per cent of the value of what they recovered. Piracy is an act of robbery at sea and *wrecking* is a particular type of piracy. Some salvagers became *wreckers* by working hulks without permission. English officials usually only enforced salvage laws when it came to English and ally vessels, requiring salvagers to pay the crown a "royal tenth" of proceeds for permission to plunder Spanish wrecks. Beginning in the late eighteenth century, after the known Spanish treasure wrecks were stripped, salvagers increasingly wrecked English vessels.[12]

GAINING PRIVILEGES IN THE DEEP

Privileges hinged on divers' ability to use African expertise to produce significant capital for enslavers. Slaveholders understood that members of certain African ethnic groups possessed knowledge and skills suited to specific labor demands.[13] Sources suggest that seventeenth-century salvage divers, like most slaves at the time, were African-born and that their skills were developed in African waters. Early travelogues documented how Atlantic Africans, particularly Senegambians and Gold Coast people, incorporated swimming and underwater diving into their work and recreational lives, alerting slaveholders to the possibilities of exploiting Africans' aquatic proclivities. Coming from societies that had largely abandoned swimming during the medieval period, European travelers were impressed by Africans' swimming and underwater diving abilities. In 1455, Venetian merchant-adventurer Alvise de Cadamosto observed two Senegambian swimmers negotiate storm-swept seas to deliver a letter to his ship "three miles off shore", proclaiming that those living around the Senegal River "are the most expert swimmers in the world". During the 1590s, De Marees observed that Gold Coast Africans "can swim very fast, generally easily outdoing people of our nation in swimming and diving", while Johann von Lübelfing expressed that Ivory Coast people "can swim below the water like a fish".[14] European shipwreck survivors reported that

12. Dawson, *Undercurrents of Power*, p. 60.
13. For example, Daniel C. Littlefield, *Rice and Slaves: Ethnicity and the Slave Trade in Colonial South Carolina* (Chicago, IL, 1991); Judith A. Carney, *Black Rice: The African Origins of Rice Cultivation in the Americas* (Cambridge, MA, 2001); James H. Sweet, *Domingos Álvares, African Healing, and the Intellectual History of the Atlantic World* (Chapel Hill, NC, 2011); Dawson, *Undercurrents of Power*.
14. G.R. Crone (ed.), *The Voyages of Cadamosto and other Documents on Western Africa in the Second Half of the Fifteenth Century* (London, 1937), pp. 34, 37; De Marees, *Description*, pp. 26,

African rulers claimed wreckage within their territorial waters, dispatching men and women to strip them.[15]

Spanish slaveholders on the Pearl Coast, which encompasses northern Venezuela and the islands of Margarita, Coche, Cubagua, and Trinidad, were the first Europeans to exploit slaves' African expertise. In 1526, they began purchasing Senegambian and Gold Coast captives to replace indigenous Guaiquerí Indian divers, whose numbers were being decimated.[16] De Marees observed how Gold Coast Africans were targeted for enslavement on the Pearl Coast, writing that they

> can keep themselves underwater for a long time. They can dive amazingly far, [...] Because they are so good at swimming and diving, they are specially kept for that purpose in many Countries and employed in this capacity where there is a need for them, such as the Island of St. Margaret in the West Indies.[17]

As discussed below, English salvagers followed Spain's example of purchasing members of African ethnic groups known to possess skilled divers (Figure 2).

Salvage divers were cosmopolitan men. Spinning webs of economic, as well as social, cultural, and political connectivity across the Atlantic world, they leveraged aquatic propensities to negotiate dynamic situations and improve their circumstances afloat and ashore, as illustrated by the HMS *Mary Rose* divers. During the 1540s, before the English crafted concepts of race or slavery, Jacques Francis, John Ik, George Blacke, and five other unnamed African divers were transported to England by Venetian salvager Petri Paulo Corsi to salvage the *Rose*. When litigation disrupted salvaging, the divers used England's High Court of Admiralty as a platform to secure their legal personhood, challenging still undefined European perceptions of race and slavery that were used during an attempt to marginalize and subjugate them.

While preparing to engage an attacking French fleet on 19 July 1545, the *Rose*, which was Henry VIII's flagship and one of the world's most modern battleships, sank off Portsmouth, with her deck lying about forty feet below the surface. English salvagers used grappling hooks to "fish" objects from wrecks or looped cables under intact wrecks, and hoisted them to the surface. Both methods failed on the *Rose*. Italian freedivers were considered the best European salvagers and, in July 1546, the Admiralty appointed Corsi to work the *Rose*. In July 1547, Corsi was also hired by Italian merchants to

32, especially 186–187; Adam Jones (ed.), *German Sources for West African History, 1599–1669* (Wiesbaden, 1983), p. 12; Kevin Dawson, "Swimming, Surfing, and Underwater Diving in Early Modern Atlantic Africa and the African Diaspora", in Carina E. Ray and Jeremy Rich (eds), *Navigating African Maritime History* (St. John's, 2009), pp. 81–116.

15. Dawson, *Undercurrents of Power*, p. 60.

16. *Ibid.*, pp. 64–65.

17. De Marees, *Description*, p. 186.

1. "Sidi-Arab" Diver with "Pince Nez."—2. The "Mosquito Fleet" at Anchor.—3. The Divers at Work Below.—4. Apparatus used by the Divers.
THE PEARL FISHERY IN THE PERSIAN GULF

Figure 2. The pearl fishery in the Persian Gulf. *The Graphic: An Illustrated Weekly Newspaper,* *1 October 1881, p. 356.*

salvage the merchantman *Sancta Maria and Sanctus Edwardus* off nearby Southampton.[18]

Francis "was born" on the "Isle of Guinea", which is probably Arguin, or Arguim, off Mauritania. Its hydrography (marine geography, including the seafloor, and effects of tides and currents on bodies of water) speaks to the divers' proficiencies as it is surrounded by "shallows of rocks and sand [bars]" that claimed many ships, providing the aquanauts with fertile training grounds. Arguin was deemed the divide between North and sub-Saharan Africa and "inhabited by black-a-moors", meaning sub-Saharan Africans. Prior to Portuguese contact, it had been occupied only by migratory fishermen from Senegal during fishing season. The Portuguese built a trade castle

18. Interrogation of and deposition made by Jacques Francis on Tuesday, 8 February 1548 (O.S.), 18 February 1548 (D.S.), PRO, HCA (London) 13/93/202v–203r [hereafter, Jacques Francis]; deposition made by Anthonius de Nicholao Rimero on 28 May 1548, PRO, HCA 13/93, pp. 275–276 [hereafter, Nicholao Rimero]. Miranda Kaufmann, *Black Tudors: The Untold Story* (London, 2017), pp. 32–55. I am indebted to Miranda Kaufmann for insights on Francis.

there in 1448 to divert commerce away from Timbuktu, transforming the island into an important port and its waters into hinter-seas where divers salvaged Portuguese and African commodities. These divers spoke the same African language, with sources suggesting they were members of Arguin's Wolof merchant/fishing community. They possibly worked wrecks around Gorée Island (Senegal), and were probably Lebu, a Wolof aquacultural ethnic group. Word of their expertise seemingly flowed northward, convincing Corsi to hire them in 1545 to work other wrecks off England.[19] Corsi could "dyve under the water", though not as well as Francis, who became head diver, while Ik and Blacke were divers and the other Africans were apparently apprentices. All were treated well, with Corsi "payeng for ther meate [a true luxury] and dryncke at the Dolphin" Inn, which was a Hampton tavern.[20]

Salvaging proceeded until the Italian merchants accused Corsi of stealing items recovered from the *Sancta Maria* and arrested and sued Corsi in the High Court of Admiralty, prompting Francis to testify. The merchants, who had applauded Francis's expertise, turned on him. Attempting to preclude Francis's testimony, win their suit, and seemingly be awarded the divers as slaves for compensation for their financial losses, they called him a "slave", "Blacke more", "morisco born where they are not christened", and "gynno [Guinea] born". (These remained imprecise idioms that could aver the inferiority of Muslims and Africans.)[21]

Evidence indicates that the divers were never enslaved, with recent scholarship explaining that sixteenth-century English society regarded Africans as cultural inferiors, yet did not racialize them or accept slavery as a legitimate

19. Jacques Francis; Nicholao Rimero, pp. 275–276. For Arguim, see Gomes Eannes de Azurara, *The Chronicle of the Discovery and Conquest of Guinea*, 2 vols (London, 1899), I, p. 58; II, pp. xi, 104, 107, especially 320; Duarte Pacheco Pereira, *Esmeraldo de Situ Orbis* (London, 1937 [1892]), pp. 72–78, especially 72, 77; John William Blake, *Europeans in West Africa, 1450–1560* (London, 1967 [1942]), pp. 14, 22, 88, 132–133, 139–140; A.C. de C.M. Saunders, *A Social History of Slaves and Freedmen in Portugal, 1441–1555* (Cambridge, 1982), pp. 5, 20–25; George E. Brooks, *Landlords and Strangers: Ecology, Society, and Trade in Western Africa, 1000–1630* (Oxford, 1993), pp. 125, 132, 197; D.P. Gamble, *The Wolof of Senegambia, Together with Notes on the Lebu and the Serer* (London, 1957); Dawson, *Undercurrents of Power*, pp. 11, 117.
20. William Mussen PRO, HCA 13/93, ff. 193v–194r?; John Westcott PRO, HCA 13/93, ff. 192v–193r; Jacques Francis; Nicholao Rimero; HCA 13/93, pp. 203–204.
21. Deposition made by Niccolo de Marini on 5 June 1548, PRO, HCA 13/5/191; Nicholao Rimero; deposition made by Domenico de Milanes on 23 May 1548, PRO, HCA 13/93/242–243; Gustav Ungerer, "Recovering a Black African's Voice in an English Lawsuit: Jacques Francis and the Salvage Operations of the 'Mary Rose' and the 'Sancta Maria and Sanctus Edwardus', 1545–c.1550", *Medieval & Renaissance Drama in English*, 17 (2005), pp. 255–271, 263; 270 n. 36. For English perceptions of Africans, see Kaufmann, *Black Tudors*; Michael Guasco, *Slaves and Englishmen: Human Bondage in the Early Modern Atlantic World* (Philadelphia, PA, 2014).

legal status in England. Corsi never claimed the divers were enslaved, while he seems to have been a member of the middling sorts without the means to purchase them. For his part, Francis testified that he was "of his own free will" in Africa and a servant in England. Ik and Blacke stated they were "servauntes" and "laboryng men".[22]

The Italians' strategy failed. The court valued Francis's acumen, allowing him to both testify and defy English notions of inferiority. With his legal personhood secured, Francis used his understanding of English society to go on the offensive, knowing Corsi's freedom would permit them to resume salvaging.[23] On 8 February 1547, he appropriated symbols of English civility, appearing in court dressed not as a slave but a skilled professional. In testimony recorded in Latin, Francis identified himself as Corsi's "famulus", meaning "servant" or "attendant", not "servus" meaning "slave", explaining they had been in a patron-client relationship for the past "two years". Francis "dyd handell and see under water" the allegedly stolen items that were "takyn and saved" and would have been restored if Corsi had not been "arreste[d]". He then accused the Italians of inhibiting the salvaging of the king's ship by arresting Corsi in "Maye", "the beste tyme" for diving, as seas were calm.[24]

Francis demonstrated that African expertise surpassed all European techniques, using African aquatics to graduate into his elevated position. As a skilled professional, he helped exonerate Corsi. Corsi, nonetheless, spent six months in the Tower of London for abandoning the *Rose* when Henry Fitzalan, Earl of Arundel, convinced the team to temporarily leave Portsmouth to "take certain of his stuff out of the sea".[25]

Here, the divers fade from the historical record, though, like watermarks upon paper, they left a lasting impression. The *Mary Rose* attracted crowds that made the divers famous while introducing the English to African salvaging techniques. From Southsea Castle, perched upon a cliff above Portsmouth, Henry VIII watched her sail into battle and watched her sink.

22. Jacques Francis; Nicholao Rimero. Kaufmann, *Black Tudors*; Guasco, *Slaves and Englishmen*, pp. 11–79, 115, especially 14, 67, 108.
23. For the manipulation of legal systems, see Graham Russell Hodges, *Root and Branch: African Americans in New York and East Jersey, 1613–1863* (Chapel Hill, NC, 1999), pp. 7–68; Anthony S. Parent, Jr., *Foul Means: The Formation of a Slave Society in Virginia, 1660–1740* (Chapel Hill, NC, 2003), pp. 105–172; Katherine Howlett Hayes, *Slavery Before Race: Europeans, Africans, and Indians at Long Island's Sylvester Manor Plantation, 1651–1884* (New York, 2013); Kevin Dawson, "The Cultural Geography of Enslaved Ship Pilots", in Jorge Cañizares-Esguerra, Matt D. Childs, and James Sidbury (eds), *Black Urban Atlantic in the Age of the Slave Trade* (Philadelphia, PA, 2013), pp. 163–186; Kevin Dawson, "Enslaved Ship Pilots in the Age of Revolutions: Challenging Notions of Race and Slavery between the Boundaries of Land and Sea", *Journal of Social History*, 47:1 (2013), pp. 71–100.
24. Jacques Francis. For racial/social inversion, see Dawson, "Enslaved Ship Pilots".
25. Kaufmann, *Black Tudors*, pp. 53–54.

Africans and swimming were novelties in sixteenth-century England and crowds gathered upon Portsmouth's waterfront to watch the divers part the English brine and land recovered goods upon its wharves, speculating upon underwater possibilities with the Earl of Arundel and others hiring them to work England's hinter-seas.[26]

The *Mary Rose*, Spanish pearl fisheries, and sixteenth- and seventeenth-century Spanish successes using enslaved divers to salvage treasure galleons inspired seventeenth-century colonists, especially from Barbados, Jamaica, Bermuda, the Bahamas, Antigua, and the Cayman Islands to begin plundering Spanish wrecks. While Spain remained the owner of treasure ships that went down decades earlier, English colonists viewed these "enemy ships" as the abandoned "Possession of the Devil", making them legitimate arenas of "frequent and abundant harvest". Thus, salvagers transformed Spanish shipping lanes into English hinter-seas, reaping Spain's hinterland-produced commodities at very little upfront cost, as illustrated below.[27]

Settled in 1609, Bermuda illustrates how early colonists sought skilled African divers to facilitate personal and colonial success. In 1615 Governor Daniel Tucker proclaimed: "Wee hold yt fitt and have given order that Mr. Willmot" should go to the "Savadge Islands", or Lesser Antilles, which includes Pearl Coast islands, where it "is hoped he shall there gett [...] negroes to dive for pearles" before Bermuda focused on salvaging, as its waters lacked pearl oysters. In 1707, English physician Hans Sloane portrayed this shift as a legitimate process, penning: "Divers, who are us'd to Pearl-fishing, &c. and can stay under Water for some Minutes [were] bought or hir'd at Great Rates and a Ship sent out to bring home Silver". Early seventeenth-century divers were probably obtained through theft. It is unlikely that Spain sold aquanauts to English salvagers so they could strip Spanish hulks in Spanish-claimed waters. It is equally improbable that Bermudians had the funds to purchase divers. Other sources indicate that Bermudians turned to piracy and the slave trade. In May 1683, Bermudian pirate Jacob Hall participated in a raid on Vera Cruz, Mexico, which possessed a pearl fishery. Seizing "1,230 Negro, Indian, and malato prisoners",

26. *Ibid.*

27. Hans Sloane, *A Voyage to the Islands Madera, Barbados, Nieves, St. Christophers and Jamaica*, 2 vols (London, 1707), I, pp. lxxx–lxxxi; Jean Hector St. John Crevecoeur, "Description of Bermuda: Extract from 'Letters d'un Cultivateur Americain' by Jean Crevecoeur", *Bermuda Historical Quarterly*, 3:4 (1946), p. 202. Hope, "Description of Bermuda"; Dawson, "Enslaved Swimmers", pp. 1348–1350; Kaufmann, *Black Tudors*, pp. 53–54; Schoepff, *Travels*, pp. 284–285; Virginia Bernhard, *Slaves and Slaveholders in Bermuda, 1616–1782* (Columbia, SC, 1999), p. 24. For scholarship on these colonies, see Jarvis, *Eye of All Trade*; Michael Craton and Gail Saunders, *Islanders in the Stream: A History of the Bahamian People: From Aboriginal Times to the End of Slavery* (Athens, GA, 1999); Roger C. Smith, *The Maritime Heritage of the Cayman Islands* (Gainesville, FL, 2000).

he sold slaves to Bermudian and Jamaican slaveholders.[28] Later, in the seventeenth century, Gold Coast people were among Bermuda's unwilling colonists. Anchored off Komenda in 1682, an English slaver complained that captives were diverted to a Bermudian slave ship offering African traders better prices. By 1628 many of Bermuda's captives were employed as salvors, perfecting their techniques on old Spanish and Portuguese wrecks.[29]

The recovery of Spanish galleon *Nuestra Señora de la Concepción* was another important salvaging event that had far-reaching repercussions. In 1641, the *Concepción*, also called the *Almiranta* or "Ambrosia wreck", sank in sixty feet of water on Ambrosia Banks (now Silver Bank) off Hispaniola. In 1686, William Phipps colluded with Bermudian captains William Davis and Abraham Adderley, with Phipps providing the financing and the Bermudians the technical expertise, to recover over twenty-five tons of gold and silver worth some £300,000 sterling. They were Atlantic men, with Adderley holding property in Jamaica while Davis had financial interests, and perhaps an estate, in Barbados. Davis arrived at the wreck in a Bermudian "Sloope" that he "fitted" with "ten gunns" in Barbados. Their diver contingents were comprised of captives from Bermuda, Jamaica, and Barbados.[30]

Phipps apparently learned of the wreck's location along Havana's waterfront from Cuban inter-island merchants who saw her submerged hulk. Taking this information to England, he obtained backing from investors who formed a joint-stock company headed by Charles Monck, Duke of Albemarle, who received the exclusive "Patent for all such wrecks" from King James II. Purchasing two ships in London, the *Henry* and the *Bridgewater*, Phipps renamed the latter *James and Mary* after the King and Queen. Sailing for Barbados in September 1686, they re-provisioned and Francis Rogers boarded the *Henry* as captain, bringing one dugout canoe,

28. Sloane, *Voyage*, I, pp. lxxx–lxxxi; J.H. Lefroy, *Memorials of the Discovery and Early Settlement of the Bermudas or Somers Islands, 1515–1685*, 2 vols (London, 1877), I, pp. 60–61, 72, 115–116, 159–160, especially 115–116; Vernon A. Ives (ed.), *The Rich Papers: Letters from Bermuda, 1615–1646* (London, 1984), p. 401; David Marley, *Sack of Veracruz: The Great Pirate Raid of 1683* (Ontario, 1993).
29. Robin Law (ed.), *The English in West Africa, 1681–1683: The Local Correspondence of the Royal African Company of England, 1681–1699*, 3 vols (Oxford, 1997), I, p. 273; Jarvis, *Eye of All Trade*, pp. 80–82.
30. Jarvis, *Eye of All Trade*, pp. 80–82; 502 n. 34; William Phipps Papers, VII, p. 14, Frederick Lewis Gay Transcripts [Massachusetts Historical Society, Boston]; Peter Earle, *The Wreck of the Almiranta: Sir William Phips and the Search for the Hispaniola Treasure* (London, 1979), pp. 155, 168–180; U1515/O10, William Yarway, "A Journal of our Voyage Intended by Divine Asistance in the Ship Henry, Frances Rogers Com: Bound for Ambroshia Banks on ye North Side off Hispaniola, in Company with ye James & Mary, Cap: W.^m. Phips Com^er: Both in Pursuits of a Spanish Wreck in Search with God for our Guide Henry", 27 February 1686, Kent History and Library Centre [hereafter, "Yarway, Journal of the Henry"]; Inventory of Abraham Adderley, 4 April 1690, Bermuda Wills, III, pp. 107–111 [Massachusetts Historical Society, Boston].

and John Pasqua, Francis Anderson, and Jonas Abimeleck, who were enslaved divers from Port Royal, Jamaica.[31] On 20 January 1687, William Covill, second mate of the *James and Mary*, and "Francis & Jonas Abimeleck" took the canoe to look for the *Concepción*. Remarkably, they found her "in 2 hours", spotting bronze cannons against the seafloor's white sand in forty feet of water.[32]

Numerous other vessels from Bermuda, Jamaica, the Bahamas, Barbados, and Turks Islands descended upon the wreck.[33] The *Concepción* was worked by approximately sixty aquanauts, who were probably African-born, as the documented names suggest. Phipps manned the *James and Mary* with four Mosquito Indians; one was named Amataba, another Sancho. All were pearl divers who had fled Nicaragua.[34]

Divers' value was measured not by the duration of their labors, but by the value of the goods raised. During brief moments beneath the sea, they produced tremendous wealth. For instance, Adderley hired an unnamed "Negroe" diver, who was probably James Locke, from Mary Robinson of Bermuda. Locke's share (probably between one-tenth and one-twentieth of what Adderley's crew recovered) amounted to 2,358 "pieces of eight", or *Spanish dollars*. Pasqua, Anderson, and Abimeleck were similarly productive, with the *Henry's* log keeping daily tallies of what this team recovered, including several silver bars and plates and over one hundred dollars in silver coin, and other valuables per day. Indeed, 24 February was exceptionally productive, as they gathered 10,105 dollar coins and 518 half-dollar coins.[35]

As Phipps departed "towards England" on 27 April 1687, word of the *Concepción* rippled across maritime channels of communication, allowing salvagers from English, French, and Dutch colonies to converge upon her before Phipps reached London. Bermudians recovered the most. Adderley and Davis declared three tons of coins and plate worth £27,000. At least

---

31. Cotton Mather, *Pietas in Patriam: The Life of His Excellency Sir William Phips, Knt. Late Captain General and Governour in Chief of the Province of the Massachuset-Bay, New England, Containing the Memorable Changes Undergone, and Actions Performed by Him* (London, 1697), pp. 11, 104; Yarway, "Journal of the Henry", 24 September 1685–16 November 1686.

32. Yarway, "Journal of the Henry", 24 September 1685 to 16 March 1686, especially 20 January 1686; Peter Earle, *Treasure Hunt: Shipwreck, Diving, and the Quest for Treasure in an Age of Heroes* (New York, 2007), pp. 60–61.

33. Yarway, "Journal of the Henry".

34. Phipps Papers, VI, pp. 66–68; VII, especially pp. 12, 14, 17, 20; Lieutenant's logbooks for HMS *Foresight* 1687–1690; HMS *Fowey* 1696–1716; HMS *Falcon* 1778-1782, ADM/L/F/198 [National Archives, Kew, Great Britain]; Yarway, "Journal of the Henry", 24 September 1685 to 16 March 1686, especially 20 January 1686; Jarvis, *Eye of All Trade*, pp. 80–82, 502 n. 34, 503 n. 36.

35. Bermuda Colonial Records, 1615–1713, vol. 8, p. 190, Bermuda Archives; Jarvis, *Eye of All Trade*, 503 n. 36; Yarway, "Journal of the Henry".

thirteen other Bermudian vessels declared almost 17,000 pounds of silver and one ton of gold, worth over £48,000 sterling. Bermudians also mounted twelve salvaged brass cannons in the island's fort to guard their wealth and divers against pirates and a vengeful Spain. Undeclared treasure was also smuggled into Bermuda, and other ports. It was believed that Adderley and Davis underreported their salvage by £15,000-£16,000. Even Governor Robert Robinson engaged in clandestine salvaging. Claiming King James II granted him rights to one-tenth of whatever he salvaged for the colony, Robinson impressed twenty-four enslaved divers and mariners, primarily employing them for his personal benefit. He further profited by collecting the crown's royal tenth on all salvage, underreporting the amount to London, and embezzling the difference.[36]

Phipps demonstrates how salvaging could realign one's stars, while shaping English overseas expansion, with historians concluding that the *Concepción* "was sufficient to alter the course of England's financial history". Receiving an investment of £3,200, Phipps reached London with proceeds of between £205,000 and £210,000, making investors' returns great, even after James II received his royal tenth. Historians believe such returns encouraged the formation of many future joint-stock companies, contributing "substantially to the expansion of the market in stocks in the early 1690s and thereby to the foundation of the Bank of England". In 1707, Sloane noted that the operation inspired many similar "Projects of the same nature". For his part, Phipps, who was of humble frontier New England origins, received £8,000, fame, and a knighthood, going on to become Massachusetts' first royally appointed governor.[37]

Concepción divers changed many Bermudians' fortunes. Adderley and his salvors each declared shares of 2,358 pieces of eight. Prior to the *Concepción*, Adderley was a man of modest socio-economic standing. His 1690 estate inventory reflects a sharp economic rise. He purchased eighty-seven acres of land, filling his home with a surprising number of luxury items, including £448 in cash, 1,856 ounces of bullion, a substantial collection of English-made silver spoons, plates, and tankards, two mirrors, topped off by candlesticks plated with recovered Spanish coins. He also purchased fourteen slaves, twenty-five cows, several boats and small ships, and two ship-cannons.[38]

Much of these hinter-seas proceeds were invested in terrestrial production and comfort. Adderley's purchase of land, slaves, and livestock reveals plans

36. Phipps Papers, IV, VII, pp. 14, 19, 22, 24, especially I, pp. 14-15; Yarway, "Journal of the Henry"; Jarvis, *Eye of All Trade*, pp. 80–82, 502 n. 34, 503 n. 36.
37. Emerson W. Baker and John G. Reid, *The New England Knight: Sir William Phips, 1651–1695* (Toronto, 1998), pp. xi, 53–54; Sloane, *Voyage*, I, pp. lxxx–lxxxi.
38. Phipps Papers, VII, pp. 25, 40; Inventory of Abraham Adderley, 4 April 1690, Bermuda Wills, III, pp. 107–111, Bermuda Archives; Jarvis, *Eye of All Trade*, p. 503 n. 36.

for using hinter-seas proceeds to pursue terrestrial production. Phipps's benefits were equally tangible. The Duke of Albemarle gave Phipps's wife "a Present of a *Golden Cup*, near a Thousand Pound in value" for Phipps honestly delivering the salvage to London. In Boston, where most homes were wood, Phipps "built himself a Fair Brick House". Additionally, the now *Sir* William Phipps ascended into the ranks of the nobility, expanding his social, political, and economic connections and opportunities throughout the English Empire.[39]

White salvors incentivized work to extract incomes from divers' minds and bodies. Most divers were hired out, using this labor system to destabilize typical slaveholder-slave relations by, among other things, exercising varying degrees of control over their lives. Hiring out permitted captives to construct social and political spaces in between slavery and freedom, where they challenged notions of African inferiority by forming work contracts honored by white employers and government officials and making their own shoreside living arrangements. It was lucrative for slave owners, who received a portion of hirelings' incomes, while employers benefited from slaves' wisdom and brawn.[40] Divers' expertise allowed them to gain far greater benefits than slaves hired into other occupations. Instead of solely relying upon wages to motivate divers, white salvors created hybridized wage-share systems in which divers also received shares.[41]

Affidavits of the *Ann* from Barbados exemplify this process. Praising the five divers who worked the *Concepción*, it read "four of ye aforsaid five Divars by name Keazar, Salsbury, Tony & Tom were as good as any that went from Barbados", and these "Divers [received] four single shares", while "the Negro Bamko the other Diver, one share". The *Ann* also evidences divers' origins. Most seventeenth-century Barbadian slaves were African-born, and Bamko and Keazar seemingly bore African names.[42]

Divers did not passively wait for white authority to bequeath privileges. They knew their numbers were few, they were not easily replaced, and, without divers, salvagers were largely left to gaze at shipwrecks through clear Caribbean waters. Bermudians knew well-treated divers were more productive, prompting Phipps to hire "Spanish hunt[rs]" to obtain upwards of twenty-nine "wild hoggs" per day. Those suffering from diving disorders and other ailments were granted time off. To reduce injury, diving was performed only

---

39. Mather, *Pietas in Patriam*, pp. 6, 14–15, 18; Baker and Reid, *New England Knight*, pp. 54–69. Also see the discussion of Sam Lord below.
40. See Dawson, "Enslaved Ship Pilots", p. 80.
41. Instead of strictly adhering to hiring-out traditions, salvagers seemingly rented divers, paying slaveholders a monthly fee. For hiring out, see Jonathan D. Martin, *Divided Mastery: Slave Hiring in the American South* (Cambridge, MA, 2004); Dawson, "Enslaved Ship Pilots".
42. Phipps Papers, VI, pp. 33–38; Charles Vignoles, *Observations upon the Floridas* (New York, 1823), p. 125. For other Barbadian ships, see Phipps Papers, VI and VIII.

in calm seas, often precluding work for several days.[43] Divers also kept themselves from being sucked into the churning whirlpools of verbal and physical abuse that punctuated the daily experiences of sailors and agricultural slaves. They informed captains that physical punishment prolonged recovery times, and could render them unfit to dive. Indeed, Phipps was notoriously violent towards white officers and sailors, yet refrained from abusing Indian and black divers, and there were only two reported deaths among the approximately sixty *Concepción* divers.[44] Hence, divers were well treated – for slaves.

Ashore, aquanauts received roughly the same food, clothing, and shelter as their owners, prompting Governor John Hope of Bermuda to state, in 1722: "They are Strong well Bodied Fellows and well fed". Many became literate, using this skill to advance their opportunities.[45] Some free and enslaved salvors became ship captains, commanding white and black mariners. Unfortunately, sources do not describe shipboard relationships under slaves' captaincies. For instance, Governor Hope simply noted that Turks Island slaveholders dispatched "vessels navigated by negro's" to go "fishing for turtle, diving upon wrecks, and sometimes trading with pyrates".[46]

Hinter-seas also produced colonists. On 7 December 1781, the *Nelly*, en route from Calabar (Nigeria) to Jamaica, grounded off Grand Cayman, where Caymanians saved 321 of the 429 captives and all but one crewmember. The vessel's recovery was a pivotal moment in the archipelago's development. Salvaging offered a much-needed economic boost for this backwater Jamaican territory as many of the slaves were sold in Jamaica "to pay salvage". Some rescued captives, along with bond people saved from subsequent wrecks, became unwilling colonists. A permanent English population dates to 1734, yet the slave population remained small prior to the import of the *Nelly's* slaves. By 1802, 551 of the 933 inhabitants were of African descent. Salvaging redefined Cayman's shoreside population,

---

43. Phipps Papers, VII, pp. 3, 6–8; Yarway, "Journal of the Henry", 9 January 1687, 28 May 1686; Earle, *Almiranta*, p. 184. For time off when ill, see Phipps Papers, VII, pp. 14, 17, 20; Yarway, "Journal of the Henry". For dive conditions, see Phipps Papers, VI, VII; Yarway, "Journal of the Henry", 24 September 1685 to 16 March 1686.

44. For Phipps' violence, see John Knepp's Journal of a Voyage from the Downes to Boston in the Ship Rose, William Phipps Commander, 1683, Frederick Lewis Gay Transcripts, Massachusetts Historical Society [hereafter, John Knepp's Journal]; Baker and Reid, *New England Knight*, pp. 22, 41, 91, 211. For ill divers, see Phipps Papers, VII, pp. 14, 17, 20.

45. Hope, "Description of Bermuda"; Daniel McKinnen, *A Tour Through the British West Indies, in the Years 1802 and 1803* (London, 1804), pp. 140–141; Jarvis, *Eye of All Trade*, pp. 217, 281, 283.

46. "Lt. Governor Hope to the Duke of Newcastle", in Cecil Headlam and Arthur Percival Newton (eds), *Calendar of State Papers: Colonial, America and West Indies*, vol. 34 (London, 1936); Anonymous, "Voyage from Halifax to Bermuda", in *Mariner's Chronicle of Shipwrecks, Fires, Famines and Other Disasters at Sea*, 2 vols (Boston, MA, 1834), I, pp. 326–327; Miller, *Nassau, Bahamas*, p. 43. For black captains, see W. Jeffrey Bolster, *Black Jacks: African American Seamen in the Age of Sail* (Cambridge, MA, 1998).

providing it with a black majority, while transforming it from a society with slaves into a slave society that cultivated hinter-seas rather than plantations.[47]

Salvaging equally benefited colonies committed to plantation bondage, with Barbados demonstrating planters' involvement in salvaging. By the 1650s, Barbadian plantation slavery was deep-rooted, allowing sugar to "dominate the Barbadian export sector" in what "was a slave society by at least 1680". In 1840, Robert Schomburgk reported that "repeated instances of shipwrecks have attracted the attention of successive commanders-of-chief on the West Indian station", while goods also fell overboard in Barbadian waters and planters hired out divers to work distant wrecks, all of which allowed slaveholders to capitalize on the debris of consumer cultures. As noted above, during the mid-1680s, the *Ann* from Barbados employed slave divers to work on *Concepción*. While sources document the regularity of shipwrecks in Barbadian waters and lighthouses were built during the late nineteenth century to reduce their frequency, records detailing salvaging in Barbadian waters have not been located. For example, between 1820 and 1834 sixteen ships wrecked on Cobbler Reef in Long Bay off Sam Lord's cotton plantation. Male and female slaves saved mariners and plundered these wrecks, which apparently provided capital necessary to construct Lord's "Long Bay Castle". Completed in 1831, it was "one of the finest mansions in the West Indies", making it "an oasis in the desert" of far more modest neighboring estates. Its elaborately carved ceiling took English and Italian craftsmen three years to complete and Lord lavishly furnished it with an array of fine English furniture, silverware, china, glass, books, and decor. Perhaps to conceal his duplicity, Lord provided no written record of these shipwrecks.[48]

Divers in maritime and plantation colonies gained similarly, benefiting from the flexibility of maritime bondage. Enslavers promoted arduousness by avoiding coercive discipline, nurturing a sense of mutual obligation arising from collective responsibilities, and extending material rewards. They cultivated reciprocal relationships binding slaves to multi-racial crews and the

---

47. Quoted in Neville Williams, *A History of the Cayman Islands* (Grand Cayman, 1970), p. 21; Voyages: The Trans-Atlantic Slave Trade Database, available at: http://www.slavevoyages.org/voyage/82894/variables; last accessed 22 June 2010. Gomer Williams, *History of the Liverpool Privateers and Letters of Marque with an Account of the Liverpool Slave Trade* (London, 1897), p. 566; Smith, *Cayman Islands*, pp. 170–174; Michael Craton, *Founded upon the Seas: A History of the Cayman Islands and Their People* (Kingston, 2003), pp. 57–60, 63, 111, 433 n. 1.
48. Russell R. Menard, *Sweet Negotiations: Sugar, Slavery, and Plantation Agriculture in Early Barbados* (Charlottesville, VA, 2006), especially pp. 30, 44–45, 48; Schomburgk, *Barbados*, pp. 323–325, 218–219, especially 181, 219; Richard S. Dunn, *Sugar and Slaves: The Rise of the Planter Class in the English West Indies, 1624–1713* (Chapel Hill, NC, 1972), pp. 3–187. For Sam Lord, see A.H. Wightwick Haywood, "Sam Lord and His Castle", *Journal of Barbados Museum and Historical Society*, XXX:4 (1964), pp. 114–125; Neville Connell, "Sam Lord's Castle", *Journal of Barbados Museum and Historical Society*, XXX:4 (1964), pp. 126–129; Anonymous, *A Guide to Sam Lord's Castle* (Barbados, n.d.).

islands where their families lived, while implicit threats of selling family members transformed them into hostages, compelling divers to return home. As the eighteenth century progressed, multi-racial kinship ties increasingly bolstered shipmate affiliations. Many whites went to sea with biracial men whom they owned. Some recognized divers as relatives, allowing aquanauts to use white familial ties to advance their positions. For instance, by 1824 it was said that "most" Bahamians "have a dash of dark blood in their veins & many are mulattoes".[49]

Divers cloistered their wisdom, creating semi-fraternal orders that precluded slaveholders from appropriating and propagating their aquatic fluencies, as occurred when South Carolina planters integrated African rice-producing methods "within applicable European farming strategies without the need to offer compensation".[50] Beneath the sea, African wisdom outperformed European technology and techniques, providing aquanauts with sway. Concurrently, gender prejudices impeded white attempts to control divers. Skilled labor was a "gendered phenomenon" favoring bondmen as "enslaved women found themselves confined to the monotony and drudgery of the field more regularly than their male counterparts". Many African-descended women were expert divers. Yet, beliefs that maritime labor was a male occupation precluded women from salvaging. In the absence of this gendered bias, slaveholders could have swelled divers' numbers to increase their control over salvaging.[51]

FORGING BONDS BETWEEN SEAPORTS AND HINTER-SEAS

Divers' ability to retain privileges in homeports hinged on more than linking seaports to hinter-seas. They had to inform white port residents of their

49. Miller, *Nassau, Bahamas*, pp. 25, 43; Anonymous, "Halifax to Bermuda", pp. 326–327; Jarvis, *Eye of All Trade*, pp. 30–31, 147–151, Michael J. Jarvis, "Maritime Masters and Seafaring Slaves in Bermuda, 1680–1783", *The William and Mary Quarterly*, 59:3 (2002), pp. 585–622, 608; Michael J. Jarvis, "The Binds of the Anxious Mariner: Patriarchy, Paternalism, and the Maritime Culture of Eighteenth-Century Bermuda", *Journal of Early Modern History*, 14:1 (2010), pp. 75–117, 86; Bernhard, *Slaves and Slaveholders*, pp. 50–52, 123, 238–272; Dawson, "Enslaved Ship Pilots"; Bolster, *Black Jacks*, especially pp. 268–269; Craton and Saunders, *Islanders*, pp. 179–396; Craton, *Founded upon the Seas*, pp. 52–3, 111, 146–147, 217; Smith, *Cayman Islands*, pp. 73–74; McKinnen, *British West Indies*, pp. 140–141.
50. S. Max Edelson, *Plantation Enterprise in Colonial South Carolina* (Cambridge, MA, 2011), pp. 62–63, 97, 156–158, especially 84; Carney, *Black Rice*, especially p. 81; Littlefield, *Rice and Slaves*.
51. Follett, *Sugar Masters*, pp. 127–128; Jennifer L. Morgan, *Laboring Women: Reproduction and Gender in New World Slavery* (Philadelphia, PA, 2004), pp. 144–165, especially 146–147; Daina Ramey Berry, *Swing the Sickle for the Harvest is Ripe: Gender and Slavery in Antebellum Georgia* (Chicago, IL, 2007), pp. 14–19.

ability to transform what would have otherwise been production-less shipping lanes into arenas of substantial economic production. Many New World ports were small, while maritime colonies functioned as ports that were home to small interconnected populations. This spatial arrangement and related social geography allowed most residents to palpably experience how salvagers benefited them. For instance, the historian Michael Jarvis explained that the spending practices of salvagers who worked the *Concepción* infused Bermuda with considerable amounts of capital, "spreading much of their cash throughout the island", in ways benefiting all Bermudians. This seemingly convinced them, in some important ways, to treat divers like free, skilled laborers.[52]

Smuggling salvage into port strengthened the bonds between seaports and hinter-seas. Divers were central in producing salvage and smuggling it across imperial borders and into homeports, as demonstrated when English salvors secreted *Concepción* salvage out of the Spanish Empire and into English ports. Even though most of the salvage was declared in London and colonial ports, much went undeclared. Scholars have convincingly argued that intra- and inter-imperial seaborne smuggling benefited most seaport residents. Most seaport residents understood how smuggled salvage improved their material circumstances and that divers offloaded, hid, and helped launder undeclared wealth. The *Concepción's* unreported salvage was a poorly kept secret, with many Bermudians, including officials, openly discussing and displaying their smuggled wealth. Likewise, Caymanians exemplify how cargoes and ships were used to build and ornament salvagers/wreckers' homes. Ships' hinges, latches, windows, and timber were repurposed, while French tiles pulled from one wreck adorned the floors of several homes. Duplicity in smuggling and wrecking probably provided divers with privilege-extracting leverage bolstered by white people's understanding that aggrieved divers could disclose their unlawful activities.[53]

---

52. Jarvis, *Eye of All Trade*, pp. 82, 503 n. 36. In 1802, the Cayman Islands had fewer than 1,000 residents. During the 1770s, Bermuda had a population of about 10,500. In 1807, the Bahamas were home to 3,525 people. Plantation island ports were also relatively small. Bridgetown's seventeenth-century population hovered around 3,000 and remained at about 10,000 until the mid-eighteenth century, before rising to 14,000. In 1730, Kingston, Jamaica, was home to 4,461 people, a figure that increased dramatically. Craton, *Founded upon the Seas*, p. 60; Jarvis, *Eye of All Trade*, p. 262; Craton and Saunders, *Islanders in the Stream*, p. 180; Pedro Welch, *Slave Society in the City: Bridgetown Barbados, 1680–1834* (Kingston, 2003), p. 53; Trevor Burnard, "Kingston, Jamaica: Crucible of Modernity", in Cañizares-Esguerra *et al.* (eds), *Black Urban Atlantic*, p. 126.

53. Hope Masterton Waddell, *Twenty-Nine Years in the West Indies and Central Africa: A Review of Missionary Work and Adventure, 1829–1858* (London, 1863), pp. 212–217; Smith, *Cayman Islands*, p. 175. For smuggling, see Wim Klooster, *Illicit Riches: Dutch Trade in the Caribbean, 1648–1795* (Leiden, 1998); Kenneth J. Banks, "Official Duplicity: The Illicit Slave Trade of Martinique", in Peter A. Coclanis (ed.), *The Atlantic Economy during the*

Divers continually endeared themselves to white elites by employing hydrographic and maritime aptitudes in corollary professions. Between salvage operations they worked as ship pilots, fishermen, sea turtlers, sponge and conch divers, and coastal and inter-island sailors. These occupations allowed divers to cultivate nuanced understanding of hydrography and weather patterns that precipitated shipwrecks while situating them to find recent wrecks.[54]

Using their incomes and white connections, some obtained freedom, becoming independent salvagers, while improving family members' circumstances, as James Locke demonstrates. Abraham Adderley helped Locke purchase his liberty from Mary Robinson and then purchase his sister, Betty, and her son, "Jethrow". Sources suggest that most freed divers maintained bonds with white patrons, who advanced their interests and shielded them from abuse. For instance, Adderley and Locke seemingly colluded to gain Locke's freedom so they could salvage without Robinson's interference.[55]

As divers circulated the Atlantic world, seaports became concentric links in the sprawling constellation of communities created as aquanauts and other maritime slaves cast far-reaching lines of connectivity.[56] Seaports were important places and structures for harnessing skilled labor, while converging human currents accumulated, interlaced, and disseminated global knowledge that had been developed on African, European, and New World hinter-seas. There "was no center to the Atlantic, although there were nodal points with their own centripetal political, economic, and cultural forces, notably in urban areas, where Atlantic peoples met, shared information, and circulated ideas, things, and people between themselves in ongoing, reciprocal, contestable networks". Seaport residents, including divers, were "quintessential Atlantic people".[57]

At docks, aquanauts exchanged salvaging techniques, speculated on how recent storms exposed sand-covered wreckage, learned how shipping and weather patterns conspired to sink and accumulate colonial wealth in somewhat predictable places, and considered the possible locations of missing

Seventeenth and Eighteenth Centuries: Organization, Operation, Practice, and Personnel (Columbia, SC, 2005), pp. 229–252; Dawson, "Enslaved Ship Pilots", pp. 71–100.

54. Dawson, "Enslaved Ship Pilots", pp. 79–87.

55. Bermuda Colonial Records, 1615–1713, vol. 8, p. 190, Bermuda Archives.

56. Julius S. Scott, "Afro-American Sailors and the International Communication Network: The Case of Newport Bowers", in Colin Howell and Richard Twomey (eds), *Jack Tar in History: Essays in the History of Maritime Life and Labour* (Fredericton, 1991), pp. 41–42; Alexander X. Byrd, *Captives and Voyagers: Black Migration Across the Eighteenth-Century British Atlantic World* (Baton Rouge, LA, 2008), especially pp. 177–253; Peter Linebaugh and Marcus Rediker, *The Many-Headed Hydra: Sailors, Slaves, Commoners, and the Hidden History of the Revolutionary Atlantic* (Boston, MA, 2000), pp. 174–210; Bolster, *Black Jacks*, pp. 23, 186–187; Dawson, "Enslaved Ship Pilots", pp. 75, 79–81.

57. Burnard, "Kingston, Jamaica: Crucible of Modernity", p. 143.

vessels. Seaports contained vibrant multiracial institutions catering to maritime workers' desires while serving as marketplaces of information that advanced black and white salvagers' economic opportunities. The murmurings of the Atlantic world floated into taverns and brothels, where prostitutes, customers, and barkeepers gleaned information about shipwrecks, passing it on to receptive divers and white salvagers.[58] It was along Boston's waterfront that William Phipps acquired his initial lessons on salvaging. On 16 October 1683, three years before salvaging the *Concepción*, shipmaster Peres Savage boasted how he "consorted" with six other captains to assemble thirty "good divers" to partially salvage a Spanish wreck in the Bahamas. This foray informed Phipps of the importance of enslaved divers. Similarly, Petri Corsi, Jacques Francis, and the other African divers frequented English taverns, where they were hired by merchants whose ships had sunk in England's hinter-seas.[59] As rumors of shipwrecks drifted into seaports upon the lips of mariners and pages of newspapers printed in far-off ports, white salvagers amassed teams of enslaved divers, slipping off to create new hinter-seas.

Port Royal, Jamaica was an important center for salvaging, providing a unique opportunity for divers to create a new hinter-sea. It was also the largest seventeenth-century Caribbean city and "one of the world's great harbors". White pirates and salvagers assembled teams of "Diving Negroes" to work wrecks around its shipping lanes, amassing their treasure in waterfront homes. On 7 June 1692, an earthquake caused much of this seaport to slide beneath the ocean, transforming it into a hinter-sea for Kingston and what remained of Port Royal. The submerged town became the long-term training ground for over 200 enslaved divers who, for more than thirty years, entered its partially collapsed structures. It can be inferred that its waters, wharves, and taverns were important places for concentrating, perfecting, and disseminating techniques. In 1687, John Pasqua, Francis Anderson, Jonas Abimeleck, and other divers carried their expertise from Port Royal to Barbados, then to the *Conceptión*. After the earthquake, they probably swam along streets they had once walked. While there are no known descriptions of this salvage operation, twentieth-century underwater archaeologists reported that enslaved divers were "quite thorough and good at their work; missing very little of value", stripping structures so "there was absolutely nothing to be found".[60]

---

58. Dawson, "Enslaved Ship Pilots", pp. 75, 79–81.
59. John Knepp's Journal, pp. 86–87; Sloane, *Voyage*, I, p. lxxx; Mather, *Pietas in Patriam*, p. 104; Kaufmann, *Black Tudors*, p. 40.
60. Dunn, *Sugar and Slaves*, pp. 21, 36, 43–45, 177–179, especially 36; Robert F. Marx, "Divers of Port Royal", *Jamaica Journal*, 2:1 (1968), pp. 15–23; especially 21; "A Letter from Hans Sloane, M.D., with Accounts of the Earthquakes in Peru, Oct. 20. 1687; and at Jamaica, Feb. 19. 1687–8; and June 7. 1692", in *Philosophical Transactions, Giving Some Account of the*

Port Royal divers quickly mobilized to other hinter-seas. In September 1730, the fifty-four gun "Spanish Man of War" *Genoesa* wrecked upon Pedro Bank (about forty miles south-west of Jamaica) carrying a "great Treasure". Sea turtlers rescued the Spaniards, depositing them ashore, and began stripping the *Genoesa*. To preserve the *Asiento*, or contract, allowing Britain to import slaves into the Spanish Americas, Governor Robert Hunter of Jamaica sought to secure the vessel, requesting English "Ships of War to guard the Wreck" and asked "the Gentlemen" of Port Royal to lend their divers to recover "all such Treasures" they could. Arriving at the *Genoesa*, Captain Ware, who commanded a "Sloop", encountered unsanctioned salvagers, turned wreckers, pillaging her. Instead of safeguarding the vessel, Ware colluded with them and "fish'd up a great deal of Treasure. The third day while they were at work upon her", the HMS *Experiment* arrived. Ware claimed to be securing the treasure and "readily promised" to load it aboard the *Experiment* the following morning, but slipped off in the night. The *Experiment* gave chase before leaks forced her to return to Port Royal, allowing wreckers to descend upon the *Genoesa* before she was secured by the HMS *Tryall*, which recovered 31,695 gold and silver coins, 105 silver ingots, and eight bars of gold. Spaniards also "fish'd up and brought from the said wreck a good deal of treasure etc.". Regardless, Governor Hunter concluded that wreckers made off with most of the treasure, accusing Neal Walker, commander of a sloop belonging to the South Sea Company, of looting gold and 16,000 pieces of eight, which was "shar'd and divided the same among themselves in a private and clandestine manner", on Little Cayman Island. Hunter also exclaimed that "there had been other vessels in a clandestine manner fishing upon her, and that part of the treasure had been landed in remote parts and there concealed and secreted".[61]

Among other things, the *Genoesa* illustrates divers' ability to quickly strip wrecks, while underscoring the acceptance of wrecking and smuggling. Wreckers secreted salvage into Jamaica and Cayman Islands, where merchants accepted Spanish coins as payment. Furthermore, English officials openly engaged in wrecking, as both Ware and Walker were employees of public-private trading companies and both seemingly escaped punishment.

Present Undertakings, Studies and Labours of the Ingenious in Many Considerable Parts of the World, XVIII, issues 207–214 (London, 1695), pp. 77–100; J.W. Fortescue (ed.), *Calendar of State Papers: Colonial, America and West Indies*, vol. 13 (London, 1902), pp. 651–711.
61. "Hunter to Lord of Trades", 19 September 1730, 24 December 1730, PRO, CO 137/18, fos 70–71, pp. 120–122; Proclamation of 26 September 1730, list of treasure, PRO, CO 137/19, fos 3, 5; "Governor Hunter to the Council of Trade and Plantations", 19 September 1730, 1 October 1730, 24 December 1730, in Cecil Headlam and Arthur Percival Newton (eds), *Calendar of State Papers: Colonial, America and West Indies*, vol. 37 (London, 1937); Smith, *Cayman Islands*, p. 170.

Divers' ability to link seaports to lucrative hinter-seas afforded privileges that made them targets of those seeking to appropriate their bodies and wisdom, as illustrated by Ned Grant, a Charleston, South Carolina diver. Grant was stolen by pirates and, after he had been recovered, Charleston officials conspired to appropriate him. On 27 September 1718, Grant and nine other slaves were captured in North Carolina's Cape Fear River, with Barbadian planter-turned-pirate Stede Bonnet. The ensuing piracy cases were tried by Judge Nicholas Trott in the South Carolina Vice Admiralty Court.[62] As typical in piracy cases, on 17 November Grant became part of the litigation over Bonnet's "Sloop Revenge", her "Negroes Goods & Merchandise". William Rhett, a planter and slave trader, led the expedition against Bonnet, claiming Grant as "Salvage", meaning Rhett was entitled to a *share* of his value. Grant's owner, the widow Catherine Tuckerman, sought his return, explaining she "hired" him "to one Captain Barrett" who "took him to the Wrecks for a Diver", referring to the 1715 Spanish Plata (Silver) Fleet that sank in a hurricane off Cape Canaveral, Florida. Known as the "Bahama Wrecks", pirates from Port Royal, the Bahamas, Bermuda, and elsewhere drove Spanish salvagers off to plunder the hulks. There, Grant was "taken [stolen] by one Capt. Burgess a pirate and by him Carried to the Bahama Islands". Grant escaped to New England, where he boarded a vessel "bound for Great Britain which was afterwards taken by Stede Bonnett the Pirate". At this juncture, Grant was apparently recognized as a diver or disclosed his aquatic acumen to escape harsh treatment, for Bonnet took him back to the "Bahama Wrecks", and then North Carolina.[63]

Judge Trott detested pirates as "Enemies of Mankind", believing salvagers "gave birth and increase to all the Pirates in those Parts" as both preyed upon others' misfortune. There was no evidence that Grant engaged in piracy and Trott could have returned him to Tuckerman. Instead, Trott ruled that Grant was "a notorious Renegade", sentencing him to be "publicly sold", with half

---

62. *Sloop Revenge*, 19 November 1718, South Carolina Vice Admiralty Court Records, A–B vols, pp. 276–300, Library of Congress, Manuscripts Division, Washington, DC; *The Tryals of Major Stede Bonnet, and Other Pirates* (London, 1719). Special thanks to Lee B. Wilson for informing me of this case. Lindley S. Butler, *Pirates, Privateers, and Rebel Raiders of the Carolina Coast* (Chapel Hill, NC, 2000), pp. 51–72.

63. *Masters et al. v. Sloop Revenge*, South Carolina Vice-Admiralty Court Records, A–B vols, pp. 276–300 [Library of Congress, Manuscripts Division, Washington, DC], pp. 279, 289–291, 300; *Tryals*, pp. 8, 45; Mark G. Hanna, *Pirate Nests and the Rise of the British Empire, 1570–1740* (Chapel Hill, NC, 2015), pp. 371, 389. There are no known descriptions of diving at the 1715 "Bahama Wrecks" that were worked by slaveholders from North America, Jamaica, Barbados, the Bahamas, or Bermuda. Charles Leslie, *A New History of Jamaica, from the Earliest Accounts, to the Taking of Porto Bello by Vice-Admiral Vernon* (London, 1740), p. 274; *Tryals*, pp. 8, 4.

the proceeds going to Tuckerman, the other to Rhett, who was Trott's brother-in-law.[64]

Grant's ability to link the small but significant port of Charleston[65] to fertile hinter-seas made him an important fixture in this seaport. Trott seemingly condemned Grant so Rhett would profit from his sale. To Trott's chagrin, Tuckerman paid "the Salvage" to repurchase her slave for far less than he would have been sold for at auction. Undoubtedly motivated to regain and exploit her property, Tuckerman's actions, nonetheless, rescued Grant from an uncertain future, reuniting him with family and friends.[66] Grant demonstrates the limits of divers' humanity, made palpable when, like all slaves, whites sought to possess and control their wisdom and expertise.

While hinterlands lay close to seaports, hinter-seas could be far off, allowing colonists to profoundly expand their arenas of economic production. Seventeenth- and early eighteenth-century divers' success in stripping known Spanish treasure ships prompted salvors to engage in wrecking and cross the Atlantic. The *Hartwell* exemplifies these shifts in the pursuit of profits. On 23 May 1787, the *Hartwell*, the largest and one of the "finest ships" in the British East India Company's (EIC) fleet, sank in forty feet of water off Boa Vista Island, in the Cape Verde Islands off West Africa. Carrying money and trade goods with which to purchase Indian commodities, it contained sixty chests of silver coins worth £153,642, three chests belonging to the ship's owner, "several packages of private trade", and one hundred lead ingots. London newspapers chummed the channels of maritime communication with exaggerated tales of her fortunes while describing how enslaved and free Cape Verdians worked her, luring wreckers across the Atlantic.[67]

William Braithwaite of London and his sons, John and William, Jr, secured the EIC contract giving them exclusive rights to salvage the *Hartwell*. They had developed a steam engine to pump air into diving bells, believing this modern technique was the most efficient way to salvage wrecks. Working the wreck during summer months from 1787 to 1790, the EIC hired British warships to guard the site before deeming it unnecessary in the early summer of 1789. By mid-summer "five Piratical vessels" were "lurking

---

64. *Tryals*, p. 8; *Sloop Revenge*, pp. 297, 299.

65. Charleston had a population of about 5,000 people. Walter J. Fraser, Jr, *Charleston! Charleston!: The History of a Southern City* (Columbia, SC, 1989), pp. 26, 55; Emma Hart, *Building Charleston: Town and Society in the Eighteenth-Century British Atlantic World* (Charlottesville, VA, 2010).

66. *Sloop Revenge*, p. 297. Records do not state the salvage amount Tuckerman paid, though it would have been a fraction of Grant's value.

67. *London Chronicle*, 11–14, 14–16, 16–18 August 1787; *The Times* (London), 13 August 1787, 22 October 1787, 11 November 1788, 5 January 1789, 24 April 1790, especially 15 February 1787.

about", like hyenas circling lions' kill, "plundering the *Hartwell*" whenever the Braithwaites chased one wrecker off. On 29 August 1789, five heavily armed wreckers drove the Braithwaites off and teams of divers stripped her faster than the Braithwaites could.[68]

The wreckers worked unmolested until the HMS *Pomona*, captained by Henry Savage, who was part of Britain's West Africa Squadron, arrived on 29 October, capturing the *Brothers*. From John English, one of the *Brothers*'s seven enslaved divers, Savage gleaned the wreckers' Atlantic origins. The sloop was from St Eustatius in the Dutch West Indies and sailed under the Danish flag. Captain Thomas Hammond was from New York, the mate was Scottish, and they "procured seven Negroes Men Divers", from St Thomas in the Danish West Indies. Hammond partnered with a slave ship's "Tender belonging to St. Thomas" and commanded by "a native of Ireland". These divers recovered some 20,000 silver coins. Aquanauts belonging to the other wreckers were equally productive. *Mary* was captained by "a native of Rhode Island", flew a Dutch flag, and recovered "10,000 Dollars" before returning to its homeport of St Eustatius. The *Swift*, also of St Eustatius, flew "Swedish Colours" and "got about 8,000 Dollars", but "lost their best diver". Another sloop was stolen "from some English Port" by "an Englishman" and commanded by "Lumbard" of Cape Cod, Massachusetts.[69]

Westerners routinely believe in the unfaltering "triumph of modernity over tradition" and the EIC was both an instrument of British imperialism and juggernaut of corporate sovereignty.[70] The London *Times* praised the Braithwaites' "extraordinary genius" as a monumental improvement over "Dr. [Edmund] Hailey's diving-bell" (Figure 3), allowing them to remain "underwater for six weeks, or any length of time". Regardless, freedivers' centuries-old wisdom capsized this assumption, as African-descended aquanauts stripped this EIC leviathan faster than the Braithwaites could with the steam-driven technology of a modern industrializing Britain. Diving bells were difficult to negotiate around wrecks, too big to enter holds, while the

---

68. "Short Journal of Commodore Inglefield's Transactions on the Coast of Africa", *The Times* (London), 1 June 1790; *Universal Daily Register*, forerunner to *The Times*, 9 November 1785, 22 September 1786, 14 July 1786; William Braithwaite, "A New Line of Business: The Pioneering Braithwaites", *Diver* (June 1986), pp. 18–19; William Braithwaite, "A Short History of the Braithwaites", *Family Tree Magazine*, 18:11 (1992), pp. 8–9.

69. ADM 1/2488/12, Henry Savage to Philip Stephens, 27 May 1790, "Narrative of the Capture of the Pirate Sloop Brothers"; ADM 51/703/2, log of the *Pomona*, 30 October 1789, Kent History and Library Centre.

70. Erik Gilbert, *Dhows and the Colonial Economy of Zanzibar, 1860–1970* (Athens, GA, 2004), pp. 4–6, especially 5. For the EIC, see Philip J. Stern, *The Company-State: Corporate Sovereignty and the Early Modern Foundations of the British Empire in India* (Oxford, 2011); S. Chaudhury and M. Morineau (eds), *Merchants, Companies and Trade: Europe and Asia in the Early Modern Era* (Cambridge, 1999).

Figure 3. Halley's diving bell, engraved for the Universal Magazine, Printed by J. Hinton, London, eighteenth century.
©*Museum of the History of Science, University of Oxford.*

masts, yardarms, and rigging of recent wrecks threatened to capsize bells and snare their lines and air hose. Methods for replenishing air supplies were unreliable, frequently causing divers to suffocate. The Braithwaites' technique was a significant improvement. Regardless, their engine could only pump air twelve feet deep, requiring the bell to be frequently raised from the *Hartwell*, while its limited mobility enabled nimble, incentivized freedivers to outperform it.[71]

The *Brothers* punctuates aquanauts' potentially fragile circumstances. Captain Hammond apparently told the owners of the captured divers that they would legally salvage a shipwreck. Upon returning home, their shares were to benefit their lives and those of their enslaved family members. Charged with piracy, they never returned home. The divers became salvage, and six were sold to compensate the EIC for its losses. John English was "kept on Board the Pomona as an Guidance [perhaps meaning pilot]" and cook, which raises provocative questions. His surname and ability to speak English imply previous British associations, while Savage's decision to retain him as a pilot in the West Africa Squadron intimates understandings of African hydrography.[72]

CONCLUSION

We routinely consider the past with our backs to the ocean, assuming seas were watery roads that connected ports to each other while social, cultural, and economic production occurred ashore. We leave water out of maritime histories, treating them as dry experiences that unfolded upon ship's decks and docks, while ignoring non-Westerners' maritime traditions. Likewise, scholars regularly situate seaports between hinterlands and overseas markets. As important areas of rural production, hinterlands rise to the analytical foreground while seaports slip to intellection horizons, becoming mere entrepôts – sometimes metaphors – for connecting countrysides to distant consumers. Divers directed ports' eye to hinter-seas of production. This essay encourages scholars to view the world from different perspectives. Face seaward; slip into the intellectual drink to consider immersionary cultures and how divers informed seaports' structures and functions.

Seas were places of hope and opportunity for those capable of negotiating them. Standing upon wharves while gazing towards hinter-seas, black and white salvagers knew unique prospects lay beyond horizons and beneath the water's surface. Using African-derived expertise to harvest the human

71. *Universal Daily Register*, forerunner to *The Times*, 22 September 1786; Earle, *Treasure Hunt*, especially pp. 33–36, 174–190, 255–256, 264–265.
72. ADM 1/2488/12, Henry Savage to Philip Stephens, 27 May 1790, "Narrative of the Capture of the Pirate Sloop Brothers", Kent History and Library Centre.

debris of commercial capitalism, divers transformed shipping lanes into hinter-seas.

Even as white people enslaved African bodies and colonized dry spaces, the turbulence of maritime slavery destabilized their authority afloat, providing shipboard opportunities for captives.[73] Divers found still greater benefits beneath the waves. Even as planters imposed high rates of suffering and death on manacled field-hands, salvagers treated divers well.

Enslaved divers were not simply carried by the tides of others. From the deep, aquanauts generated undercurrents of wealth and power that, in some important ways, allowed them to chart their own course even while remaining enslaved. Employing their expertise, they deflected the prevailing winds of racial/social subjugation. As planters, capitalists, and manufacturers increasingly imposed clock discipline on laborers, divers harnessed the ocean's rhythms to resist such regulation.[74] Salvaging was largely limited to spring and summer months and, then, only during the morning calm, requiring aquanauts to dive less than two hours per day, while their enslaved brothers and sister toiled the length of their days in agricultural fields. Divers retained premodern share systems that compensated them far more than wages. They also pushed the boundaries of what is typically imagined by the "Black Atlantic" and "greater Caribbean", bringing European and African hinter-seas, seaports, and port communities into their orbits of understanding.[75]

It is time to take the deep intellectual dive. By incorporating the ocean into Atlantic history and immersionary traditions into maritime deliberations, we can expand our intellectual horizons by thousands of miles, both across and below the water's surface. But, oceans are not one vast environmental expanse. Examining seaports' relationships with hinter-seas, we can begin to understand how discrete maritime regions informed human circumstances in different ways. Hopefully, "History Below the Waterline" will be the breath before the plunge as we plumb the depths of African-descended people's aquatic cultures.

73. Dawson, "Enslaved Ship Pilots", pp. 75; 95 n. 33; Bolster, *Black Jacks*.
74. Mark M. Smith, *Mastered by the Clock: Time, Slavery, and Freedom in the American South* (Chapel Hill, NC, 1997).
75. Dawson, "Enslaved Ship Pilots", p. 73; *idem*, *Undercurrents of Power*, p. 69; Scott, "Afro-American Sailors".

IRSH 64 (2019), pp. 71–93 doi:10.1017/S0020859019000038

The Household Workers of the East India Company Ports of Pre-Colonial Bengal*

TITAS CHAKRABORTY

Duke Kunshan University
8 Duke Avenue, Kunshan, Jiangsu, China 215316

E-mail: titas.chakra@gmail.com

ABSTRACT: This article examines the various experiences of slavery and freedom of female household workers in the Dutch and English East India Company (VOC and EIC, respectively) ports in Bengal in the early eighteenth century. Enslaved household workers in Bengal came from various Asian societies dotting the Indian Ocean littoral. Once manumitted, they entered the fold of the free Christian or Portuguese communities of the settlements. The most common, if not the only, occupation of the women of these communities was household or caregiving labour. The patriarchy of the settlements was defined by the labour and subjection of these women. Yet, domestic service to VOC/EIC officials only partially explains their subjectivity. This article identifies the agency of enslaved and women of free Christian or Portuguese communities in their efforts to resist or bypass the institution of the European household in the settlements. These efforts ranged from murdering their slave masters to creating independent businesses to the formation of sexual liaisons and parental/fraternal/sororal relationships disregarding the approval or needs of their settlement masters.

The East India Company settlements in early eighteenth-century Bengal were primarily trading settlements. The largest ones, Hugli and Calcutta – the respective headquarters of the Dutch East India Company (VOC) and the English East India Company (EIC) – were ports. Much like other port cities across the globe, these settlements were crucibles of new social relationships. This article explores the origins and labours, oppressions, and aspirations of the enslaved, free Christian and Portuguese women, who formed the majority of the household workers – caregivers who worked in private homes, taverns, mess-houses, and brothels – in the East India Company ports in pre-colonial Bengal. Living in close proximity to their employers,

* I finished writing this article during my time as a Postdoctoral Research Fellow at the Institute of Historical Studies, University of Texas at Austin. I am extremely grateful to the Institute for its support.

primarily officials of all ranks of the East India companies, these women proved to be a defining element in the social composition of the early company settlements.

This paper shows that the origins of the Anglo-Indian family[1] lie not in the sexual encounter between local women and European men, but in the complex interaction amongst enslaved women coming from all over the Indian Ocean world, free Christian and Portuguese women, and European men. Demographic information on enslaved women workers in European households in early eighteenth-century Bengal shows that they came from all over the Indian Ocean littoral – from Mando, Makassar, Banda, and Batavia in the present-day Indonesian archipelago, from Ceylon, Patna, and Bengal – where they were captured and sold into slavery.[2] Once manumitted they entered the fold of the free Christian or Portuguese communities of the settlements. Because of their ambivalent identities, the enslaved, free Christian, and Portuguese women have escaped the attention of the historians of the informal Portuguese Empire as well as historians of women in European settlements. The Bay of Bengal region was a frontier zone of the Portuguese Empire in Asia.[3] The Portuguese presence in this region has been studied as that of independent merchants, renegades, imperial aspirants, soldiers, and subordinate agents of the EIC Empire.[4] The women of the Portuguese community, who worked as caregivers in various capacities in all European settlements, are hardly ever discussed in this literature. Even though women in the European settlements of the Indian Ocean world are now a long-discussed topic, the literature focuses on relationships between native/local women and Europeans.[5] Non-European, but non-indigenous women

1. Durba Ghosh, *Sex and Family in Colonial India: The Making of Empire* (Cambridge, 2006).
2. For the demographics of the slave trade in eighteenth-century Bengal, see Titas Chakraborty, "Work and Society in the East India Company Settlements in Bengal, 1650–1757" (Ph.D. dissertation, University of Pittsburgh, 2016); manumission documents, too, give us similar demographic information. Tamil Nadu State Archives [digitized by the National Archive, The Hague, available at: http://www.gahetna.nl/collectie/archief/ead/index/zoekterm/tamil%20nadu/aantal/20/eadid/1.11.06.11; last accessed 6 December 2018, hereafter 1.11.06.11], 1677B, fos 5, 120–132, 254, 284; 1.11.06.1/1694, fos 747, 1031.
3. George Winius, "The 'Shadow-Empire' of Goa in the Bay of Bengal", *Itinerario*, 7:2 (1983), pp. 83–101.
4. Sanjay Subrahmanyam, *The Portuguese Empire in Asia, 1500–1700: A Political and Economic History* (Malden, MA, 2012), pp. 261–283; Maria Augusta Lima Cruz, "Exiles and Renegades in Early Sixteenth Century Portuguese India", *Indian Economic and Social History Review*, 23:3 (1986), pp. 249–262; Jorge Manuel Flores, "Relic or Springboard: A Note on the 'Rebirth' of Portuguese Hughli, c.1632–1820", *Indian Economic and Social History Review*, 39:4 (2002), pp. 381–395; Stefan Halikowski Smith, "Languages of Subalternity and Collaboration: Portuguese in English Settlements across the Bay of Bengal, 1620–1800", *The International Journal of Maritime History*, 28:2 (2016), pp. 237–267.
5. Some representative works are Jean Gelman Taylor, *The Social World of Batavia: Europeans and Eurasians in Colonial Indonesia* (Madison, WI, 1983); Leonard Blussé, *Bitter Bonds: A Colonial*

find no place in this scholarship. Yet, as this paper shows, the majority of the household workers in the early eighteenth-century European settlements were non-indigenous female enslaved and "free" workers, and their labour and subjection as slaves, housekeepers, domestic help, and sexual partners within the families of European company servants, and as proprietors, slaves, and workers of the taverns and brothels, shaped the patriarchy of the settlements.

As once-uprooted people, these women figured out ways of surviving in Bengal while also subverting the class and gendered order of the settlements. The agency of enslaved female domestics, especially concubines, is a much-discussed subject. The literature can be divided into two broad groups. One group asserts the agency of women especially as cultural intermediaries and creators of Eurasian cultures and families.[6] The other group emphasizes the lack of agency of these women in making choices in their work, sexuality, and family.[7] Both groups, however, have only examined the lives and actions of these women strictly ordained in relation to, and in the presence of, European men. This paper investigates and locates the agency of women in their efforts at self-creation, autonomous of the control of their European masters/employers. The self-activity of household workers shaped their manifold trajectories within and outside the bounds of company settlements in Bengal – from slavery to freedom, from foreigner to native, from worker to employer. Most importantly, these women – both enslaved and free – formed familial structures separate from the households of the men they served that were based not just on labour, but also on creative kin relations. Their ability to form friendships or affective ties with various people within the settlements proved not just their resilience, but also their drive to break free from the subject position created through labour and bondage.

Divorce Drama of the Seventeenth Century (Princeton, NJ, 2009); Ann Stoler, "Sexual Affronts and Racial Frontiers: European Identities and the Cultural Politics of Exclusions in Colonial Southeast Asia", *Comparative Studies in Society and History*, 34:3 (1992), pp. 514–551; Erica Wald, "From *Begums* to *Bibis* to Abandoned Females and Idle Women: Sexual Relationships, Venereal Disease and the Redefinition of Prostitution in Early Nineteenth-Century India", *Indian Economic and Social History Review*, 46:1 (2009), pp. 5–25; Ratnabali Chatterjee, *The Queen's Daughters: Prostitutes as an Outcast Group in Colonial India* (Bergen, 1992); Ghosh, *Sex and Family in Colonial India*; Indrani Chatterjee, "Colouring Subalternity: Slaves, Concubines and Social Orphans in Early Colonial India", in Gautam Bhadra, Gyan Prakash, and Susie Tharu (eds), *Subaltern Studies*, No. 10 (New Delhi, 1999), pp. 49–97; Margaret Strobel, "Women's History, Gender History, and European Colonialism", in Gregory Blue, Martin Bunton, and Ralph Croizier (eds), *Colonialism and the Modern World* (Armonk, NY, 2002), pp. 51–70.

6. Taylor, *The Social World of Batavia*; Strobel, "Women's History, Gender History, and European Colonialism"; Ghosh, *Sex and Family in Colonial India*.

7. Chatterjee, "Colouring Subalternity"; idem, *The Queen's Daughters*.

SLAVES, "FREE CHRISTIAN" AND "PORTUGUESE WOMEN", AND THE SETTLEMENT HOUSEHOLD

By the mid-eighteenth century, both Calcutta and Chinsura, the headquarters of the EIC and the VOC respectively, had grown into prominent settlements. Chinsura was the Dutch sector within the larger port city of Hugli. Even though Hugli had its origins as a Portuguese settlement in the late sixteenth century, it grew as a port city only after the Mughal emperor Shahjahan's conquest of the place in 1633. He then allowed all Europeans to build their settlements in the region for trading purposes. In the early eighteenth century, the city was one long stretch along the river Bhagirathi, with the Portuguese, Dutch, and French sectors laid out from north to south. Even though the English maintained a factory in Hugli, they had acquired zamindari rights over three villages further south along the river in 1698, which became their most prominent settlement and headquarters, Calcutta. Chinsura was a conglomeration of the "village" Chinsura and the adjacent Bazar Mirzapore. It was fortified in the late 1690s, when the EIC fortified Calcutta too. By the mid-eighteenth century, the settlement around the fort in Calcutta had taken the form of a commercial, administrative, and military centre. Residential complexes with sprawling gardens belonging to Europeans had also grown within this area. In Chinsura, the VOC officials lived alongside the Portuguese, Armenians, Greeks, Banians, and Muslim merchants of various Asian origins who owned individual houses. But in Calcutta, the Armenians and Greeks shared the European quarters, while the native merchants were pushed to the north of the city, and the Portuguese were primarily sandwiched between the native and European quarters. Just north of Chinsura was the Church of the Holy Rosary, the largest Roman Catholic Church in the region, with influence over the Catholic population in most of Western Bengal, including Calcutta. The numerous Portuguese inhabitants of Chinsura, and Calcutta – many of them independent women proprietors – came under the spiritual jurisdiction of this church. These Portuguese women ran taverns, messhouses, and brothels in both Hugli and Calcutta, places that Europeans frequently visited. The mainly female proprietors of such places, as well as English, Dutch, Armenian, Greek, and Portuguese householders owned slaves.

The enslaved population in the settlements, both male and female, primarily performed the work of social reproduction, as nurses, cooks, housekeepers, and sex workers, in houses and taverns. For instance, in August 1678 an ailing Padre Manuel Gonsalves sought passage on an EIC ship. He was to be nursed by two of his slaves. Captain Stafford, relieved that the crew would not be responsible for his care, allowed the padre passage.[8]

---

8. Factory Records [British Library, London; hereafter G] 20/5, fo. 6.

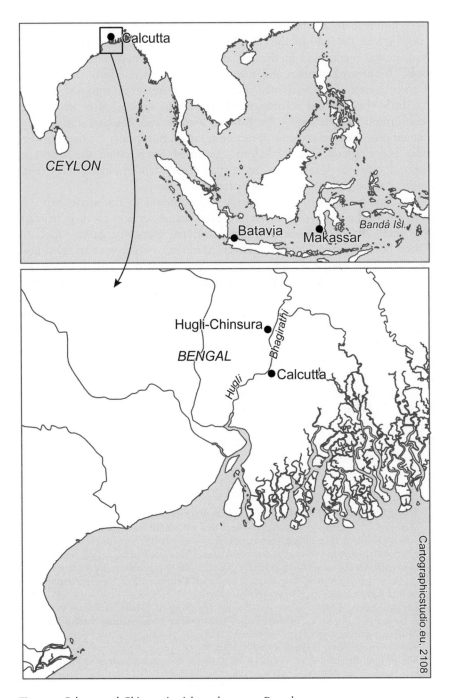

Figure 1. Calcutta and Chinsura in eighteenth-century Bengal.

When junior merchant Harmanus von Blom sold Febrauraij van Bengale and Valentijn van Bengale to the VOC director Jan Sichterman in November 1740, it was mentioned in the sale document that they were both "good cooks".[9] Enslaved women and men were critical to childcare. In the wills of their masters, enslaved men and women were often enjoined to look after little children and accompany them back to Europe, after which they were promised freedom.[10] As Rozina Visram and Michael Fisher have pointed out, this was common practice amongst Europeans moving between India and England. The "freedom" promised on reaching the shores of England, however, was nothing more than the masters' euphemism for relinquishing all responsibility for supporting their slaves.[11]

Manumission of enslaved workers was common in the settlements. In cases where the enslaved women provided sexual services to their masters, they could expect manumission and additional monetary gains, especially if they bore children of their masters. Marcella, a slave woman who bore the child of her master, George Petty, was emancipated and given fifty pagodas.[12] Maria, a female slave of John Rennald, was promised her freedom in his will and a sum of 300 rupees. She was the mother of Rennald's only son.[13] Some enslaved women could expect to inherit the houses of their masters. Nathalia Peres, a slave of a pilot, was emancipated in 1740 and she received the house of her master in the Stroobazar near Chinsura. Nathalia was the mother of the pilot's only son, Dirk.[14] Paternal guilt and a sense of obligation allowed these women to make small but significant gains.

Oftentimes, the passage from slavery to freedom was punctuated with conditions that chained the freed slaves to their old status. Henry Dallibar handed over his slave, Bastian, to his friend, Capt. Marmaduke, on the stipulation that Bastian was to serve his new master for five years before gaining his freedom.[15] Similarly, Luzia, one-time slave of Sarah Shadow, was

---

9. 1.11.06.11/1715, fo. 85.

10. Will of Elizabeth Harding, Mayor's Court Records [British Library, London]. Most files for the Mayor's Court records are unfoliated. Those that are foliated have two types of foliation – first, the entire file is foliated consistently, irrespective of bundles; second, the foliation starts anew with each bundle in a file. In the case of the latter, I have specified the bundle in parentheses and folio numbers. For unfoliated files, I have given the date of proceedings. [Hereafter, P/154 or P/155.] P/155/9 (1736 bundle), fos 1–2; will of Daniel Willeboorts P/155/9 (1736 bundle), fos 2–4; will of Sarah Guion, 1742, P/154/42, fos 2, 6–7.

11. Rozina Visram, *Ayahs, Lascars and Princes: The Story of Indians in Britain 1700–1947* (New York, 1986), pp. 11–34; Michael Fisher, *Counterflows to Colonialism: Indian Travellers and Settlers in Britain, 1600–1857* (New Delhi, 2004), pp. 53–65.

12. Will of George Petty, P/154/40 (1728 bundle), fos 14–15.

13. Will of John Rennald, 1741, P/154/55, fo. 7; similar gains were made by Sophia, slave of Thomas Hawkes, and Magdalena, slave of John Gulielmis. P/154/50, fos 19–20, Bengal Public Proceedings [British Library, London; hereafter P/1] 4, fos 414v–415r.

14. 1.11.06.11/1694, fo. 124.

15. P/1/5, fo. 255r.

bequeathed to Sarah Peris, whom she was required to serve for seven years before gaining her freedom.[16] As these examples show, freedom, though promised, could be deferred in various ways. George Downing stated in his will that Nicholas, his eight-year-old slave, was to serve his friend Richard Dean "not as a slave but as a servant" for five years, after which time he was "to be set entirely at liberty".[17] Though juridically no longer a slave, Nicholas was to continue to function as one until he gained complete freedom. Sometimes, the conditions of emancipation blurred all difference between slaves and servants. In 1736, ship captain George Penuse freed all of his slaves – Giddah, Flora, Bavenah, and Pauncheecok – but added that they were to "serve as before".[18] William Coverly gave his slave boy Caesar his freedom, but "he is to serve my well beloved wife Maria Coverly as long as it shall require him to do so".[19] It was thus not a mere slip of the tongue when the terms "servant" and "slave" were used interchangeably.[20]

For those slaves who successfully moved out of their slave status once manumitted, the social trajectory from slavery to freedom often meant entrance into the "free Christian" and/or the extremely heterogeneous Portuguese community, whose existence was primarily dependent upon various forms of services it provided to the VOC and the EIC trade and settlements in Bengal. The Portuguese had been in Bengal since the sixteenth century, both as rebels and merchants working under the legal framework of the Estado da India. Three factors – the licence to marry locally, the presence of a large number of renegades, and the proselytizing practices of the Augustinian church – led to the formation of an internally variegated community, especially in the second half of the seventeenth century, when the influence of the Estado waned. The community was fractured along race, religious, and linguistic lines. Various estimates indicate that the "black" or "brown" Portuguese, as opposed to the pure-bred Portuguese, were the overwhelming majority in eighteenth-century Bengal.[21] The Augustinian mission held only nominal sway over the Portuguese community. Especially the "black" and "brown" segments of the community often questioned the Augustinian church's moral authority.[22] Even though historians

---

16. Will of Sarah Shadow, 1755, P/154/46 (4th bundle), fos 40–42.
17. Will of George Downing, P/154/46 (6th bundle), fos 40–42.
18. Will of George Penuse, 1736, P/154/40 (1736 bundle), fos 4–5.
19. Will of William Coverly, 1751, P/154/46 (3rd bundle), fos 36–37.
20. Will of George Petty, 1728. Petty mentions his "servants" Marcella and Maria, to whom he promised "freedom" and fifty pagoda and twenty pagoda respectively, P/154/40 (1728 bundle), fos 14–15.
21. In the early eighteenth century, an Augustinian friar noted that there were 25,000 Christian Portuguese in Bengal, most of them being "brown" Portuguese. Arnulf Hartmann, "História dos Missões dos Padres Augustinianos na India nos principios do 18 sécolo escripta pelo P. Fr. Jorge da Presentação missionário", *Analecta Augustiniana*, 57 (1994), pp. 193–341.
22. *Ibid.*

have emphasized language as a cement for the highly variegated Portuguese community,[23] it is unlikely that all members of the Portuguese community spoke Portuguese. From the baptismal records of the Church of the Holy Rosary for 1698, it is clear that none of the 487 converts were of Portuguese origin.[24] Of these converts, some were twenty-five years old. It is unlikely that such mature age converts would have spoken Portuguese, though they took Lusophone names. It is evident also from various wills left by self-declared Portuguese people that only some spoke the language. Despite their internal differences, almost all Portuguese served the European companies, including the EIC or the VOC, in some capacity.[25] While some worked as merchants, the majority worked in subaltern positions, such as soldiers, pilots, and household workers. Manumitted slaves joined the ranks of these subaltern Portuguese.

The practice of conversion to Christianity upon manumission, and the prevalence of Lusophone names amongst the slaves, eased the transition of freed slaves into the free Christian and Portuguese communities. Masters such as Roger Kinsey wished that his slaves, Scipio and Pompey, be christened in the Roman Catholic Church as a condition for their emancipation.[26] In Chinsura, several emancipated slaves had Lusophone names. When Nathalia Peres, Theodara de Rosario, Rosa de Rosario, Sabina, or Domingo gained their freedom, absorption into the Portuguese community presumably was a small step (see Table 1). Portuguese women were often referred to as "free" Portuguese women, signifying their passage from slavery to freedom in a society marked by household slavery. When Anna Cordosa appeared in the Mayor's Court as a witness, she was specifically asked "to whom she belonged", to which she answered "she was her own mistress".[27] As noted in various manumission documents, wills, and inventories, slaves in the European households were able to create and maintain their own families. Such families included not only man, woman, and children, but also multigenerational members, such as grandparents and grandchildren (Table 1). In several instances, they were both listed and manumitted as families. On the eve of his departure in 1755, Jan Kerseboom, Director of the VOC in Bengal, manumitted fifteen such families (Table 1).[28] Some even received a house or part of a house as a condition of emancipation (Table 1). Since kinlessness is possibly the greatest bane that separated

23. Shihan de Silva Jayasuriya, *The Portuguese in the East: A History of a Maritime Trading Empire* (New York, 2008), pp. 71–124; Halikowski Smith, "Languages of Subalternity and Collaboration", pp. 240–241.
24. Historical Archives of Goa, Goa, India, Book No. 2760, fos 3–19.
25. Halikowski Smith, "Languages of Subalternity and Collaboration", pp. 241–252.
26. Will of Roger Kinsey, undated, P/154/45 (unfoliated).
27. P/154/46, Proceedings of 27 February, 1746/47 (unfoliated).
28. 1.11.06.11/1693, fo. 376.

Table 1. *List of selected manumissions in VOC records.*

Year	Name of slave	Master	Terms
1732	Rosa de Rosario	Joannes Anzelmus Thielen, fiscal and merchant	
1734	Sabina	Leonara van Mandhar and Jan van Boekholt	Retained right to recall manumission
1734	Theodora de Rosario	Nicolaas Buinincx, sergeant	
1740	Aron, his wife, Aurora, and their children Domingo and Sabina	Ditto	Aron's family received 100 rupees and a part of the house and garden bought by Blom outside of Chinsura
1740	Nathalia Peres	Trent Wenneber, pilot	Received a house in Stroobazar. She got patta but could not sell the house
1755	Tjelie and Rebecca	Jan Kerseboom, director, who was leaving	
	October and Dina and their children Sictie and Isabel	Ditto	
	Kamis with his grandsons Jonas, Adonis, and Joseph	Ditto	
	Elis and Patra and their children Domingo and Bouang	Ditto	
	Kloris and Lijsje with their child Saptoe	Ditto	
	Anthonij and Calista	Ditto	
	Coridon and Diana	Ditto	

(Continued)

Table 1. (*Continued*)

Year	Name of slave	Master	Terms
	Sultan and Sabina	Ditto	
	David and Juliana with their children Ontong,	Ditto	
	Dominga, Leander, Lizarda, and Lena		
	Damon and Limanada and their children Meij, Manies,	Ditto	
	and Andries		
	Titus and Regina	Ditto	
	Florentiana with her daughter Floriana	Ditto	
	Rebecca with her son Arees	Ditto	
	Alexander with his wife Magdalena and son Albert	Ditto	
	and daughter Fenisa		
	Snel and Malatie with their children Sisilia, Octavio,	Ditto	
	and Harlequin		

Source: Bengal Directorate at Chinsura and the successors (*Kantoor Bengalen te Chinsura en rechtsopvolgers*) collection at Tamil Nadu State Archives, Chennai. Boxes consulted: 1677A, 1677B, 1679A, 1679B, 1694, 1696, and 1715.

a slave from a free person, the presence of family at the moment of emancipation no doubt made the task of blending into society of freed men and women far easier.

Women of the Portuguese and the free Christian communities were extremely visible in the company records as various forms of caregivers – tavern owner, landladies or mess owners, brothel keepers, and housekeepers. In the 1670s, an English traveller, Thomas Bowrey, noted that in Hugli provisioning trades were run by the Portuguese, a significant number of whom were women. In the early eighteenth century, Portuguese women continued to be important in the provisioning and caregiving trade at both Chinsura and Hugli. In Calcutta, Domingo Ash is a unique example of an enterprising Portuguese woman. Domingo Ash was the most important supplier of arak to the EIC ships for at least forty years.[29] An arak distiller herself, Domingo Ash also maintained her own punch-house. To add to her profits, she was a moneylender and a landlady on the side.[30] Apart from Domingo Ash, Portuguese or free Christian landladies and tavern keepers abounded in both Chinsura and Calcutta.[31] Beginning in the late 1680s, Portuguese women worked as tavern keepers.[32] As a traveller in 1727 observed, the taverns doubled as lodgings in the early settlements, for tavern keepers let out rooms to lodgers.[33] Often, poor European soldiers and sailors were the lodgers, and they shared rooms, each occupying one bed. Room sharing was an old practice amongst European sailors and soldiers in Bengal.[34] For Portuguese and free Christian women proprietors who accumulated wealth, this reproductive labour remained the primary or foundational source of their income.

Several of the Portuguese and free Christian women worked as housekeepers. Durba Ghosh has noted that "housekeeper" was a term signifying "conjugal

29. Starting from 1704, Domingo Ash's licence for distilling arak was renewed until 1743/4, P/1/5–P/1/16.

30. In 1727/28, she lent a considerable sum of 200 rupees to a ship merchant, Sheikh Benaik, proceedings of 1 February 1727/28, P/155/10 (unfoliated). In the same year, she was renting out a house for ten rupees a month. Proceedings of 16 March 1727/28, P/155/10 (unfoliated). Another example of Portuguese women in the moneylending business is Dominga Araujo, who listed her creditors in her will, 1760, P/154/50 (unfoliated).

31. On 18 June 1734, a bookkeeper, Nicolaas Wendel as a tenant, and Nathalia Raposa, a free Portuguese woman as the landlady, signed a lease for a whole year, renewable on the willingness of both parties involved. 1.11.06.11/1677B, fo. 278. Examples of tavern keepers from Chinsura include Anthonica da Silva (1733) 1.11.06.11/ 1677A, fos 255–282; a woman named Lucia (1743) 1.11.06.11/1693, fo. 347; in Calcutta, Alsida de Rosario, P/155/73, fo. 58.

32. In 1686, in Chinsura, [National Archive, The Hague, Archive of the Dutch East India Company, hereafter, VOC] 1422, fos 1450r–1451v; in 1733 in Chinsura, 1.11.06.11/1677A, fos 255–282; in 1743 in Chinsura, 1.11.06.11/1693, fo. 347.

33. MssEur B 162 [British Library, London], account by Judith Weston of a voyage to Madras in East Indiamen, fo. 6r.

34. Tapan Raychaudhuri, *Bengal Under Akbar and Jahangir* (Calcutta, 1953), pp. 241–242.

domestic arrangements" of the European men.[35] "Conjugality" often translated into domestic labour – looking after men in sickness and health was the task of these housekeepers. For example, Leonara van Mandhar took care of Roger Bereneert, Director of the VOC in Bengal, in his illness. Pleased with her service, Bereneert made a handsome provision of 10,000 rupees for her in his will.[36] Before his death in 1715, Captain Herbert left "nurse money" for a woman.[37] Lodewick Demurry's housekeeper, Rosa de Rosario, who was also his sexual partner, "made the punch and dressed the victuals" for him. When he fell sick at Culpy, Rosa de Rosario went from Calcutta to look after him.[38]

During his travels in Bengal in the early eighteenth century, Alexander Hamilton summed up his impression of the oldest Portuguese quarter, Bandel, in Hugli: "The Bandel, at present, deals in no sort of commodities, but what are in request at the Court of Venus".[39] Providing sexual services formed the foremost work of the Portuguese or free Christian women of the settlements. The practice of taking native women as concubines by European men was rare in this period, in contrast to the late eighteenth and early nineteenth centuries. Since deep intrusion into the Indian heartland was not possible in this period, Europeans had to rely on the women originating from their Indian Ocean outposts for such services. Native women were thus present in the European settlements as construction workers and domestic servants. Except for three instances, native women never figured as domestic partners of the European men.[40]

As "free" women, the Portuguese or free Christian women performed the same work as their enslaved sisters. In this sense, the free Christian and Portuguese communities must be understood as being on the same continuum as slavery. Since freed slaves joined the ranks of the Portuguese and free Christian communities and then continued to do domestic labour, the community was an outgrowth of the practices of slavery in early company settlements. However, there were two major differences in being a free Christian or Portuguese female caregiver. First, through the creation and maintenance of taverns, lodging houses, and brothels, these women were able to commercialize household labour and thereby amass wealth. Secondly, for those who became housekeepers, reproductive labour was premised on fairly contractual relationships. Contractual relationships,

35. Ghosh, *Sex and the Family in Colonial India*, p. 110.
36. 1.11.06.11/ 1677A, fo. 456.
37. P/1/3, fo. 112v.
38. Proceedings of 17 February 1746/7 P/154/46 (unfoliated).
39. Alexander Hamilton, *A New Account of the East Indies* (Edinburgh, 1727), p. 21.
40. Nicholas Rowe in his will, 1731, left for the maintenance of "a Moor woman" Meddo and her son an allowance of five Madras rupees, P/154/40 (1731 bundle), fos 9–11; will of John Vass, 1752, mentioned a native servant Meapa, who bore him a son, P/154/50 (1752 bundle), fos 19–20; will of Samuel Spencer, gunner, 1741, mentioned a woman Chicka with whom he had a child, P/154/42, fos 9–10.

furthermore, reveal that households in the company settlements were cemented through labour over and above any affective ties.

THE LIMITS OF PATERNALISM

There were limits to the paternalism of European masters towards their female enslaved and free household workers. Within the context of indigenous noble families, concubinage or wet-nursing were avenues for considerable social mobility for enslaved and free women. Within Rajput, Mughal, and Bengal Nawabi households these women were important political actors with considerable land grants.[41] Moreover, in the case of the Bengal Nawabs, all children within a household shared similar agnate kinship, i.e. the patriarch extended equal paternity to all.[42] Since the concept of an "illegitimate child" did not exist within these noble families, the possibility of social mobility for concubines (enslaved or otherwise) and the children borne by them increased significantly. In contrast, within hyper-monogamous European households, domestic labour of concubinage or wet-nursing was fairly transactional. It did not create any avenue for the enslaved or free concubines or their children to be part of the master's family. European men provided for their children born of the bodies of their (enslaved) concubines as an obligation outside the realm of the family. Even then, in many cases, they made sure that the mothers of such children formally had no access to such provisions. Though the unnamed Portuguese woman from Chinsura might have secured some financial support since Jan Cornelisz had left his entire estate to their child, who lived with her, she personally did not inherit a single penny.[43] While a provision of 200 pounds was made by Charles English for his "illegitimate" son, John English, he made no provision for the mother of the child.[44] In certain cases, childbearing brought no change in the conditions of work. Jan van Latum freed his child Turkenij de Rosario, born to a slave woman. Though Turkenij got her freedom "by dint of her birth", no provision was made to free the mother or to leave her with any money.[45]

Promises of gain were always dependent upon conditions beyond the control of the enslaved women. While many slave women remained slaves

41. Ramya Sreenivasan, "Drudges, Dancing Girls, Concubines: Female Slaves in Rajput Polity, 1500–1850", in Indrani Chatterjee and Richard Eaton (eds), *Slavery and South Asian History* (Bloomington, IN, 2006), pp. 136–161; Shadab Bano, "Women Slaves in Medieval India", *Proceedings of the Indian History Congress*, 65 (2004), pp. 314–323.
42. Indrani Chatterjee, *Gender, Law and Slavery in Colonial India* (New Delhi, 1999), pp. 36–77.
43. 1.11.06.11/1677A, fo. 570.
44. Will of Charles English, 1756, P/154/40 (6th bundle), fo. 7.
45. 1.11.06.11/1696, fo. 217.

regardless of their maternity, most enslaved women bearing their masters' children were promised their freedom after the death of their masters. Such a waiting period was a major predicament in their path to emancipation, as some of them died before their masters. Flora, who bore a child for Adam Dawson, boatswain of the EIC living in Calcutta, never lived to see any gains from her childbearing.[46] In his will, John Rennald promised his slave Maria 300 rupees and her freedom as she was the natural mother of his son. Later, he made amendments to his will as Maria had passed away.[47] Any hope of gain was made even more fragile by the master's potential dissatisfaction. Mary Dottison could inherit her part of her master's property only if "she behaves herself in a proper manner till the time of my decease and not otherwise".[48] Mary's freedom depended upon her master's arbitrary definition of "good behaviour".

For free Christian and Portuguese women, contracts sometimes guaranteed no protection against the whims of their masters and even their friends. In England, from the mid-eighteenth century there was a marked move towards contractual relationships between household employers and their domestic servants. Such contracts, or "poor settlements", were often contested in courts.[49] Examples for similar contractual relations between household workers and domestic (especially female) servants are rare in Bengal. From the few examples available, it is clear that contracts were flimsy verbal arrangements. Rosa de Rosario's appeal to the Mayor's Court demanding her share of the inheritance of her client/master Lodewick Demurry's belongings reveals the vulnerability of the housekeeper in these contractual arrangements. Six years before his death, Lodewick Demurry moved in with Rosa de Rosario. Her expenses were borne by him, and he was heard saying multiple times, "If I go to Europe or marry or dye I will provide for my girl". Catherine de Rosario, Anna Cordosa, and Maria de Rosario, who were all close to Rosa and who also worked as housekeepers, confirmed the verbal promise made by Lodewick Demurry.[50] In hopes of Demurry's legacy, Rosa continued to work for him, even though she felt burdened by her work. Anna Cordosa, Rosa's friend, observed that Rosa and Lodewick had differences and that Rosa often "came and lived with deponent (Anna Cordosa) for seven or eight days and then she went back and lived with Lodewick Demurry". After Lodewick's death, four of his friends, Harman Hendrikson, John van der Hayden, Jan Carl, and Samuel Bailey, testified that they heard Lodewick say on his deathbed that he would not leave

46. P/154/40 (1733 bundle), fos 1r–2r.
47. P/154/45, fo. 7.
48. P/154/50 (2nd bundle), fos 12–13.
49. Carolyn Steedman, *Master and Servant: Love and Labour in the English Industrial Age* (Cambridge, 2007), pp. 66–86, 131–145.
50. Proceedings of 17 February and 27 February 1746/47, P/154/46 (unfoliated).

anything to his girl "who hath poisoned me". The counter evidence provided by Rosa de Rosario and her three housekeeper friends was ignored by the Mayor's Court of Calcutta. The court decided to hand over Demurry's entire property to the aforementioned Harman Hendrikson, to be divided amongst himself, Jan Carl, and John van der Hayden.[51] We do not know whether cutting Rosa from the inheritance was Demurry's deathbed wish. But it is clear from the judicial proceedings that the evidence and interests of company men were given undue importance over the voices of the housekeepers.

The main possibility for social mobility amongst the women of the free Christian population of Bengal was marriage with European men. In 1688, the EIC allowed their men in India to marry Roman Catholic women in the settlements. Such marriages were also allowed in the Dutch settlements.[52] In 1734, Leonara van Mandhar thus married a VOC sailmaker from Rijswijk, Jan van Boekholt. Had she not married, she could not have made good use of the fortune left to her by her erstwhile master, Roger Bereneert. Bereneert added a clause to his will stipulating that Leonara, his "free Christian girl", could gain access to her money only if she were married, thus limiting her chances of enjoying her new-found wealth. However, her prospects for marriage were not difficult, for with her inheritance of 10,000 rupees Leonara was presumably a sought-after maiden in Chinsura.[53] Leonara in all probability was an exception.

Marriages, though allowed, were extremely difficult to come by, especially in Calcutta, and the few existing examples show that marriage did not improve the status of the "free" women. One James Kennie was married to a Maria Texeira. Abusively describing her as "a common whore" in his will, Kennie left her three Arcot rupees.[54] Hamilton's description of the "mustice wife" of a seaman had similar overtones. In the absence of the seaman, Hamilton alleged she was "a little inclined to lewdness".[55] The sexuality of the free Christian and Portuguese women was feared and abused even in marriage.

Physical abuse, perhaps, most blatantly revealed the limits of paternalism. Tavern keepers such as Anthonica da Silva were often perceived by their neighbors as "whores".[56] Taverns were also sites of extreme violence. In 1686, Abraham, a VOC gunner, and a mate he had known from his previous ship, enjoyed drinks at a tavern not far from the EIC factory in Hugli. For some unknown reason, in the course of the first drink Abraham's friend struck the barmaid, a Portuguese woman, in her face.[57] The ugliest form

51. *Ibid.*
52. Ulbe Bosma and Remco Raben, *Being "Dutch" in the Indies: A History of Creolisation and Empire, 1500–1920* (trans. Wendie Shaffer) (Athens, OH, 2008).
53. 1.11.06.11/1677B, fo. 63.
54. Will of James Kennie, 1757, P/154/50 (3rd bundle), fos 3–4.
55. Hamilton, *A New Account of the East Indies*, p. 10.
56. 1.11.06.11/1677A, fo. 143.
57. VOC 1422, fos 1450r–1451v.

of assault was obviously rape. On 10 October 1719, Michael Cameron and John Massey, sailors on two EIC ships, broke into the house of two Portuguese women, Joanna Averiss and Maria Rodriguez, presumably tavern keepers, and gagged and tied two minor girls of that house and then raped them. The older girl, Sabina, was a nine-year-old slave, and the younger one, Biviana, daughter of Joanna Averiss, was only five. Biviana, bleeding profusely, was seriously injured. Cameron and Massey were punished with thirty-nine lashes by rattan on their bare backs.[58] This shows that in EIC settlements rape was considered a minor offense compared to petty theft, which was often punished by death.[59] As victims of the same crime, Joanna and Biviana's fate bridged the social difference between slavery and freedom. The difference between their social status in the settlement was one of degree and not of kind. As workers who could be easily denied any monetary gains or who could be physically abused at the whim of the master, they equally felt the limits of paternalism of the settlement men.

SELF-MAKING OF THE HOUSEHOLD WORKERS

It was through resistance and not just through the masters' manumission documents or provisions in wills that enslaved workers achieved their freedom. The only work that mentions South Asia within the context of slave resistance in the Indian Ocean world argues that there is very little evidence of resistance amongst slaves.[60] Since the focus has been on African slaves, other enslaved people have fallen out of the discussion. The experiences of the enslaved population in Bengal shows that they were no passive sufferers in the household. Strategies of resistance were many. Even murdering one's master was not off the charts. In 1712, a slave woman owned by Jacques Leloeu, a free burgher of Chinsura, was caught conspiring to poison her master and his wife. After she confessed, the Hugli council of the VOC hanged her.[61] On 19 November 1739, September van Mandhar, a slave of a junior merchant, killed his master and injured one of his master's palanquin bearers. He was apprehended and sentenced to the rack. Upon his death, his body was to be thrown into the Ganga.[62] The severity of punishments reveals how households were fraught with worker-employer contradictions; not all slaves were eligible for manumission. Moreover, as the two preceding sections of this article show, manumission was not in itself emancipation for the

58. P/1/4, fos 140r–v.
59. P/155/72, fo. 51.
60. Edward Alpers, "Flight to Freedom: Escape from Slavery among Bonded Africans in the Indian Ocean World, c.1750–1962", *Slavery and Abolition*, 24:2 (2003), pp. 51–68.
61. VOC 8742, fo. 527.
62. VOC 8787, fos 1132–1133.

enslaved, as freedom from slavery did not mean freedom from reproductive labour. Manumission was very much an external process – a process from above – where the household workers had very little leeway in shaping their lives.

Family formation amongst slaves sometimes could become a transgressive act, if the masters disapproved. As manumission documents show, masters allowed their slaves to maintain families under conditions of slavery. However, the master's consent was necessary for such family formation. Wherever slave masters did not approve of a match, family making became an audacious task. The tragic story of Hanna and Hackema demonstrates the high stakes of aspirations to conjugal life independent of the will of masters. In May 1728, a slave woman, Hanna, stole gold and silver ornaments worth one hundred rupees from her master, Khwaja Gregor, an Armenian merchant residing in Calcutta, and fled with her lover, a freedman, Hackema. For Hanna and Hackema theft was a crucial means to their freedom and a life not ordained by Hanna's master. Hanna and Hackema had unsuccessfully tried to steal from Khwaja Gregor six months before. Hanna was pardoned that time on her promise "never to be guilty of such actions again nor any more to keep company with Hackema".

Yet, Hanna took the risk a second time, with fateful consequences. Running away was the only avenue open for Hanna and Hackema to keep each other's company. They crossed over to the other side of the river Hooghly, where the old Mughal *thana* or toll station stood. There they went to a lodging house maintained by two merchants, Bunny Khan and Bauden, and found food and lodging for a night in exchange for some stolen jewellery. To assuage the merchants' suspicions, Hanna told them that her master had freed her and gave her the jewellery as gifts to start anew her life with Hackema, whom she would marry. Unfortunately, before Hanna and Hackema could safely pass into their free life in Bengal, they were caught by her master's search army the very next day. With the stolen goods on them, they had no safeguards against the brutal justice of the Mayor's Court and were both sentenced to death. Hanna pleaded that she was pregnant. Despite being in the early stages of pregnancy – as attested to by a jury of matrons – she was judged unworthy of life.[63]

Hanna and Hackema's journey displayed their knowledge of the politics and law of both Bengal and the EIC. The Mughal police station signified the boundary of the EIC's zamindari, beyond which point they had no legal jurisdiction. They went over to a place that came under the legal jurisdiction of the Bengal Nawab or the Mughal emperor. Apart from her knowledge of the legal boundaries of the EIC zamindari, Hanna had the necessary knowledge of English common law to defend herself in the Calcutta court.

63. P/155/72, fo. 31.

When the death penalty was passed against Hanna and Hackema, they were asked if "they had anything to urge why sentence of death should not pass against them". Hanna promptly mentioned her pregnancy – she was aware that English common law provided immunity to pregnant women on death row. Like many poor pregnant women facing the death penalty in England, her plea proved futile as the jury of matrons judged that Hanna was "not quick with child", or not in the later phases of her pregnancy.[64] Hanna and Hackema's labours of robbery and flight to carve out a life together and then Hanna's self-defence in the courtroom bore testimony to the immense efforts enslaved people put into creating an autonomous zone of interpersonal relationships.

Even though Hanna's aspirations to a family life came to a violent end, some female household workers could successfully create and maintain their own affective ties. The wills of sixteen Portuguese and free Christian women provide a rare window into what these women called "family" and how they dealt with the patriarchy of the settlement even when it impinged on their affective ties. [65] While toiling for the upkeep of the company servants, these workers, especially women, innovated different kinds of affective ties, which developed an alternative form of family life, separate from households with male company servants at their centre. The Anglo-Indian family, especially in North Indian Mughal cities in the early colonial period, has received a fair amount of historians' attention. Studies on Begum Samru and Khair un-Nissa, for example, have emphasized the agency of indigenous women in creating innovative family ties at the moment of transition from pre-colonial rule to company rule.[66] As the first women who served the domestic needs of the European men of the companies in Bengal, Portuguese/free Christian women in and around Calcutta and Chinsura in many ways pioneered the innovative family ties in the long transition to colonialism. At the crossroads of class and gender, these women defined the various possibilities of emotional ties for the household workers.

---

64. Gregory Durston, *Wicked Ladies: Provincial Women, Crime and the Eighteenth-Century English Justice System* (Newcastle upon Tyne, 2013), p. 75.

65. Wills of Susanna de Rosario, Catharina Disius, Anthonia de Rosario, 1.11.06.11/1694, fos 112, 222, 1026; will of Lucia de Piedade, Simoa de Mello, Anna de Rozario, Magdalena de Rosario, 1.11.06.11/ 1693, fos 181, 239, 247, 480; will of Roza de Costa, 1.11.06.11/1693, fo. 258 and her revised will in 1.11.06.11/1715, fo. 552; will of Elizabeth Pain, 1757, will of Dominga Araujo, 1760, P/154/50 (unfoliated); will of Adriana Mendis, will of Clara van Bengale, 1.11.06.11/ 1693, fos 39,84; will of Josepha Jesus, 1.11.06.11/1715, fos 159–160; will of Petronella Henrietta, 1.11.06.11/ 1696, fos 628–629; will of Nathalia Raposa, 1.11.06.11/ 1694, fo. 108.

66. Michael Fisher, "Becoming and Making 'Family' in Hindustan", in Indrani Chatterjee (ed.), *Unfamiliar Relations: Family and History in South Asia* (New Brunswick, NJ, 2004), pp. 95–121; William Dalrymple, *White Mughals: Love & Betrayal in Eighteenth-Century India* (New York, 2004); Ghosh, *Sex and the Family in Colonial India.*

In analysing the experience of motherhood amongst black women in the United States, Patricia Hill Collins has noted that the disjuncture between the public and the private sphere, or the domestic sphere and the labour market, was blurred for most women of color.[67] Similarly, unlike the European woman, familial ties experienced by the propertied free Christian or Portuguese women of the settlements went beyond the experience of womanhood confined to the hearth and home. For most female European women who left wills, their widowhood was their primary identity.[68] There are very few instances of VOC or EIC officials recording Portuguese or free Christian women as dependents. None of the sixteen women in their wills express any inkling of present or former marital ties. Reproductive work mainly for male company servants was the source of these women's wealth, yet in the absence of the patriarch in these units these women created affective ties in their workplace with their subservient male workers and slaves, according to a logic that went beyond the singular factor of heteronormative caregiving.

There is significant evidence to show that free Portuguese women contributed towards the making of the fortunes of quite a few European men. Alexander Hamilton described Baranagore, a place known for the brothels run by the Portuguese women, thus: "The town is famously infamous for a seminary of female lewdness, where numbers of girls are trained up for the destruction of unwary youths".[69] Though in Hamilton's representation, these women were infamous for the "destruction of unwary" men, their wills on the contrary reveal that they were generous benefactors to European men. Magdalena de Rosario from Chinsura left the bulk of her property to Simon George.[70] Petronella Henrietta also nominated a Dutch man as her sole heir. Nathalia Raposa left 868 rupees and 5.5 annas to VOC bookkeeper Joan Francois van Schie. Simao de Mello chose a VOC sergeant, Lodewijk de Giets, as her universal heir. The wealthiest of all these women, Roza de Costa, who had multiple acquaintances in Batavia, left a substantial amount of money for each of them. Particularly, a sergeant, Grimius, and a bookkeeper, Grabo, were the primary inheritors of Roza de Costa's wealth. She revised her will twelve years later in 1755 following Grimius's death and left his son, Lambertus Grimius, 1,000 Arcot rupees.[71] As has been discussed earlier, the relationship between these women and European men was normally maintained outside of wedlock. True to this practice, none of the

---

67. Patricia Hill Collins, "Shifting the Center: Race, Class, and Feminist Theorizing About Motherhood", in Evelyn Nakano Glenn, Grace Chang, and Linda Rennie Forcey (eds), *Mothering: Ideology, Experience, and Agency* (New York, 1994), pp. 45–66.
68. Married women made their wills jointly with their husbands in the Dutch settlement.
69. Hamilton, *A New Account of the East Indies*, p. 19.
70. 1.11.06.11/ 1693, fo. 480.
71. This Roza de Costa wrote her will in 1743 and she is not the same Roza de Costa who wrote a will in 1755.

wills define these women's relationship with the men, evading any effort to formally establish bonds centring these men legitimately in the eyes of settlement patriarchy. Moreover, they were not motivated by the need to compensate for caregiving work or paternal guilt for leaving behind illegitimate children. Thus, benefaction was never a one-way channel, with Portuguese/free Christian women at the receiving end.

In these houses of "female lewdness" women formed familial relationships with native men. Of the sixteen women, only Catharina Disius referred to male relatives. The first was Ram Chandra, whom Disius called her brother, and the second, Betchoe, her nephew and Ram Chandra's son. She left the former a large garden and the latter a smaller garden she owned. The non-Christian names of her brother and nephew suggest that most probably they were not her blood relations. However, not only were they included within the ambit of her family, they were also generously endowed with her wealth, in her will.

The most important innovation in kinship ties amongst these women lay in their practices of motherhood. Except for Lucia de Piedade, who had a grandson, no other woman had any consanguineous kin. In fact, four of them clearly stated that they had "no blood relations in the world". Yet, as in most wills, the possessions of these women were left for the young. "Motherwork" is a term used by Patricia Hill Collins to signify racially marginalized women's experience of raising children. According to Collins, "I use the term 'motherwork' to soften the existing dichotomies in feminist theorizing about motherhood that posit rigid distinctions between private and public, family and work, the individual and the collective".[72] These women engaged in the trade of reproductive work were performing motherwork, through bridging the divides between private and public, family and work, the individual and the collective as an expression of a collective survival strategy. Motherhood was broadly defined; biological mothers were not the only ones responsible for the upkeep of the children. Filial relationships thus had various names. Most of the women from the VOC settlements left money for their "wards" (*opvoedeling*). Susanna de Rosario chose her "ward", Sabina de Rosade, as her universal heir. Similarly, Anthonia de Rosario chose her "ward", Johanna de Rosario. Lucia de Piedade left her "ward" half of the straw house. Magdalena de Rosario left for her "foster child", Margaretha de Rosario, ten rupees. Domingo Araujo from Calcutta referred to the three children to whom she left most of her property, as "house-bred child". These "wards", "house-bred child", or "foster children" were usually not the natural children of these women. Even when Lucia de Piedade nominated her grandson, Nicolaas de Silva, as her universal heir, she mentioned no clear relationship with his natural mother, Roza de Rozario. That all three – Lucia, Nicolaas, and Roza – had different surnames

---

72. Collins, " Shifting the Center", pp. 47–48.

suggest that irrespective of blood relations, a process of kin formation, going beyond consanguineous relationship, was at play in defining maternal lineage. Similarly, Anna de Rozario left all her property to her "adopted children", Catharina and Francisco de Rozario, whose biological parents were her slave, Sara and her husband, Tam. Motherwork for these women was a process of maintaining children in the taverns and brothels, irrespective of who the biological mother was and whether their birth was planned or not. While most of these children were born as a result of the women's sexual work for the company men, the patriarchy of the settlements found no incentive to maintain these children. Moreover, as has been discussed earlier, European fathers generally considered these children as "illegitimate", and none of the children born to Portuguese/free Christian/enslaved women lived with their fathers or entered the ambit of his family, even when they inherited part of the father's property. The families of these Portuguese and free Christian women thus found novel ways of incorporating these otherwise unwanted "illegitimate" children.

These matri-focal families sustained the institution of slavery in the settlement, even though their relationship with their slaves differed considerably from the European men's relationship to their slaves. For these women, as was the case with all slave owners of the settlement, slaves were capital investments. Portuguese and free Christian women were prominent in the slave trade. For example, in 1753 a Portuguese woman from Calcutta sold her slave in Chinsura for seventy Arcot rupees – the money "saved her from poverty".[73] Anna de Rosario earned thirty-five Arcot rupees by selling her slave Sabina van Falta to the assistant merchant, Jan van Hoorn in 1743.[74] Some even "lent out" their slaves in order to make money.[75] Some women, like Leonara van Mandhar along with her Dutch husband, used the language of any other cautious European slave owner – "retained rights to recall manumission" – while freeing slaves.[76] However, except for Simao de Mello, none of these women, unlike the European slave masters, gifted slaves to acquaintances in their wills. Promising all the house slaves freedom after their death was the norm. Some, like Leonara van Mandhar, went to the length of using 1,550 of her 10,000-rupee inheritance to emancipate seven of her slaves.[77] As mistresses of taverns, lodging houses, and brothels, it is highly likely that they had exploitative control over their slaves, even though, as is clear from the tavern keeper Lucia's testimony, slaves were working alongside the mistress at her workplace.[78]

73. 1.11.06.11/1715, fo. 560.
74. 1.11.06.11/1694, fo.132.
75. 1.11.06.11/1715, fo. 117.
76. 1.11.06.11/1677B, fos 120–132.
77. 1.11.06.11/1677A, fo. 545.
78. 1.11.06.11/1693, fo. 347.

As slave mistresses, what set these free Christian and Portuguese women apart from their European male counterparts was the familial ties they created with their slaves. The wills present an insight into the interpersonal relationships between the female members of such establishments, and even between the slave-owning mistress and her female slaves. Roza de Costa left her "housebred" children, Rafael, Domingo, and September, and two female slaves Rosetta van Bengale and Anthonia 300 rupees and her house. Roza also provided for burial money for Rosetta and Anthonia in her will. In this case, motherwork performed by the propertied woman opened up a zone of cooperation between the enslaved women and their mistresses. In the "absence of blood relations", these women often depended upon their slaves to fulfill the filial duties of caregiving. Magdalena de Rozario freed her slave Susanna van Calcutta and left her 1,000 rupees. Magdalena depended on Susanna to bury her. Though Roza de Costa had several acquaintances in Batavia, her closest people in Chinsura were her eight slaves. She promised freedom to all and left them each between ten and 200 rupees in cash. One slave family of Rafael de Couto, Andre and Sophia Theodora, inherited a large amount of gold. Sophia Theodora also inherited the house in which her mistress lived, and others were to eventually inherit three other houses that Rosa owned in Chinsura. Josepha Jesus was unique amongst these women. In her will made in 1755, she left her two slaves, Allvina Jesus and Rietha de Chorea, her entire property. Both of these slaves were first entered in her will as "daughters". The word was later struck out and the word "slaves" was entered. Slaves in some of these households were subservient female members of the family. Though these relationships were unequal – the mistress exploiting the labour of the enslaved women to generate profits – such establishments provided spaces where female bonding based on trust and care could develop.

CONCLUSION

During the Battle of Buxar in 1764, some members of Mr Morgan's Battalion abducted Komaree from her village adjoining Buxar. Following her abduction, she served as a concubine to various members of the EIC army and her work took her all over Northern India. Years of service yielded a modest fortune, with which Komaree started her own business in Farukhabad in the Upper Gangetic plain, in the province of Awadh in the 1790s. Here, adjacent to the army regiment, she set up her own shop, retailing in grains, mats, carts, etc. Most importantly, a steady source of her income remained "conveying" her sister and two other slave girls to men in the army.[79] Komaree's story was very similar to many female household workers discussed in this paper.

---

79. Chatterjee, "Colouring Subalternity", pp. 60–61.

As predecessors to Komaree, the enslaved, free Christian, and Portuguese women of the EIC and VOC settlements of the early eighteenth century set the stage for sexual and familial relationships between European men and non-European women. Despite the similarities, the process of colonial expansion by the EIC after 1757 separates Komaree's story from the stories of the enslaved and freed women of early eighteenth-century settlements. With colonization, the class and gendered relationship that had emerged centring the European household in the company settlements penetrated deep into the South Asian hinterland. Unlike the household workers in the early eighteenth century, Komaree was born in the North Indian mainland. After the Battle of Buxar, EIC officers no longer had to rely on their Indian Ocean networks to supply their domestic labour force. In other words, as nodes of Indian Ocean networks of trade, the company settlements/ports in the early eighteenth century were incubators of relationships of reproductive/sexual labour that later became the foundations of the Anglo-Indian family in colonial India.

With their lives and labour, these women bridged the dualities of slavery/freedom, domesticity/market relations, and slavery/kinship. As this article shows, manumission of enslaved women in European households was common. Upon manumission, they became part of the free Christian or Portuguese communities of the settlements. However, manumission did not translate into freedom from domestic labour. Domestic service for European men was the only form of economic opportunity open to them. Even the most fortunate amongst these women, who amassed considerable wealth, made their money from running taverns or brothels providing care to European men. Caregiving work thus bridged the fates of freed and enslaved female domestic workers of the settlements. Moreover, the nature of their work, and in some cases bondage, blurred the distinction between the domestic sphere and the marketplace/workplace.

Domestic service to EIC officials only partially explains the subjectivity of these women and their agency in forming social relationships in the company settlements of pre-colonial Bengal. Some of these women formed families extraneous to the institution of the European household. For enslaved women such tasks were difficult and entailed "conspiracies" of escape and/or murder of the slave masters. Freed women created sexual liaisons and parental/fraternal/sororal relationships bypassing the needs of their male European clients. In more ways than one, these women pioneered the strategies of independent existence, albeit highly circumscribed, that Komaree adopted towards the end of the eighteenth century.

IRSH 64 (2019), pp. 95–124 doi:10.1017/S002085901900004X

Between the Plantation and the Port: Racialization and Social Control in Eighteenth-Century Paramaribo

PEPIJN BRANDON

International Institute of Social History
Cruquiusweg 31, 1019 AT Amsterdam, The Netherlands
Vrije Universiteit
De Boelelaan 1105, 1081 HV Amsterdam, The Netherlands

E-mail: pepijn.brandon@iisg.nl

ABSTRACT: Starting from an incident in the colonial port city of Paramaribo in the autumn of 1750 in which, according to the Dutch governor Mauricius, many of the proper barriers separating rich and poor, men and women, adults and children, white citizens and black slaves were crossed, this article traces some of the complexities of everyday social control in colonial Suriname. As gateways for the trade in commodities and the movement of people, meeting points for free and unfree labourers, and administrative centres for emerging colonial settlements, early modern port cities became focal points for policing interaction across racial and social boundaries. Much of the literature on the relationship between slavery and race focuses on the plantation as "race-making institution" and the planter class as the immediate progenitors of "racial capitalism". Studies of urban slavery, on the other hand, have emphasized the greater possibilities of social contact between blacks, *mestizos*, and whites of various social status in the bustling port cities of the Atlantic. This article attempts to understand practices of racialization and control in the port city of Paramaribo not by contrasting the city with its plantation environment, but by underlining the connections between the two social settings that together shaped colonial geography. The article focuses on everyday activities in Paramaribo (dancing, working, drinking, arguing) that reveal the extent of contact between slaves and non-slaves. The imposition of racialized forms of repression that set one group against the other, frequently understood primarily as a means to justify the apparent stasis of the plantation system with its rigid internal divisions, in practice often functioned precisely to fight the pernicious effects of mobility in mixed social contexts.

INTRODUCTION[1]

On Saturday, 3 October 1750, a joyful sight greeted the Governor General of Suriname, Johan Jacob Mauricius. Along Paramaribo's Waterkant, the quay adorned with tamarind and orange trees stretching out from the square where the governor's mansion was located, most of the ships ran flags and fired their guns "as if it were the birthday of the Prince".[2] However, the occasion of these festivities greatly annoyed the Dutch governor. For several years, Paramaribo had been the scene of a long feud between Mauricius and sections of the planter class well-entrenched in Suriname's governing council. The conflict can be situated in a wider Atlantic moment of Creole triumphalism in which colonial elites started to challenge the political and economic restrictions imposed by their respective motherlands, and would result in the ousting of Mauricius in April 1751.[3] In this context of increasing political tensions, Johanna Catharina Brouwer (born Bedloo), one of the most vocal members of the opposition and widow of Everhard Brouwer, the recently deceased former captain of the citizens' guard and member of the governing council, had organized a provocative ball to celebrate the birthday of her five-year-old daughter.[4] During the rowdy birthday party, which went on well into the night, fireworks and oranges were thrown at the governor's house, soldiers and slaves broke curfews regulating movement

1. I would like to thank the participants in the two workshops on "Free and Unfree Labor in Atlantic and Indian Port Cities (c.1700–1850)" held at the University of Pittsburgh in May 2016 and May 2017, and the N.W. Posthumus conference at the Radboud University in Nijmegen in June 2017 for their suggestions. Special thanks go to Seymour Drescher, Dienke Hondius, Pernille Røge, Niklas Frykman, and Lex Heerma van Voss, who commented on the paper in detail. I also want to express my gratitude to my students Annette Bosscher, Alida Jones, and Theo Mulder, who worked with me on this source material in the context of a course at the Vrije Universiteit Amsterdam. Their insightful questions and observations were helpful for me while finishing this article, and they also managed to unearth a couple of beautiful details that I integrated into the final version. The research for this article was made possible by an NWO Rubicon grant, project number 446-13-007.
2. National Archives, The Hague, Oud Archief Suriname [hereafter, NA-OAS], 1.05.10.01, Gouvernementssecretarie, no. 5, "Journaal Mauricius 1748–1750", entry for 3 October 1750.
3. The political conflicts surrounding Mauricius's governorship are described at length in Gerard Willem van der Meiden, *Betwist bestuur. Een eeuw strijd om de macht in Suriname 1651–1753* (Amsterdam, 1987). Accounts that focus more on the social aspects can be found in J. Marten W. Schalkwijk, *The Colonial State in the Caribbean: Structural Analysis and Changing Elite Networks in Suriname 1650–1920* (The Hague, 2011); and Karwan Fatah-Black, *White Lies and Black Markets: Evading Metropolitan Authority in Colonial Suriname, 1650–1800* (Leiden and Boston, MA, 2015). On the wider Atlantic moment of Creole triumphalism, see Bernard Bailyn, *Atlantic History: Concept and Contours* (Cambridge, MA, 2005), p. 101; and Jeremy Adelman, *Sovereignty and Revolution in the Iberian Atlantic* (Princeton, NJ and Oxford, 2006), pp. 146–147.
4. Biographical background information on Johanna Catharina Brouwer can be found in Fred. Oudschans Dentz, "De fortuinlijke loopbaan in Suriname van den Zweed C.G. Dahlberg", *De West-Indische Gids*, 23:1 (1941), pp. 269–279.

in the city at night, and the authorities were taunted and mocked by adults and children. Only at midnight did the bailiff succeed in finally disbanding the riotous birthday party of Brouwer's happy five-year-old. Three days later, the exasperated Mauricius wrote a long report of the incident to the authorities of the Reformed Church and the directors of the Society of Suriname in Amsterdam, in which he warned that "all respect for God and Government has *broken down* here, how these are being *mocked openly, and spat in the face. Yes, how little children and slaves are being taught to cuss at them*".[5]

A long line of social history on medieval and early modern Europe has concentrated on the way in which internal conflict among sections of the ruling classes could open up spaces for wider social explosions, laying bare existing tensions between political and economic elites and subalterns. In this literature, special importance is attached to rites, festivities, and acts of public shaming, such as rough music, as moments in which social norms and barriers were simultaneously revealed and transgressed.[6] As the reference to the slaves in Mauricius's outcry reminds us, such transgressions were even more dangerous in a plantation colony in which the bedrock of all social relations was slavery. This article takes a thick description of the many social norms invoked and transgressed in the evening of 3 October 1750 as a starting point to examine everyday practices of social control in Paramaribo, the town of five to six thousand inhabitants that stood at the centre of the colonial Suriname's commerce. In particular, it will look at the way in which, in an Atlantic slave port, more familiar and generally applied aspects of enforcing social order – restricting movement, maintaining social distinctions, effecting taboos on interaction – intersected with a process of racialization, by which skin colour itself became a key determinant of one's position in society. Racialization has not been a prominent theme in the study of the

---

5. Salomon du Plessis (ed.), *Recueil van egte stukken en bewyzen ... tegens Mr. Jan Jacob Mauricis etc.* 5 vols (s.l., 1752), IV, p. 295, Report by Mauricius to the Society of Suriname of 6 October 1750. Italics in the original. The fact that women and children were among the key protagonists drawing Mauricius's ire is important. While this article is about racialization rather than the enforcement of gender differences, in practice the two intertwined in intricate ways. The subsections that follow draw attention to this at several points, but the theme deserves further development. See the contributions by Titas Chakraborty and Melina Teubner in this Special Issue.

6. Classic texts are Natalie Zemon Davis, "The Reasons of Misrule: Youth Groups and Charivaris in Sixteenth-Century France", *Past & Present*, 50 (1971), pp. 41–75; Edward P. Thompson, "'Rough Music': Le Charivari Anglais", *Annales. Histoire, Sciences Sociales*, 27:2 (1972), pp. 285–312; Natalie Zemon Davis, "The Rites of Violence: Religious Riot in Sixteenth-Century France", *Past & Present*, 59:2 (1973), pp. 51–91. See also the exchange of letters between these two authors in Alexandra Walsham, "Rough Music and Charivari: Letters Between Natalie Zemon Davis and Edward Thompson, 1970–1972", *Past & Present*, 235:1 (2017), pp. 243–262.

Figure 1. Diorama of the Paramaribo Waterfront (Waterkant), Gerrit Schouten, 1820. *Rijksmuseum, Amsterdam.*

Dutch Atlantic.[7] This dovetails with more general trends in Dutch historiography, which has often treated the social construction of race as a non-issue.[8] When historians have discussed race at all, they have done so frequently in a way that treats the emergence of phenotypical differences as key markers of distinction as an almost self-explanatory fact. Starting from places where we can see interaction between different social groups at work – from the squares and the loading docks, the bars and the neighbourhood brawls – can help us to look beyond the apparent naturalness of the success of racially segregationist policies pursued by colonial authorities.[9]

7. Typically, a recent volume that summarizes the results of the current wave of interest in Atlantic studies in the Netherlands barely mentions race or racialization, and only marginally discusses slavery. Gert Oostindie and Jessica V. Roitman (eds), *Dutch Atlantic Connections, 1680–1800: Linking Empires, Bridging Borders* (Leiden and Boston, MA, 2014).
8. Kwame Nimako, Amy Abdou, and Glenn Willemsen, "Chattel Slavery and Racism: A Reflection on the Dutch Experience", in Philomena Essed and Isabel Hoving (eds), *Dutch Racism* (Amsterdam, 2014), pp. 31–51. For some exceptions focusing on the development of racialized representations in the metropole, see Allison Blakely, *Blacks in the Dutch World: The Evolution of Racial Imagery in a Modern Society* (Bloomington, IN, 1993); Angelie Sens, *"Mensaap, heiden, slaaf". Nederlandse visies op de wereld rond 1800* (The Hague, 2001); and Dienke Hondius, *Blackness in Western Europe: Racial Patterns of Paternalism and Exclusion* (New Brunswick, NJ, 2014). An East Indian perspective is provided in Ulbe Bosma and Remco Raben, *Being "Dutch" in the Indies: A History of Creolisation and Empire, 1500–1920* (Athens, OH, 2008), pp. 21–25.
9. This is, of course, true for the study of urban slavery more generally. Peter Wood talks about the "efforts to prohibit Negro socializing" in Carolina in the early eighteenth century, citing

However, choosing the port city as a focal point in this research is not simply a matter of convenience. For understandable reasons, studies of social control in eighteenth-century Suriname have put most emphasis on plantation life.[10] In the context of the plantation, with its rigid social division between white masters and overseers and the black slaves, outnumbering whites by a ratio of more than ten to one, the almost complete overlap of social and racial distinction hardly appears as strange. The only real question for debate seems to be whether the growing racial exclusivity of plantation slavery was the result of latent prejudices that had always been present in European society, or whether race as a category was created from the outset as an ideological justification for an essentially economic system.[11] The everyday functioning of social and racial distinctions was much less straightforward in port cities, where intermingling between social groups was extensive and hard to control, movement of people and goods was a given due to their commercial function and geographical location straddling sea and hinterlands, and society was much more socially diverse.[12] However, the notion of two separated worlds, the static and simple world of the plantation and the complex and dynamic world of the town, is based on an illusion. Constant movement between these worlds was the norm. This included the movement of many

---

1712 legislation "against the numerous Negroes who entered Charlestown on Sunday and holidays in order – according to the whites – 'to drink, quarrel, fight, curse and swear, and profane the Sabbath, [...] resorting in great companies together, which may give them an opportunity of executing any wicked designs'". Peter H. Wood, *Black Majority: Negroes in Colonial South Carolina from 1670 through the Stono Rebellion* (New York and London, 1974), p. 272.

10. Gert Oostindie, *Roosenburg en Mon Bijou. Twee Surinaamse plantages, 1720–1870* (Dordrecht, 1989); Alex van Stipriaan, *Surinaams contrast. Roofbouw en overleven in een Caraïbische plantagekolonie 1750–1863* (Leiden, 1993); and Ruud Beeldsnijder, *"Om werk van jullie te hebben". Plantageslaven in Suriname, 1730–1750* (Utrecht, 1994).

11. Among the vast literature on this question, see H. Hoetink, *Slavery and Race Relations in the Americas: An Inquiry into their Nature and Nexus* (New York, 1973); Alden T. Vaughan, "The Origins Debate: Slavery and Racism in Seventeenth-Century Virginia", in *idem, Roots of American Racism: Essays on the Colonial Experience* (Oxford and New York, 1995), pp. 136–174; Barbara Jeanne Fields, "Slavery, Race and Ideology in the United States of America", *New Left Review*, I/181 (1990), pp. 95–118; James H. Sweet, "The Iberian Roots of American Racist Thought", *The William and Mary Quarterly*, 54:1 (1997), pp. 143–166; and Jorge L. Giovannetti, "Slavery, Racism and the Plantation in the Caribbean", *Latin American and Caribbean Ethnic Studies*, 1:1 (2006), pp. 5–36.

12. Douglas Catterall and Jodi Campbell (eds), *Women in Port: Gendering Communities, Economies, and Social Networks in Atlantic Port Cities, 1500–1800* (Leiden and Boston, MA, 2012), and Jorge Cañizares-Esguerra, Matt D. Childs, and James Sidbury (eds), *The Black Urban Atlantic in the Age of the Slave Trade* (Philadelphia, PA, 2013). For what follows, see the powerful argument for mobility as a key factor in understanding slave societies presented by Julius S. Scott, *The Common Wind. Afro-American Currents in the Age of the Hatian Revolution* (London, 2018).

slaves, who, individually or in small groups, went to the port for chores, as rowers for the master or his goods, to perform hard labour on the fortress for the government as hired slaves, or to receive punishment. It also included the movement of slaves who had received temporary leave from the plantation to visit their families or sell goods in the market, and of those who had managed to escape and sought refuge in the town. It is exactly this perpetual movement between plantation and port – a crossing of boundaries in its own right – that made towns like Paramaribo focal points for the racialization of social control. Starting from a seemingly innocuous moment of contention, this article tries to capture this process of creating and enforcing boundaries in a sea of movement and intermingling.

DISREPUTABLE DANCES, SWINGING BODIES

What was the Paramaribo in which the widow Johanna Catharina Brouwer organized the "disreputable dance" (in Dutch: *eclatant bal*) for her daughter, and where did it fit into patterns of colonial sociability? In the decades after the capture of Suriname by a Zeeland fleet in 1667, the Guyana settlement remained a fragile plantation colony built around the three villages Torarica, Jodensavanne, and Paramaribo nearest to the coast. The eighteenth century saw a rapid expansion of the colony's population and a steady growth in its economic importance to the Dutch Republic. Both reached their zenith in the first half of the 1770s. The importance of Paramaribo grew accordingly, while the other two settlements remained villages. By 1752, Suriname had a slave population of 37,835, of whom 2,264 lived in Paramaribo. In the same year, the white, *mestizo*, and free black population (excluding maroons and the indigenous) numbered 2,062, half of whom lived in Paramaribo. In addition, around 700 soldiers were stationed in Suriname, many of them garrisoned in Fort Zeelandia, which overlooked the Suriname River at the northern edge of Paramaribo.[13] Beyond Paramaribo, the plantation colony stretched out in two divergent strips along the Suriname and Commewijne Rivers. The middle of the eighteenth century formed a moment of rapid expansion and change, in which the value of coffee exports overtook that of sugar. The steep rise in the number of coffee plantations, from none in 1713 to around 140 by 1745 and 295 around 1770, lay behind the financial boom that made West Indian mortgages all the rage on Amsterdam's capital market.[14] Dutch Atlantic trade steadily grew to

---

13. Figures taken from Van Stipriaan, *Surinaams contrast*, pp. 311 and 314. See also Karwan Fatah-Black, "Paramaribo as Dutch and Atlantic Nodal Point, 1650–1795", in Oostindie and Roitman, *Dutch Atlantic Connections*, pp. 52–71.
14. Van Stipriaan, *Surinaams contrast*, pp. 33–35.

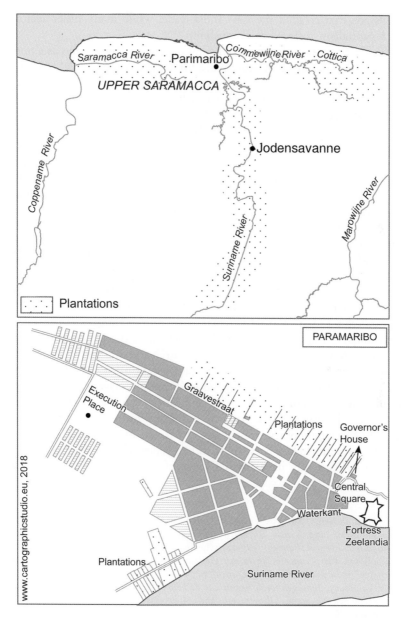

Figure 2. Top: map indicating the spread of plantations in mid-eighteenth-century Suriname. Bottom: map of Paramaribo including some of the main locations mentioned in this article.

dimensions that rivalled the East India trade, while many other sectors of Dutch capitalism suffered a severe slump.[15]

With the growth of the colony, the importance of Paramaribo as a node of urban production and a meeting place for transactions, for gathering news, and for participating in a more diverse social life increased. In this way, in the words of the Surinamese-Dutch scholar Rudolf van Lier, the town "became the centre around which all life in the colony revolved".[16] Social and cultural life for the white planter class in Paramaribo included occasional balls of the type organized by the widow of Captain Brouwer, as well as visits to the theatre and the expensive coffee houses and taverns near the waterfront.[17] When whites went out in the evening, it was not uncommon for them to bring several of their slaves to serve on them.[18] For masters as well as for large numbers of slaves, though to a lesser extent for the latter owing to their more limited freedom of movement, Paramaribo became an important place of work, where they could obtain news and sometimes drink and socialize around the improvised bars and small shops (*vettewariers*) that were considered a continuous threat to social order by the colonial authorities.[19] Fatah-Black details the street peddling done in the town by both slaves and poor whites, and the growth of markets where slaves sold the goods that they produced independently on the *kostgronden* (provisioning grounds) of the plantations. Markets "were mainly found in the less affluent parts of town, on the square near the church and on the waterfront".[20] Of course, Paramaribo was itself an important location for slave labour. Many slaves in Paramaribo were employed as domestic slaves, but occupations also included traditional dock work and labour on the plantations on the outskirt of the town. Slaves carried out tasks for the plantation owners that required a temporary presence in the town, or worked there permanently as carpenters, butchers, or in other types of skilled labour.[21] Their paths must frequently have crossed those of free blacks and mulattos who

15. Victor Enthoven, "An Assessment of Dutch Transatlantic Commerce, 1585–1817", in Johannes Postma and Victor Enthoven (eds), *Riches from Atlantic Commerce: Dutch Transatlantic Trade and Shipping, 1585–1817* (Leiden and Boston, MA, 2003), pp. 385–445, 443.
16. Rudolf van Lier, *Samenleving in een grensgebied. Een sociaal-historische studie van de maatschappij in Suriname* (The Hague, 1949), p. 79.
17. A.F. Lammens, *Bijdragen tot de kennis van de kolonie Suriname* (Amsterdam, 1982), p. 41, notes the high prices in some of these taverns and coffee houses, which were within reach only of the quite well off.
18. Van Lier, *Samenleving*, p. 81.
19. As can be gauged from the many regulations and cases of infringement surrounding official and improvised taverns and shops, gathered in NA-OAS, Archief Raad van Politie, 1.05.10.02, no. 953, "Register van publicaties, notificaties en reglementen betreffende herbergiers, tappers, vettewariers, slachters, broodbakkers en pontevoerders over 1717–1824".
20. Fatah-Black, *White Lies*, p. 143.
21. J.D. Kunitz, *Surinam und seine Bewohner* (Erfurt, 1805), p. 72.

carved out their livelihood in Paramaribo, indigenous hunters, white artisans, or sailors and soldiers who worked in town. Waged artisans, crewmen, and slaves often found themselves working side by side on a single project.[22] Adriaan François Lammens, whose early nineteenth-century description of Suriname gives the most detailed picture of urban life in the colony, describes the scene of work and social and ethnic intermingling along the quay in a passage mixing admiration and class prejudice:

> The view of the riverside, where forty to seventy, and sometimes more, seagoing vessels are anchored, is most agreeable: the loading and offloading of the ships, with the continuous coming and going of tent boats, ferries, carrying vessels, and *corjaren*; the strange sight of Indians, who come to visit Paramaribo; the general activity on the water. A daily, well-stocked fish market opposite the Jewish Broad Street produces an unpleasant sensation for the nostrils, which is not improved by the smells eluded by the working lower class; but one finds for this ample compensation in seeing the abundance of fish, crabs, fruit, and birds available at the market.[23]

Despite this lively portrait, the visible marks of repression and violence were never far off. Fort Zeelandia, which overlooked the governor's mansion, served as the place to which plantation owners had to bring slaves for punishment exceeding the maximum number of lashes they could administer privately. The square between the fortress and the mansion was the place of punishment for soldiers condemned to run the gauntlet.[24] And a short walk along the Western outskirts of the town brought one to the funeral site reserved for non-whites, as well as the place of execution containing "the remnants of the unlucky ones, who as a warning to others and as punishment for their evil deeds had to end their lives there".[25] The close proximity between violence, work, and festivities, both in spatial and in symbolic terms, is well illustrated by a casual remark in the diary of the famed chronicler of the Surinamese Maroon Wars John Gabriel Stedman. On 9 March 1773, he noted:

> I return to Paramaribo. N.B. During my absence 3 negroes were hang'd on the boat, and 2 whipt below the gallows. On the 8th [March], being the Prince of Orange his birthday, Colonel Fourgeoud gave a genteel supper and ball to the ladies and gentlemen, *la sale de danse* [in the] officers' guardroom.[26]

---

22. Fatah-Black lists cases of enslaved "carpenter-negroes" and waged shipwrights or ships' carpenters being employed to construct transport vessels: Karwan Fatah-Black, "Scheepsbouw en reparatie in achttiende-eeuws Suriname", *Tijdschrift voor Zeegeschiedenis*, 36:2 (2017), pp. 68–88, with, for example, a case from January 1744 on p. 80.
23. Lammens, *Bijdragen*, p. 53.
24. NA-OAS, Archief Gouvernementssecretarie, 1.05.10.01, no. 615, "Reglement voor de Militaire Troupen in de Colonie Suriname, 1778", p. 38.
25. *Ibid.*, p. 51.
26. Stanbury Thompson (ed.), *The Journal of John Gabriel Stedman 1744–1797, Soldier and Author: Including an Authentic Account of his Expedition to Surinam, in 1772* (London, 1962), p. 122.

This, then, was the social and physical environment in which Johanna Catharina Brouwer organized her disreputable dance.²⁷ According to Mauricius, when first announced, the plans for the party had already raised a murmur within polite society. The minister of the Reformed Church had ordered the sacristan to inquire with the widow whether she was aware that her ball would be taking place on the night before the Lord's Supper. In answer to these criticisms, Johanna Catharina replied that the ball would only be a children's party.²⁸ Persisting against the wishes of the Reformed Church and high society's perceptions of good taste, she asked another widow, her aunt Wossink, for the use of her house. The request was far from innocent, for the house was strategically located between the commander's lodgings and the governor's mansion. It was an excellent place for a spectacle, for the same square also functioned as the parade ground of the garrison of Fort Zeelandia during festivities or official inspections.²⁹ Around five in the afternoon of that fateful day, bystanders witnessed the arrival of the guests. These included, in Mauricius's words, "all the children of the Cabal" (meaning the youth from oppositional planter families).³⁰ An hour later, to the sound of trumpets, the dance started. To add insult to injury, not long afterwards, one of the prominent guests started throwing fireworks and oranges towards the house of the commander and the governor's mansion, supported by "loud cries of slaves".³¹

The exact timing of events is important to our understanding of the combination of digressions of the prevailing social order that followed. Mauricius is meticulous in establishing this timeline. According to him, at eight o'clock in the evening the clamour quietened down. Mauricius ascribed this to the fact that regulations prohibited slaves from being on the street without a lantern after this time of night. But shortly after nine, the trumpets started blowing again. This contained a second infringement on lawful restrictions of nightly activities, for among the musicians appeared to be a soldier, the army drummer Lorsius, who was required to be back in his barracks before nine on pain of running the gauntlet.³² The latter infringement of discipline provided the pretext for trying to shut the party down. But when Mauricius sent a non-commissioned officer, Hendrik Hop, to arrest Lorsius, the party-goers allowed the soldier to escape through the backdoor. When Hop inquired politely about the drummer, the lady of the house told him that

27. Report of the Dance of Widow Brouwer, 3 October 1750, du Plessis, *Recueil*, IV, p. 295.
28. Letter of Minister Yver to Governor Mauricius, 3 October 1750, *ibid.*, p. 298.
29. Lammens, *Bijdragen*, p. 31.
30. Report of the Dance of Widow Brouwer, 3 October 1750, du Plessis, *Recueil*, IV, p. 296.
31. A fortnight later, the Suriname government council prohibited the throwing of fireworks in the colony. NA-OAS, Gouvernementssecretarie, 1.05.10.01, no. 556, Kopie-notulen Hof van Politie en Criminele Justitie, 20 October 1750.
32. Report of the Dance of Widow Brouwer, 3 October 1750, du Plessis, *Recueil*, IV, p. 296.

Figure 3. Nineteenth-century view of the government house and adjacent square of Paramaribo, Eduard van Heemskerck van Beest, after Gerard Voorduin, 1860–1862. *Rijksmuseum, Amsterdam.*

Lorsius had already left by eight, and that "they had no need for soldiers in the house". After this, she shut the door in Hop's face.[33]

The enraged Mauricius sent the bailiff, but he, in turn, was intercepted by Johanna Catharina, who defiantly told him that "the Governor might be master in his house, but she was the master in hers".[34] Meanwhile, new musicians had taken the place of the escaped soldier, the most notable of them a violinist referred to as "the young Crepy", a clerk at the Paramaribo secretariat and son of a prominent planter. One of the most ominous moments of the evening came when this young clerk interrupted the music to shout a mocking challenge to the authorities: "Tomorrow, all the citizens will eat Blakke Breddie". Employing a phrase in Sranan Tongo or "Negro English", as the English-based Creole language of Surinamese slaves was then commonly known, this supposedly meant as much as "tomorrow, all the citizens will be in jail".[35] It was followed

33. Testimony of *Landspassaat* Hop, 4 October 1750, *ibid.*, p. 299.
34. Mastery of the house was also of course a crucial element of gendered power divisions. For comparison, see Susanah Shaw Romney, *New Netherland Connections: Intimate Networks and Atlantic Ties in Seventeenth-Century America* (Chapel Hill, NC, 2014).
35. The modern name is Sranan Tongo. For the social significance of its use, see also Natalie Zemon Davis, "Creole Languages and their Uses: The Example of Colonial Suriname", *Historical Research*, 82:216 (2009), pp. 268–284.

by "Hurrays" taken over by the children. To top it off, a trumpeter "had the temerity to blow on his trumpet, not orderly, but with the most infamous sound in the world, while wenches, children, and slaves loudly laughed and shouted". The shouts and "mocking trumpet blows" lasted until close to midnight, when Talbot, a member of the government council, came down from Fort Zeelandia and finally managed to disperse the crowd.[36] In a separate series of comments on the events, added to the official report, Mauricius underlined the reason for his outrage:

> To loudly shout under the Governor's windows at night that the citizens will be brought into the fortress in the morning and call out "Hurray!" for this, is such great and coarse rebellion as one can imagine. Just one step further, and the Citizens come and tear the house down.[37]

THE CITIZENS WILL EAT BLAKKE BREDDIE

The "children of the Cabal", who behaved in such a rowdy way right in front of the governor's house, in fact hailed from the higher echelons of Dutch Surinamese society. All the more powerful therefore was the symbolic inversion of social roles that was implied in the notion that the citizens were jailbound. Alleging that they had included "Negro English" in their mocking shouts, and to do so in reference to a fortress that also functioned as the central slave prison, further added to the scandalous nature of their utterance. Whether or not Mauricius really believed that the relatively minor infringements that caused him such irritation on the night of 3 October 1750 opened the road to all-out rebellion, his repeated insistence on this in his reports and letters suggests that his superiors in the Dutch Republic would at least recognize the subversive potential of the inversion. Conflicts over class belonging and social status played an important role in the political clashes between increasingly self-confident planters and the governor that divided the colonial state. Behind the anger expressed by each party over the lack of respect shown by the other loomed a greater fear: the existential angst that, while the colonists shouted, the slaves laughed.

---

36. Report of the Dance of Widow Brouwer, 3 October 1750, du Plessis, *Recueil*, IV, p. 296. As is clear from this and several other of the passages cited, gender and age play an important role in Mauricius's moral outrage. In this context, the pairing of children and slaves is highly significant, since in developing colonial law as well as in developing European conceptions of Africans in general both groups were frequently equated for being "dependent" and therefore unable to speak on their own behalf (*onmondig*). Hondius, *Blackness in Western Europe*, ch. 2.
37. "Remarks on the Report of the Dance", du Plessis, *Recueil*, IV, p. 297. The soldier Coenraad Noltmyer, one of the guards in front of Mauricius's house, gave a statement in which he repeated the phrase of Crepy as "tomorrow we shall eat black bread", without using Negro English. He declared he had heard a woman speaking similar words to the children who were present. "Verklaringe van den Canonier Coenraad Noltmyer", *ibid.*, p. 300.

Behind the conflicts that erupted in Suriname in the late 1740s ultimately lay economic trends. In order to exploit the opportunities provided by the growing market for Atlantic products in Europe and burgeoning intercolonial trade and smuggling, planters worked to escape the restrictions imposed from above. In 1738, private West Indian traders forced the Dutch West India Company to relinquish its monopoly on the slave trade to Suriname. From the 1740s onwards, a lively legal and illegal trade with the British North American colonies developed that would grow to enormous proportions by the end of the century. As a result, the planters could muster increasing economic power against the governor, who acted as a representative of mercantilist policies enforced by the Society of Suriname, and demanded to be treated with the respect that their wealth in their eyes bestowed upon them.[38] Economic success also fostered a more assertive attitude towards the motherland. In one of his first petitions to the States General, Samuel du Plessis, one of the most vocal members of the opposition within Suriname's government council, pointed out that "all inhabitants of these lands [i.e. the Dutch Republic], as well as the State itself, would be drawing considerable advantages and prosperity" as a result of the success of the colony.[39] Suriname planters thus demanded acknowledgement of their role as important contributors to the wealth of the nation. However, colonial governors and their overseas directors tended to see the local elites as rabble and adventurers who had been able to outgrow their proper social sphere to live a life of debauchery in the colony.[40] A particularly striking example of someone who, in the eyes of Governor Mauricius, had refused to observe the limits imposed by low provenance was Carl Gustav Dahlberg. For the course of events in October 1750, it is significant that, at the time of the scandalous ball, Dahlberg was eating the proverbial black bread. Even more significantly, he was Johanna Catharina Brouwer's lover.

Like many white soldiers and labourers who came to Suriname, Carl Gustav Dahlberg was of non-Dutch origin. In an angry rant in his journal, Mauricius alleged that the Swedish corporal had come to Suriname as part

---

38. Van der Meiden, *Betwist bestuur*; Fatah-Black, *White Lies*.

39. "Request, door Salomon du Plessis den 31 July 1747 aan Haar Hoog Mog. gepresenteerd", *Recueil*, I, p. 1.

40. The idea that in Suriname only knaves could make a fortune clearly comes to the fore in a play published in 1771, in which a plantation director echoes the common perception: "O Land vol list en schelmeryen, / Die Eerlyk is koomt in den noot, / Opregte deugt loopt hier om broot, / Genoopt van honger luydt te schryen." ["O Country of thievery and deceit, / Honest persons will fall into distress, / Sincere virtue will force you on the street, / To cry of hunger and beg for bread"]. *Het Surinaamsche Leeven, toneelwyse verbeeld door Don Experientia* (s.l., 1771), p. 19. The perception, which also existed in other Atlantic empires, might have had a real social basis. The Atlantic provided many opportunities for captains and new merchants to establish themselves as large-scale traders. Robin Blackburn, *The Making of New World Slavery: From the Baroque to the Modern, 1492–1800* (London and New York, 2010), pp. 232–233.

of a transport organized by *zielverkopers*.[41] This Dutch term refers to recruiters who used debt traps to force people into the army, the navy, or the service of the colonial companies. Being the victim of a *zielverkoper* thus automatically designated someone as poor. With some help, once in Suriname Dahlberg had apparently managed to climb to the rank of sub-lieutenant. It was enough of an advance in status for Dahlberg to become an attractive partner for the widow of a member of the government council and plantation owner Johanna Catharina Brouwer, a fact that in itself enraged Mauricius. In the latter's eyes, Dahlberg's engagement with the widow Brouwer, "one of the most impertinent and hellish shrews of the Cabal", only served him to build his fortune.[42] Dahlberg would indeed marry Johanna Catharina Brouwer in March 1751, making him the owner of the plantations Brouwershaven and Carlsburg. In 1752, he quit military service and the couple settled in a house in the Heerenstraat in Paramaribo, for which they paid the very high annual rent of 1,000 guilders.[43] However, as long as he was in the military his love life put him directly at odds with his superiors. On 14 September 1750, his commander had put him under house arrest for unspecified "insolent words", for which he refused to apologise.[44] Mauricius was quick to blame the wily ways of women for Dahlberg's behaviour, for "[a]ll his bravado is only to please his Infante".[45]

Among the oppositionist planters, the arrest became instant proof of the tyrannical mode of operation of the governor and his cronies. In a session of the Military Court on 23 September, four against three council members voted for Dahlberg's release against Mauricius's advice, leading him to overrule the decision and refer the case to a later full session.[46] In the week that followed, Dahlberg's house was the scene of daily solidarity visits by "the Ladies of the Cabal", who were received "with music".[47] On 3 October, the arrestee even went as far as asking for a temporary release "because he would like to visit the dance" later that night.[48] Not without reason, Mauricius was convinced that the prime reason behind the provocative gestures that took place at Johanna Catharina Brouwer's party was "that this *Amante* is piqued by the arrest of her beloved Dahlberg".[49]

---

41. NA-OAS, Gouvernementssecretarie, 1.05.10.01, no. 5, "Journaal Mauricius 1748–1750", entry for 1 October 1750.
42. *Ibid.*
43. Oudschans Dentz, "Dahlberg", p. 275.
44. NA-OAS, Gouvernementssecretarie, 1.05.10.01, no. 5, "Journaal Mauricius 1748–1750", entry for 14 September 1750.
45. *Ibid.*, 1 October 1750, significantly again linking supposed inferiority directly to childhood, although in this case the inferiority is based on gender rather than on status or race.
46. *Ibid.*, 23 September 1750.
47. *Ibid.*, 1 October 1750.
48. *Ibid.*, 3 October 1750.
49. "Remarques", *Recueil*, IV, p. 297.

The class anger apparent from Mauricius's comments on the relationship between Dahlberg and Brouwer was wholly in keeping with his general attitude to the oppositionist planters. When first confronted with a petition to the Dutch authorities signed by forty prominent whites, he had used similar slurs to describe his adversaries on the council. He referred to the planter du Plessis as "a raving upstart of a wig-makers apprentice", Taunay as an "old hunger-comrade", and the citizens' captain Amand Thomas as "a real Judas, who in his youth as a regimental barber-surgeon has escaped the gallows twice, now to make his fortune here".[50] Whereas Mauricius claimed that the planters blurred social distinctions by rising from rags to riches, the planter oppositionists, in response, charged him with blurring social lines by degrading them in the eyes of ordinary soldiers and slaves. In 1747, sixteen oppositionists, including Taunay, Thomas, and Brouwer (then still alive), complained about Mauricius's pardoning of two deserters who had been sentenced to death. After recalling that the freed soldiers had immediately deserted to a French privateer, they rhetorically asked: "Would it not be better to be a bit more rigorous towards the Soldiers, and a bit less towards Citizens?".[51] In a further protest against the "tyrannical regime" of Mauricius, planters retold with even greater indignation the story of a government slave who in the eyes of the opposition had been unjustly released after attacking a free person.[52] Again charging the governor with irresponsible laxity towards the upholding of social distinctions, they insisted that

> an act of Connivance of that nature can only be of dangerous consequence, and must give the Negroes reason to set free their natural penchant towards evildoing even further. And so it is in this case [...] since aforementioned slave has later told [Sluyter] in public on the street: "Scoundrel, what good did your complaints do you? I will beat you with a stick, etc."[53]

The idea that the greatest danger of blurring class distinctions among the white population was to set free the forces of slave rebellion was widely shared on all sides of the conflict. During a meeting in Amsterdam, a supporter of Mauricius in the Society of Suriname emphasized that if the conflicts in the colony had been between Europeans alone, it would have been easy for the authorities to come to a settlement. The real threat from the

---

50. Van der Meiden, *Betwist bestuur*, p. 103.

51. "Aan den Edele Agtb. Heer Salomon du Plessis tot Amsterdam, 6 February 1747", *Recueil*, I, p. 24.

52. The free person was Frans Sluyter, who in May 1745 had walked along Paramaribo's Waterkant when five "negroes", including the slave of the government, had called him a "damned Mulatto" and thrown stones at him. "Poincten en Consideratien, dienende ter betoog van de nadeelige despotique en verre gaande geïnteresseerde Regeeringe van Mr. J.J. Mauricius, Gouverneur Generaal over de Colonie van Surinamen, Rivieren en Districten van dien, &c. &c. &c.", *Ibid.*, p. 32.

53. *Ibid.*

planter opposition arose from the fact that the forty social upstarts who put their signature under the protest could mobilize a force of ten to twelve thousand slaves. To make sure this never happened, it was imperative to prevent "turbulent spirits" from entering the Suriname planter class. The oppositionists again presented their own variant of this argument. Not their demands, but the tyrannical actions and lack of respect shown by Mauricius for his council would lead the slaves to lose the necessary reverence for their masters, threatening "a general massacre of all the Europeans".[54] Thus, the invocation of largely imaginary class differences among the white planters became firmly attached to the question of the stability of the fundamental dividing line underlying colonial social order: that between African slaves and white masters.

FORCES OF REPRESSION, SOURCES OF REBELLION

The rulers' fears became all the more urgent since one of the key questions over which politics split in these years was how to deal with the rapid growth of actual slave resistance in the form of mass marronage and "slave conspiracies". For both parties, maintaining the slave-based social order was their primary concern. But whether this would be done best by increasing the planters' power on the plantation, or by strengthening the central institutions of state power based in Paramaribo became an issue that divided the colonial state up to the highest echelons. Fort Zeelandia, in the shadow of which the citizens danced and the slaves laughed on 3 October 1750, was a focal point for these conflicts.

Practically from the start, colonial authorities had deemed the presence of a sufficient number of white labourers and supervisors on the plantation as the first line of defence against slave resistance. It is important to remind oneself that making white or European labour synonymous with supervision constituted an element of racialization, in the same way that equating the word "negro" with "slave" did.[55] A string of new rules to solidify this division accompanied the transfer of control over the colony from Zeeland to the Society of Suriname in 1683. On 24 January 1684, the governor ordered owners to hand over lists that specified the number of white servants and the number of slaves on their plantations, prescribing that all plantations should have one white person as overseer for ten slaves.[56] While frequently

---

54. Van der Meiden, *Betwist bestuur*, pp. 106–108.
55. Vincent Brown makes a similar observation in *The Reaper's Garden: Death and Power in the World of Atlantic Slavery* (Cambridge, MA, and London, 2008), pp. 22–23. See also Edmund S. Morgan, *American Slavery, American Freedom* (New York and London, 1975), pp. 338ff; and Theodore W. Allen, *The Invention of the White Race*, 2 vols (London and New York, 2012), II, pp. 239ff.
56. J.T. de Smidt and T. van der Lee (eds), *West Indisch plakaatboek. Plakaten, Ordonnantiën en andere wetten, uitgevaardigd in Suriname 1667–1816*, 2 vols (Amsterdam, 1973), I, p. 137.

repeated during the eighteenth century, the intended ratio of white servants to slaves proved to be wildly unrealistic. Lists handed over by the citizens' captains for 1740 mention the presence of 87 whites and 3,910 slaves on the plantations in the Thorarica region, and 79 whites and 1,872 slaves in Jodensavanne. These examples were representative for the entire period and for plantations throughout Suriname.[57] Furthermore, while notoriously cruel towards the slaves, the white overseers especially were far from being a disciplined force. They mostly came from poor sections of the European population, under some of the worst conditions of employment available for colonial white labour. Table 1, based on a sample of almost 600 contracts of recruitment for eighteenth-century Suriname in the Amsterdam notarial archives, shows white overseers at the bottom of the hierarchy of white labour in terms of wages and length of obligatory contracts. Of the main groups of white labourers in the colony, with their wage of ninety guilders a year only soldiers earned less.[58] Soldiers and sailors were sometimes recruited to serve as overseers, but their record of alcoholism and physical and sexual abuse was so infamous that an important manual for plantation managers from the late eighteenth century suggested that the chances of slave unrest would decrease by employing fewer of these guards.[59] To strengthen the numbers and quality of their white personnel, plantation owners also tried to recruit skilled labourers such as carpenters, coopers, or barber-surgeons. However, as their average salaries and the frequent clauses for additional earnings indicate, the presence of these skilled labourers on the plantation was often only transitory, with many intending to set up shop for themselves as soon as the opportunity arose.[60]

Given the clear deficiencies of this small and divided white workforce as a barrier to slave rebellion, successive governors sought to create an apparatus of repression separate from the plantations. This included strengthening the army, fortresses, and guard posts, requisitioning citizens and slaves for patrol duties and hunts for maroons, and shifting some of the prerogatives in relation to punishing slaves from the individual planters to their collective representatives in Paramaribo.[61] However, planters frequently opposed this buttressing of the colonial state. They insisted that instead of creating security it destabilized the self-contained order of the plantation. In April 1744, the

---

57. NA-OAS, Archief Raad van Politie, 1.10.05.02, no. 580, "Opgaven van blanken, vrijen en slaven", figures from reports by Dirk Guldensteeden, 1740, David de Nassy, 1740.

58. Beeldsnijder, *Plantageslaven*, p. 42.

59. Anthony Blom, *Verhandling over den landbouw, in de colonie Suriname, volgens eene negentien-jaarige ondervinding zamengesteld* (Haarlem, 1786), pp. 365–366.

60. Van Stipriaan, *Surinaams contrast*, pp. 284–285.

61. On the development of central institutions for repression, see Jean Jacques Vrij, "Wapenvolk in een wingewest. De slavenkolonie Suriname, 1667–1799", in Victor Enthoven, Henk den Heijer, and Han Jordaan (eds), *Geweld in de West. Een militaire geschiedenis van de Nederlandse Atlantische wereld, 1600–1800* (Leiden and Boston, MA, 2013), pp. 45–74.

Table 1. *Employment contracts for West Indies in the Amsterdam notarial archives, eighteenth century.*

Job	Number	Average duration (months)	Average wage (guilders, first year)	Average wage (guilders, final year)*	Contains provision for extra earnings	Receives advance on wages
Director / Administrator	54	67	460	506 (12)	40 (74%)	1 (2%)
Barber-surgeon	81	49	290	320 (32)	39 (48%)	34 (42%)
Clerk / writer**	63	47	207	261 (42)	1 (2%)	14 (22%)
Carpenter	150	46	349	372 (45)	21 (14%)	89 (59%)
Manual labourers (other)	147	49	226	257 (58)	15 (10%)	81 (55%)
Overseers	101	51	131	163 (55)	0 (0%)	46 (46%)
Total	596	50	269	301 (244)	116 (19%)	265 (44%)

Source: The sample of contracts is compiled from Simon Hart's inventory of Amsterdam notarial records, Stadsarchief Amsterdam (SA), Notariële Archieven, collectie S. Hart, nos 433–434.

* Between brackets: number of contracts that provided for a wage increase between the start and the end of the term.

** In practice, writers (*schrijvers*) often also acted as overseers. However, on average, contracting terms for those signified as writers were substantially better than for those hired as overseers, and closer to those hired as clerks.

citizens' captain Pieter van Baerle from Cottica wrote a request defending masters in his precinct, who preferred to organize their own hunts for runaways, rather than employ government patrols. Van Baerle would later become fiscal council, the Paramaribo official responsible for punishing slaves brought to Fort Zeelandia. But as citizens' captain, he argued that the masters were right to hand out pardons on their own authority to recaptured runaways, and to refuse to bring slaves to the fortress.[62] A year later, another planter defended evading the obligation to bring captured runaways to Paramaribo by lugubriously claiming that "nothing else but their heads" had returned from the hunt.[63] The planters' allegation that the need to send slaves to Paramaribo for punishment could actually stimulate resistance finds some confirmation in a defiant saying used by slaves: "Tangi vo spansi boko mi bin si foto" – Thanks to the Spanish Bock I have seen the town.[64] In addition, for many slaves, to be sent on a forest patrol provided the ultimate opportunity to join the maroons.[65] Planters therefore often did not comply with a summons for patrol duty.

Plantation owners and directors raised similar complaints against the requirement to hire out slaves for building and maintaining the fortresses near the city. Like the obligation to supply slaves for patrols, in the eyes of the planters this weakened the workforce on the plantations. Furthermore, planters complained that they did not have enough white servants to guard their slaves on the way to and from Paramaribo, increasing rather than preventing possibilities of marronage. At the fortress itself, black supervisors frequently allowed slaves some time to go hunting and fishing to earn some money on the urban markets.[66] Finally, Mauricius himself affirmed the complaint by the masters that working at the fortress brought slaves into contact with slaves from other regions, which tended to make them more rebellious and allowed them to learn new means of resistance, such as the use of poison.[67] In part, the protests by the masters might have been a strategy in negotiating rent prices for their slaves. Before the arrival of Mauricius, they had managed to set a rate of twenty-four *stuivers* a day, twice the ordinary price for hiring a slave in Suriname.[68] In comparison, in 1745 free day labourers at the fortress succeeded in obtaining a wage raise from six to twelve *stuivers* a day, and soldiers protested their

---

62. NA-OAS, Archief Raad van Politie, 1.05.10.02, no. 286, "Ingekomen stukken, afgezonden door particulieren 1740-1748", 12 April 1744.
63. *Ibid.*, 31 January 1745.
64. Beeldsnijder, *Plantageslaven*, pp. 132–133. The Spanish Bock was a severe form of corporal punishment employed in Suriname, where a slave was bent over a contraption and whipped.
65. Wim Hoogbergen, "De binnenlandse oorlogen in Suriname in de achttiende eeuw", in Enthoven *et al.*, *Geweld in de West*, pp. 147–182, 161.
66. *Ibid.*, p. 79.
67. Van der Meiden, *Betwist bestuur*, p. 95.
68. *Ibid.*

employment at this twelve-*stuiver* rate.[69] The first conflict between the planters and Mauricius resulted from the latter's attempts to renegotiate the rate at which planters rented out slaves for work at the fortress.

The disputes over responsibilities in supplying the forces and building the infrastructure of colonial power were certainly not theoretical. The numerical weakness and divided nature of white society, combined with the geographical conditions of Suriname, provided the opportunity to build one of the more successful examples of resistance through mass marronage in Caribbean history. In total, Mauricius estimated the number of maroons living in independent communities surrounding the plantations or deeper inland at 3,000. By 1749, their combined strength had become so great that Mauricius was compelled to conclude a temporary peace with the maroons in Upper Saramacca. This peace was heavily contested by planters, who felt that any sign of compromise would encourage other slaves to follow the example of the "bush-negroes".[70] In turn, Mauricius insisted that it was the arbitrariness of repression on the plantations combined with the lack of central forces to fight the maroons that put the colony in acute danger. Both sides found proof for their position in the uprising on the plantation of Armand Thomas that broke out on the evening of 21 February 1750. Only two days before, to suppress rumours caused by the peace treaty, the government council had ordered a stern warning to be read out on all the plantations that every slave who tried to join the maroons in Upper Saramacca would suffer beheading. Furthermore, the order emphasized that the peace treaty did not include any of the other maroon communities. Those "would be persecuted by fire and the sword with the utmost rigour".[71] However, it is an open question whether this announcement helped to suppress attempts at mass marooning or provided a final push.

The course of the rebellion on the plantation of Armand Thomas, which was the largest uprising on a plantation in the entire period in Suriname, and the brutal repression that followed, has been well described in the literature.[72] On the evening of 21 February, Thomas, whom we have already encountered as a citizens' captain and one of the leaders of the opposition to Mauricius, was beaten to death with a hammer by a group of slaves. His scribe, the only other white person on the plantation, soon followed his fate. The lifeless body of Thomas was severely beaten, and his whip was put in his mouth under shouts of "now eat it", signifying that Thomas's reign of terror on the plantation was one of the prime reasons

69. Beeldsnijder, *Plantageslaven*, p. 42.
70. Van der Meiden, *Betwist bestuur*, p. 109.
71. NA-OAS, Archief Gouvernementssecretarie, 1.05.10.01, no. 556, "Kopie-notulen Hof van Politie en Criminele Justitie, 2 February 1750 – 27 January 1751", entry 19 February 1750.
72. Van der Meiden, *Betwist bestuur*, pp. 110–111, and Beeldsnijder, *Plantageslaven*, pp. 231–234.

for the revolt. The rebels then took about thirty guns and tried to mobilize slaves on surrounding plantations. They were captured, and a long series of severe interrogations and torture started. The trial itself again revealed the divisions within the planter state. Mauricius blamed Thomas's arbitrary and violent rule on the plantation and his licentious sexual behaviour, including that towards an Indian slave called Eva, who, after the revolt, gave birth to Thomas's son, for causing the rebellion. As a result, he favoured a combination of exemplary death penalties for the leaders of the revolt and pardons for others. Members of his council insisted that the peace with the maroons in Upper Saramacca had inspired Thomas's slaves to rebel. They blamed Mauricius for undermining the authority of the planters on their own plantation. To restore their authority, they demanded the most brutal punishment for every slave involved. Showing the weakness of Mauricius's position in the council, they got their wish. At least thirty-four participants in the rebellion were sentenced to gruesome deaths.[73]

MAINTAINING A CURFEW SOCIETY

The uprising on the plantation of Armand Thomas preceded the central event in this article by eight months. While these were moments of contention of completely different magnitude and consequence, they are not entirely unconnected. In the wake of the partial peace with the Saramacca maroons and the uprising on Thomas's plantation, fears of conspiracies were running wild. These were not confined to slaves on the plantations nearer to the maroon villages; they were raised, too, against slaves who lived and worked in and around Paramaribo, as well as against members of the free population suspected of collaborating with them.

A particularly interesting case that highlights the importance of slave mobility and the diversity of contacts between free and unfree persons was the charge brought against Askaan and April. Both were owned by the "separated wife of Johan van Hertsberg", Willemina Schroder. Their captors found six guns with April belonging partly to him and partly to Askaan, and the prosecutor stated that these were intended for "fighting against the whites, or making attempts at rebellion".[74] Even under torture, the two captives maintained that they planned to use the guns only for hunting.[75]

---

73. The interrogations and sentences of those involved in the uprising on Thomas's plantation fill several hundred pages in NA-OAS, Archief Raad van Politie, 1.05.10.02, no. 801, "Processtukken betreffende criminele zaken 1750".
74. *Ibid.*, 268r°.
75. An astoundingly rich description of criminal justice in Suriname, white practices of torture and disfiguring, and sources of the African slaves' resilience under duress can be found in Natalie Zemon Davis, "Judges, Masters, Diviners: Slaves' Experience of Criminal Justice in Colonial Suriname", *Law and History Review*, 29:4 (2011), pp. 925–984.

However, they did reveal an interesting network of contacts through which they had acquired these arms. Askaan said that April had bought one gun from Sockelaet (or Chocolate), who was a slave at the almshouse, received two from the free black man Adoe, bought or hired one other for eight shillings, and had bought two older guns from the "Jew negro" Agouba or Prins, who lived on the Waterkant. The "negress Europa, who used to belong to the ensign Meijer", had supplied a calabash of gunpowder. In addition, an earlier interrogation had led to the conclusion that gunpowder and bullets had been bought from an "Indian". During his trial, his interrogators asked Askaan whether he was not aware "that one white person has enough courage to take aim at a hundred slaves".[76] However, when push came to shove his persecutors preferred not to take the risk. Despite his insistence under torture that he had not planned to use the guns against his masters, on 5 June 1750 Askaan was sentenced "to the cord", his head to be put on a stake, and his "cadaver to be burnt to ashes".[77] Similar attitudes were shown in a simple case of marronage that occurred around that time. Quater Cheureua from the plantation of Jacques de Crepij near Paramaribo was brought to Fort Zeelandia accused of wanting to join a village of runaways. To the "very pernicious design to desert", the authorities added the charge of conspiracy. Quater was sentenced to be brought to the execution terrain, where he was bound on a cross, his bones broken "from the bottom upwards", and beheaded. His lifeless body was then subjected to the same ritual disfiguring as Askaan's.[78]

Next to the mounting slave resistance, the internal division of the white community and the apparent weakness of the apparatus of repression, authorities considered the mobility of slaves and the poor, whether black, *mestizo*, or white, to be one of the greatest potential dangers to social order. A crucial tool for the regulation of colonial society was an intricate web of curfews and passports restricting the movement of different groups among the lower classes. The breaking of such curfews by slaves who remained on the square before the governor's house after sunset, and by a soldier who did not return to his barracks after nine in the evening, played an important role in Mauricius's description of the "disreputable dance" of early October 1750. This was a direct reflection of the importance attached to upholding curfews in Suriname everyday life. Of course, the idea that controlling the movement of working people and the poor was imperative to maintaining order was nothing new. Especially in the dire persecution of beggars and the restrictions imposed on itinerant day labourers not attached

76. NA-OAS, Archief Raad van Politie, 1.05.10.02, no. 801, "Processtukken betreffende criminele zaken 1750", 271vs°.
77. *Ibid.*, 268r°-271vs°, and *Recueil*, IV, pp. 290–291.
78. NA-OAS, Archief Raad van Politie, 1.05.10.02, no. 801, "Processtukken betreffende criminele zaken 1750", 230r°–230vs° and 243r°.

to a master or guild, European states and town governments had long experience in regulating who could be where to do what, and under what conditions.[79] Frequently, such practices arose simultaneously from fear of rebellion and more immediate concerns about property and theft. Similar motivations existed in the imposition of a regime of curfews in colonial contexts.[80] However, the more limited reach of authority, the semi-militarized conditions and legal structures under which the lower classes were forced to operate, and the presence of large indigenous and enslaved populations greatly amplified their use.

Already in 1669 and 1670, just a few years after the Dutch takeover of Suriname, ordinances were published admonishing plantation owners to control the movement of their slaves more strictly by allowing them to move off the plantations only with passports, within set times, and for clearly delineated purposes.[81] Attempts to limit the unsupervised movement of slaves conspicuously mixed with concerns about tying wage labourers to a single place of employment. Significantly, these first regulations already entailed divisions between black and white labourers that went beyond the simple substitution of the word negro for slave. A separate clause in the March 1670 labour regulation addressed the status of manumitted Africans, saying:

> That all negros that have received their liberty from their masters, will be obligated to hire themselves out to one master or another, on penalty of being severely whipped every time of being found without employment or being in someone's service.[82]

Fears that uncontrolled movement or a life outside employment for free and unfree blacks would create openings for smuggling and the sale of stolen goods provided the initial thrust for such racialized legislation. A 1679 ordinance prohibited "any boats without white people on board" from travelling on rivers or creeks without express permission of plantation owners, alleging that "several boats with negroes [...] go up and down the river to ravage here

---

79. John Torpey, *The Invention of the Passport: Surveillance, Citizenship and the State* (Cambridge, 2000), pp. 18–19. However, Torpey's account of the pre-history of the passport also reveals an important difference. Focusing on local regulations, he states: "Until the ultimate triumph of capitalism and the nation-state in nineteenth-century Europe [...] controls on movement remained predominantly an 'internal' matter". In a colonial context where the state often started as an urban settlement with its surroundings, controls on movement were from inception a prerogative of the central authorities.
80. For example, see the 1638 regulations prohibiting sailors from being on shore at night, and ordering work bosses to strictly control the time at which their labourers in New Amsterdam arrived and left, in E.B. O'Callaghan (ed.), *Laws and Ordinances of New Netherland, 1638–1674* (Albany, NY, 1868), pp. 10–12.
81. De Smidt and Van der Lee, *West Indisch plakaatboek*, I, Ordinance of 13 June 1669 and Ordinance of 12 March 1670, pp. 44–45 and 57 respectively.
82. *Ibid.*, p. 57.

and there". If the black passengers of such a boat without whites failed to show their passes at first call, their vessel should be shot at "as if at public enemies, because for the service of the land and the preservation of the colony, they should be viewed as such".[83] Another prohibition to trade goods with slaves in June 1684 and a similar one against trading with slaves or soldiers in May the next year followed this.[84] Perhaps the most striking rule, effectively introducing an early form of racial profiling, allowed sentries to shoot on sight any black person on the streets later than half an hour after sundown "as if they were runaways". As a justification, the regulation explained that this was necessary "because at night one cannot tell the good from the bad negroes, since one cannot tell the difference from their cloths".[85]

In the heated atmosphere of the late 1740s, maintaining slave curfews became a particularly important element in enforcing public order. To assist in this task, the government council decided on 5 September 1747 to install a clock in the tower of Fort Zeelandia.[86] Even a full century later, a traveller in Suriname noticed that every day at eight o'clock in the evening a cannon would be fired from the fortress, which contained the only public clock in Paramaribo, to mark the moment when slaves should be indoors.[87] In the summer of 1749, new rules followed prescribing that slaves could be on the streets of Paramaribo at night only if carrying a lantern, and that the citizens' guard should start making its rounds at seven in the evening.[88] However, given the prevailing tensions among white citizens the mode of operation of these citizens' guards created its own problems. On 4 December 1749, the government council discussed at length the disorders created by citizens, who randomly opened fire on slaves who merely sat on the pavement outside their masters' houses, or were walking the streets in the presence of their masters "so that shots of hail flew around and through the company". Apparently, several of the inhabitants of Paramaribo had already been shot in such altercations. When the NCO Bulke, who was responsible for opening fire, was questioned by his lieutenant, he had answered: "We want to shoot at slaves, and if not, you should dissolve the citizens' guard".[89] Based on this testimony, the council considered only the possibility that shootings at night were a form of protest against guard

83. *Ibid.*, p. 102.
84. *Ibid.*, pp. 143 and 155–156.
85. *Ibid.*, p. 144.
86. NA-OAS, Archief Raad van Politie, 1.05.10.02, no. 165, "Register", 5 September 1747.
87. Gaspard Philippe Charles van Breugel, *Dagverhaal van eene reis naar Paramaribo en verdere omstreken in de Kolonie Suriname* (Amsterdam, 1842), pp. 23–25.
88. NA-OAS, Archief Raad van Politie, 1.05.10.02, no. 165, "Register", 4 August 1749.
89. NA-OAS, Archief Raad van Politie, 1.05.10.02, no. 43, "Minuut notulen 1749", 4 December 1749.

duty. However, Bulke's answer also suggests how easily policing the street could slip into vigilante actions against the slaves.

A safer, less contentious way of maintaining order on the street was to try to close down venues for unguarded activity after hours, especially where such venues provided a space for interaction between slaves and free whites and blacks. Many rules and regulations were aimed at enforcing separation, especially in the context of travelling back and forth to Paramaribo. Among the most notorious were the draconian mutilations introduced as punishment for black and Indian slaves found drinking and playing games with white people in taverns (1698), and punishment by death for any "negro" having sexual relations with a white woman (1711).[90] Curfews on soldiers and sailors also helped to limit interaction. This included the rule that, after the evening call, soldiers should remain confined in their barracks on pain of running the gauntlet.[91] However, in such attempts the authorities were up against what was perhaps the most powerful enemy of the curfew and of social segregation in general in the port city: the underground bar. In early February 1750, the court in Paramaribo sentenced the German immigrant Christiaan Crewitz for inviting "several Negroes into his house, where sitting at his Table, he served them beer and soup", as well as selling alcohol to several others.[92] One of the most interesting elements of the case is that Crewitz, who declared that before opening a small bar he had made a living by "catching tortoises with the Indians in the river Marrewyne", repeatedly professed that he did not believe he had done anything wrong by serving drinks to black men.[93] Crewitz was condemned to pay a fine of 500 guilders, the equivalent of between two and four years' salary for an unskilled worker in Suriname, and was banished from the colony for life.[94]

The trigger-happy NCO Bulke and Crewitz can be seen as presenting opposite ends of white society in Paramaribo. However, these opposites might not always have been as far apart as they seem. Their everyday context brought lower-class whites into continuous contact with the enslaved, sometimes as overseers, sometimes as colleagues, buyers and sellers, gamblers or drunks. This could be the basis for reflections on shared miseries, as well as for the exploitation of their whiteness as a protective shield against the

90. De Smidt and Van der Lee, *West Indisch plakaatboek*, I, pp. 219–221 and 277. White women who were found in such relationships would be severely whipped, for the "great scandal they caused the entire colony".
91. NA-OAS, Archief Gouvernementssecretarie, 1.05.10.01, no. 615, "Reglement voor de Militaire Troupen in de Colonie Suriname, 1778", p. 63.
92. NA-OAS, Archief Raad van Politie, 1.05.10.02, no. 800, "Processtukken betreffende criminele zaken, 1750", 3r°–3vs°.
93. *Ibid.*, 5r°–5vs°, 6r°–6vs°, and 13r°–13vs°.
94. *Ibid.*, 3vs°.

masters. The two attitudes could even exist side by side. John Gabriel
Stedman described the working conditions of many common sailors:

> In every part of the colony they are no better treated, but, like horses, they must
> (having unloaded the vessels) drag the commodities to the distant storehouses,
> being bathed in sweat, and bullied, with bad language, sometimes with blows;
> [...] The planters even employ those men to paint their houses, clean their
> sash windows, and do numberless other menial services, for which a seaman
> was never intended. All this is done to save the work of their negroes, while
> by this usage thousands are swept to the grave, who in the line of their profession
> alone might have lived for many years; [...] I have heard a sailor fervently wish he
> had been born a negro, and beg to be employed amongst them in cultivating a
> coffee plantation.[95]

As an answer to real or perceived social degradation, many embraced cruel
displays of racial superiority, as did the sailor who, in passing, "broke the
head of a negro with a bludgeon, for not having saluted him with his
hat".[96] In this case, as in Bulke's, racist attitudes among the white population
became a powerful instrument for maintaining the curfew society.

COLONIAL ROUGH MUSIC

The previous sections have examined how the physical surroundings, the
context of political tension within the planter class and slave resistance,
and the importance of curfews for the maintenance of racialized social
order all provide elements for understanding the contentious nature of
Johanna Catharina Brouwer's dance. This final brief section will look at
the significance of the most carnivalesque aspect of the confrontation that
took place on the night of 3 October 1750: rough music, both in its literal
and its symbolic sense represented by the trumpeter playing "the most
infamous sound in the world, while wenches, children, and slaves loudly
laughed and shouted". Music and dance played a crucial role in Suriname
slave life. It provided not only one of the rare instances for truly independent
social interaction, but also a vehicle for passing on secret messages undetect-
able to the ear of the masters, concealed in song, rhythm, or dance movements.[97] From the other side, a vehement dislike of African song and
dance was one of the important cultural markers of the distance between

---

95. John Gabriel Stedman, *Narrative of a Five Years' Expedition against the Revolted Negroes of
Surinam* (Amherst, MA, 1972), p. 58. See also Karwan Fatah-Black, "Slaves and Sailors on
Suriname's Rivers", *Itinerario*, 36:3 (2012), pp. 61–82.
96. Stedman, *Narrative*, p. 58.
97. Alex van Stipriaan, "Muzikale creolisering. De ontwikkeling van Afro-Surinaamse muziek
tijdens de slavernij", *OSO. Tijdschrift voor Surinaamse Taalkunde, Letterkunde, Cultuur en
Geschiedenis*, 19:1 (2000), pp. 8–37. Cf. Frantz Fanon, *Les damnés de la terre* (Paris, 2002
[1961]), pp. 57–58.

civilized (white) society and the world of the slaves. In his nineteenth-century travelogue, Gaspard van Breugel attested to his understanding of the importance of this marker by inserting the following description of a *banja*, a slave dance:

> To unite their voices with their instruments, one sees the so-called musicians seated on the ground in a row; hitting their also so-called instruments, twisting their bodies and nodding their heads, while drawing faces with which one could immediately scare the naughtiest children to bed [...] Behind them stands a crowd that shouts, more than sings, in such a way that one needs a bale of cotton to plug one's ears not to hear that beautiful music.[98]

Well aware of the power of music as an instrument to mock the white masters, or worse, colonial authorities throughout the period of slavery waged an uphill battle to prevent the slaves from singing, playing the drums, and dancing. Funerals in particular became moments of contention.[99] On 6 February 1750, the government council discussed the "frequent assembly of slaves [in Paramaribo – PB] for funerals". The immediate cause of this discussion was the funeral of one of the slaves of S. Clijn. A large crowd had gathered in front of his house, "making much noise and rumour, creating confusion and murmurs".[100] The council reconvened to discuss concrete measures on 26 February, a few days after the news of the uprising on the plantation of Armand Thomas had reached Paramaribo. In this session, the council decided to allow masters who owned houses or gardens outside the city to bury their slaves there instead of in the town's slave graveyard. For slave funerals that did take place in Paramaribo, the bailiff was ordered to make sure that no "noise" accompanied the ceremony. Masters who allowed any form of *baljaaren* (dancing) during a funeral would be fined 500 guilders. Slaves arrested during a funeral for contravening this order would receive the Spanish Bock.[101]

Was Mauricius's remark on the quality of the trumpet playing at the party of Johanna Catharina Brouwer an allusion to yet another barrier of social order and racial distinction being crossed? This will have to remain a speculation. However, it is interesting to note that almost all reports on neighbourhood brawls in Suriname in this period mention noise and loud music as major affronts to public decency. On 20 November 1748, Pieter Brouwer returned from his plantation to his house in Paramaribo to nurse his sick wife. The next evening, at around nine-thirty, a loud party began in the house of his neighbour Dirk Brendt. Musicians played the violin and blew

98. Van Breugel, *Dagverhaal*, p. 63.
99. As they did elsewhere, as is shown by Brown, *Reaper's Garden*, ch. 2.
100. NA-OAS, Archief Gouvernementssecretarie, 1.05.10.01, no. 556, "Kopie-notulen Hof van Politie en Criminele Justitie, 2 February 1750 – 27 January 1751", entry 6 February 1750.
101. *Ibid.*, entry 26 February 1750.

horns, "accompanied by continuous shouts of Hurrays and other noise". Brouwer alleges that Brendt was too drunk to pay a visit to his house and complain, so that the party continued until half an hour before midnight. However, the next morning the party resumed. What most upset Brouwer was that, "probably to increase the noise", to the horns was now added "the sound of a drum, again accompanied by continuous shouts of Hurray, at which hundreds of black boys gathered in front of the door". This was the final straw that led Brouwer to complain about his neighbour's behaviour, but Brendt did not take this well. Instead, he came to Brouwer's door to shout: "Canaille, did you have the heart to complain about me to the Fiscal, I will goddamned tear you to pieces." Fighting ensued, and ended only when soldiers came to take Brendt to the fortress.[102] In this 1748 case, the actual overstepping of the proper time for celebration and dancing, playing noisy music, and involving slaves in a public spectacle figured in ways very similar to the descriptions encountered in Mauricius's October 1750 complaint to underline a breakdown in public order.

References to slave dances or *baljaaren* could also be employed to hint at even greater digressions, connected to both gendered and racialized distinctions. This is revealed by an explosive brawl that took place just a few years earlier in the Gravestraat or Soldiers' Street, which ran between the central square and the gardens on the outskirts of Paramaribo. In the late afternoon of 22 October 1745, violence erupted between Moses Levy Ximenes and David and Rachel Moateb, a mulatto. The root of the fight was that earlier, David and Rachel had visited Moses's father to complain about the noise emanating from his house. The old Ximenes had had a loud argument with one of his enslaved female servants. According to Rachel, Moses' father had responded to the complaint by "calling her husband a mulatto". Despite the fact that she herself was of mixed descent, she took this as a grave insult since her husband "was a legitimate white man" like Moses's father.[103] According to Moses, the real insult had been David and Rachel's interference with a domestic affair, since it was his father's right "to chastise [*kastijden*] his negroes with words".[104] Between the two parties, testimonies differed over the question of who at this point was the first to resort to physical violence. However, one other small difference between the statements given in this case

102. NA-OAS, Archief Raad van Politie, 1.05.10.02, no. 920, "Processtukken aangaande criminele en politieke zaken", 1747–1749, Testimony Pieter Brouwer, 25 November 1748.

103. NA-OAS, Archief Raad van Politie, 1.05.10.02, no. 800, "Processtukken betreffende criminele zaken, 1750", 103r°, testimony Rachel, mulatto. The question of the complex in-between status of mulattoes in Surinamese society is too complicated to go into here. However, the fact that Rachel saw the employment of the word "mulatto" for someone who was "legitimately white" as a grave insult is itself proof of the extent to which social difference had become racialized.

104. NA-OAS, Archief Raad van Politie, 1.05.10.02, no. 800, "Processtukken betreffende criminele zaken, 1750", 123vs°.

matters more for the current purpose. One of the neighbours gave testimony to support Moses's plea. In this statement, rather than talking about his father's chastising of his slaves, Moses was presented as saying: "What do you have to do with the quarrel [*ruzie*] of my father, as he danced [*baljaerden*] with his slaves."[105] The word *baljaeren* in this context is so strange that one cannot help suspecting an unspoken meaning, pertaining to violence, sex, or both. In any case, it helps to underline a point that is crucial for understanding what happened on the night of 3 October 1750. When involving masters and slaves, a dance was never just a dance.

CONCLUSIONS

Starting from an incident in colonial Paramaribo in the autumn of 1750 in which, according to the Dutch governor Mauricius, many of the proper barriers separating rich and poor, men and women, adults and children, white citizens and black slaves were crossed, this article has traced the complexities of everyday social control in colonial Suriname. The rowdy ball for the birthday of Johanna Catharina Brouwer's daughter, which drew the governor's ire, can easily be understood as a minor skirmish in the long-lasting conflict between the increasingly confident colonial planter class in Suriname and the local representatives of Dutch company rule. In the middle of the eighteenth century, such conflicts occurred throughout the Atlantic world as a result of the rapid rise of a Creole colonial elite, which self-confidently asserted its role in expanding capitalist networks across European empires. However, as so often in the history of popular rebellion, divisions within the ruling class also brought to the fore deeper fissures between the political and economic elites on the one hand and the lower classes on the other. Through the prism of the different transgressions mentioned by Mauricius in his report and letters about the "disreputable dance", we can observe essential characteristics of repression and rebellion in mid-eighteenth-century Suriname. In particular, it can be shown how instruments of social segregation with a long pedigree – enforcing distinctions of class and status, invoking taboos to limit the free interaction between men and women and adults and children, restricting the movement of labourers and the poor through passports and curfews – intersected with the harsh racialized separations of an eighteenth-century Atlantic slave society.

Much of the literature on the relationship between slavery and race focuses on the plantation as race-making institution and the planter class as the immediate progenitors of racial capitalism. Studies of urban slavery on the other hand have emphasized the greater scope for social contact between

---

105. *Ibid.*, 125r°, testimony Schröder.

blacks, *mestizos,* and whites of various social status in the bustling port cities of the Atlantic. This article has attempted to understand practices of racialization and control in the port city of Paramaribo, not by contrasting the city with its plantation environment but by underlining the connections between the two social settings that together shaped colonial geography. Continuous movement between plantation and port, including the unsupervised movement of slaves, was a crucial aspect of the political economy and the cultural life of a society like Suriname. The article has focused on everyday activities in Paramaribo (dancing, working, drinking, arguing) that reveal the extent of contact between slaves and non-slaves. The imposition of racialized forms of repression that set one group against the other, frequently understood primarily as a means to justify the apparent stasis of the plantation system with its rigid internal divisions, in practice functioned precisely to fight the pernicious effects of mobility in mixed social contexts. In the process, plantation owners and the state that they at least in part controlled could sometimes find themselves at loggerheads, but, ultimately, they found themselves united in their primordial fear – that of slave rebellion.

One charge that could be made against this article is that the impact of mobility has not been researched through systematic quantification. Instead, it has illuminated key aspects of social relations in colonial Paramaribo through discursive practices at a moment of widespread contention. The new social historians of the 1970s employed this method to reveal the importance of rituals, culture, and perceptions of justice at a time when their colleagues were mostly concerned with hard material factors. This article has in a way tried to retrace their steps. Starting from cultural practices and real and imagined distinctions of status, gender, age, and race surrounding an apparently innocuous birthday party, it has sought a way back to the brutal realities of colonial control in which these imaginings obtained their violent urgency.

IRSH 64 (2019), pp. 125–147 doi:10.1017/S0020859019000051
© 2019 Internationaal Instituut voor Sociale Geschiedenis

Securing Trade: The Military Labor of the British Occupation of Manila, 1762–1764*

M E G A N C. T H O M A S

Department of Politics, University of California, Santa Cruz
1156 High St., Santa Cruz, CA 95060, USA

E-mail: mcthomas@ucsc.edu

ABSTRACT: Military labor played a key role in conquering and preserving ports as nodes in trading networks. This article treats the military labor of the British occupation of Manila from 1762 to 1764, during the Seven Years War. It examines the motley crew that formed the British forces, exploring British categories of military laborers sent from Madras. The particular combination of forces composed for this expedition had more to do with the East India Company's concerns in Madras than with what was thought to be needed to take and hold Manila. These military laborers were sometimes unruly, insisting on better pay, and deserting when it was not forthcoming. The story of the British occupation of Manila highlights how ideas about desertion traveled along with military laborers from one port city to another in the Indian Ocean world, and what happened when they did.

INTRODUCTION

In 1762, a few days before leaving the British East India Company's port of Madras (now Chennai) on a military expedition to seize the Spanish port of Manila, the British commander Brigadier General William Draper wrote to the Secretary at War in London complaining that most of his men were

a composition of deserters of all nations who I take with me more to ease the fears and apprehensions of the people at Madrass, than from any service I can expect from them; as, perhaps, I shall only carry recruits to the enemy, but I

* I would like to thank the editors for inviting me to contribute to this Special Issue, and especially Pernille Røge and Pepijn Brandon for guiding revisions; workshop participants, Catherine Jones, and Christina Welsch for crucial comments on earlier drafts; Christina Welsch for generously sharing with me her knowledge of and work on the Madras military of this period; and Bettina Ng'weno for sharing with me her knowledge about the histories of Africans in India.

have no choice. Those or none; such banditti were never assembled since the time of Spartacus.[1]

Draper likely worried sincerely about the quality of his personnel, and also sought to lower his superiors' expectations, to shield himself from blame should the endeavor fail. But his words also reflect truths about military labor's composition in South Asia in this period. It was composed of a motley crew, managed through categories that corresponded less to how the men identified themselves than to how they were treated by their superiors: the work for which they were deployed, the conditions under which they labored, and the pay they would receive.

This motley military labor produced global commerce. Along with diplomacy, war aimed to produce the access and security on which the profits of long-distance trade depended. Imperial expansion required a great deal of military labor to secure markets and access to raw materials, and to create the conditions that yielded workers available perform the labor of extraction and production. As Peter Way has argued, because war is central to capitalism's emergence, "it is necessary to reconceptualize soldiers as war workers, indeed, as transnational laborers whose martial toil around the globe proved integral to the development of international capitalism".[2] Much of that martial toil was in port cities; commercial empires depended on the work that secured access to and control over a port's trade. As key nodes in emerging global trade, port cities were critical sites of military labor, and targets in wars of imperial rivalry.

Military labor, therefore, was a significant part of port cities' labor. Often, like other laborers in port cities, these military workers came from elsewhere, having been made mobile by processes of dispossession and accumulation. In port cities, military labor was itself a sort of commodity of more or less trained and disciplined bodies, moving in and out of port cities along with other products of emerging imperial commercial trade. So, while military labor often worked to secure port cities, port cities were also points at which the motley military crew was gathered, mustered, garrisoned, trained, disciplined, paid (or not), and sent into the field. The port city was also a place where military laborers sometimes disobeyed, mutinied, or deserted.

As Way's work has shown of military labor in the Atlantic world, in the Indian Ocean armies drew on labor that had traveled great distances in coercive if not technically unfree conditions. The Atlantic context, however, has no real counterpart to the British East India Company's own military. The

---

1. The UK National Archives [hereafter, TNA]: War Office records [hereafter, WO] 1/139, pp. 355–356. Transcribed in Nicholas Cushner (ed.), *Documents Illustrating the British Conquest of Manila, 1762–1763* (London, 1971), p. 34.
2. Peter Way, "'Black Service ... White Money': The Peculiar Institution of Military Labor in the British Army during the Seven Years' War", in Leon Fink (ed.), *Workers Across the Americas: The Transnational Turn in Labor History* (Oxford, 2011), pp. 57–80, 62.

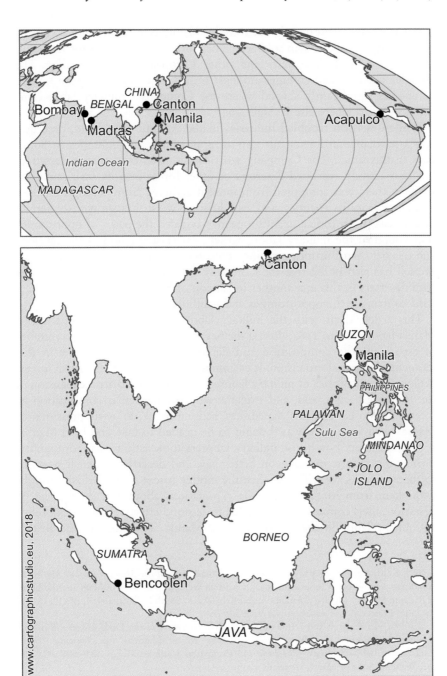

Figure 1. Island Southeast Asia (East Indies).

Company's military grew significantly in this period, increasingly incorporating a long-mobile Indian soldiery.[3] The Company competed for that military labor with Indian states and other European companies alike. The complex alliances and enmities amongst Indian states and European trading companies significantly shaped where the Company's military labor came from, but also where else it might go.

While desertion troubled militaries in the Atlantic world too, desertion was a particular problem, but also an opportunity for militaries in South Asia in this time.[4] The Company worried about its own troops deserting, but also actively recruited deserters of other forces into its own ranks. Its military, then, was composed from those it gathered from amongst its allies as well as from its enemies, and, as Christina Welsh has shown, soldiers in South Asia (both Indian and European) navigated the paths of opportunity they found in the military labor market as it existed amongst the tensions and ties between European trading companies and Indian states and rulers.[5] Welsch has also noted that the Company was unusually lenient toward its own deserters in this era, another indication of how Company commanders tried to manage the opportunities and liabilities of desertion.[6]

This article deals with the military labor of the British occupation of Manila from 1762 to 1764, during the Seven Years War, exploring a number of aspects of the composition and deployment of military labor in this moment of imperial expansion. It examines the composition of British forces, explores the categories of military laborers that powered British expansion in the Indian Ocean world, and explains why the particular combination of forces composed for this expedition had more to do with pressures in Madras than with what was thought to be needed to take and hold Manila. It also considers how those military laborers took actions that confounded their commanders: insisting on better pay, and deserting when it was not forthcoming. As we will see, when the motley forces of the British brought with them from Madras to Manila expectations about and experiences of desertion, their commanders struggled to respond effectively to the mobility of military labor in the environment of Manila. The story of the British

---

3. Dirk Kolff, *Naukar, Rajput and Sepoy: The Ethnohistory of the Military Labour Market in Hindustan, 1450–1850* (Cambridge, 1990); Christina Welsch, "The Sons of Mars and the Heirs of Rustam: Military Ideology, Ambition, and Rebellion in South India (1746–1812)" (Ph.D. dissertation, Princeton University, 2017), especially ch. 1.

4. Matthias van Rossum and Jeannette Kamp (eds), *Desertion in the Early Modern World: A Comparative History* (London, 2016), especially ch. 8: Matthias van Rossum, "From Contracts to Labour Camps? Desertion and Control in South Asia", pp. 187–202, 187, 188, 194; Welsch, "Sons of Mars", especially ch. 3.

5. Welsch, "Sons of Mars".

6. *Ibid.*, p. 160; cf. Pepijn Brandon, "'The Privilege of Using Their Legs': Leaving the Dutch Army in the Eighteenth Century", in Van Rossum and Kamp, *Desertion in the Early Modern World*, pp. 73–93, 83; Van Rossum "From Contracts to Labour Camps?", p. 195.

occupation of Manila, then, shows what could happen when military laborers were sent across the Indian Ocean from one port city to conquer another.

BRITISH PLANS FOR MANILA'S OCCUPATION

Manila played an important role in eighteenth-century global trade. It was on the western edge of the Spanish trade across the Pacific, part of southern Chinese trading networks across the South China Sea, and on the easternmost limb of British networks in the Indian Ocean. For the Spanish, Manila was a crucial node in the galleon trade linking Spain and the Americas with China across the Pacific. At Manila, American silver was exchanged for luxury goods from China, which were shipped to the Americas and eventually to Spain.[7] From China's southern coast, merchants, artisans, and seafarers knew Manila as part of the South China Sea trading networks. Those networks were essential for the "Spanish" city; Chinese junks brought porcelains, silks, and other goods to Manila, and the commerce of the city was more Chinese than Spanish.[8] Periodically, the Spanish administration wrought violence on the Chinese in Manila, and in 1755 non-Christian Chinese were expelled; hundreds had become baptized in order to stay.[9] At the time of the British occupation, Manila and its surrounding suburbs and towns probably had a population of between 70,000 and 100,000.[10]

The plan to occupy Manila was in part a continuation of the East India Company's China trade. Manila was on the eastern periphery of its Indian Ocean trade, and a crucial source of silver, valued in Canton unlike British and Indian goods. Though technically barred from trading in Manila, British merchants regularly circumvented the ban, trading for silver that in Canton bought the luxury goods so valued in Europe.[11] Seeking an alternative to silver, the Company had, for some time, aspired to establish a base in the realm of the Sultan of Sulu (which extended north to Palawan, west to Borneo, and east to Mindanao), where they hoped to exchange British and

7. William Lytle Schurz, *The Manila Galleon* (New York, 1939).

8. O.D. Corpuz, *The Roots of the Filipino Nation*, 2 vols (Quezon City, 2005 [1989]), I, pp. 358–358; Arturo Giraldez, *The Age of Trade: The Manila Galleons and the Dawn of the Global Economy* (Lanham, MD, 2015), pp. 160–161; T'ien Ju-K'ang, "The Chinese Junk Trade: Merchants, Entrepreneurs, and Coolies, 1600–1850", in Klaus Friedland (ed.), *Maritime Aspects of Migration* (Cologne and Vienna, 1989), pp. 381–389.

9. Corpuz, *Roots of the Filipino Nation*, pp. 306–307.

10. This estimate is drawn from Madras Presidency Records Office, *Records of Fort St. George, Manilha Consultations*, 8 vols (Madras, 1940–1946), III, p. 12, as well as Linda Newson, *Conquest and Pestilence in the Early Spanish Philippines* (Quezon City, 2011), pp. 42–43, 309, 311, 312, 383.

11. Serafin D. Quiason, *English "Country Trade" with the Philippines, 1644–1765* (Quezon City, 1966).

Indian goods for regional forest and sea products that were highly valued in Canton. When Spain belatedly joined the French side of the war against Britain, Manila became an enemy target, and its occupation an opportunity for the Company to pursue its trading base plans. The Company also hoped to seize silver arriving in Manila from the Acapulco galleon, to fund investments in the upcoming trade season at Canton. For the Crown, occupying Manila had strategic value as a bargaining chip to be used in negotiations with Spain and France at the war's end. The British occupation of Manila, then, was envisioned not so much to secure that port's trade for Britain, but instead to secure British trade with Canton.

Manila was also thought to be an economical target, requiring only a relatively small investment of British troops and capitalizing on the proximate location of relatively inexpensive South Asian military labor based in the Company's presidency of Madras on the Coromandel coast. The institutional processes and pressures that came to bear on these plans, however, would shape the force in ways not originally envisaged. As the planning process unfolded, we see much more concern about the Company's position in India than about what would actually be required to take and hold Manila.

Plans were first drawn up in London but significantly revised in Madras in ways that reflect the Company's strong priorities for maintaining security along the Coromandel coast of the Carnatic, and British conviction that European troops were more valuable than Indian troops. Initial plans hatched in London called for about 2,000 infantrymen, accompanied by "a moderate train of artillery", officers, and an engineer.[12] Of the infantrymen, between seventy and eighty per cent were to be Europeans, and between twenty and thirty per cent would be "sepoys", South Asian infantrymen trained in European styles of warfare but paid just over half what European infantry were.[13] Because of company concerns that security on the Coromandel coast might be compromised by sending so large a force,[14] the commander of the expedition, William Draper, was to make the final determination about the composition of forces in consultation with Company officials in Madras.[15] In Madras, the proposal became more ambitious than the original London plans in terms of overall numbers, increasing the total by forty per cent (from 2,000 to 2,805), mostly by quadrupling the number of sepoys (from 500 to 2,000), but also by adding the labor of eighty-four "Coffreys", about whom we will hear more below. But the plan had become more conservative in terms of using European

12. Cushner, *Documents Illustrating the British Conquest of Manila*, p. 13.
13. *Ibid.*; [Madras Army], *Orders, Rules, and Regulations to be Observed Respecting the Troops on the Coast of Choromandel* (s.l., 1766), pp. 9, 21.
14. Cushner, *Documents Illustrating the British Conquest of Manila*, p. 15.
15. *Ibid.*, p. 19.

troops, halving their numbers.[16] The council was concerned that even though the plan drastically scaled back the number of European troops to be sent, British forces in Madras would be dangerously depleted, and they approved the plan only because they hoped the troops would return before their absence would pose a danger.[17]

But there were also some European Company troops whose *presence* in Madras worried the Company: French deserters. The French deserters were men who had been serving in the French military in India; in their struggles against the French, the British had decided in 1758 to form companies of French deserters within British ranks, "to encourage desertion among the enemy's troops".[18] The numbers of French deserters had swollen during the brutal British siege of the French garrison at Pondicherry in 1760, when many starving soldiers defected. After this, the number of French prisoners and deserters in Madras was a source of worry for the Company.[19] The British feared that the defeated French might regroup against them, whether under their own banner or that of another hostile power.[20] French soldiers, whether deserters or prisoners, needed to be kept alive but harmless, and, preferably, they would be sent away. Several months before the Manila expedition left Madras, the Military Council there was "desirous of letting no opportunity slip of getting transported to Europe as many French Prisoners as possible", proposing to send them by way of Bombay or Canton.[21] In the midst of this dilemma, the Manila expedition offered an opportunity: transporting them to distant Manila seemed a reasonable way to prevent them from rejoining French forces in the Carnatic, and, at the same time, doing so allowed the Company to contribute troops that counted as "European" without actually sending troops that it valued.

Company officials likely doubted the value of the French deserters as soldiers, for reasons that did not make it into the record of these deliberations. Some French deserters were serial deserters: having deserted from French forces in Europe, they signed up for Indies service in exchange for amnesty, and so would already have deserted at least twice (in Europe and in India) before being sent to Manila.[22] To complicate matters, many French

16. British Library (BL): India Office Records (IOR)/P/251/48 bk. 2, pp. 102–105. A copy is transcribed, with one apparent minor error, in Cushner, *Documents Illustrating the British Conquest of Manila*, pp. 27–29.

17. *Ibid.*

18. W.J. Wilson, *History of the Madras Army*, 5 vols (Madras, 1882–1889), I, p. 122.

19. *Ibid.*, pp. 173–174.

20. Many French deserters ended up in the forces of Haider Ali, the later commander of Mysore. Maya Jasanoff, *Edge of Empire: Lives, Culture, and Conquest in the East, 1750–1850* (New York, 2005), pp. 154–155.

21. BL: IOR/P/251/48 bk. 1, p. 98 (quote, and Bombay), and bk. 2, pp. 45–46 (Canton).

22. John Malcom, *The Life of Robert, Lord Clive: Collected from the Family Papers*, 3 vols (London, 1836), I, pp. 368–369.

European infantrymen were not from France, but were Catholics from else-where in Europe. Some were, for example, Swiss mercenaries, but others were Britain's Catholics whose loyalty to the Crown was suspect: Scottish Jacobites, i.e. Catholics or supporters of a Stuart monarch, and Irish Catholics.[23] No one in Madras considered – or more likely, no one wanted those thoughts committed to the record – that the French deserters' Catholicism might become a liability if they were supposed to be fighting Catholics in Manila.

The commanders had other reservations and complaints. Most notably, Company officials worried that "it may be a difficult matter to find the Number of Seapoys [...] required [2,000] willing to go".[24] Their solution was to offer them significant advance pay, as well as allowing their families to receive their pay directly from the company at Madras, while the men themselves were on the expedition.[25] These enticements were, however, insufficient. Just before leaving Madras, Draper wrote that he expected only about a quarter of the sepoys that he had been promised, a decrease that he attributed to religious rather than financial concerns: "their averseness to sea voyage [thought to be connected with caste], the difference of religion & particular methods of diet".[26] In the end, only 600 sepoys embarked for Manila, and they were not all the experienced "disciplined" sepoys initially imagined; instead, as Draper later complained, half of them were "Raw & new raised".[27]

In sum, the British in Madras planned for the occupation with their atten-tion focused more on Madras than on Manila. The Crown and Company each stood to gain from a successful venture at Manila, but they stood to gain different things, and for the Company the attendant risks at Madras were greater. The Company felt pressures at Madras to cut down on its over-all commitment of troops to the expedition, and also to compose those troops strategically, seeking to eliminate the threat posed by the presence of many French deserters in their own ranks by sending them off to Manila. Though the Company hoped their troops – particularly their British troops – would return from Manila relatively quickly, they also maneuvered to send troops whose absence they would not particularly lament.[28] Thus, Draper was absolutely correct when he wrote that he

---

23. Jasanoff, *Edge of Empire*, p. 26.
24. BL: IOR/P/251/48 bk. 2, pp. 118–123.
25. *Ibid.* Family benefits were important in the Madras military in particular, as Christina Welsch has explored in "'An Indulgence Which Can Never Be Denied Them': The Question of Family Benefits in the East India Company's Madras Army, 1746–1812", paper presented at the Association for Asian Studies annual meeting, Chicago, 2015.
26. Cushner, *Documents Illustrating the British Conquest of Manila*, p. 35.
27. *Ibid.*, pp. 13–14 ("disciplined"); TNA: WO/1/139 ("raw & new raised").
28. Cushner, *Documents Illustrating the British Conquest of Manila*, pp. 40–42.

thought the expedition's troops were chosen "more to ease the fears and apprehensions of the people at Madrass, than from any service I can expect from them".

THE COMPOSITION OF BRITISH MILITARY LABOR

Overall, British land forces in the Manila operation were a crew cobbled together by economic and political forces in India and beyond. Who, in the end, comprised that crew? Sources vary, but the most comprehensive single account enumerates 1,478 total rank-and-file land troops, composed of royal infantrymen (571), sepoys (468), "The Honorable Company's Troops" (310), royal artillerymen (57), "the Nabob's Irregulars" (43), and Company artillerymen (29).[29] They were accompanied by 335 officers, for a total of 1,813 land forces. British royal naval forces were also landed as part of the initial attack on Manila: 632 private seamen (with 47 officers) and 274 Marines (with 64 officers), for a total of 1,017 members of the sea forces landed.[30]

Of the land troops, 600 were rank-and-file "sepoys" and their South Asian officers.[31] In addition to being paid less that European troops, sepoys served in separate units, and while they had South Asian officers, they were always commanded at the highest levels by Europeans.[32] Sepoys were used in the South Asian militaries of European companies and Indian rulers alike, but the British and French increasingly relied on them during the Carnatic Wars.[33] While on campaign, unlike European infantrymen who were provisioned, sepoys had to buy their own food, for which they were allotted a subsistence cash allowance called a *batta*. Sepoys, therefore, were "absolutely

29. Unless otherwise indicated, these numbers are derived from troop returns in BL: IOR H/77, pp. 48–49, transcribed imperfectly in Cushner, *Documents Illustrating the British Conquest of Manila*, p. 57.
30. "An Account of the Number of Seamen and Marines Landed from His Majesty's Squadron [...]", in Cushner, *Documents Illustrating the British Conquest of Manila*, p. 56; the same numbers are given in the map "Draught of the Great Bay of Manilla and Harbour of Cavita [...] Surveyed & Drawn [...] by William Nichelson", 1764. These numbers exclude those on the ships but not landed.
31. As was typical of Madras Company returns at the time, "European" troops are listed separately from "sepoy" troops. BL: IOR H/77, pp. 48–49.
32. Much of what we know about sepoys comes from later years, when the number of sepoys shot up and systems for recruitment, pay, and discipline became centralized and standardized, and from which more records survive. An important corrective is Welsch, "Sons of Mars", especially ch. 1.
33. Jasanoff, *Edge of Empire*, pp. 90–92; P.J. Marshall, "Western Arms in Maritime Asia in the Early Phases of Expansion", *Modern Asian Studies*, 14:1 (1980), pp. 13–28, 26, citing G.J. Bryant, "The East India Company and its Army 1600–1778" (Ph.D. dissertation, University of London, 1975).

dependent on their pay and ready to mutiny or desert if payment was seriously delayed".[34] The Manila operation may have been the first time that sepoys had been deployed overseas, though it would not be the last. We have already heard Draper blame the sepoys' reluctance to go to Manila on their "averseness to sea voyage", but material concerns were at least as pressing. Some of these sepoys had likely previously been on campaign in Bengal, while others, as Draper complained, were inexperienced and on their first campaign.[35] Most of these sepoys had family near Madras, though as part of the itinerant military market many would also have had roots further afield.[36] Some were Muslim and probably most were Hindu, many low caste and Dalit; commanding ranks comprised both Muslim and Hindu men.[37]

Once British commanders were in the Philippines with sepoys, they articulated why these troops were, they thought, particularly useful in this case: "they are [...] formidable to the [local] Indians, who hold moors in the highest Detestation".[38] Some but not all of the sepoys were Muslim, so the British perception that the locals "[held] moors in the highest Detestation" might reflect locals' conflation of sepoy with "moro" [Muslim], or British generalization. The statement probably reflected panic in coastal Christian settlements that were sometimes raided by seafaring Muslim groups of the Sultanate of Sulu, whose captives became part of the Indies' slave trade. But the comment also reflects a British effort to capitalize on these military laborers of empire through how they arranged types of people in relation to each other. Sepoys' labor was more valuable when transported to the Philippines because of locals' ideas about "moors".

An additional forty-three to sixty of the land forces on the Manila expedition were "irregulars" on loan from the Nawab of Arcot, who, other than a few European officers, were "Topasses" in the parlance of the Company's military.[39] Topasses were South Asian Indo-Portuguese Catholics, a capacious category (see Chakraborty, in this Special Issue). Many of these

---

34. Daniel Baugh, *The Global Seven Years War, 1754–1763* (Harlow, 2011), p. 465.
35. They were offered and insisted on the same *batta* rate as had been paid on that expedition; see *Manilha Consultations*, II, p. 15.
36. On sepoys' families in Madras: *Manilha Consultations*, I, pp. 33, 60; *Manilha Consultations*, II, p. 21; *Manilha Consultations*, V, pp. 2–3. On military markets and mobility: Kolff, *Naukar, Rajput and Sepoy*, and Welsch, "Sons of Mars".
37. From W.K. Elles's characterization of W.J. Wilson's notes about rare surviving sepoy nominal rolls of those who eventually returned from the expedition, in [Office of the Adjutant General], *Precis of the Services of the Madras Native Army, with a Note on its Composition* (Ootacamund, 1886), app. II.
38. BL: IOR/P/251/49, bk. 1, p. 83.
39. "Nabob's irregulars" BL: IOR H/77, pp. 48–49; *Manilha Consultations*, I, p. 4, enumerates somewhat higher numbers. Other than the highest-ranking officers, these men were probably all topasses, since some are referred to as such in BL: IOR/P/251/51A bk. 3, p. 42.

Indo-Portuguese in South Asia had come into the employ of the Dutch and English militaries, as well as militaries of Indian rulers, often serving as gunmen (artillerymen).[40] They also served as infantrymen – in their own distinct units – as was the case in this instance. Their status vis-à-vis "European" was ambiguous. In troop returns, they were listed in a table alongside European troops, though in a column separate from them; in contrast, the sepoys were generally counted in a separate table. On this expedition, they were paid the same as "European" troops, but that may not have been the general rule.[41] The sepoys and topasses on the Manila expedition – rank and file as well as officers – were overseen at their units' highest levels by officers who were European.[42]

As part of the infantry, the Company also contributed seventy-four "Coffreys", men from sub-Saharan African areas historically sources of Portuguese military and seafaring labor, particularly from the Cape, the Swahili coast, and Madagascar.[43] In the Company parlance of the Coromandel coast, the term "Coffrey" had gone from designating religious status ("unbeliever", i.e. non-Muslim, a term derived from Arabic but learned by Portuguese from their Swahili allies and rivals) to having a racial meaning.[44] As one Englishman explained in 1761 with reference to the Carnatic Wars, "Coffrees, (By the French called Cafres) is now become the general name for all negroes who are brought to India from the Cape, the coast of

40. Marshall, "Western Arms in Maritime Asia", pp. 25–26; Pradeep Barua, "Military Developments in India, 1750–1850", *The Journal of Military History*, 58:4 (1994), pp. 599–616, 602; Channa Wickremesekera, *"Best Black Troops in the World": British Perceptions and the Making of the Sepoy 1746–1805* (New Delhi, 2002), pp. 86–87. For some contemporary references, see Richard Owen Cambridge, *An Account of the War in India between the English and French, on the Coast of Coromandel, From the Year 1750 to the Year 1760* (London, 1761); and Henry Davidson Love, *Vestiges of Old Madras, 1640–1800*, 4 vols (1913), II, pp. 82, 196, 295, 352.

41. Those on the Manila expedition were accustomed to being paid "as Europeans" at the rate of two pagodas and twenty-one fanams per month (*Manilha Consultations*, I, pp. 2, 4), equivalent to European infantry rates, and quite a bit more than the sepoy rate (*Orders, Rules and Regulations*, pp. 9, 21); as this was an exception, they were likely not generally so well paid.

42. BL: IOR H/77, pp. 48–49; *Manilha Consultations*, I, p. 4.

43. BL: IOR H/77, pp. 48–49 (the main table indicates fifty-four, but a note below it records that twenty additional "coffereys" were embarked). On Portuguese labor, see Shihan de Silva Jayasuriya, "Identifying Africans in Asia: What's in a Name?", *African and Asian Studies*, 5:3–4 (2006), pp. 275–303, 286. It is unclear whether "Coffreys" of Madras might also have included those with roots in Africa's Horn, historically a source for military labor in western India. See *idem*, *African Identity in Asia: Cultural Effects of Forced Migration* (Princeton, NJ, 2008), ch. 4; Richard Pankhurst, "The Ethiopian Diaspora to India: The Role of Habshis and Sidis from Medieval Times to the End of the Eighteenth Century", in Shihan de Silva Jayasuriya and Richard Pankhurst (eds), *The African Diaspora in the Indian Ocean* (Trenton, NJ, 2003), pp. 189–221.

44. Jeremy Prestholdt, "Portuguese Conceptual Categories and the 'Other' Encounter on the Swahili Coast", *Journal of Asian & African Studies*, 36:4 (2001), pp. 383–406, 386, 390.

Guinea, or any other parts of Africa, and chiefly from Madagascar: they are brave and steady in the field", a characterization that reflects their importance as military laborers.[45] In the Company's Madras military of this period, "Coffrey" companies listed in infantry rolls are segregated from sepoys, and appear alongside but distinct from Europeans and topasses.[46] "Coffreys" from Madagascar also worked, enslaved, at the Company's plantations in Bencoolen, Sumatra.[47] According to Wickremesekera, military "Coffreys" were enslaved; at least during the British occupation, however, they were paid.[48]

Filling out the ranks of the Company's infantry were two companies (totaling 165 rank and file) of French deserters, about which we have already heard.[49] The only rank and file with English origins were 571 royal infantrymen, those whom the Company was most anxious to have returned to Madras as soon as possible, and probably the Royal Artillery's 57 gunners and matrosses (gunner's assistants). Less clear are the origins of the Company's 29 artillerymen and 71 "Pioneer" infantrymen (categorized with Europeans).[50]

Somewhere amongst these British military personnel who set foot on Philippine soil were a good number of men referred to in other records as "lascars", though it is unclear from the sources in which of the above categories, if any, they may have been counted. This term is even more slippery than the other somewhat arbitrary categories through which the company understood its military labor.[51] East India Company officials referred to non-European laborers who manned the company's ships as "lascars", but also described as lascars men who performed menial labor in company encampments, including "gun lascars", who worked as part of the artillery hauling equipment.[52] Lascars laboring for the Company in encampments and as part of the artillery may have been distinct from most of the seafaring

45. Cambridge, *An Account of the War in India*, unnumbered page of the Glossary preceding the Introduction.

46. For example, BL: IOR/L/MIL/11/109.

47. BL: IOR/E/4/301.

48. Wickremesekera, *"Best Black Troops"*, p. 91; BL: IOR/P/251/53, p. 1080.

49. BL: IOR H/77, pp. 48–49. In that document, Pioneers are listed with the Company's other non-sepoy troops. Later, the Manila board refers to "Europeans including the Pioneers" (*Manilha Consultations*, V, p. 8).

50. BL: IOR H/77, pp. 48–49. Overall, these numbers of land forces correspond neatly to the numbers given as landed in "Draught of the Great Bay of Manilla and Harbour of Cavita". That data may have the same source.

51. Aaron Jaffer, *Lascars and Indian Ocean Seafaring, 1780–1860: Shipboard Life, Unrest and Mutiny* (Rochester, NY, 2015), Introduction.

52. BL: IOR/P/251/48–49. Wilson, *History of the Madras Army*, I, and the 1766 regulations refer to the categories of "European Infantry", "Sepoys", "Artillery", and "Lascars", consistent with the relationships being analogous such that European infantry is to sepoy as European artillery is to lascar.

lascars, whose skills would have been more specialized, but some of the gun lascars may also have been seafarers grounded between sailing seasons.[53]

In the end it is unclear how many lascars were part of the expedition, and how they were enumerated amongst the personnel captured in the sources treated above, but their number was significant. Just a couple of weeks before the whole embarked from Madras, Company officials were planning for a force of 350 lascars (with eighteen lascar officers).[54] A few months into the occupation, more than 200 must have been present, because the Manila board suggested sending that number on an expedition to the countryside.[55] Lascars in the Manila occupation performed grueling manual labor – digging, clearing, constructing fortifications, and hauling guns and ammunition.[56] As part of the artillery, lascars on the expedition were paid more than sepoys, though, consistent with general practice in the Madras military at the time, probably only about a third as much as the lowest-ranking European artilleryman.[57] Most of these lascars probably hailed from around Madras, as Company officials there, worrying that they would not be able to recruit enough of them, offered advance pay to them that they could leave with their families before departing – the same offer they made to sepoys.[58] As with the sepoys, many were likely veterans of the expedition to Bengal.[59] Some of these lascars had seafaring skills.[60]

Finally, these British forces brought from India were supplemented in the Philippines with Chinese laborers, referred to by the British usually as "Chinese coolies", "coolies", or "coolie lascars", reflecting the fact that they were employed in much the same way as the lascars from Madras: hauling gun carts and other heavy loads, or performing other demanding physical labor, and indeed they are often mentioned in the same breath.[61] The coolies were paid, though officials were clear that they were not to be put on the same terms as other Company military personnel. The British had counted

53. Janet J. Ewald, "Crossers of the Sea: Slaves, Freedmen, and Other Migrants in the Northwestern Indian Ocean, c.1750–1914", *American Historical Review*, 105:1 (2000), pp. 69–91, 73.

54. IOR/P/251/48 bk. 2, p. 120.

55. *Manilha Consultations*, V, p. 8.

56. Hauling military equipment: *Manilha Consultations*, II, pp. 4, 14.

57. Part of artillery: *Manilha Consultations*, VI, p. 118; Pay: *Manilha Consultations*, V, p. 65. *Orders, Rules, and Regulations*, pp. 7, 9, 21, 38.

58. Some seafaring lascars were likely to have been Muslim and spoke Tamil. George Dodwell, *A Narrative of the Principal Transactions betwixt the Agents, and Officers of the Hon. East India Company, and George Dodwell, Esq. Commander of the Ship Patty* [...] (London, 1773), pp. 71–83.

59. Lascars (like sepoys) complained that they had been promised the same pay and *batta* as the Bengal expedition (*Manilha Consultations*, VI, p. 12).

60. BL: IOR/P/251/51A bk. 2, p. 461.

61. *Manilha Consultations*, I, p. 60; *Manilha Consultations*, II, pp. 4, 6–8, 9, 11; *Manilha Consultations*, VI, pp. 67, 71, 106, 115.

on Manila's Chinese welcoming them with open arms, in light of the regular and brutal expulsions that the Chinese suffered from Manila's Spanish authorities. It is not possible to give a full account here of the various ways that Chinese skills and labor were central to British dreams for the occupation, but we will see one part of it in this military labor.

The British envisioned, organized, and disciplined their military force through these categories. It is sometimes difficult to see past the British imagination to how the people who were interpolated in these categories saw their own affinities and affiliations. The categories – as well as the difficulty of pinning down their contents – reveal the motley nature of the crew, and the broad reach of forces that produced these people as British military labor en route from Madras to Manila in late 1762. As we will see when we follow them to Manila, the ties that bound them to their commanders were tenuous, and sometimes broke.

TROUBLE IN MANILA

The British occupation of Manila lasted from September 1762 until April 1764.[62] When British forces first arrived, they were challenged by Spanish forces (a mix of soldiers from New Spain, probably mestizos and *criollos*, and people native to central Luzon), but the British took Manila proper more easily than they had anticipated they would. The Spanish were caught unprepared. Manila was awaiting a new Governor General from Spain, and the acting Governor General was Archbishop Rojo, who had no military training. Furthermore, Rojo had not yet received word from Spain that they were at war with the British.

Spanish forces quickly capitulated to the British, agreeing to accept British sovereignty in Manila, and also agreeing that the city would pay a significant ransom in return for its citizens being spared from further looting of their property – looting that had begun when British troops breached the walls of the city.[63] Although the British were technically in control, outside of Manila, a high-ranking Spanish official, Simon de Anda, led a growing military resistance of Spanish military and locals. The British may not even have cared about the situation outside of Manila except that the city depended on the surrounding areas for food, and also the British sought word of the galleon's arrival from Acapulco, hoping to seize its silver to fund, along with the ransom money, the upcoming season's investments in Canton. This very abbreviated account of early events sets the stage on which we can see

---

62. On the British occupation of Manila, see Nicholas Tracy, *Manila Ransomed: The British Assault on Manila in the Seven Years War* (Liverpool, 1995); on the geopolitical context of the Seven Years War, see Baugh, *The Global Seven Years War*.
63. Tracy, *Manila Ransomed*, pp. 35–55.

how British commanders experienced significant problems controlling their military labor.

De Anda's resistance early on posed military and labor challenges for British officials. "The great extent of the Place & present situation of affairs in the country", the board reported soon after the capitulation of Manila, "have induced the General to leave all the Troops that came upon the Expedition" rather than sending many of them back, as had been planned. Even with all the troops staying, they were "but barely sufficient for our Garrisons" and so the board "intend[ed] applying to the Presidency [Madras] for reinforcements of seapoys by all opportunities", "thought by the General to be absolutely necessary".[64] General Draper's words were a bit spicier. Though he praised the royal infantrymen, he lamented that he could not send any of them back because "We have no Troops besides who can be Depended upon".[65] Amongst those least trustworthy, according to Draper, were the French deserters.

Indeed, almost immediately, the French deserters began deserting.[66] In late December, Manila company officials wrote that "We have the Mortification to inform you that no fewer than twenty Men have deserted" and that "all of them to a Man wou'd have certainly have gone off" had they kept using them for patrols and detachments, because de Anda had sent "Numbers of Emmissaries to entice them particularly, as they are Catholicks".[67] Friars supporting de Anda indeed sought to encourage French deserters to join the Catholic side of the conflict; some friars offered only a "prevaricating defence" when confronted with letters showing that they had been "encouraging the Desertion of our [the Company's] People".[68] The losses were significant enough that the Manila board asked commanders to pardon deserters who voluntarily surrendered themselves.[69]

By February, the desertions of the French deserters had reached a crescendo such that Company commanders decided they were more useful to the occupation if they were shipped back to Madras. Since they had "deserted in great numbers" to de Anda's side, one wrote, "least [sic] the rest shou'd follow which I have great reason to apprehend we have been obliged to petition the Admiral to take them off the Island".[70] In early March, the Manila council, explaining why "the frequent Desertions from the French Companies have put us to the disagreeable necessity of sending them to

---

64. *Manilha Consultations*, III, p. 3.
65. TNA: WO/1/139, p. 411 (Cushner, *Documents Illustrating the British Conquest of Manila*, p. 147).
66. TNA: WO 1/139, p. 445.
67. BL: IOR/P/251/49 bk. 1, pp. 83–84.
68. *Manilha Consultations*, V, p. 72.
69. *Manilha Consultations*, II, p. 12; *Manilha Consultations*, V, p. 11.
70. TNA: WO 1/139, p. 445.

the Coast [of Coromandel]", blamed Catholics and Catholicism: "to have continued them here might have been attended with very bad Consequences, as they are most of the Romish Religion, the Fryars would by degrees have carried off the whole".[71] The Admiral's assessment was characteristically more cutting. Responding to the Company's request that he ship them back, he wrote, "I learn with more concern than surprize the Considerable Desertion which has happened in the Company's Troops", and pointedly reminded the Company that it had only itself to blame: "with regard to the French Company's [desertion] I shall say the less as my opinion was well known to the Council of Madras before they Embarked".[72] He ultimately granted their request in terms that emphasized his benevolence and generosity, and suggested the incompetence of those who had overridden his objections: "If you judge the safety of the Garrison to depend on sending them away I will receive them on board his Majesty's ships[. B]ut [...] I am on guard against them as Enemies".[73]

It was in part because of early problems with the French deserters that, by December, officials in Manila were urgently requesting that reinforcements to the tune of 2,000 more sepoys be sent from India, as well as more armed vessels.[74] Sepoys were both particularly valued by Company officials, but also the source of challenges. It will be recalled that British commanders worried about sepoy and lascar discontent before the troops even left Madras. In order to persuade sepoys and lascars to go on the expedition, the Company offered them two months' advance pay – which most left with their families – and the option of having any part of their pay at Manila disbursed directly to their families in Madras.[75] This benefit caused problems. By mid-November, the Manila council noted that since they "had left the greatest part of the pay advanced them at Madras with their families there" they had been "reduced [...] to great hardships since their arrival here" – recall that sepoys had to provision themselves from their pay – and so they were to be advanced one additional month's pay out of their prize money.[76]

If many sepoys arrived in Manila with nothing, and could not expect pay until December, that might go some way toward explaining why they were blamed for the looting that took place during the early days of the siege. British commanders tended to minimize the plunder their troops had committed during the early days of the siege of Manila, though what they admitted, they blamed on the motley crew, a "Variety and Confusion of People,

---

71. *Manilha Consultations*, III, p. 37.
72. *Manilha Consultations*, V, pp. 67–68.
73. *Ibid*.
74. *Manilha Consultations*, III, p. 12; BL: IOR/P/251/49, bk. 1, p. 77.
75. *Manilha Consultations*, I, p. 60.
76. *Ibid*., p. 33.

who differed as much in Sentiments and Language, as in Dress and Complexion", who were not easily restrained.[77] Sepoys were convenient scapegoats, to be sure. But likely, too, the sepoys who entered the battle for Manila without prospects for the means to sustain themselves for over a month may have sought those means in what they could seize during the battle. It helps to consider how these men might have encountered or participated in plunder elsewhere. Plunder was widely used in the Carnatic Wars, on all sides, sometimes clearly according to commanders' orders, and other times supposedly the unsanctioned actions of unruly troops.[78] Plunder was an established form of military pay, and so while it was only sometimes officially sanctioned, at other times it would likely have been unofficially tolerated as a way to effectively supplement troops' pay. It may be, then, that the officers of the Manila assault encouraged their troops to plunder, despite their protestations otherwise and their condemnation of what they characterized as errant actions of unruly sepoys. Troops may also, however, have plundered in insubordination and in defiance of their commanders, as a form of direct action to ensure their pay.

Early on in the occupation, British commanders tried to take steps to ameliorate sepoys' discontent, appealing again to sepoys' desires to support their families: they offered that sepoys might opt to send their pay or a portion of it back to their families with the first Madras-bound ship, rather than receiving it in Manila.[79] It quickly became clear, however, that sepoy discontent was a significant strategic problem. One of the bones of contention was around *batta*, the per diem allowance from which sepoys were accustomed to provision themselves while in the field. In early December, the sepoys were "disappointed" and "much dissatisfied, at not receiving Batta at the rate allowed upon the Bengal Expedition, which they alledge was promised them before embarking at Madras".[80] The sepoys agitated around this issue, "appealing to Captain Flint their Commandant" who confirmed their account; the board decided in their favor, noting the principle that "they are justly entitled to every reasonable Indulgence, in those distant parts".[81] But practical matters were at least as pressing, for the board described their decision as "Politic", both "to pacify" the sepoys as well as "to facilitate [...] encouraging others to come here".[82] Indeed, "every cause of disgust ought to be avoided if possible, otherwise the [Madras]

77. William Draper, *Colonel Draper's Answer to the Spanish Arguments* [...] (London, 1764), p. 21.
78. See, for example, Cambridge, *An Account of the War in India*, p. 132; Baugh, *Global Seven Years War*, pp. 465, 466.
79. *Manilha Consultations*, V, p. 2.
80. BL: IOR/P/251/49, bk. 1, p. 83; *Manilha Consultations*, II, p. 15.
81. *Manilha Consultations*, II, p. 15.
82. BL: IOR/P/251/49, bk. 1, p. 83.

Presidency may find it a difficult matter to send us the reinforcements of this useful Corps that are necessary".[83] Sepoy discontentment only increased. In March, when the Admiral wrote to the council agreeing to relieve them of the problem of the remaining French deserters, he added:

> the Desertion of Sepoys is an event you may perhaps account for better than I, I have observed they have served here with great dissatisfaction and frequently complained the Engagements they entered into at Madras were not made good to them, if this is the case, the remedy is in your [East India Company officials'] own hands.[84]

The French and sepoys were not the only problems. British commanders of the Manila garrison warned the board in March that "the desertion of the Soldiers, Seapoys and lascars has been very great", and British records from the Manila operation are replete with accounts of their own forces deserting – French, "European" (likely also the French), sepoys, and lascars – as well as with reports of those deserters fighting with enemy forces.[85] Pay was thought to be an issue in all cases, and the British commanders inconsistently tried to remedy discontent about pay. In late January 1763, one of the British commanders reported from the field that he planned to try to lure back the French deserters to the British side by offering them "Pardon with a Bounty".[86] Lascars complained that they were promised the same pay and *batta* as on the Bengal Expedition, but instead "are paid 8 Fanams less than at Madras", and so the Board agreed to make up the difference.[87] Yet, these steps did not have the desired effect. In March, commanders of the Manila garrison warned that the "clamours [of the soldiers, sepoys, and lascars] on account of their Pay being so small grow stronger dayly", and so recommended that "an augmentation be made to their subsistence which considering the excessive Prices of the necessaries of Life is really much too small as may enable them to support themselves with Comfort and put a stop to their desertion".[88] In response, the Manila board ordered that "the Military &ca [presumably European troops] be daily allowed 2 Drams" of alcohol – apparently hoping that increased rations of booze would be sufficient to stem their discontent – and that "the Sepoys and Lascars [be allowed] 1 Dollar Pr. Month Gratuity".[89] These small steps were not enough to effectively combat desertion.

The issues of pay and food were connected ones, not just for the military personnel in the Manila garrison, but for commanders as they planned efforts

---

83. *Manilha Consultations*, II, p. 15.
84. *Manilha Consultations*, V, pp. 67–68.
85. *Ibid.*, p. 70; see also pp. 72, 107, 108.
86. *Ibid.*, p. 27.
87. *Manilha Consultations*, VI, p. 12.
88. *Manilha Consultations*, V, p. 70.
89. *Ibid.*, p. 71.

to get at the root of both problems. They sent parties into the countryside to secure food, and also in search of the silver supposed to be arriving in the galleon from Acapulco. They worried that should the galleon's silver reach de Anda first, he would even more effectively woo deserters from British forces. In fact, that seems to be exactly what happened. The commanders of the Manila garrison reported in March that their intelligence told them that British soldiers were being offered by de Anda's agents one hundred dollars up front, and a dollar a day, to desert.[90] The material rewards promised by de Anda's agents – or perhaps even the rumor of them – might have spoken volumes to these men, aggrieved as they were over pay. Though the Manila board approved only paltry pay increases, they offered a two-hundred-dollar reward for helping to convict those who were recruiting British forces to join the Spanish resistance, planned to hire one hundred Chinese to patrol the bridges over which garrison deserters had to pass, authorized a thirty-dollar reward for catching a deserter, and banned the use of covered litters, in which soldiers were thought to escape the city.[91] While many deserted from the field or while on detachment, these measures show that some soldiers deserted from their garrison within the walled city of Manila itself; the bridges that connected it to its suburbs, and the covered litters in which its wealthier residents would themselves travel, were routes by which garrison soldiers could escape the more easily surveilled interior of the walled city into the more populous suburbs which housed so many of the city's markets, its commerce, and many other laborers.

The situation only deteriorated: a year into the occupation, the Governor of Madras wrote to London that "We have reason to believe the Troops we sent to Manilha, are greatly reduced by death and desertion, if we receive one half of the number sent it will exceed our expectation".[92] Several months later, they received word that "Our Troops were reduced by Death & desertion to about 400 Europeans & as many Seapoys", and that "upwards of 100 of Our Deserters" were fighting for de Anda.[93]

Members of the sea forces were troublesome, too, when they were on Philippine soil. One of the commanders of an expedition around Laguna de Bay, in search of food and the galleon's silver, expressed "great Mortification and sorrow that the Sailors [who were on patrol in the large lake] have plundered some of the Houses in the Village" and deplored "the actions of those Villians", as they undid his careful work to win over locals' cooperation.[94] For this reason, he preferred to take on patrol lascars

---

90. *Ibid.*, p. 70.
91. *Ibid.*, p. 71.
92. BL: IOR/E/4 300, pp. 212–213; abstracted in Henry Dodwell, *Calendar of the Madras Despatches 1754–1765* (Madras, 1930), p. 344.
93. BL: IOR/P/251/51A bk. 1, pp. 203–204.
94. *Manilha Consultations*, II, p. 11.

and Chinese coolies, whom he trusted better. The same commander praised both the coolies and the lascars on his expedition as having "behaved like Angels", and noted that the lascars in particular had "done more in the working way than ever the same number of Men did in the time", despite enduring extreme hardship.[95] Because they had behaved so well, he "found it necessary to be liberal" with some of them on account of their hard work under dire conditions.[96]

In the reports of this expedition, we can see some of the ways that the categories of British labor were enacted, and other ways that they were flexible. Though the expedition had lascars and coolies, the Pioneers (categorized as European) were not exempt from particularly onerous physical labor: they worked alongside lascars clearing particularly thick bamboo in order to construct an esplanade around a church that had been captured.[97] In another mark of the ways these categories might have some flexibility, the commander at one point described himself as having been "obliged to convert" a number of the royal infantrymen on the expedition "into Lascars, by rewards and fair speeches", as he did not have enough lascars to haul the artillery equipment.[98] Another example of flexible use of labor, and labor's categories, was when the Company decided that since the "Lascars are willing to act as Sepoys", they would be "tought twice a Week to load and Fire". This change in work had to be carefully categorized, however, to avoid grumbling over pay:

> to prevent the Sepoys from murmuring which if they were put on an equal Footing they would not fail to do, as they receive less Pay than the Lascars Agreed that they (lascars) be called the Artillery Volunteers that they nevertheless continue in their former employment under the Engineer and Military Storekeeper.[99]

In other respects, however, these categories of labor could not be bridged: the same commander wrote that: "The Chinese are good Cooleys, but I have had inexpressible Trouble for want of some one among them invested with authority [so] it would still be of great use if you could get me such a person", and the Manila council agreed to send such.[100] While the Chinese coolies had some agency in determining their pay, the Manila council was determined to keep expenses down and to retain rigid boundaries between the terms of coolies' labor and the other Company employees: the paymaster of the expedition was instructed that "the Custom of Batty should by no

95. *Manilha Consultations*, II, pp. 6, 8; see also pp. 4, 11, 14, 17, 50; *Manilha Consultations*, V, p. 8; *Manilha Consultations*, VI, p. 12.
96. *Manilha Consultations*, II, pp. 4–6, 8.
97. *Ibid.*, p. 10.
98. *Ibid.*, p. 17.
99. *Manilha Consultations*, V, p. 65.
100. *Manilha Consultations*, II, pp. 8–9.

means be introduced" for the Chinese coolies. He could offer them one-half *real* more than what was paid in garrison, and even one full *real* if they refused to accept just one-half, but the board reminded the paymaster that "we rely on your Endeavours to settle it in the cheapest manner possible".[101]

Finally, on the question of troublesome or cooperative labor, we might note that by the end of this most vexed occupation, the remaining board members at Manila reported back to Company officials in Madras that "As the Coffres in the Companys Service have behaved remarkably well during the Expedition, and the times have been very hard on their earnest representation we granted to them the same pay as the Nabob's Irregulars".[102] It may be remembered that the "Nabob's irregulars", Indo-Portuguese, had been granted pay "as Europeans" in the way that they were accustomed to being paid by the Nawab.[103] These African soldiers, then, persuaded the board to grant them pay "as Europeans".

CONCLUSION

While all of these laborers of the British occupation were paid, the conditions under which these men labored – even the most valued members of the Royal 79th – could hardly be said to be of their own choosing. Way describes how even the formally free labor that comprised most of the British army in America during the Seven Years War had many qualities that made it closer to other forms of contract labor in which the terms of employment are highly coercive and conscripted, such as indenture: even "freely" recruited military laborers enlisted for long stretches of employment, lived with their employers, and were not part of independent households.[104] In these respects, we find much of the same coercion in the experiences of these other British troops in another theater of that war.

Many, though, opted out. Weighing the likely risks and opportunities of remaining under their British commanders against those of leaving to pursue their livelihood by other means, they deserted, as many would have already done in India. These deserters likely brought with them from Madras the expectation that, as in India, deserters in Manila and its environs could expect to be welcomed by "enemy" forces, as indeed many were. When food was short and pay not forthcoming as promised from their British commanders, they set their sights on the other side – with easier access to food, and of whose silver they would have heard. Yet deserting in the Philippines must also have seemed a different proposition from deserting in India, for

101. *Manilha Consultations*, I, pp. 60, 61–62.
102. BL: IOR/P/251/51A bk. 2, p. 401.
103. *Manilha Consultations*, I, pp. 2, 4.
104. Way, "'Black Service'", pp. 24–25.

Manila and its environs were for nearly all utterly unfamiliar in landscape and languages. And aside from this exceptional moment when two different employers competed for military labor, it had no military labor market to speak of. If one came from France, or Scotland, or India's Coromandel coast, it must have seemed a great risk to leave the ranks of those who would at least in principle go back to Madras at the end of the conflict, and instead opt to join an army of Mexicans, Kapampangans, Tagalogs, and a few Spaniards. For some, Catholicism would have made the otherwise foreign life more familiar. Also, deserters may have thought that from the port city of Manila they could find their way on some ship to Canton and from there back to India or Europe. Those with seafaring skills could have easily done so, for there was always a market for seafaring labor in Manila.

We also see in this Indian Ocean story a strikingly complicated combination of highly differentiated categories of labor, somewhat haphazardly combined. The categories of labor that were part of this expedition reveal something about how the Company thought of the people whose labor it might coerce, if little about how those people thought of themselves. The formation of these categories, and the ways they composed this expedition, were utterly inseparable from financial prospects for the East India Company. The Company functioned by composing complex assemblages of labor, drawn from near and far, allies and enemies. Company officials in Madras believed that they could most safely afford to spare from Madras those who were sepoys, lascars, "Coffreys", and the Nawab's topasses, but they sought to keep in Madras as many royal and European troops as possible, with the significant exception of French deserters, who they were eager to send away. These exigencies of the Company – concerned as it was about the security of its Coromandel and Bengal ports, and eager to capitalize on its support for the Nawab of Arcot – conflicted with the expedition's more narrowly military focus as the commanders of royal forces understood it.

What might be more surprising is that even those at the bottom of the hierarchies of labor might, under the extraordinary circumstances of the occupation of Manila, be able to push for better pay. The flexibility that commanders sometimes showed, in terms of pay and in pardoning deserters, attests to the challenges the East India Company faced when it moved from Madras to Manila. As in the South Asian context, its troops had ample opportunity to desert, but, unlike in South Asia, in Manila the Company could not recruit from enemies' deserters or draw on allied rulers' forces. Instead, its only local sources of new military labor were local Chinese. The challenges of the British in Manila show in part that when cut off from South Asian military markets, those trying to command forces had fewer options, whereas their troops still found the opportunity to desert. These British commanders, then, generally could not enforce the corporal and capital punishment that disobedience and desertion typically merited in the Atlantic context, though there, too, we see leniency when an army depleted by desertion had few prospects for fresh recruits.[105]

The labor of both British and Spanish colonies changed substantially after the British occupation. In British India, systems of sepoy recruitment, pay, and discipline became much more standardized and bureaucratic, and the British focused on producing opium to trade with Canton rather than trying to trade its other manufactures for the sea and forest products of the Indies Seas. In the Spanish Philippines, the city of Manila and the surrounding countryside were transformed by the introduction of the tobacco monopoly, the first significant Spanish effort to manufacture in the colony, and the tribute system was overhauled to raise more revenue: in short, the colony was to be made profitable.[106]

The British occupation of Manila is an exceptional moment, but in tracing its labor we see interconnections of the wider Indian Ocean world and the Philippines as part of it – interconnections that form a web of human labor and struggle, commercial aspirations, and material goods. This story, unfolding as older forms of empire were fading but newer ones were just emerging, shows new commerce emerging as an uncertain, sometimes improvised, sprawling network of trade, diplomacy, and military force.

105. *Ibid.*; Brandon, "'The Privilege of Using Their Legs'", p. 83.
106. Ed. C. de Jesus, *The Tobacco Monopoly in the Philippines: Bureaucratic Enterprise and Social Change, 1766–1880* (Quezon City, 1980); Newson, *Conquest and Pestilence*, p. 130.

IRSH 64 (2019), pp. 149–171 doi:10.1017/S0020859019000075
© 2019 Internationaal Instituut voor Sociale Geschiedenis

The Path to Sweet Success: Free and Unfree Labor in the Building of Roads and Rails in Havana, Cuba, 1790–1835*

EVELYN P. JENNINGS

St. Lawrence University
Vilas Hall 103, Canton, NY 13617, USA

E-mail: ejennings@stlawu.edu

ABSTRACT: Havana's status as a colonial port shaped both its infrastructure needs and the patterns of labor recruitment and coercion used to build it. The port city's initial economic and political orientation was maritime, with capital and labor invested largely in defense and shipbuilding. By the nineteenth century, Cuba had become a plantation colony based on African enslavement, exporting increasing quantities of sugar to Europe and North America. Because the island was relatively underpopulated, workers for infrastructure projects and plantations had to be imported through global circuits of coerced labor, such as the transatlantic slave trade, the transportation of prisoners, and, in the 1800s, indentured workers from Europe, Mexico, or Asia. Cuban elites and colonial officials in charge of transportation projects experimented with different mixes of workers, who labored on the roads and railways under various degrees of coercion, but always within the socio-economic and cultural framework of a society based on the enslavement of people considered racially distinct. Thus, the indenture of white workers became a crucial supplement to other forms of labor coercion in the building of rail lines in the 1830s, but Cuban elites determined that these workers' whiteness was too great a risk to the racial hierarchy of the Cuban labor market and therefore sought more racially distinct contract workers after 1840.

INTRODUCTION

The construction of infrastructure in Cuba, whether for imperial defense or private economic interests, was carried out by a shifting combination of state and local actors, often with motley crews of forced and free laborers. Because Cuba did not have a substantial indigenous population beyond the middle of the sixteenth century, many of the laborers for construction projects were

* The author would like to thank Pepijn Brandon, Niklas Frykman, Pernille Røge, Marcus Rediker, and all the participants in the "Free and Unfree Labor in Atlantic and Indian Ocean Port Cities (c.1700–1850)" conference and workshop at the University of Pittsburgh for helpful criticisms and suggestions for revising this essay.

involuntary migrants from Africa or from other regions of the Spanish Empire. In this sense, Havana's port was also the site of first arrival for many of the people who built and labored in the city and extended the empire's economic and political reach into the countryside. The port's infrastructure projects also served as a testing ground for different mixes of forced and free laborers in completing difficult, unskilled work. The consolidation of the social and economic structures of plantation slavery in the first third of the nineteenth century in Cuba framed all later experiments with labor. The experiences of Cuban officials in the road and rail projects from 1790 to 1835 informed their successors' resort to indenture to supplement enslavement in both public and plantation work by the 1840s, and their insistence on maintaining the controls of slavery over workers who were legally freer.

As this brief summary suggests, freedom and unfreedom were not absolute opposites in theory or practice for workers in Cuba in the eighteenth and nineteen centuries. The levels of violence and constraint experienced by the laborers discussed in this essay in the areas of recruitment, compensation, and "control over the working body" demonstrate most clearly the range of coercion that employers applied to workers of varying status in Cuba, from the enslaved and indentured to convicts and to those who were legally free.[1] In the context of a society in which enslavement was deeply embedded and expanding, employers sought to extend the controls applied to slaves – shackles and chains, the lash, and the barracoon – to workers who were not enslaved by law, though workers' resistance did limit the success of these efforts. At this time, Spanish law defined "free" persons as those not bound by the strictures of slavery, by which another person owned both the slave's body and labor, or by a judicial sentence or contract to labor for a given period. This essay seeks to illuminate the many ways that both the free, the enslaved, and those in between in colonial Cuba were subject to violence and coercion as part of their work for the state. Thus, the terms free and unfree highlight the contingent and broad nature of both categories in the work regimes imposed on laborers in road and rail projects of colonial Cuba.

FROM IMPERIAL SERVICE TO PLANTATION EXPORT

For the first two centuries of colonial rule, Havana's orientation and connections were largely maritime. Goods, capital, and labor arrived from other Spanish Caribbean ports such as Cartagena de Indias or Veracruz, or from the metropole across the Atlantic. The Spanish Crown sought to control imperial trade and migration to the island by funneling it through designated

---

1. Sabine Damir-Geilsdorf *et al.* (eds), *Bonded Labour: Global and Comparative Perspectives 18th to 21st Century* (Bielefeld, 2016), p. 12.

ports such as Seville and later Cádiz, and Veracruz. However, unlike many other colonial ports in Spain's American empire, initially Havana's primary function was not to be an outlet for goods produced in Cuba. Rather, as historian Alejandro de la Fuente has noted, "it was the port that made the hinterland", though this process was a slow one.[2]

Havana became the gathering site for the convoys returning to Spain in the 1550s and maintained that role into the late eighteenth century. Infrastructure investment around the port by the crown from the late 1500s to the 1700s focused on securing the city and its bay with forts and a wall to deter pirate or imperial rivals' attacks from the sea. In addition, the vast majority of the people who built and sustained the city and its port also arrived by sea or were descended from those who had done so, making Havana a diverse and cosmopolitan place even in its first century as a Spanish colonial port.[3]

Unlike other Caribbean colonies such as Barbados or Saint Domingue, the Havana region developed into a major producer of tropical products for export only after 1750, recasting the port's role in the empire and its infrastructure needs.[4] Though the port's maritime connections continued to be vital and expand throughout the eighteenth and nineteenth centuries, by the 1790s the orientation of infrastructure investment shifted inward to extend a network of roads, and later rails, to link Havana's widening plantation hinterland to its port to ensure the transport of sugar and coffee to overseas markets.

Cuba's shift to slave-based plantation production also transformed its demography as the white population was overshadowed by a rapidly growing enslaved and free population of African descent in the first third of the nineteenth century. Enslavement and other forms of forced labor were long-standing practices of conquest and colonization in the Spanish Empire. Though full-blown plantation economies were a late development, the execution of defense works for the key imperial ports such as Havana often relied on coerced laborers.[5] For example, by the eighteenth century, as the Spanish monarchy contended with growing French and English power in the Americas, the Spanish crown expanded its use of state-owned enslaved workers to better fortify Cuba after the British occupation of Havana ended in 1763. Over the next three decades, colonial officials on the island also

---

2. Alejandro de la Fuente, *Havana and the Atlantic in the Sixteenth Century* (Chapel Hill, NC, 2008), p. 9.
3. *Ibid.*, p. 6.
4. Allan J. Kuethe, "Havana in the Eighteenth Century", in Franklin W. Knight and Peggy K. Liss (eds), *Atlantic Port Cities: Economy, Culture, and Society in the Atlantic World, 1650–1850* (Knoxville, TN, 1991), pp. 13–39.
5. Evelyn P. Jennings, "The Sinews of Spain's American Empire: Forced Labor in Cuba from the Sixteenth to the Nineteenth Century", in John Donoghue and Evelyn P. Jennings (eds), *Building the Atlantic Empires: Unfree Labor and Imperial States in the Political Economy of Capitalism, ca. 1500–1914* (Leiden, 2016), pp. 25–53.

experimented with ways of forcing legally free people to do defense and civil construction and to serve in the military through levies during the revolutionary era in the Caribbean.[6]

For Cuba, militarization and state investment in defense were coupled with Crown concessions to liberalize trade and state-private efforts to foment economic development. By the time slave rebellion in nearby Saint Domingue had destroyed that island's booming planation sector, Cuba was poised to take its place. Hence, the period from 1790 to 1840 saw major transformations in Cuba as elites and colonial officials collaborated to foster plantation development and to better defend the island. At the heart of these transformations was the shift in the island's economy from imperial service to plantation production of coffee and sugar for export.[7] This transformation was demographic and geographic; plantations spread out from the Havana region into new parts of the island, creating explosive demand for enslaved workers. This demand for labor and the relaxation of imperial controls on the slave trade brought more than 536,000 enslaved Africans to Cuba over the fifty-year period.[8]

These demographic transformations prompted concerns among the Cuban elite about the "Africanization" of the island's population, particularly in light of the revolutionary upheaval in Saint Domingue that culminated in the declaration of a black republic in 1804.[9] Proposals debated over the next forty years all sought to increase white migration to Cuba, though members of the elite differed over whether continuing the importation of African slaves was wise. The proponents of white immigration also differed on whether to recruit white families with offers of modest plots of land for farming or single white men to work for a wage on plantations.[10] How best to increase the numbers of available laborers in Cuba for both state-sponsored projects and agriculture remained a challenge throughout the first half of the nineteenth century, but there was little debate about the desirability of increasing sugar production to fill the void left in the world's supply after the collapse of Saint Domingue. The experiments to recruit labor for

6. Evelyn P. Jennings, "War as the 'Forcing House of Change': State Slavery in Late-Eighteenth-Century Cuba", *William and Mary Quarterly*, 62:3 (2005), pp. 411–440.

7. For a more recent examination of these transformations, see Ada Ferrer, *Freedom's Mirror: Cuba and Haiti in the Age of Revolution* (New York, 2014). The classic and still indispensable work is Manuel Moreno Fraginals, *El ingenio. Complejo económico social cubano del azúcar* (Barcelona, 2001 [1978]).

8. Derived from the Transatlantic Slave Trade Database: Cuba/disembarkation/ 1790–1840, available at: http://www.slavevoyages.org/estimates/oCxk1QIw; last accessed 10 February 2018.

9. Consuelo Naranjo Orovio, "La amenaza haitiana, un miedo interesado: poder y fomento de la población blanca en Cuba", in María Dolores González-Ripoll *et al.* (eds), *El rumor de Haití en Cuba: Temor, raza y rebeldía, 1789–1844* (Madrid, 2004), pp. 83–99. See also Ferrer, *Freedom's Mirror*.

10. Naranjo Orovio, "La amenaza haitiana", pp. 101–178.

infrastructure projects informed and were informed by the consolidation of plantation slavery in Cuba. Elites were particularly concerned about where a given group of workers would fit in the racial hierarchy and whether the costs to recruit, maintain, and control those workers were sustainable.

In addition to recruiting labor, the geographic expansion of plantations necessitated the construction or repair of roads to ensure the efficient transport of export products to the port of Havana, especially for the more perishable export, sugar. Into the eighteenth century, road building and repair had been carried out by private householders in the countryside, employing local, free, and enslaved laborers. Many travelers to Cuba reported on the disastrous state of its roads, especially during the rainy season. The most famous traveler of the early nineteenth century, Alexander von Humboldt, noted from his visits in 1800–1801 and 1804 that the streets of Havana were "disgusting [...] because one walked up to the knees in mud". Roadways leading out of the capital were no better as "[t]he interior communications of the island [were] laborious and costly, in spite of the short distance [...] between the northern and southern coasts".[11] Decades of local efforts brought little progress in road repair and construction, as weather and wear took their toll. Von Humboldt favored the digging of a canal to improve north-south transport, but this project never came to pass.[12]

After an intense period of the colonial state employing enslaved and other coerced workers to build and repair the defense works of Havana (1763–1790), Crown officials, many of whom had become planters themselves, began to intervene to speed road construction and repair to outlying plantation districts. Initially, the captains general tried to encourage, then force, free householders to do the work of road and bridge construction themselves, with scant success as many claimed their military service as grounds for an exemption from road work.[13] The failure to coerce local free people to extend the road network stimulated Cuban elites and colonial officials to explore other options. By the 1790s, wealthy creole planters petitioned the Spanish Crown for control of the labor of captured fugitive slaves to advance road construction, again with only limited success. Finally, the obstacles to transportation construction were overcome by recruiting contract laborers abroad and undermining the liberty of Africans freed by British anti-slave trade treaties to build the first rail line in Latin America, from Havana south and east to Güines; the line was finished in 1838.[14]

---

11. Alexander von Humboldt, *Ensayo político sobre la isla de Cuba* (Madrid, 1998 [1827]), pp. 108 and 273. The translations from the Spanish are my own.
12. Von Humboldt, *Ensayo político sobre la isla de Cuba*, pp. 273–276.
13. Sherry Johnson, *The Social Transformation of Eighteenth-Century Cuba* (Gainesville, FL, 2001), pp. 121–145.
14. These liberated Africans were often called *emancipados* in Cuba. Inés Roldán de Montaud, "Origen, evolución, y supresión del grupo de negros 'emancipados' en Cuba 1817–1870",

Thus, capitalist development of the export economy in Cuba was closely intertwined with the imperial state's policies and practices of labor recruitment and deployment in public works. The state and its contractors sought to hold down labor costs and exert control over workers' mobility and pace of work by experimenting with a range of coercive labor forms, such as enslavement, penal labor, and apprehensions of vagrants and fugitive slaves. The analysis here shows that the experiments with varied types of forced labor that successfully completed road and rail networks shaped later labor experiments on plantations, when African slavery was disrupted by the long process of abolition in the Atlantic world.

COLONIAL PRECEDENTS IN LABOR RECRUITMENT BEFORE THE 1790s

Much of the colonial infrastructure of Havana was built with combinations of forced and free labor. The construction of the earliest forts to guard the port employed state- and privately owned slaves, prisoners, and free workers from the local population, Africa, and Europe.[15] By the mid-eighteenth century, as the city's strategic importance to the empire grew, the Spanish Crown subsidized Havana's defenses with Mexican silver and increasing numbers of forced laborers, both slaves and convicts, employed in defense works.

The height of the use of state slavery for Havana's defense works came immediately after the British occupation of Havana in 1762. The Spanish Crown purchased over 4,000 African slaves in the king's name to build and repair its fortifications. The costs of maintaining such a large cohort of state slaves quickly led the Crown to reduce their numbers and supplement them with more imperial prisoners, mainly those sent from Mexico to the forts of Havana as part of their sentence.[16]

Revista de Indias, 42:169–170 (1982), pp. 574–576; Luis Martínez-Fernández, "The Havana Anglo-Spanish Mixed Commission for the Suppression of the Slave Trade and Cuba's *Emancipados*", *Slavery & Abolition*, 16:2 (1995), pp. 209–213. For the experiences of liberated Africans in the British Caribbean, see Rosanne Marion Adderley, *New Negroes from Africa: Slave Trade Abolition and Free African Settlement in the Nineteenth-Century Caribbean* (Bloomington, IN, 2006).

15. De la Fuente, *Havana and the Atlantic*, pp. 5, 70–71; Reneé Méndez Capote, *Fortalezas de la Habana colonial* (Havana, 1974).

16. Jennings, "War as the 'Forcing House of Change'", pp. 411-440; Francisco Pérez Guzmán, *La Habana clave de un imperio* (Havana, 1997); Jorge L. Lizardi Pollock, "Presidios, presidiarios, y desertores: Los desterrados de Nueva España, 1777–1797", in Johanna von Grafenstein (ed.), *El Caribe en los intereses imperiales, 1750–1815* (San Juan Mixooc, 2000), pp. 20–45; Ruth Pike, "Penal Servitude in the Spanish Empire: Presidio Labor in the Eighteenth Century", *Hispanic American Historical Review*, 58:1 (1978), pp. 21–40; Christian G. De Vito, "Connected Singularities: Convict Labour in Late Colonial Spanish America (1760s–1800)", in C.G. De Vito and Anne Gerritsen (eds), *Micro-Spatial Histories of Global Labour*

The Crown's efforts to better defend Havana and wage war over the eighteenth century brought more Spanish troops to the city, increasing concerns about the disorderly behavior and desertion of military men and others.[17] Colonial officials also faced the devastation of recurring hurricanes, which damaged roads and bridges with frustrating regularity.[18] The exigencies of wartime and environmental disasters resulted in greater state intervention in infrastructure projects, particularly in the recruitment and coercion of labor. With Crown support, colonial officials expanded the definitions of vagrancy and even resorted to forced levies to keep order and complete the port's defense works during the cycles of Caribbean warfare in the late 1700s.[19]

In a series of royal orders over the eighteenth century, the Spanish Crown defined more clearly the category of vagrant and its negative connotations. A royal order from 1717 defined those who could be subject to levies of vagrants as "bad living people" with "no honor".[20] By 1745, the Crown had issued another order that expanded its definition of vagrancy and delinquency to cover all who had no trade, home, or income, and lived "not knowing from what licit and honorable means their subsistence might come".[21] The order included both the unemployed and the underemployed who did not find productive activities to occupy their time during dead seasons. The delinquent included gamblers, drunks, the sexually promiscuous or adulterous, pimps, and disobedient children. Crown officials also distinguished between "deserving" beggars, who merited compassion and charity, and "false", able-bodied beggars, who were to be prosecuted as vagrants.[22]

The metropolitan approach also revealed a growing effort to centralize the holding of captured vagrants under royal control and to harness their labor. In the 1730s and 1740s, the Crown ordered that vagrants be detained and

(New York, 2018), pp. 171–202; Jason M. Yaremko, *Indigenous Passages to Cuba, 1515–1900* (Gainesville, FL, 2016), pp. 66–79.

17. On the militarization of Cuba after 1763, see Allan J. Kuethe, *Cuba, 1753–1815: Crown, Military, and Society* (Knoxville, TN, 1986), and Johnson, *Social Transformation*.

18. On the interactions of cycles of storms and droughts with warfare and revolution in the eighteenth-century Spanish Caribbean, see Sherry Johnson, *Climate and Catastrophe in Cuba and the Atlantic World in the Age of Revolution* (Chapel Hill, NC, 2011).

19. On sweeps of Havana that netted men for Spanish ships stationed there, see Josef Solano to Juan Manuel Cagigal, 8 January 1782, and Juan Manuel Cagigal to José de Gálvez, 20 February 1782, Archivo General de Indias [hereafter, AGI], Santo Domingo [hereafter, SD], legajo [hereafter, leg.] 1234, no. 180. On the Spanish state's increasing preoccupation with vagrancy, see Rosa María Pérez Estévez, *El problema de los vagos en la España del Siglo XVIII* (Madrid, 1976), and in Cuba, Juan B. Amores, *Cuba en la época de Ezpeleta (1785–1790)* (Pamplona, 2000), pp. 117–123.

20. Royal Order, 21 July 1717, quoted in Pérez Estévez, *El problema de los vagos*, p. 61.

21. Royal Order, 30 April 1745, quoted in Pérez Estévez, *El problema de los vagos*, p. 61.

22. Pérez Estévez, *El problema de los vagos*, pp. 56–81. Similar characterizations were articulated and drove policy in late eighteenth-century Mexico. See Silvia Marina Arrom, *Containing the Poor: The Mexico City Poor House, 1774–1871* (Durham, NC, 2001), p. 23.

held in jails, sending the able-bodied among them to army service or public works. In 1775, Charles III authorized annual levies to round up vagrants, and in the later 1770s shelters were established in Madrid to hold them. In 1779, when Spain joined France to intervene in the American War of Independence, the king set the term of service at eight years for captured vagrants sent to the army. The Crown continued to publish bans against vagrants, beggars, and foreigners every few years over the next two decades.[23]

In Cuba, colonial officials employed metropolitan directives to extend their authority out from Havana into the countryside. Before 1762, the deputizing of patrols to track down enslaved fugitives and military deserters had rested with the local town governments, but this power was appropriated in moments of crisis. For example, in 1765, Captain General Ricla created a rural police and judiciary force that reported directly to him and the captains of *partidos* (districts of the interior).[24] As the Captain General's representatives in the countryside, the captains of *partidos* were charged with maintaining good order and seeing to the needs of the local population. After a terrible hurricane in 1768, Captain General Bucareli also sent out groups of soldiers to round up escapees. The king ordered that those apprehended as vagrants be employed in Crown projects or on public works, or be exiled from Havana altogether.[25]

Times of emergency allowed the colonial state to extend its power and create new corps to enforce that power. Once extended, the state rarely returned power to the localities. Still, as historian Sherry Johnson has argued, for several decades after the British occupation the governors in Havana maintained a reputation for good government, at least with the "better" classes, through their attention to the public welfare during disasters, which helped justify and control resistance to their extension of power.[26] The constant stream of desertions and reports of delinquency from the captains of *partidos* suggests that many of those pressed into military service or defense construction were less appreciative.[27]

Bucareli's successor as Captain General, the Marqués de la Torre (1771–1777), enjoyed a brief respite from warfare and was able to perfect the mechanisms of capture and deployment of a range of transgressors to

23. Luis Miguel Enciso Recio, "Prólogo", in Pérez Estévez, *El problema de los vagos*, pp. 16–17, lists bans published in Madrid on vagrants, the idle poor, and foreigners in 1783, 1786, 1789, 1790, 1791, and 1798.
24. Juan B. Amores Carredano, "Ordenanzas de gobierno local en la isla de Cuba (1765–1786)", *Revista complutense de Historia de América*, 30 (2004), pp. 95–109.
25. "San Lorenzo, 19 de Noviembre de 1769=Yo El Rey", Escoto Collection, Houghton Library, Harvard University, bMS Span 52, 858. Johnson, *Crisis and Catastrophe*, p. 88.
26. Johnson, *Crisis and Catastrophe*, ch. 4, pp. 92–122.
27. See, for example, Amores, *Cuba*, pp. 117–120, on the mid-1780s.

carry out a major program of urban renewal that included street paving in Havana and the building of bridges on thoroughfares out of the city. To stem the tide of military desertions and flight from work sites, De la Torre established both uniformed and plain-clothes (*disfrazados*) patrols to search for fugitives, centralizing some components of the apprehensions begun under his predecessors.[28] Captors notified the Captain General of an apprehension and requested reimbursement for maintenance costs, transport, and fees.[29] His office began keeping track of the deserters recaptured in 1775, reporting a total of sixty-four rounded up by the end of his term in 1777.[30] The growing size and complexity of Havana, in both its spatial and human dimensions, spurred De la Torre and his successors to expand the state's powers of coercion to control the swelling numbers of people trying to escape military service or the more restrictive norms of decent behavior, with the approval of Cuban elites.

When De la Torre turned over the reins of government to his successor Diego Navarro in 1777, he highlighted his efforts at improving policing to ensure the "tranquility and good order" of Havana and its benefits in recruiting labor for public works.[31] He claimed to have sent 8,263 people to jail in less than six years, though most spent little time behind bars because the usual punishment was to "send them to public works for more or less time according to the crime".[32] Colonial officials scrambled to find labor for fort projects in the 1760s and had looked outside Cuba for forced labor – purchasing the king's slaves in the mid-1760s – and then shifted to requesting more imperial convicts from Mexico. While De la Torre continued to use both state slaves in smaller numbers and convicts to finish defense works, he turned the state's coercive power on the island population to find labor for civil construction projects in the 1770s. His successors continued to persecute and prosecute the "vice-ridden and evilly entertained", but found diminishing returns with this policy for staffing road-building projects.

28. El Marqués de la Torre, "Apuntes de las principales providencias", Del Monte Collection, Manuscript Division, Library of Congress [hereafter, LOC] (Havana, 11 June 1777), Box 3, nos 3–4, fos 2–3.
29. See AGI, Papeles de Cuba, leg. 1153, for numerous examples.
30. "Cargos y Esculpaciones del Sr. Mqs de la Torre", Archivo Histórico Nacional [hereafter, AHN], Consejos, 20892, 2a (Havana, 25 October 1777), fo. 195.
31. For descriptions of civil projects completed during De la Torre's term in office, see Miguel Josef de Azanza, "Noticia formada de orden del Señor Marqués de la Torre, Gobernador y Capitán General de la Isla de Cuba, de los caudales que se han invertido en la Havana y sus cercanías, y de los repartimientos y arbitrios que los han producido", AHN, Consejos, 20892 6a (Havana, 12 April 1777), fos 30–36.
32. De la Torre, "Apuntes sobre las principales providencias", Del Monte Collection, Manuscript Division, LOC, Box 3, no. 4, fos 2–3.

During the years of Spain's intervention in the American War for Independence (1779–1783), the captains general of Cuba resorted to levies on the free population to recruit troops for the army and navy and laborers for defense works.[33] Many free people, both white and of color, also volunteered for militia service during the war. The end of hostilities in 1783 found much of the Cuban population exhausted after the considerable sacrifices demanded by the war effort; this complicated the search by state officials for labor to build and repair roads.

PRESSURE ON FREE PEOPLE FOR ROAD WORK

The captains general who served from the mid-1780s to the mid-1790s found free Cubans less willing than they had been in the late 1760s and 1770s to volunteer for road construction. Of particular concern were the roads and bridges to the south and east of Havana toward Güines and Matanzas, where some of the greatest sugar and coffee expansion was concentrated. Even before the revolution in Saint Domingue in 1791 opened greater opportunities for Cuban planters in the world market, sugar production had begun to grow substantially. Sugar exports through Havana doubled in the decade from 1776 to 1785, then more than doubled again between 1785 and 1800. By 1840 sugar exports from Havana had reached 26.6 million *arrobas*, an almost twelvefold increase (Table 1).

Already by the mid-1780s, colonial officials were meeting resistance in recruiting labor for road and bridge works, though some progress was made by sending out groups of coerced workers in the state's charge to the projects. Captain General Ezpeleta (1785–1790) sent numerous requests to his captains of *partidos* in the region to require local householders (*vecinos*) to give two days per week to road and bridge building and repair or to send several slaves or farmhands in their stead. He often received long reports of reasons why local *vecinos* could not or would not comply, particularly from those whose military privileges freed them from labor in public works. To advance the road projects, Ezpeleta gave the contractor in charge of the works access to a number of captured deserters, fugitive slaves, and escaped convicts. Ultimately, this infusion of forced laborers had some success in improving the road networks between Havana and the growing

---

33. For example, in 1781, Captain General Juan Manuel de Cagigal rounded up men to serve in his expedition the following year against Providence Island in the Bahamas. Antonio J. Valdés, *Historia de la Isla de Cuba, y en especial de la Habana*, 2 vols (Havana, 1813), I, p. 192. On sweeps of Havana that netted men for Spanish ships stationed there in this same period, see Josef Solano to Juan Manuel Cagigal, 8 January 1782, and Juan Manuel Cagigal to José de Gálvez, 20 February 1782, AGI, SD, leg. 1234, no. 180.

Table 1. *Sugar exported from Havana 1776–1840 in* arrobas.

Five-year intervals	Sugar exports
1776–1780	2,295,456
1781–1785	4,939,984
1786–1790	5,191,552
1791–1795	6,718,416
1796–1800	11,008,144
1801–1805	14,253,040
1806–1810	14,090,704
1811–1815	13,327,728
1816–1820	16,544,360
1821–1825	20,031,424
1826–1830	20,988,495
1831–1835	21,877,219
1836–1840	26,606,316

Sources: Pablo Tornero Tinajero, *Crecimiento económico y transformaciones sociales: esclavos, hacendados, y comerciantes en la Cuba colonial (1760–1840)* (Madrid, 1996), Appendix 3, p. 383, for 1776–1820 and 1826–1840; Von Humboldt, *Ensayo político*, p. 218, for 1821–1825.

plantation areas in the second half of the 1780s.[34] Ezpeleta's successor was not so fortunate.

In the summer of 1790, Luis de Las Casas arrived in Cuba as the new Captain General and a dedicated supporter of sugar expansion. Plantation owners sought to ensure his long-term favor by presenting Las Casas with a plantation of his own, complete with machinery and enslaved laborers.[35] One way that Las Casas sought to reward their generosity and reap the maximum benefit from his plantations was to advance the road-building projects. He had an ambitious plan to connect Havana to other Cuban ports by land, with trunk lines to the port of Matanzas to the east and Batabanó to the south, as well as roads to inland regions with essential timber and plantation products such as Güines.[36]

Las Casas began his road building program with an order in late 1790 for all able-bodied men to report for road work. Almost immediately, captains of *partidos* began reporting resistance, such as an unruly crowd in a small town southeast of Havana refusing to report for road duty. The ringleaders were sent to Havana for a personal admonishment by the Captain General, who

34. Amores, *Cuba*, pp. 405–408.
35. It was illegal for Las Casas to own plantations in his own name, so they were registered to others, but he soon purchased a second plantation that grew to be one of the largest in Cuba. Ferrer, *Freedom's Mirror*, pp. 29–31.
36. Las Casas, "Plan de Caminos", Mapas y Planos, Santo Domingo, 583, reproduced in Johnson, *Social Transformation*, p. 131.

warned them to respect the authority of their local captains of *partidos*.[37] Las Casas continued to press the captains of *partidos* to force locals to do road work, but *vecinos* claimed military privileges, illness, and even bad roads as reasons why they could not comply.[38] In short order, even the government's representatives in the countryside joined the effort to resist the Captain General's orders for free *vecinos* to perform road work. When pressed by Las Casas to produce workers, town mayors and some of the captains of *partidos* themselves responded with excuses or not at all.[39]

A severe hurricane in 1791 caused extensive loss of life and washed out bridges and roads, but further orders from Las Casas to round up the "idle" and "evilly entertained" yielded few laborers. When the Captain General ordered the captains of *partidos* to conduct censuses of their jurisdictions' population, several submitted drastically reduced numbers or tried to resign their posts. Las Casas then tried to arrest resisters, putting some in stocks as an exemplary punishment or sending them to road projects as prisoners. Ultimately, the Captain General failed to win the compliance of his underlings or the people they were supposed to recruit. By October 1796, he had admitted defeat on advancing road projects with free laborers and was recalled to Madrid.[40]

EXPERIMENTS WITH CAPTURED FUGITIVE SLAVES

Las Casas's failure to compel free people to do road work necessitated finding other groups of people with fewer ways to resist. The demographic transformation of the Havana region with the influx of thousands of enslaved Africans provided a new group that could be coerced by the state for road work. Captain General Las Casas worked with Havana-area planters through quasi-governmental organizations to advance their mutual interests in road expansion. Organizations such as the Havana Consulado brought together wealthy planters and merchants with colonial officials to foment plantation development and adjudicate commercial disputes. The Consulado also became a new vehicle through which to execute infrastructure projects.[41]

---

37. Johnson, *Social Transformation*, p. 130, describes a rowdy demonstration that turned hostile to the captain of *partido* in the town of San José de las Lajas.
38. Amores, "Ordenanzas", p. 104 ; Johnson, *Social Transformation*, p. 128.
39. Johnson, *Social Transformation*, p. 130.
40. *Ibid.*, pp. 137–145.
41. Its full title was the Real Consulado de Agricultura y Comercio de la Habana. See Peter J. Lampros, "Merchant-Planter Cooperation and Conflict: The Havana Consulado, 1794–1832" (Ph.D., Tulane University, 1980). For a report on the state of Cuba's roads and possible sources of funding for their repair, see AGI, Ultramar, leg. 170, and Nicolas Calvo y O'Farrill, "'Memoria sobre los medios que convendrá adopter para que tuviese La Havana los caminos necesarios'. Presentada al Consulado por la diputación que con este objeto nombró",

In the wake of the slave rebellion in Saint Domingue, planter members of the Consulado, Joseph Manuel de Torrontegui and Francisco Arango y Parreño, proposed to the Crown the centralization of the capture and warehousing of fugitive slaves as a necessary security measure and a remedy for the challenges of recruiting laborers for road work. Showing parallels to state policies of the previous twenty years centralizing the disposition of military deserters, Torrontegui and Arango suggested that the Consulado regulate expeditions of capture and control the disposition of fugitive slaves thereafter.[42] Their report asked the king to allow all captured fugitive slaves to be assigned to public works and to remain in that service without time limit, unless the owner came forward and could pay the costs of the slave's capture.[43] In late 1796, the king agreed and the Consulado became the major beneficiary of their labor on the island.[44]

In spite of having a reasonably low-cost group of laborers at its disposal, the Consulado was not successful in greatly expanding the road system of Cuba over the next thirty-five years. The perennial problem of torrential rains and geographically scattered sites bedeviled the Consulado's projects, such that only 25.4 kilometers were completed by 1831.[45] In contrast to the road-building projects of the 1830s and 1840s, in the expanding British Empire in Asia discussed in Clare Anderson's essay in this Special Issue, by the mid-nineteenth century the shrinking Spanish Empire did not have significant cohorts of convicts to transport to Cuba for such projects. Dramatic improvements in internal transport in Cuba had to await the construction of railroads in the late 1830s and the resort to coerced laborers from beyond the island and the empire.

Biblioteca Nacional de España [hereafter, BNE], VE 1233–14 (Havana, 1795). For the Torrontegui and Arango report see "Informe que presentó en 9 de Junio de 1796 a la Junta de Gobierno del Real Consulado de Agricultura y Comercio de esta ciudad e isla cuando examinó la mencionada Real Junta el Reglamento y Arancel de capturas de esclavos cimarrones y propuso al Rey su reforma", BNE, 5 (Havana, 1796).

42. Torrontegui and Arango, "Informe", pp. 11–14.

43. The report's authors did not think the slave owner should have to pay for the slave's maintenance when under the charge of the Consulado, only for the slave's maintenance and transport to Havana, but nor did they think that the Consulado should have to pay wages to the owners for the public labor of their slaves. *Ibid.*, p. 28.

44. The registers of the Havana Depósito, which housed the captured runaways, show almost 16,000 fugitive slaves entered there between 1797 and 1815. The Depósito program was reasonably effective in eventually returning fugitive slaves to their owners, with eighty-six per cent of the fugitives (13,801) being returned over the first eighteen years. Even though this group of laborers was not a static and permanent labor force, in a given year the Consulado had at its disposal the labor of hundreds of fugitive slaves for whom it had to pay only the cost of capture and maintenance. Gabino La Rosa Corzo, *Los cimarrones de Cuba* (Havana, 1988), p. 34.

45. *Ibid.*, p. 149.

EXPERIMENTS WITH *EMANCIPADOS*
AND CONTRACT LABORERS

The Cuban railroad-building projects of the mid-nineteenth century show well the patterns of coercion that were most successful for infrastructure building in Cuba. Unlike railroad building in other colonial settings, the main actors in organizing the first rail project included Havana-dwelling Cubans who also owned plantations outside the city. These planters used their connections in Europe and North America to find the necessary capital, technology, and skilled and unskilled labor to build the first rail line to the growing sugar area of Güines, southeast of Havana.

Though there was a growing enslaved population, high slave prices privileged their employment in the most profitable sectors of the economy. Relatively high wages in other sectors and miserable working conditions on rail projects kept most free workers from choosing labor in public works. Additionally, similar to planters in the private sector, the railroad projects' promoters had to recruit labor in a vastly different labor market from 1820 onward. Anti-slave trade treaties with Great Britain in 1817 (taking effect in 1820) and 1835 succeeded in disrupting the flow of African slaves to Cuba and raising prices. Spain abolished slavery in the metropole in 1836 and the British officially emancipated the slaves in their empire by 1838, causing Cuban slave owners to fear the eventual end of slavery on their island as well.[46] Colonial officials began to experiment with contract labor in the 1830s to ensure lower costs and sufficient work discipline to complete the first railroad line in Cuba. Their experiments with contract labor for infrastructure building were adapted to the needs of the plantation sector less than twenty years later, as legal access to enslaved workers from Africa through the transatlantic slave trade contracted by the late 1840s.

The labor force for building the first rail line out of Havana into its hinterland came to include virtually every kind of forced and free laborer ever employed in the colony. The work, similar to plantation labor, fort building, and road work, was arduous and largely unskilled labor, rarely attracting free laborers at the low wages the promoters were willing to offer. An 1837 report from the commission that oversaw the first rail project, lamented that, in Cuba, where "daily wages are so high and hands always scarce for the urgent work of agriculture, workers are not to be found".[47] From 1835 to 1838 the rail line's workforce contained some slaves owned by or housed in the Havana Depósito for runaway slaves and the nominally free Africans

---

46. David R. Murray, *Odious Commerce: Britain, Spain and the Abolition of the Cuban Slave Trade* (Cambridge, 1980), pp. 68–88; Christopher Schmidt-Nowara, *Empire and Antislavery: Spain, Cuba, and Puerto Rico, 1833–1874* (Pittsburgh, PA, 1999), pp. 14–36.
47. AHN, Ultramar, leg. 37, expediente [hereafter, exp.] 1, no. 30.

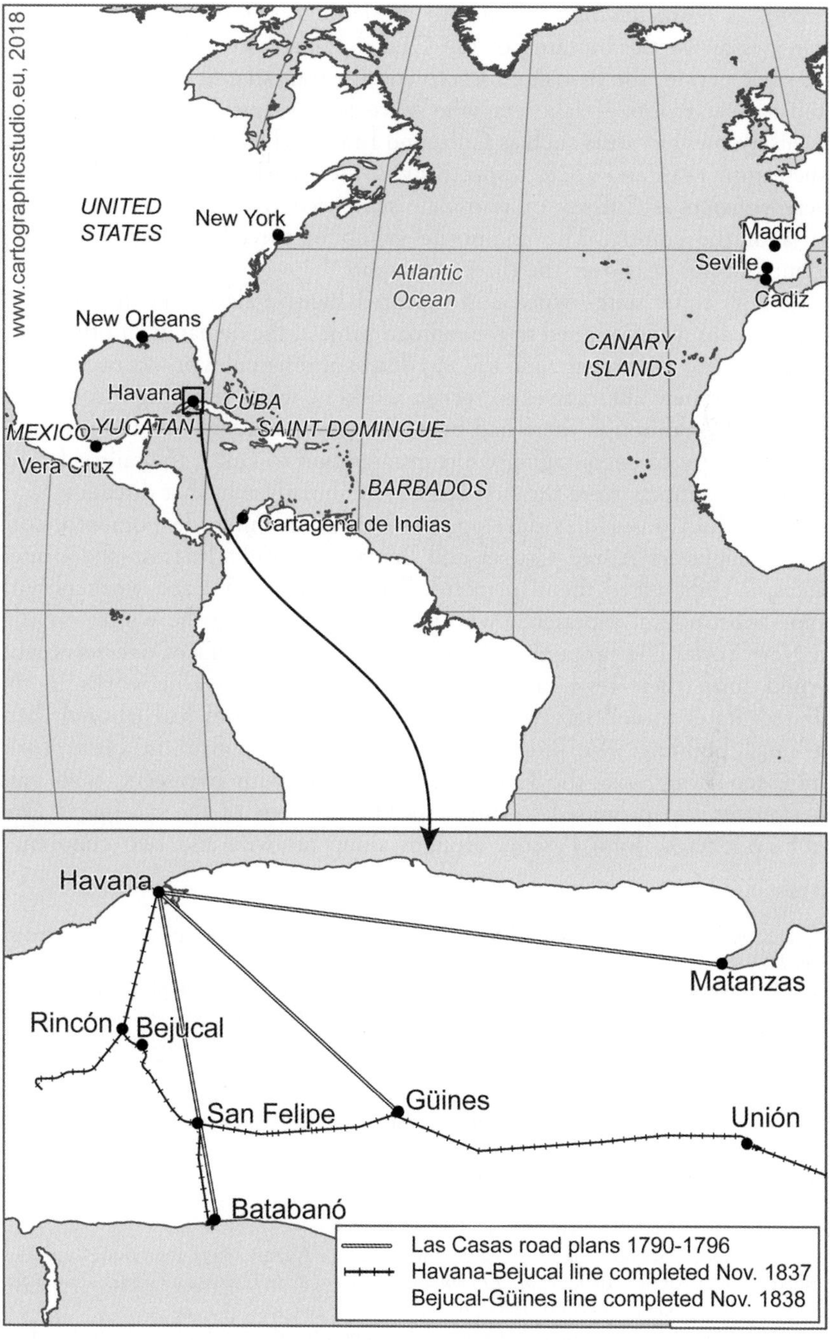

Figure 1. Roads Proposed and Rail Lines Built, Havana Region, 1790–1850.

known as *emancipados*.[48] Similar to the labor crews discussed in Martine Jean's essay on the building of the Casa de Correção in Rio de Janeiro in the same period, the British efforts to end the transatlantic slave trade generated a new group of laborers who were legally free but suffered virtual re-enslavement in areas such as Cuba and Brazil, where slavery was not abolished until 1886 and 1888, respectively. Other workers on the rail projects were convicts – Cubans or criminals sentenced to the island from other parts of the empire. The composite group of forced laborers numbered about 500 per year over the three-year span.[49]

Though some state-owned and captured fugitive slaves and hundreds of *emancipados* were assigned to the railroad project, the demands of other public works, like road repair, and the 209 deaths among rail workers necessitated a search for new alternatives to recruit workers, while retaining mechanisms of control.[50] Although there had been discussion since at least the late eighteenth century of encouraging white immigration to Cuba, the railroad commission's contracts were the first large-scale initiatives in that direction.[51]

When the Consulado's development board, the Junta de Fomento, contracted engineers Alfred Cruger and Benjamin Wright Jr. from the United States, it empowered them to recruit between 800 and 1,200 workers with some construction experience who might be idle during the winter months in New York. The Junta also allowed for the recruitment of overseers who would form their own crews. Wright used established networks in the United States to contract with workers, some of whom had labored there in canal building. Working through the Spanish consul in New York, Francisco Stoughton, the Junta made contracts with overseers, who paid their crews and promised to finish specific portions of the rail line.[52] One such contractor, John Pascoe, brought along his wife and two children.[53]

---

48. The *emancipados* were enslaved Africans freed by the terms of the anti-slave trade treaty signed by Spain and Great Britain in 1817. After 1820, any Africans illegally shipped to Spanish colonies could be seized by the British navy, then freed. In an example of creative coercion by the Spanish state, beginning in 1824 the *emancipados* were consigned to the captains general of Cuba to be allocated to private individuals for training and Christianization rather than returned to Africa and possible re-enslavement. Murray, *Odious Commerce*, pp. 271–297; Roldán de Montaud, "Origen, evolución, y supresión", pp. 574–576; Luis Martínez-Fernández, "The Havana Anglo-Spanish Mixed Commission", *Slavery & Abolition*, 16:2 (1995), pp. 209–213.
49. La Rosa Corzo, *Los cimarrones*, p. 68.
50. AHN, Ultramar, leg. 37, exp. 1, no. 30 (26 July 1837).
51. Naranjo Orovio, "La amenaza haitiana", pp. 83–178.
52. "Acuerdo. En Sesión de la Rl. Junta de fomento…" (5 August 1835), reproduced and transcribed in Berta Alfonso Ballol *et al.*, *El Camino de Hierro de la Habana a Güines: Primer ferrocarril de Iberoamérica* (Madrid, 1987), p. 78.
53. "List of Mechanicks Laborers & Overseers employed for the real Junta de Fomento of the Island of Cuba – Dispatched by brig Havre to Havana Nov 1, 1835", reproduced and transcribed in Ballol *et al.*, *El Camino de Hierro*, p. 80.

Another contractor, named Erastus Denison, was hired by the Junta because he had shown his knowledge of the "construction and use of machinery in general, in the construction of works in the water, in all branches of common works of mechanics, including steam machines and locomotives". He would be paid 110 pesos per month for at least six months, though the contract could be extended to one year.[54]

Those who contracted to go to Cuba as *peones* and *operarios* (unskilled workers) were to be paid only twenty-five pesos per month, though this wage was almost double or more than the wages offered to any of the other groups of the unskilled. Those laborers working with explosives would be offered "something more". The contracts were for six months but could be extended to one year at the discretion of their employer. The Junta would provide shelter, but all other maintenance would be at the expense of the workers. Their contracts also required them to pay back the costs of their passage and provisions for the voyage through deductions from their wages. The Junta clearly had high hopes that this white, largely Anglophone cohort would prove to be exemplary workers, with some knowledge of either canal or railroad building, at a relatively modest cost.[55]

In Cuba these contracted workers from North America were called *irlandeses*, "Irish", although there were some other nationalities in the group. There are varying estimates of the size of this group. British abolitionist David Turnbull, who visited Cuba in 1837, reported that "upwards of a thousand Irishmen" came to work on the railroad. Margaret Brehony has confirmed Turnbull's guess, estimating between 800 and 1,200 *irlandeses* in the cohort that built the Havana to Güines rail line.[56]

The *irlandeses* began arriving in November 1835. Even though their pay was high by Cuban standards, some were already heavily indebted to the Junta before leaving New York, meaning that their first few months in Cuba would have been lean indeed.[57] By spring of 1836, some of the *irlandeses* had returned home; some had deserted the railroad sites, but did not

54. "Contratas", n.d., reproduced and transcribed in Ballol *et al.*, *El Camino de Hierro*, p. 81.
55. *Ibid.* There are many parallels in the genesis, financing, management (especially the resort to contractors), and labor recruitment and exploitation between this analysis of railroad building in Cuba and canal building in North America over a similar period. See Peter Way, *Common Labour: Workers and the Digging of North American Canals, 1780–1860* (Cambridge, 1993). There were direct connections as well. Benjamin Wright was one of three head engineers on the building of the Erie Canal and other North American projects. His son, Benjamin H. Wright, recruited the first groups of *irlandeses* for the construction of the first rail line in Cuba. *Ibid.*, pp. 56–57.
56. David Turnbull, *Travels in the West: Cuba; with Notices of Porto Rico and the Slave Trade* (London, 1840), p. 190; Margaret Brehony, "Irish Migration to Cuba, 1835–1845: Empire, Ethnicity, Slavery, and 'Free' Labour" (Ph.D., National University of Ireland, Galway, 2012), p. 35.
57. Brehony, "Irish Migration to Cuba", pp. 35–36.

have the resources to book a return passage. Both the American and the British consuls received pleas from destitute workers from North America for help paying for a passport and passage back home. The American consul Nicholas Trist reported paying sixty dollars to a young woman, who had come to Cuba with her husband, to help her return via New Orleans with her two young children.[58]

The Junta decided that their resort to North American contract laborers, at least the unskilled *peones*, was too expensive and created problems even after the workers had left the rail works. The chief engineer Cruger blamed the workers themselves, angered by what he called their "drunken state", insubordination, disobedience, and complaints about low pay and work conditions. He thought any who were unhappy could go back to the US "at their own expense".[59]

The *irlandeses* were a short-lived experiment with indenture that helped advance the first railroad line only briefly and revealed some of the dangers of importing culturally alien workers who could not be subjected to the lash and shackles, as were the enslaved and prisoners. The *irlandeses* resisted through drink, disobedience, and desertion. Since the state refused to pay for their return to the US or allow them to work on their own account elsewhere, some of them appeared idle and destitute in the streets of Havana after their contracts were completed.

The Junta de Fomento initiated another experiment with contract labor within the Spanish Empire that succeeded in recruiting a similar number of workers as the North American venture, but at a lower cost and with more control. In 1835, the Junta contracted several Spanish ship captains to recruit bonded laborers in the Canary Islands for work on the rail line. One contract with Captain Nicolás Domínguez in April 1836 stipulated that the captain would be paid up to forty-five pesos for the passage and passport or license of each worker. Those contracted had to be between twenty and forty years old and "apt to be employed" in building the railroad. The workers had to agree to be employed in the rail works or on another Junta project at least long enough to pay back the costs of their passage, paying three pesos per month until the debt was cleared. They would be paid nine pesos per month and provided with shelter, food, and medical care for up to one year. Though the Canary Islanders, called *isleños* in Cuba, received some maintenance, unlike the *irlandeses*, their pay was even less than the wage offered to hired slaves. These workers also had to agree not to desert the rail works before covering the costs of their passage, under penalty of a hefty fine of twenty-four pesos, plus the cost of their

---

58. *Ibid.*, pp. 51–52.
59. Quoted in *ibid.*, p. 51.

apprehension.[60] This strategy produced the largest group of contract laborers for the first rail project, a total of 927 Canary Islanders. However, by the time the rail line opened two years later in 1837, only seven remained working on the railroad, in part due to the miserable conditions under which they labored. One hundred and fifty-six of the Canary Islanders had died, another thirty-five were incapacitated, and eighty-four had fled the rail works.[61]

Some of the Canary Islanders tried to remedy what they saw as ill treatment by complaining to authorities that they were not paid regularly and were given disgusting food. Some protested with sticks and knives about their miserable living and working conditions. In both cases their complaints were either ignored or repressed. To the charges of late pay and rotten food, the Junta countered that their contracts did not stipulate when exactly they would be paid and that the *isleños* only ate cornmeal and fish at home, so the food in Cuba was sufficient. In response to the more vigorous armed resistance, the Intendant the Count of Villanueva ordered that the protesters who were apprehended be sent back to the rail project in chains for two months.[62]

It is not surprising, therefore, that the contracted Canary Islanders suffered high rates of death and frequently tried to flee the rail works. Death and desertion among them rose to almost twenty-six per cent over two years. When added to those workers who were incapacitated, the Junta's losses rose to almost thirty per cent. The Junta was particularly concerned about desertion among the Canary Islanders, since they could easily blend into the larger Hispano-Cuban population. The Junta tried to impose high fines on anyone who might harbor a fugitive worker. Most of the *isleños* would have been fluent in Spanish and, as the Junta reported, there were "sound reasons to fear that they might desert, favored by the multitude of persons of the same origin who were well established on the island".[63]

Both schemes for white immigration from the United States and the Canaries were bedeviled by high mortality and desertion, a testimony to the difficult and unhealthy conditions under which these workers labored. Still, their work ultimately may have ensured the successful completion of the first rail line, extending opportunities for successful plantation expansion far beyond the port of Havana to the south and east.[64]

---

60. Antonio de Escovedo, "Condiciones del contrato para el embarque de operarios procedentes de Islas Canarias entre la Real Junta de Fomento y el Sr. Nicolás Domínguez, 30 April 1836", reproduced and transcribed in Ballol *et al.*, *El Camino de Hierro*, p. 84.
61. AHN, Ultramar, leg. 37, exp. 1, no. 29.
62. Violeta Serrano, *Crónicas del primer ferrocarril de Cuba* (Havana, 1973), p. 36.
63. Quoted in Oscar Zanetti and Alejandro García, *Sugar and Railroads, A Cuban History, 1837–1959*, trans Franklin W. Knight and Mary Todd (Chapel Hill, NC, 1998), p. 29; Serrano, *Crónicas*, p. 36.
64. Zanetti and García, *Sugar and Railroads*, pp. 117–118. However, according to Zanetti and García the Junta had greater success importing labor when they began bringing in Chinese contract laborers in 1847, p. 121.

By 30 June 1837, the total number of workers on the rail line was 742 men; only seven of the contracted *isleños* continued working on the railroad. Various contingents of enslaved and recently freed men of African descent remained, almost sixty-five per cent of the total workforce – eighty-seven *emancipados* diverted by the Junta from work on Havana's aqueduct, 145 of the Junta's own slaves, and between 200 and 250 of the Junta's fugitive slaves. The remaining workers were employed by the various contractors in transport of materials, stone work, and excavation, though the Junta did not keep track of their numbers or fortunes.[65]

After one year of extensive use of contract workers on the railroad project, the Junta returned to using mostly enslaved workers from among those at its disposal. Similar to the hasty purchase of large numbers of state slaves in the defense works of the 1760s, the Junta's recruitment of European, North American, and Canary Island contract workers provided the surge of coerced labor that the project needed to initiate rail construction. The costs and problems encountered with the resort to thousands of kings' slaves in the 1760s and hundreds of contract workers in the 1830s encouraged the return to employment of coerced workers whose recruitment did not involve major investments and over whom the projects' supervisors had significant control. In the case of the first rail line, slaves, some owned by the Junta and some captured in flight from their owners, came at lower cost and could be more easily controlled, due to their unfree status.

The contracting of white laborers for plantation work would not be the long-term answer to the vagaries of the illegal slave trade to Cuba. Indentured Canary Islanders, especially, could desert too easily due to their whiteness and Spanish language. Similar to other Caribbean plantation colonies in the mid-nineteenth century, Cuban elites and officials eventually turned their attention to Asia and Mexico for laborers perceived as racially different enough to provide low-cost, bound labor on plantations. Funds were invested in the immigration of *yucatecos* (largely Mayans or mestizos from the Yucatan peninsula) and Chinese as indentured laborers, whose contracts obligated them to accept wages well below the Cuban norm for both free wage earners and hired slaves.[66] The prices that planters paid to purchase their contracts were also considerably lower than the prices for African slaves; from 1845 to 1860 prices for Chinese indentures were less than half those of slaves.[67] Though the numbers of *yucatecos* imported into Cuba were small, Chinese indentured laborers arrived in much larger numbers,

65. "Cuadro del camino de hierro de la ciudad de la Habana a la villa de Güines en 30 de Junio de 1837", AHN, Ultramar, 37, exp. 1, no. 29.
66. Naranjo Orovio, "Amenaza", p. 162.
67. Lisa Yun, *The Coolie Speaks: Chinese Indentured Laborers and African Slaves in Cuba* (Philadelphia, PA, 2008), Table 1.2, p. 17.

Figure 2. Railroad Bridge over the Almendares River near Havana.
Library of Congress Prints and Photographs Division, Washington D.C., USA.

over 120,000 from 1847 to 1874.[68] Conditions for these contract workers were so terrible that the governments of their home countries ultimately curtailed their trade to Cuba.[69]

68. *Ibid.*, p. 19, Table 1.3, cites 138,156 Chinese as having embarked from China to Cuba from 1847–1873, and 121,810 who actually landed. Estimates of *yucateco* migrants imported to Cuba vary widely, from 730 to as many as 10,000, but even the highest number was small compared to African- and even Chinese-bound immigrants. See Paul Estrade, "Los colonos yucatecos como sustitutos de los esclavos negros", in Consuelo Naranjo Orovio and Tomás Mallo Gutiérrez (eds), *Cuba la perla de las Antillas: Actas de las I Jornadas sobre "Cuba y su historia"* (Madrid, 1994), p. 97. Yaremko, *Indigenous Passages*, pp. 115–118. Many were captured and sold to Cuban traders by Mexican officials during the Caste Wars in the Yucatan in the 1840s. See Nelson A. Reed, *The Caste War of Yucatán* (Stanford, CA, 2001), p. 142; Yaremko, *Indigenous Passages*, pp. 92–118, on migration, both forced and free, from the Yucatan to Cuba from the sixteenth to the nineteenth centuries.

69. For more detail on the contract laborers from Yucatan and China, see Evelyn P. Jennings, "'Some Unhappy Indians Trafficked by Force': Race, Status and Work Discipline in Mid-Nineteenth Century Cuba", in Raphael Hörmann and Gesa Mackenthun (eds), *Human Bondage in the Cultural Contact Zone* (Münster, 2010), pp. 209–225. On conditions for Chinese contract workers in Cuba, in addition to Yun, *The Coolie Speaks*, see Denise Helly, "Introduction", *The Cuba Commission Report: A Hidden History of the Chinese in Cuba* (Baltimore, MD, 1993), pp. 21–27; and the transcript of the Commission's Report.

CONCLUSION

This examination of forced labor in road and railroad construction reveals several insights about the state's use of coercion for public works to connect Havana's port with the rapidly expanding plantation sector in its hinterland. The vast majority of workers employed in infrastructure building in Cuba entered through the port of Havana as migrants under some form of coercion – enslavement, a prison term at hard labor, or, after 1800, an indenture contract. As the island's plantation boom took place parallel to the growing movement to abolish the transatlantic slave trade and slavery itself, for state officials the costs of purchasing enslaved workers rose prohibitively over much of the period from 1790–1838. State- or privately owned slaves were usually too valuable to be employed in large numbers in public works. Hence, Cuban elites and their state collaborators sought out other vulnerable groups who could be forced to do road and rail work at lower costs and under sufficient control to advance the projects.

Free householders successfully rebuffed those efforts. Convicts had little choice, but their numbers and lengths of sentence fluctuated widely. Captured fugitive slaves rarely provided years of labor for public projects, because they were often in poor health when captured and their owners were likely to reclaim them. State officials and Cuban planters had more success, forcing the unfortunate *emancipados* into both public works and plantation labor, because the anti-slave trade treaties allowed Cuban captains general to consign them for years of coerced labor, in spite of their nominally free status.

Ultimately, contract laborers provided the mix of low cost and unfreedom that both planters and state officials desired, after some experimentation. Unlike free workers, contract laborers' resistance or desertion could result in arrest and return to work as a convict, but the racial hierarchy of a plantation society set both state and private employers' expectations for necessary subservience. "Irish" workers, whose whiteness was initially seen as an asset, were ultimately deemed too disobedient and their recruitment was abandoned. Canary Islanders were white and Hispanophone and therefore too likely to successfully flee work sites.

These problems were outweighed in the short term as the contracted labor of North Americans and Europeans was the supplement to other forms of forced labor needed to establish the first rail connection between Havana's port and growing plantations to the south and east. However, after 1838, both planters and colonial officials sought a new group of racially and culturally different contract workers, especially from China, to supplement enslavement on plantations and on rail lines, as the fate of slavery in the Atlantic world became more uncertain. The railroad promoters' problems and losses with white contract workers in the early 1830s led Cuban Captain General Alcoy in 1849 to petition the Crown for permission to use the tools of enslavement to control contracted workers from Yucatan and China – "the whip, shackles, and stocks". Queen Isabella II agreed that such control was essential because without them "the subordination of the African race so indispensable for the tranquility of [Cuba] would be altered".[70] The experiments with white contract workers showed state officials and planters that coerced labor without the controls allowed by enslavement were too risky in Cuba once the sugar boom and slavery dominated the island's economy and society.

70. Captain General Alcoy to Minister of Governance, 25 April 1849, in *Colonos yucatecos en Cuba*, MSS/13857, 1848–1849, 15–19ff. and 33f., BNE, Madrid, Spain.

IRSH 64 (2019), pp. 173–204 doi:10.1017/S0020859019000105
© 2019 Internationaal Instituut voor Sociale Geschiedenis

Liberated Africans, Slaves, and Convict Labor in the Construction of Rio de Janeiro's Casa de Correção: Atlantic Labor Regimes and Confinement in Brazil's Port City*

MARTINE JEAN

Weatherhead Research Cluster on Global Transformations
1727 Cambridge Street, Cambridge, MA 02138, USA

E-mail: mjean@wcfia.harvard.edu

ABSTRACT: From 1834 to 1850, Latin America's first penitentiary, the Casa de Correção in Rio de Janeiro, was a construction site where slaves, "liberated Africans", convicts, and unfree workers interacted daily, forged identities, and deployed resistance strategies against the pressures of confinement and the demands of Brazil's eclectic labor regimes. This article examines the utilization of this motley crew of workers, the interactions among "liberated Africans", slaves, and convict laborers, and the government's intervention between 1848 and 1850 to restrict slave labor at the prison in favor of free waged workers. It asserts that the abolition of the slave trade in 1850 and the subsequent inauguration of the penitentiary augured profound changes in Rio's labor landscape, from a predominantly unfree to a free wage labor force.

In his 1849 annual report to the Brazilian parliament, Justice Minister Eusébio de Queiroz Mattoso da Camara observed that most of the workers employed in the construction of Rio de Janeiro's penitentiary, the Casa de Correção, were slaves, and he concluded that it would be less expensive for the government to hire free laborers to complete it. Queiroz's main concern was that, after nearly sixteen years of construction, the Casa de Correção was only halfway done. Only one of its planned four pavilions was near completion. Meanwhile, Rio's civil jail, the Aljube, stood as a "shameful anachronism" in the Brazilian capital, where convicted criminals

---

* I am grateful to the editors and contributing authors of this Special Issue. I would also like to thank the participants and organizers of the "Free and Unfree Labor in Atlantic and Indian Ocean Port Cities (c.1700–1850)" conference and workshop held at the University of Pittsburgh in May 2016 and May 2017.

shared cells with other detainees awaiting formal arraignment.[1] Queiroz emphasized the necessity to inaugurate the penitentiary to modernize Rio's penal system.

This article analyzes the utilization of a motley crew of slaves, convicts, liberated Africans, and free laborers to build the Casa de Correção between 1833 and 1850. It probes a crucial nexus point centered on Rio's significance as Brazil's preeminent commercial port city, where transformations in the labor regimes of the Atlantic from unfree to free labor reverberated. It argues that the deployment of slaves, convicts, liberated Africans, and unfree workers to build the Casa de Correção demonstrates that until the first half of the nineteenth century the boundaries between free and unfree labor were very porous in the Brazilian capital. The significance of slaves in the city's population and the availability of pauperized legally free workers allowed the authorities to constantly combine free and unfree laborers to clean Rio's streets and to build public infrastructures associated with social control and progress, such as repairing public fountains, aqueducts, and the seawall in the harbor. The permutation of labor arrangements in public works allowed legally free and enslaved laborers to interact daily in the capital. The abolition of the slave trade in 1850 engendered a politics to transform the Casa de Correção into a site for re-articulating the geography of free and unfree labor in Rio through a hardening of the distinctions between salaried slaves and legally free wage workers. Brazilian authorities intervened over time to restrict bonded labor to plantation agriculture and maintained various forms of free and unfree labor, including contract labor, apprenticeship, and prison reformatory work, on Brazil's coastline, particularly in Rio, the capital.

The penitentiary belongs to Brazil's postcolonial nation-building process, which rested on concretizing the country's aspiration to modernity through prison reforms and engendering a law-abiding free working-class citizenry to abate the dependency on slave labor.[2] In this way, Brazil participated in two interrelated ideological shifts in the Atlantic World that restricted freedom for unruly and criminal social elements of the poor through confinement

---

1. Brasil, *Relatório do ministério da justiça do anno 1849, 1A apresentado a assembléa geral legislativa na 1era sessão da 8a legislativa em 1850* (Rio de Janeiro, 1850), pp. 50–53.
2. Carlos Aguirre, "Prisons and Prisoners in Modernising Latin America (1800–1940)", in Frank Dikötter and Ian Brown (eds), *Cultures of Confinement: A History of the Prison in Africa, Asia, and Latin America* (Ithaca, NY, 2007), pp. 14–54. Ricardo D. Salvatore and Carlos Aguirre, "The Birth of the Penitentiary in Latin America: Toward an Interpretive Social History of Prisons", in Ricardo D. Salvatore and Carlos Aguirre (eds), *The Birth of the Penitentiary in Latin America: Essays on Criminology, Prison Reform, and Social Control, 1830–1940* (Austin, TX, 1996), pp. 1–43; Martine Jean, "'A Storehouse of Prisoners': Rio de Janeiro's Correction House (Casa de Correção and the Birth of the Penitentiary in Brazil, 1830–1906", *Atlantic Studies: Global Currents*, 14:2 (2017), pp. 216–242.

while advocating the gradual abolition of slavery.[3] As Clare Anderson's contribution to this Special Issue argues, the abolition of slavery in the Atlantic engendered the spread of penal transportation and convictism in the Indian Ocean as part of the "circuit of repression and coerced labor extraction" that defined the global economy.[4] That Brazil was a major recipient of African slaves through the traffic rendered its reception and implementation of penal reform ideas and anti-slavery problematic. Brazilian port cities, foremost Rio de Janeiro, became the experimenting ground for the deployment of these concepts because of their significance as international ports of trade and urban centers with a cosmopolitan working class that included African slaves, free people of color, and sailors of multinational origins, foreign immigrants, soldiers, and skilled artisans. Rio shared this pattern with other port cities in the Americas and seaports in the Atlantic and Indian Ocean.[5]

As an Atlantic port city, Rio de Janeiro connected Brazil's hinterland with commercial networks that integrated the African coast to the Americas through the slave trade and to Europe through export-driven agriculture (Figure 1). The city was in the center of the transformation of slavery in the Atlantic, a process that Dale Tomich conceptualized as a Second Slavery, evidenced by its "partial relocation" and the "invention of new forms of unfree labor" that saw the institution gaining ground in Brazil, Cuba, and the US South while disintegrating in the British and French Caribbean in the nineteenth century.[6] Between 1831 and 1855, an estimated 718,000 slaves entered Brazil, or equivalent to twenty per cent of the total slave traffic during its three centuries of existence.[7] The majority of the

3. On anti-slavery and the penitentiary, see Diana Paton, *No Bond But the Law: Punishment, Race, and Gender in Jamaican State Formation, 1780–1870* (Durham, NC, 2004), p. 5; David B. Davis, *The Problem of Slavery in the Age of Revolution, 1770–1823* (Ithaca, NY, 1975), p. 242; Melanie Newton, "Freedom's Prisons: Incarceration, Emancipation, and Modernity", in *No Bond But the Law*", *Small Axe*, 15:1 (2011), pp. 164–175; Thomas Holt, *The Problem of Freedom: Race, Labor, and Politics in Jamaica and Britain, 1832–1938* (Baltimore, MD, 1992), pp. 21–53; Peter Beattie, *Punishment in Paradise: Race, Slavery, Human Rights, and a Nineteenth-Century Brazilian Penal Colony* (Durham, NC, 2015), pp. 200–226.
4. See Clare Anderson, "Convicts, Commodities, and Connections", abstract, in this Special Issue.
5. David Montgomery, "The Working Classes of the Pre-Industrial American City, 1780–1830", *Labor History*, 9:1 (1968), pp. 3–22; Seth Rockman, *Scraping By: Wage Labor, Slavery, and Survival in Early Baltimore* (Baltimore, MD, 2009).
6. Dale W. Tomich, *Through the Prism of Slavery: Labor, Capital, and World Economy* (Lanham, MD, 2004), pp. 56–71; Rafael de Bivar Marquese and Tâmis Peixoto Parron, "Internacional escravista: a política da segunda Escravidão", *Topoi*, 12 (July–December 2011), pp 97–117; Sidney Chalhoub, "The Politics of Ambiguity: Conditional Manumission, Labor Contracts, and Slave Emancipation in Brazil (1850s–1888)", *International Review of Social History*, 60:2 (2015), pp. 161–162.
7. See: http://www.slavevoyages.org/estimates/zbsnLoVK; last accessed 26 October 2018; Joseph C. Miller, *Way of Death: Merchant Capitalism and the Angolan Slave Trade, 1730–1830* (Madison, WI, 1988), pp. 455–458; Roquinaldo do Amaral, "Brasil e Angola no tráfico

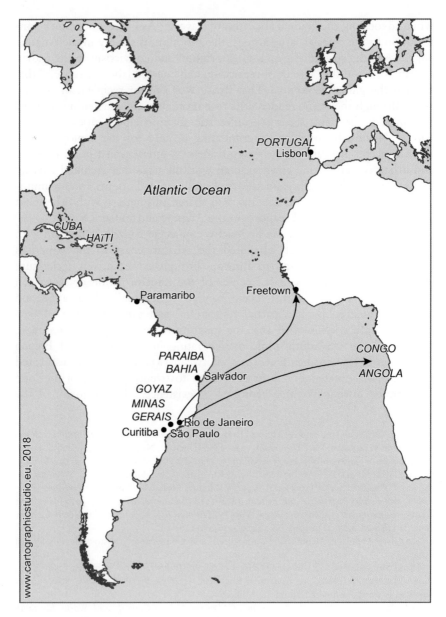

Figure 1. Some of the major port cities with which Rio de Janeiro was linked in the nineteenth century through the slave trade and commerce in colonial products.

ilegal de escravos, 1830–1860", in José Flávio Sombra Saraiva (ed.), *Angola e Brasil nas rotas do Atlântico Sul* (Rio de Janeiro, 1999), pp. 143–193.

enslaved were destined to work in the prosperous coffee plantations of Brazil's central-south region, notably the Vale do Paraiba, or Paraiba Valley. The increased volume of the traffic through Rio transformed the city demographically, but also created a local economy around the port that provided the goods and services that transient sailors depended upon for survival. As Melina Teubner's contribution to this Special Issue highlights, food-selling women played an important role in the informal economy around Rio's port by feeding the multitude of workers, sailors, waged slaves, and fugitives who worked in the city or aboard the slave ships that tied Rio to other domestic seaports, the African coast, and Europe. Mule traders from Rio's hinterland depended on street commerce to sustain them while passing through the capital.[8] Police surveillance was particularly necessary to control the circulation of slaves and freedmen in the city, and the availability of prisons was a fundamental aspect of regulating Rio's economic and social life.[9] Following the abolition of the traffic in 1850, the internal slave trade relocated slaves from north-eastern sugar plantations to the coffee economy of the central-south region. Rio served as an important corridor from whence these slaves were distributed to the Paraiba Valley.[10]

The Casa de Correção was fundamental in regulating this process, whether through the imprisonment and flogging of fugitive slaves, the custody of enslaved men and women in the process of being sold out of the city, or the detention of vagrants and beggars who challenged the new geography of labor unfolding.[11] Most of Rio's slaves originated from Angola and the Congo in the nineteenth-century and the Casa de Correção housed a microcosm of that population as a result of the prohibition of the illegal slave trade. In early July 1834, the Casa de Correção received 249 emancipated Africans from the *Duquesa de Bragança*, and 118 liberated Africans from the *Patacho Santo Antonio*, two vessels which were condemned in July 1834. The police

8. Melina Teubner, "Street Food, Urban Space, and Gender", in this Special Issue; for a comparative study of food selling in Brazil's seaport, see Richard Graham, *Feeding the City: From Street Market to Liberal Reform in Salvador, Brazil, 1780–1860* (Austin, TX, 2010).

9. Leila Mezan Algranti, "Slave Crimes: The Use of Police Power to Control the Slave Population of Rio de Janeiro", *Luso-Brazilian Review*, 25:1 (1988), pp. 27–48; Thomas Holloway, *Policing Rio de Janeiro: Repression and Resistance in a 19th-Century City* (Stanford, CA, 1993).

10. Robert Slenes, "The Brazilian Internal Slave Trade, 1850–1888: Regional Economies, Slave Experience, and the Politics of a Peculiar Market", in Walter Johnson (ed.), *The Chattel Principle: Internal Slave Trades in the Americas* (New Haven, CT, 2004), pp. 325–370; Herbert Klein, "The Internal Slave Trade in Nineteenth-Century Brazil: A Study of Slave Importations into Rio de Janeiro in 1852", *Hispanic American Historical Review*, 51:4 (1971), pp. 567–585.

11. Tom Brass and Marcel van der Linden (eds), *Free and Unfree Labour: The Debate Continues* (New York, 1997); Marcel van der Linden, *Workers of the World: Essays Toward a Global Labor History* (Leiden, 2008).

also sent illegally enslaved Africans from land seizures to the prison. Slaves aboard the *Santo Antonio* were all identified as from Gabon in Congo while the *Duquesa de Bragança*'s Africans were a mixed ethnicity from Benguella and Angola. As a result, the Africans did not experience their confinement aboard the ship and the Casa de Correção in isolation, and could converse among themselves and with other slaves.

THE POLITICS OF BUILDING THE PENITENTIARY IN POSTCOLONIAL BRAZIL

The impetus to build the Casa de Correção originated from Brazil's independence from Portugal in 1822 under a constitutional monarchy, followed by the adoption of a criminal code in 1830. The code called for prisons to be "hygienic, secure, and well-organized", and established confinement as punishment for most crimes through "prison with work", "simple imprisonment", and *galés*, or hard labor in public works in fetters (Figure 2).[12] "Prison with work" reflected the influence of liberal penal ideas, which hinged on the view that confinement was a site to reform criminals through compulsory labor and silence. Through its adoption, Brazil embraced a positive view of work as having the capacity to reform criminals into citizens.

Subsequent decrees and police regulations empowered local justices of the peace to investigate and issue sentences for "public crimes" such as vagrancy and the unlicensed carrying of pistols, daggers, and other perforating instruments. Participating in riots or the illegal assembly of groups of five or more could lead to a "prison with work" sentence of one to six months.[13] Justices of the peace such as João José da Cunha of the Sacramento district utilized this new authority to call on lawful citizens to aid the police to identify "vagrants and idlers" who had broken into various houses of the parish in 1832.[14] A year earlier, in 1831, a deputy justice of the peace calmed the public about the lack of repression against vagrants by assuring them that he had recently sentenced "eleven vagrants to 24 days of prison with labor" at the navy yard. He had also previously sent ten individuals to the army arsenal after they "approached him alleging that they could not find an occupation".[15] "Prison with labor" sentences were applied to convicts who disturbed the peace, constituted a threat to private property, and committed

12. Evaristo de Morães, *Prisões e instituições penitenciarias no Brasil* (Rio de Janeiro, 1923), pp. 1–15; on Brazilian liberalism, see Thomas Flory, *Judge and Jury in Imperial Brazil, 1808–1871: Social Control and Political Stability in the New State* (Austin, TX, 1981), pp. 50–64.
13. See Law of 26 October 1831, published in *Diário do Rio de Janeiro*, 3 November 1831.
14. Juiz de Paz, João José da Cunha, Freguesia do Sacramento, 28 February 1832, in *Diário do Rio de Janeiro*, 29 February 1832.
15. Juiz de Paz, Saturnino de Souza e Oliveira, 6 August 1831, in *Diário do Rio de Janeiro*, 8 August 1831.

Figure 2. T. Hunt, "Criminals Carrying Provisions to the Prison", London, 1822.
*Biblioteca Nacional, Rio de Janeiro, available at: http://acervo.bndigital.bn.br/sophia/index.asp?
codigo_sophia=2807; last accessed 26 October 2018.*

homicide. They were individuals of free legal status in Brazilian society. For example, José Antonio da Conceição, born in Lisbon, was punished with two years and a month of "prison with labor" in 1838 for stealing slaves.[16] By contrast, Joaquim Mina, a West African slave from the Mina coast, was sentenced to 400 lashes for a similar offence.[17]

Before the completion of the penitentiary, individuals who were sentenced to "prison with work" joined the pool of unfree workers whose labor power was utilized by public institutions in small- and large-scale work associated with modernizing the city, such as road building, constructing the seawall at Snakes Island, or repairing municipal fountains. The ethnic and racial profile of this dangerous class reflected Rio's importance as an international port city with slave and legally free workers of color as well as European

16. Jury Tribunal, extraordinary session of April 1838, in *Diário do Rio de Janeiro*, 25 May 1838.
17. Jury Tribunal, session of 31 January 1838, in *Diário do Rio de Janeiro*, 5 February 1838; in prison records and other official sources, slaves' "surnames" were attributed based on their African or Brazilian ancestry, which also indicated their place of birth or port of purchase, color, status, and provincial origins at times. See Mary Karasch, *Slave Life in Rio de Janeiro, 1808–1850* (Princeton, NJ, 1987), pp. 3–28.

immigrants. In late December 1833, a group of prisoners who escaped from their work site at the navy arsenal with the help of a prison guard included three Brazilians, a freed person of color – *pardo* – chastised with hard labor in perpetuity for murder, two other *pardos* – one an ex-soldier convicted of desertion and another sentenced for robbery – and a thirty-six-year-old Prussian skilled in saddlery who was sentenced to "prison with labor". They were all reduced to unfreedom, despite their differing legal status outside of confinement and coerced labor.

Hard-labor sentences were designed to chastise slave criminals, especially those who committed mastercide or fomented rebellion.[18] *Galés* – hard labor in public works in fetters – also applied to free people who committed property crimes such as slave thefts and counterfeiting, activities which attacked the economic basis of society. In 1833, a list of *galé* convicts who had completed their sentences included three free individuals, one of whom was punished for theft. Another convict was chastised with two years of *galés* for stealing slaves, while the last one was punished to four years of hard labor for highway robbery.[19] In February 1834, from among ten *galé* convicts who had escaped from the dungeon at Snakes Island, four were white, including two Portuguese immigrants, two were *pardos*, and one of the fugitives was a West Central African slave named João Benguella, who had been condemned to ten years of forced labor at the dike for homicide.[20] The convicts originated from the north-east and south-east of Brazil. Soldiers like Manoel Gomes Pimenta, a white man from north-east Brazil, and Paulino dos Santos, a free person of color from Rio, often found themselves among *galé* convicts for desertion and insubordination in the army or the navy, which were important social control institutions that thrived on the recruitment of coerced workers, especially free people of color.[21] *Galé* inmates were therefore a heterogeneous group that included mostly slaves but also some free offenders. They included Brazilian, European, and

---

18. João Luiz Ribeiro, *"No meio das galinhas as baratas não têm razão": a lei de 10 de junho de 1835, os escravos e a pena de morte no império Brasileiro* (Rio de Janeiro, 2005), pp. 22–38; Alexandra K. Brown, "'A Black Mark on Our Legislation': Slavery, Punishment, and the Politics of Death in Nineteenth-Century Brazil", *Luso-Brazilian Review*, 37:2 (2000), pp. 95–121; Peter Beattie, "'Born Under the Cruel Rigor of Captivity, the Supplicant Left it Unexpectedly by Committing a Crime'": Categorizing and Punishing Slave Convicts in Brazil, 1830–1897", *The Americas*, 66:1 (2009), pp. 11–55.

19. *Correio Official*, 30 October 1833.

20. "Repartição da Polícia", in *Correio Official*, 24 February 1834.

21. Peter Beattie, "Conscription Versus Penal Servitude: Army Reform's Influence on the Brazilian State's Management of Social Control, 1870–1930", *Journal of Social History*, 32:4 (1999), pp. 847–878; Zachary R. Morgan, *Legacy of the Lash: Race and Corporal Punishment in the Brazilian Navy and the Atlantic World* (Bloomington, IN, 2014), pp. 50–52; Patricia Ann Aufderheide, "Order and Violence: Social Deviance and Social Control in Brazil, 1780–1840" (Ph.D. dissertation, University of Minnesota, 1975), pp. 14–19; see Megan Thomas's contribution on military labor in the Special Issue.

African-born, as well as legally enslaved and free persons. Convicts worked manacled to one another at their ankle or neck, which was the condition under which chained gangs of slaves carried water to various venues in Rio. If one were not a slave, to be chastised to *galés* and to "prison with work" before the advent of the penitentiary constituted a reduction to the status of a judicial slave.

URBAN SLAVERY AND PRISON LABOR IN NINETEENTH-CENTURY RIO

The prison population reflected Rio's multi-ethnic inhabitants and its significance as Brazil's preeminent commercial seaport in the nineteenth century. With a significant urban slave population and an extensive harbor that linked its agrarian hinterland to European commercial centers and the African Slave Coast, Rio was a city marked by the interaction of slave and free workers. As other port cities in the Atlantic and Indian Ocean, Rio had been "a crucial component of European expansion" since the sixteenth century and a "fulcrum of European activity" by the nineteenth century.[22] Its economic life depended on the manual labor performed by thousands of Brazilian and African slaves, enslaved female domestic workers, laundresses, cooks, sailors, Portuguese cashiers, porters as well as white civil servants, impoverished policemen, and soldiers.

Rio became a center of the Lusophone Empire between 1763 and 1808, when gold and diamond mines were discovered in its interior and the Portuguese crown relocated to Brazil. Thousands of impoverished Portuguese immigrants and Brazilian north-easterners flocked to the mining region through Rio's harbor.[23] The volume of the traffic increased, resulting in the slave population as a proportion of the total population increasing from 34.6 per cent in 1799 to 45.6 per cent in 1821 (Table 1). Fifty per cent of enslaved Africans sold to Brazil between 1808 and 1821 passed through Rio's port.[24] In 1808, an estimated 15,000 Portuguese courtiers migrated to the city, which created a housing crisis and a boom in construction. The crown liberated Rio's port for free trade, leading to hundreds of British commercial agents establishing residences in the city, along with Frenchmen and Germans. French tailors owned fashionable boutiques on

22. Franklin Knight and Peggy Liss (eds), *Atlantic Port Cities: Economy, Culture, and Society in the Atlantic World, 1650–1850* (Knoxville, TN, 1991), pp. 1–7.
23. A.J.R. Russell-Wood, "Ports of Colonial Brazil", in *ibid.*, p. 201; Mary Karasch, "Rio de Janeiro: From Colonial Town to Imperial Capital (1808–1850)", in Robert J. Ross and Gerard J. Telkamp (eds), *Colonial Cities: Essays on Urbanism in a Colonial Context* (Dordrecht, 1985), pp. 139–141.
24. Karasch, "Rio de Janeiro: From Colonial Town to Imperial Capital", pp. 139–141.

Table 1. *Composition of the population of Rio de Janeiro, 1799–1849 (%).*

	1799	1821*	1834*	1838*	1849
Slaves	34.6	45.6	44.4	38.2	38.3
Free	45.1	54.4	33.8	52.3	38.9
Free people of color	20.3	–	14.9	–	5.2
Foreigners	–	–	6.9	9.5	17.6

Sources: Karasch, *Slave Life in Rio de Janeiro*, pp. 62–66, and Yedda Linhares and Barbara Lévy, "Aspectors da história demográfica e social do Rio de Janeiro (1808–1889)", in *L'Histoire Quantitative du Brésil de 1800 à 1930. Colloques Internationaux du Centre National de la Recherche Scientifique*, no. 543 (Paris, 1973), pp. 128–130. The 1821 censuses included free people and freed persons as a single group. The 1834 and 1838 censuses undercounted the city's slave population as well as the number of foreigners.

Ouvidor Street. Portuguese artisans and small businessmen established their shops in St Peter's Street.[25] Much more diluted in the population were the Germans, Chinese, Prussians, South Americans, and North Americans who passed through the city. Foreigners represented 9.5 per cent of the city's population by 1838, which undercounted their presence in the city. Historian Mary Karasch estimated that Rio's slaves likely represented 56.7 per cent of the city's total population in 1834 and 51.6 per cent in 1838 based on studies of estimated numbers of slaves owned per household.[26] The drop in the slave population in 1849 reflected the increase in the number of European immigrants in the city. The city's diverse population was well represented in jail records, and after 1850 the number of foreigners in the central police station jail regularly surpassed the number of Brazilian nationals there.[27]

Rio's slaves operated in a wage labor market that was inserted in a slave society. There were two kinds of wage-earning slaves in the city: slaves-for-hire – *escravos ao ganho* – who, in agreement with their owner, sold their services after fulfilling their obligation to their masters, to whom they paid an agreed portion of their earnings, and leased slaves – *escravo de aluguel* – whose services were rented out by their owners to an

25. Zephyr Frank, "Layers, Flows and Intersections: Jeronymo José de Mello and Artisan Life in Rio de Janeiro, 1840s–1880s", *Journal of Social History*, 41:2 (2007), pp. 307–328.
26. Karasch, *Slave Life in Rio de Janeiro*, p. 61. The author estimated that there were 3.6 slaves owned per household.
27. Criminal statistics became more organized after 1850. For example, in 1857–1858, of 6,495 detainees admitted to the city jail, 4,956 were foreigners; see the annual reports of Chief of Police of Rio de Janeiro published in the annex to Brasil, *Relatório do ministério da justiça*, 1825–1928, available at: http://ddsnext.crl.edu/brazil; last accessed 26 October 2018.

employer.[28] Slaves-for-hire worked on short-term commissions and exerted more control over their meager earnings, while leased slaves did not directly participate in the exchange between their employers and their owner. Slaves toiled as seamstresses, porters, peddlers, barbers, carpenters, masons, and were the bedrock of Rio's economic life. Many leased slaves were owned or hired by foreign skilled artisans, who possessed twenty per cent of the city's slave population.[29] Rio's slaves were ethnically diverse and divided between Brazilian-born slaves known as *Crioulo* and African-born slaves, who represented sixty-five per cent of the urban slave population. The majority originated from West Central Africa.[30]

Rio also disposed of a substantial free poor class who constituted a "reserve labor force".[31] They were a subset of the "Atlantic proletariat", which were temporarily employed and often did the work of slaves.[32] The city's free poor were manumitted slaves, mixed-race descendants of Portuguese and Africans, and poor Portuguese immigrants. In a racially stratified society where landownership and slaveholding were markers of wealth and status, the free poor, especially those who did not possess at least one slave, remained on the margins of society.[33] Liberal reformers identified them as the object of penal discipline to engender a law-abiding working class. Known as the *desprotegidos* or the dishonorable poor, they were targeted by the police for recruitment in the navy and army for vagrancy and disorder because of their vulnerable position in the social hierarchy that unfolded from an economy based on slave labor. This was part of the apparatus of security and racialization that characterized port cities, as Brandon has argued in his studies on Paramaribo.[34]

In 1833, sixty *galé* convicts were relocated from the São José fortress at Snakes Island to Catumby to work on the construction of the Casa de Correção. Given the racial, ethnic, regional, and national diversity of convicts

---

28. Leila Mezan Algranti, *O Feitor Ausente: Estudos Sobre a Escravidão Urbana No Rio de Janeiro, 1808–1822* (Rio de Janeiro, 1988), pp. 40–55; Luis Carlos Soares, "Urban Slavery in Nineteenth-Century Rio de Janeiro" (Ph.D. dissertation, University of London, 1988); Luis Felipe de Alencastro, "Prolétaires et Esclaves: Immigrés Portugais et Captifs Africains a Rio de Janeiro, 1850–1872", *Cahiers Du CRIAR*, 4 (1984), pp. 127–137.
29. Frank, "Layers, Flows and Intersections", p. 318.
30. Karasch, *Slave Life in Rio de Janeiro*, pp. 65–66.
31. Algranti, "Slave Crimes", pp. 27–48.
32. Peter Linebaugh and Marcus Rediker, *The Many-Headed Hydra: Sailors, Slaves, Commoners, and the Hidden History of the Revolutionary Atlantic* (Boston, MA, 2000); Van der Linden, *Workers of the World*.
33. Karasch, "Rio de Janeiro: From Colonial Town to Imperial Capital", p. 143.
34. Holloway, *Policing Rio de Janeiro*, pp. 7–9; Algranti, "Slave Crimes", pp. 31–32; Aufderheide, "Order and Deviance", pp. 14–19; Morgan, *Legacy of the Lash*, pp. 50–53; Peter Beattie, *The Tribute of Blood: Army, Honor, Race, and Nation in Brazil, 1864–1945* (Durham, NC, 2001); Pepijn Brandon, "Between the Plantation and the Port", in this Special Issue.

in the 1830s, the sixty convicts were probably a very heterogeneous group that included mostly slaves but also free people of color, poor white Brazilians, and foreigners.[35] In the following years, they were joined by prisoners from other worksites. In February 1834, the Director of the Navy Arsenal dispatched convict José da Silva to be employed "in the construction of the Casa de Correção".[36] It is quite possible that the official was disposing of a troublesome inmate by relocating da Silva from the navy yard in Rio's harbor to Catumby, which was situated at the edge of the city. The convicts would have walked for one hour, chained to one another and under heavy supervision, from the harbor to Catumby. The government had purchased a farm in Catumby that included a two-storied house that served as a jail for the convicts. Catumby was selected owing to its relative distance from the city center and its location at the foot of a hill – Catumby Mountain – which the authorities believed would provide the stone and gravel to build the prison.[37]

The utilization of enslaved and legally free prisoners to build the Casa de Correção strategically relocated convicts from Rio's commercial and artisan-owned shop area, where they routinely evaded their dungeons, to the rustic Catumby region. Rio's prisons were notoriously overcrowded and *galé* convicts were kept aboard hulks in the city's harbor. Aside from the dungeon at Snakes Island and the prison ships, there were three other main jails in the capital: the Aljube, a civil prison; the Calabouço, a dungeon for slaves in custody; and a reformed prison on Santa Barbara Island (Figure 3).

The city's prisons were entrenched in its export economy and in the web of power relations and a social hierarchy that was deeply connected to the plantation and mining economy of its hinterland. Snakes Island, where a dungeon filled with *galé* convicts was located, served as a station for commercial boats and the prison-hulks.[38] The Calabouço was situated in a fortress atop Castello Hill at the entrance to the city. The Aljube was imbedded in Rio's slave market in Santa Rita parish in the Valongo, where African slaves first set foot on land after the traumatic voyage across the Atlantic. The Aljube was located in the center of Rio's slave markets, which until 1831 was at Praia do Valongo. The streets and alleys that spread from the harbor were under close police surveillance because of the economic activities that abounded around the port. Before the construction of the Casa de Correção (in Rua do Conde, Catumby Hill on the map, Figure 3) prisoners were held at the Aljube, the Calabouço, the São José Fortress at Snakes

35. Brasil, *Relatório do ministério da justiça do anno 1833* (Rio de Janeiro, 1834), pp. 18–19.
36. *Correio Official*, 23 February 1834, vol. 48.
37. Brasil, *Relatório do anno 1833*, p. 19.
38. J.B. Debret, *Voyage Pittoresque et historique au Brésil, ou Séjour d'un Artiste Français au Brésil, depuis 1816 jusqu'en 1831 inclusivement*, 3 vols (Paris, 1834–1839), II, p. 30.

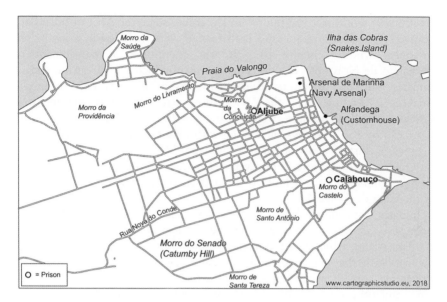

Figure 3. The evolution of Rio de Janeiro from the port region towards its hinterland, with the location of various prison sites.

Island, and the Santa Barbara jail located in the Santa Barbara island off of the Morro da Saúde. The Navy Arsenal near the customhouse was an important cog in the carceral ring around the port because of its use of conscripted labor, mostly free people of color and liberated Africans. In the 1830s, there were at least two prison hulks – *pressiganga* – filled with *galé* convicts, named the *Animo Grande* and the *Não Pedro II*. Although the traffic had been abolished in 1831, there were still warehouses in the Valongo where enslaved African men, women, and children were stored before they were sold to the interior. Walking through the straight and narrow streets that extended from the harbor to Catumby and beyond, a foreign visitor to Rio would "continuously encounter convoys of mules which intersected and succeeded one another".[39] These chains of people and commodities linked the capital to the provinces of Minas Gerais, São Paulo, Goyaz, and Curitiba among others.

The government deployed the need for compulsory labor at the penitentiary to reform its most decrepit dungeons by relieving them of excess residents. *Galé* inmates were not only sent to work in Catumby, many had their sentences commuted to banishment and were transported to Fernando de Noronha, a penal colony in the north-east, which a mixed slave and legally

39. Debret, *Voyage Pittoresque*, p. 5.

free convict workforce had built.[40] In December 1834, the African-born slave convicts José Moçambique and João Congo were included in a list of ten prisoners whose sentence to *galé* was commuted to banishment to Fernando de Noronha. The decision aimed to reduce the "great number of inmates who had accumulated in Rio's prisons at great cost to public finances".[41] In June 1834, the African-born slaves João Cabinda and José Grande, each sentenced to twenty years of *galés*, were sent to the Casa de Correção by Rio's Police Chief, along with João Feitor, who had been condemned to thirteen years of "prison with labor".[42] On 25 June 1834, Eusébio de Queiroz, who served as Police Chief, requested the Commander of the *Animo Grande*, a prison hulk, to send twenty-four *galé* convicts to work at the Casa de Correção.[43]

Inmates from the city's jails preferred to be sent to the Casa de Correção because conditions there were much better than at the Aljube or at Santa Barbara Island, which was too distant from the city and afforded them little contact with the mainland, and especially few opportunities for escape. Preference was given to detainees skilled in masonry, carpentry, ditch digging, and others who had demonstrated good behavior. The government considered paying select exemplary inmates a daily wage as an incentive and as a means of control. Other punitive forms of control were necessary. *Galés* and criminals sentenced to "prison with labor" worked in chains, which controversially blurred the lines between the two groups. The police dispatched prison guards to prevent escapes.[44] Still, it was not impossible to escape the Casa de Correção. In 1834, Luciano Lira, a convict of free legal status, fled from the worksite.[45]

The relocation of Rio's inmates to the penitentiary also applied to enslaved detainees in custody at the Calabouço. In 1837, 188 slaves in custody were transferred from the Calabouço at Castello Hill to the Casa de Correção, where they were incarcerated in a new reformed jail, also called Calabouço.[46] In June 1830, the justice of the peace of Lagoa, a rural parish to the south of the harbor, ordered the detention of the slave woman Theodora at the Calabouço after she was arrested on a farm near Rodrigo de Freitas Lake.[47] Slave owners regularly brought their bondsmen to the

---

40. Beattie, *Punishment in Paradise*, pp. 14–22.
41. *Correio Official*, 20 December 1834.
42. *Ibid.*, 2 June 1834.
43. *Ibid.*, 25 June 1834.
44. Aureliano de Souza e Oliveira Coutinho to the Brazilian Parliament in *Correio Official*, 26 May 1834.
45. *Correio Official*, 22 March 1834.
46. *Ibid.*, 8 August 1837; Brasil, *Relatório do ministério da justiça do anno 1837* (Rio de Janeiro, 1838).
47. *Diário do Rio de Janeiro*, 26 June 1830.

Calabouço to be flogged for a fee and detained as punishment for disobedience, routine flights, and rebellion.[48]

Slaveholders utilized the Calabouço, before and after its transfer to the Casa de Correção, as a warehouse to contain and correct unruly slaves while negotiating for their sale outside of Rio. It was common to find notices in the city's gazette advertising the sale of slaves like Joaquim, an African from Benguella in West Central Africa, which encouraged interested buyers to visit the Calabouço to inspect them. Joaquim was a skilled blacksmith and compelled his owner to sell him by "refusing to work".[49] Joaquim Antonio Insua, a petty slave owner who lived in Rio's Valongo, advertised the sale of his Brazilian-born slave, Manoel, a carpenter, under the condition that he was sold "outside of the province".[50]

Owners of Calabouço slaves often resided in the city's commercial districts in streets such as Rua do Carmo, where Januario, an enslaved master goldsmith, lived; Castello Street, where the owner of a slave identified as a "good cook" resided; or Fishermen's Street, where the owner of a master tailor, a Brazilian-born slave, resided.[51] These notices identified the enslaved by skills, such as cooks, master gilder, apprentice tailors, master tailors, sailors, master goldsmith, carpenters, and barbers. A substantial segment of enslaved detainees were therefore skilled urban slaves. The relocation of the Calabouço to Catumby gave the Casa de Correção access to an enslaved workforce that comprised skilled artisans and semi-skilled slaves, including female slave detainees who worked as cooks and washerwomen. Slave detainees surpassed the number of convicts because they originated from routine police actions and from slave owners who confined them at the Calabouço. The convict population was divided into two groups: minors – fourteen years or younger – who were under a correctional regime for vagrancy-related charges, and adult criminals.

The government also deployed the Casa de Correção's construction to reform vagrants and beggars, including delinquent minors under the authority of local justices of the peace. In 1831, the *Aurora Fluminense* commented on a communication from the navy arsenal for mechanics and other skilled workers to present themselves at the armory in order to be hired. The invitation was especially extended to "free or emancipated (*liberto*) officer technicians", which suggests that free people of color were particularly targeted as the recipients of this policy.[52] The program "would produce good results

---

48. Holloway, *Policing Rio de Janeiro*, pp. 55–58.
49. *Diário do Rio de Janeiro*, 2 January 1830.
50. *Ibid.*, 11 February 1830.
51. *Ibid.*, 20 March 1830, 29 February 1830, 24 April 1830.
52. *Correio Mercantil*, 8 June 1831, also published in *Aurora Fluminense*, 6 June 1831; on the utilization of naval labor to control the growing free black population, see Morgan, *Legacy of the Lash*, pp. 50–51.

by decreasing the number of vagrants who passed through the streets" by disciplining them in the "habit of work".[53] In 1836, the legislature discussed how to liberate the streets from the "high number of beggars" who harassed residents and considered employing them in their home so that they could provide for themselves.[54] A citizen's letter emphasized that small shops and vendors' stalls maintained by slaves and which specialized in selling groceries and cooked food "provided to the lower classes their means of honest subsistence". However, these places of commerce were unregulated and constituted points of conglomeration for "idlers, drunkards, thieves, gamblers, and ruffians of all caste".[55] These preoccupations with vagrancy coalesced in a vigorous police campaign in 1838 to deliver the city of the "infestation" of vagrants, beggars, and their "harmful effects" on society.[56] The police paid duty officers for each pauper brought to the Casa de Correção, where they were compelled to work on the construction of the prison. A total of 170 vagrants were sent to work at the penitentiary; forty others were sent to the navy. The policy backfired because the Casa de Correção was unable to absorb this surplus labor, which tasked the government's ability to control the prison population.[57]

CONFINEMENT AND THE CHANGING LABOR REGIME OF THE ATLANTIC

What made the labor arrangement at the Casa de Correção novel compared with previous employment practices in Brazil was its utilization of liberated Africans as involuntary "apprentice" laborers and their distribution to other public institutions and private employers. Convict laborers were an important pillar in Portuguese colonial expansion in Asia, Africa, and Brazil.[58] European empires traditionally relieved the streets of the burden that a free flowing, unattached vagrant population represented in metropolitan and colonial port cities.[59] In the Lusophone world, colonial armies and troop

53. *Correio Mercantil*, 8 June 1831.

54. Brasil, *Relatório do ministério da justiça do anno 1836* (Rio de Janeiro, 1837), p. 19.

55. *O Chronista*, 23 June 1838.

56. Holloway, *Policing Rio de Janeiro*, pp. 134–135.

57. Thomé Joaquim Rodrigues, Director of the Casa de Correção, to Eusébio de Queiroz Mattoso, Rio's Police Chief, on 2 October 1838, *Jornal do Commercio*, 6 October 1838.

58. Timothy J. Coates, *Convicts and Orphans: Forced and State-Sponsored Colonizers in the Portuguese Empire, 1550–1755* (Stanford, CA, 2001), pp. 42–64.

59. Gwenda Morgan and Peter Rushton, *Banishment in the Early Atlantic World: Convicts, Rebels and Slaves* (London, 2013); Clare Anderson and Hamish Maxwell-Stewart, "Convict Labour and the Western Hemisphere, 1415–1954", in Robert Aldrich and Kirsten McKenzie (eds), *The Routledge History of Western Empires* (London, 2013), pp. 102–117; Ruth Pike, "Penal Servitude in the Spanish Empire: Presidio Labor in the Eighteenth Century", *Hispanic American Historical Review*, 58:1 (1978), pp. 21–40; Timothy J. Coates, *Convict Labor in the*

regiments were filled with the unattached and unprotected poor, who expanded the colonial and postcolonial frontier in Brazil. The Casa de Correção's labor scheme therefore constituted an extension of the traditional imperial practice of dragooning unfree people – through the justice system and enslavement – into public work tasks around Rio. The prison's labor scheme was a response to the ripple effects of the changing labor regimes of the Atlantic, from slavery to free labor, by contracting the labor power of liberated Africans for the prison's own use and consigning this commodity to privileged landowners and other public institutions.

"Liberated Africans", known as *emancipados* in Cuba and "recaptives" in other Atlantic shores, refers to the estimated 11,000 men, women, and children that the Mixed Commission Court in Rio emancipated between 1821 and 1845.[60] A subset of that population, 150 on average, was employed at the Casa de Correção after 1834, when the government authorized the penitentiary to utilize liberated Africans "giving preference to those who were already learning a trade and had shown a love of work".[61] As salaried apprentice laborers, liberated Africans represented a significant segment of the prison's workers. Their wages were paid to the government, which acted as a corporate employer when it consigned emancipated Africans to public institutions and to slaveholders. Liberated Africans who worked at the Casa de Correção received a *vintém*, or ten per cent of their wage, which they could use to buy tobacco and other necessities. The government retained the remainder of their wage for food, clothing, and the cost of confinement. Liberated Africans were also employed at the city's Our Lady of Mercy Charity, the telegraph service, the ironsmith factory in São Paulo province, the light company, and a gunpowder workshop. They were utilized in the repair of Rio's roads, aqueducts, and public fountains, where they worked in a racially mixed workforce of salaried enslaved laborers and legally free workers with skills in carpentry, ditch digging, and masonry.

Portuguese Empire, 1740–1932: Redefining the Empire with Forced Labor and New Imperialism (Leiden, 2014).

60. This estimate is based on the calculations of Brazilian official Pedro Paulino da Fonseca in 1868. He included not only enslaved Africans liberated by the Anglo-Brazilian Mixed Commission between 1821 and 1845, but also 4,700 additional Africans emancipated *after* the Mixed Commission ceased its operations. Paulino da Fonseca estimated the number of liberated Africans in Brazil at 10,700 in 1868. In 1864, Reginaldo Muniz Freire tallied from official registries 7,366 liberated Africans in Brazil, more than 3,000 of whom were liberated after 1845. See "Estado em que se acham a escripturação da matrícula geral dos diversos carregamentos livres na corte, e provincias do império", *Arquivo Nacional do Rio de Janeiro*, ANRJ-OI (GIFI) 5B–519, and ANRJ–ZU Juizo Municipal 1era Vara do Rio de Janeiro Maço 646 # 5473 "Reginaldo Muniz Freire".

61. See the instructions on the consignation of the labor of free Africans, 29 October 1834, available at: http://legis.senado.gov.br/legislacao/ListaTextoIntegral.action?id=67373; last accessed on 8 November 2016.

After 1850 liberated Africans employed at the Casa de Correção laid the railroad tracks that connected Rio's harbor to the rural parishes where coffee plantations thrived. The new railroad system symbolized the city's modernization and booming coffee economy.

The legal status of liberated Africans was circumscribed by British and Brazilian laws and the anti-slavery discourse about freedom that linked the Atlantic and the Indian Ocean in the politics of labor exploitation that was inherent to the process of the formation and consolidation of capitalism in the nineteenth century.[62] Evelyn Jennings's study of road building in nineteenth-century Havana in this volume demonstrates the local and diasporic connections among various systems of regulating unfree labor through apprenticeship which articulated both a liberating labor policy and a recasting of slavery.[63] The Anglo-Portuguese Treaty of 28 July 1817 instituted the Mixed Commission Court on the African coast and in Rio to adjudicate the legality of slave vessels. The court provided certificates of emancipation to enslaved Africans captured aboard slave vessels and turned the freedmen to local authorities for guardianship to be "employed as servants or free laborers" for fourteen years before being declared "fully free".[64] The

---

62. See Robert Edgar Conrad, *World of Sorrow: The African Slave Trade to Brazil* (Baton Rouge, LA, 1986), pp. 56–61. On the 28 July 1817 convention, including the regulation of the Mixed Commission, see Lewis Hertslet, *A Complete Collection of the Treaties and Conventions, and Reciprocal Regulations, at Present Substituting Between Great Britain and Foreign Powers ... so Far as They Relate to Commerce and Navigation, and to the Repression and Abolition of the Slave Trade, and to the Privileges and Interests of the Subjects of the High Contracting Powers* (London, 1820), II, pp. 81–123; on the 23 November 1826 treaty, see Hertslet, *A Complete Collection* (London, 1841), III, pp. 33–35.
63. Tomich, *Through the Prism of Slavery*, pp. 56–71; Thomas C. Holt, "The Essence of the Contract: The Articulation of Race, Gender, and Political Economy in British Emancipation Policy, 1838–1866", in Frederick Cooper, Thomas C. Holt, and Rebecca Scott (eds), *Beyond Slavery: Explorations of Race, Labor, and Citizenship in Postemancipation Societies* (Chapel Hill, NC, 2000), pp. 33–59; Ada Ferrer, *Freedom's Mirror: Cuba and Haiti in the Age of Revolution* (New York, 2014), pp. 12–13.
64. There were courts in, for example, Cuba, Sierra Leone, New York, and South Africa, where liberated Africans were also settled. On the number of *emancipados* in Cuba, see Inés Roldán de Montaud, "Origen, evolución, y supresión del grupo de negros 'emancipados' en Cuba 1817–1870", *Revista de Indias*, 42:169–170 (1982), pp. 559–641; also Robert Conrad, "Neither Slave Nor Free: The *Emancipados* of Brazil, 1818–1868", *Hispanic American Historical Review*, 53:1 (1973), pp. 50–73; Edward L. Cox, *Free Coloreds in the Slave Societies of St. Kitts and Grenada, 1763–1833* (Knoxville, TN, 1984); the latest study on liberated Africans in Brazil is Beatriz Gallotti Mamigonian, "To be a Liberated African in Brazil: Labour and Citizenship in the Nineteenth Century" (Ph.D. dissertation, University of Waterloo, 2002), recently published as Beatriz G. Mamigonian, *Africanos Livres: A Abolição Do Tráfico de Escravos No Brasil* (São Paulo, 2017). For comparative studies on the experience of free Africans, see Christopher Saunders, "Liberated Africans in Cape Colony in the First Half of the Nineteenth Century", *The International Journal of African Historical Studies*, 18:2 (1985), pp. 223–239; Samuël Coghe, "Apprenticeship and the Negotiation of Freedom: The Liberated Africans of the Anglo-Portuguese Mixed Commission in Luanda (1844–1870)", *Africana Studia*, 14 (2010),

Portuguese crown promulgated a royal decree in 1818 that incorporated into Brazilian laws the guidelines of the Mixed Commission and clarified the legal position of liberated Africans in the slave society, including the fourteen-year apprenticeship requirement.[65]

Port cities like Rio were crucial nodal points for articulating and circumscribing the meaning of freedom for liberated Africans due to their significance as doorways for enslaved Africans from the slave trade and the residence of the Mixed Commission courts. The introduction of coffee in the Paraiba Valley had a profound effect on Rio's economy and demography. Coffee cultivation required little technological innovation, but like sugar it thrived on enslaved labor. Enslaved Africans fueled coffee's ascent in Brazil's economy between 1831 and 1850 (Figure 4).[66] Coffee cultivation gave rise to a powerful slaveholding aristocracy whose influence extended to all levels of the Brazilian administrative state, especially after 1837, when the rise to power of the Conservative Party marked the end of the liberal era (1831–1837).[67]

Eusébio de Queiroz, who called for the discontinuation of slave labor at the Casa de Correção in 1849, was an influential member of the Conservative Party. He was well connected to the coffee elite through marriage and was directly in charge of the allocation of "liberated Africans" as free coerced laborers to socially privileged individuals. Queiroz was at the helm of the policy to confine and compel vagrants to work in city projects. He implemented the policy that led to the routine incarceration of free people of color suspected of being fugitive slaves at the Calabouço.[68] Queiroz's role in the distribution of liberated Africans was an extension of the

---

pp. 255–273; Rosanne Adderley, "'A Most Useful and Valuable People?' Cultural, Moral and Practical Dilemmas in the Use of Liberated African Labour in the Nineteenth-Century Caribbean", *Slavery & Abolition*, 20:1 (1999), pp. 59–80; and *idem, New Negroes from Africa: Slave Trade Abolition and Free African Settlement in the Nineteenth-Century Caribbean* (Bloomington, IN, 2006). For a study of the interconnectedness of the transformation of labor migration in the Atlantic and the Indian Ocean, see Richard B. Allen, "Slaves, Convicts, Abolitionism and the Global Origins of the Post-Emancipation Indentured Labor System", *Slavery & Abolition*, 35:2 (2014), pp. 328–348; and Clare Anderson, "Convicts and Coolies: Rethinking Indentured Labour in the Nineteenth Century", *Slavery & Abolition*, 30:1 (2009), pp. 93–109.

65. Robert Edgar Conrad, *Children of God's Fire: A Documentary History of Black Slavery in Brazil* (Princeton, NJ, 1994), pp. 332–333; on the 1831 law, available at: http://www2.camara.leg.br/legin/fed/lei_sn/1824-1899/lei-37659-7-novembro-1831-564776-publicacaooriginal-88704-pl.html; last accessed 26 October 2018.

66. Stanley J. Stein, *Vassouras: A Brazilian Coffee County, 1850–1900: The Roles of Planter and Slave in a Plantation Society* (Princeton, NJ, 1986).

67. Jeffrey Needell, *The Party of Order: The Conservatives, the State, and Slavery in the Brazilian Monarchy, 1831–1871* (Stanford, CA, 2006).

68. Sidney Chalhoub, "The Precariousness of Freedom in a Slave Society (Brazil in the Nineteenth Century)", *International Review of Social History*, 56:3 (2011), pp. 405–439.

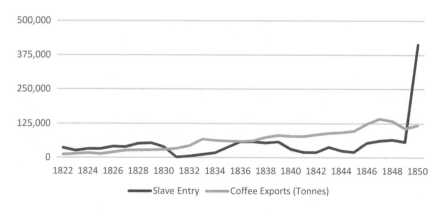

Figure 4. Brazilian Coffee Exports and the Traffic in Slaves, 1822–1850.
Corrected statistics for the volume of commodity exports from Brazil are taken from Christopher David Absell, "Brazilian Export Growth and Divergence in the Tropics during the Nineteenth-Century", IFCS – Working Papers in Economic History, WH, May 2015, pp. 1– 41. Data on the volume of the slave trade originate from the Trans-Atlantic Slave Trade Database, available at: http://www.slavevoyages.org/; last accessed 26 October 2018.

conservative strategy to identify people of color – enslaved and free – as slaves unless proven free, but also part of a broader process of statecraft that involved establishing the rule of law in the policing of the illegal slave trade.[69] Coffee's rise as Brazil's chief agrarian export corresponded with the expansion of the illegal traffic and a crucial period of postcolonial state formation. A 7 November 1831 law abolished the traffic, branded traffickers as pirates, and criminalized their activities. The law recommended *repatriating* liberated Africans to their homeland, which represented an important legal departure from British abolitionist policies because it did not envision incorporating emancipated Africans as "apprentices of freedom" in Brazilian society.[70] Liberal legislators who supported the 1831 law viewed the slave trade as a problem for postcolonial nation-building and advocated slavery's gradual abolition while building the penitentiary to discipline the free poor into workers. They viewed the entry of new Africans as introducing an "internal enemy" into Brazil that was incompatible with progress.[71]

69. See Registro da correspondencia da maior importancia de Euzébio Q. C. M. da Camara, quando Chefe da Polícia da Corte, 1833-1850, AN, *Códice* 1004, vol. 1.
70. Jennifer Nelson, "Apprentices of Freedom: Atlantic Histories of the *Africanos Livres* in Mid-Nineteenth Century Rio de Janeiro", *Itinerario*, 39:2 (2015), pp. 349–369.
71. For a study on anti-slavery ideas in the first half of the nineteenth century, see Jaime Rodrigues, *O Infame Comercio: Propostas e Experiencias No Final Do Trafico de Africanos Para o Brasil (1800–1850)* (Campinas, 2000).

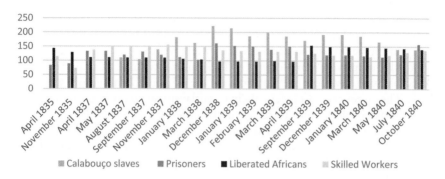

Figure 5. Slaves, Convicts, Liberated Africans, and Skilled Workers at the Casa de Correção, 1835–1840.
Compiled from the monthly reports on the prison's workforce. "Relatório dos Trabalhadores e Operários Empregados nas Obras da Casa de Correção", in Diário do Rio de Janeiro, O Despertador, Correio Official, 1835–1840.

The general consensus among liberals and conservatives was that Brazil constituted a territory of slavery for Africans.[72] At best, radical politicians believed that it was dangerous for liberated Africans to remain in Brazil because they would be immediately re-enslaved and sold to the interior.[73] Indeed, gangs of thieves often attacked the slave vessels which were anchored in Rio's harbor, filled with enslaved Africans during the adjudication process.[74] Studies on the *Emilia* and the *Brilhante*, two slave vessels captured in 1821 and 1842 respectively, show that confinement aboard these ships and at the Casa de Correção constituted an important period of identity formation for the captives and transfer of diasporic knowledge about slavery and freedom. Slaves aboard the *Brilhante* primarily spoke Kimbundu – forty per cent of the captives – and could therefore converse with one another about the trauma of enslavement, the middle passage, and the emancipation process. The other slaves spoke Bantu languages but were not isolated. Likewise, slaves from the *Emilia* were of Congo-Angolan origins and were able to establish close, interpersonal relationships that allowed them to make sense of the social, economic, and political underpinnings of Rio's port society and to deploy strategies of resistance and survival. The

---

72. See the discussions on the Barbacena Bill to revoke the 1831 law in Conrad, *World of Sorrow*, pp. 92–97; Sidney Chalhoub, "Illegal Enslavement and the Precariousness of Freedom in Nineteenth-Century Brazil", John D. Garrigus and Christopher Morris (eds), *Assumed Identities: The Meanings of Race in the Atlantic World* (Austin, TX, 2010), pp. 88–115.
73. Justice Minister Diogo Antonio Feijó in *Relatório do anno 1831* (Rio de Janeiro, 1832), p. 6.
74. Beginning in February 1834, the government began to relocate illegally enslaved Africans from land seizures to the Casa de Correção. See, AN, *Códice 1,004*, Vol. 1 and *Códice 399*. The first group of liberated Africans from ship confiscation to be sent to the prison originated from the *Duquesa de Bragança* and the *Santo Antonio* slavers which were sentenced in July 1834.

records of the *Brilhante* and other captured slave ships in Cuba and
Freetown reveal that families often experienced the traffic, adjudication,
and confinement together, though they were eventually separated once distributed to private employers.[75] The mortality rate among enslaved
Africans who awaited the decision of the Mixed Commission was very
high. The necessity to prevent their re-enslavement, reduce their mortality,
and ultimately the failure to repatriate them led to their confinement at the
Casa de Correção *in depósito* or under legal guardianship.[76] Confinement
became a formative regulatory aspect of the emancipation process for liberated Africans, while also entrenching slavery through the incarceration of
rebellious slave detainees.

Liberated Africans were held at the Casa de Correção because they were a
symbolically dangerous group in the slave society. In 1834, Manoel Alves
Branco, a government minister, admitted that "it was still not possible to
re-export any of the liberated Africans out of the empire". As a result, he
argued, the government "was forced to distribute" them to privileged
employers based on the 1818 decree which authorized utilizing them in public works.[77] It was inconceivable that liberated Africans could be released
into the Brazilian population as "free men" as Branco acknowledged that
"even their distribution did not satisfy the *great purpose* of ridding the country of *an ever dangerous population*".[78] Branco's statements expressed the
ambivalence of the Brazilian authorities about the politics of regulating the
presence of liberated Africans. Even as the government distributed liberated
Africans to politically connected civil servants, officials expressed the fear
that this population could introduce subversive ideas among the slave population, a great number of whom were illegally enslaved after 1831. The

---

75. Nelson, "Apprentices of Freedom", pp. 350–356; Walter Hawthorne, "'Being Now, as it
Were, One Family': Shipmate Bonding on the Slave Vessel Emilia, in Rio de Janeiro and
Throughout the Atlantic World", *Luso-Brazilian Review*, 45:1 (2008), pp. 53–77; Daniel
Domingues da Silva *et al.*, "The Diaspora of Africans Liberated from Slave Ships in the
Nineteenth Century", *The Journal of African History*, 55:3 (2014), pp. 347–369.

76. *Depósito* was an Iberian practice to protect vulnerable groups and was used in colonial times
to regulate the honor of women who divorced their husbands or to protect slaves petitioning
crown authorities against their masters on the grounds of excessive use of violence. I interpret
depósito – known as *recogimiento* in the Spanish Atlantic – as confinement because in practice
liberated Africans did not receive the legal protections that the term implied; on women and
guardianship, see Nancy van Deusen, "Determining the Boundaries of Virtue: The Discourse
of Recogimiento among Women in Seventeenth-Century Lima", *The Journal of Family
History*, 22:4 (1997), pp. 373–389; on enslaved Africans placed into government custody, see
Sherwin Bryant, "Enslaved Rebels, Fugitives, and Litigants: The Resistance Continuum in
Colonial Quito", *Colonial Latin American Review*, 13:1 (2004), pp. 7–46.

77. The government issued two instructions in 1834 and 1835 authorizing the employment of
liberated Africans. See Mamigonian, "To Be a Liberated African in Brazil".

78. My emphasis. Minister Manoel Alves Branco, *Relatório do anno 1834* (Rio de Janeiro, 1835),
p. 8.

authorities feared that the consignment of liberated Africans could "become unbearable after they have become acculturated and circulating *with the opinion of free men among slaves*".[79] In the aftermath of the Haitian Revolution and the Malê/Muslim slave rebellion in Bahia, liberated Africans appeared as a particularly incendiary group. In 1835, Paulino Limpo de Abreu, another government minister, published a letter in which he raised the specter that the Bahian insurgency would expand to Rio due to its "territorial proximity" to Salvador and "the size of its slave population". Abreu understood that it was Rio's standing as a seaport which made it susceptible to the spread of the rebellion from the north-east. In the 1830s, mutinies by troop regiments in the north-east spread through Rio from the sea through navy sailors and mariners who traveled between the two cities and carried the wind of insurgency with them. Abreu argued that it was the "impolitic conservation of liberated Africans among us" that raised the alarm. There existed "secret societies", he continued, "which worked systematically to foment slave insurrections by preaching the Haitian doctrine of a mass slave uprising".[80] The idea of freedom that liberated Africans and Haiti symbolized was regarded as a colossal threat to the expansion of slavery in the coffee region.

Small-scale slave owners and Rio residents also expressed a fear of the ideological powder keg that liberated Africans represented on the streets. A resident who identified as a "victim" implored Police Chief Eusébio de Queiroz to continue the "wise measures to cleanse the city" of liberated Africans. The author argued that liberated Africans were "harmful" to the slave order and concluded that most emancipated Africans were "corrupt and seduced slaves" into freedom "by taking them to their residences".[81] The persistence of the Brazilian authorities in referring to liberated Africans as "Africanos livres", which literally translates as "free Africans", offers an interesting window onto the ambivalence of slavery's expansion in the nineteenth century. The term "Africanos livres" distinguished liberated Africans from other African-born slaves who had been manumitted by their owners or freed through self-purchase and were known as "Africanos libertos", or emancipated Africans. The persistence of the term "Africanos livres" in Brazil, where the "second slavery" expanded most massively in the nineteenth century, points to the conflicting politics of liberation and unfreedom that defined the labor landscape of the Atlantic. The Casa de Correção was a key site for articulating this process because of its significance as employer and distributor of liberated Africans as well as its significance as a penitentiary.

79. *Ibid.*
80. *Correio Official*, 30 March 1835, # 70; on the Malê rebellion, see João José Réis, *Slave Rebellion in Brazil: The Muslim Uprising of 1835 in Bahia*, trans Arthur Brakel (Baltimore, MD, 1995).
81. *Diário do Rio de Janeiro*, 10 December 1839.

THE MOTLEY CREW

In total, 450 to 700 slave detainees, free prisoners, leased slaves and free craftsmen, vagrants, and liberated Africans built the original pavilion of the Casa de Correção between 1834 and 1850. Workers carried the stone to erect the tall walls that sealed the prison from the city and dug into the hard clay ground of Catumby Hill to build the penitentiary's foundations. It was grueling work. The government hired a company to provide the food and clothing for the prison's residents and builders. Though most prisoners were men, there were many women who contributed to the prison's construction as cooks and seamstresses after 1850.

The authorities established a hierarchy among the workers according to skills and legal status. Skilled workers were recorded separately in monthly reports on the prison's workforce. There were on average 54 stonemasons, 15 carpenters, 4 cart pushers, 17 stone cutters, 1 to 2 cooks, 1 overseer, and 6 or 7 foremen among the skilled laborers. Skilled craftsmen were a mixture of leased slaves, Calabouço slaves, convicts of legally free status, and hired skilled craftsmen of Portuguese descent. Skilled craftsmen included individuals like Manoel José Soares, an immigrant from Trás-os-Montes in north-eastern Portugal who arrived in Rio de Janeiro in May 1836. By 1838, he was employed as a stonemason at the Casa de Correção. He lived in Conde Street, in the immediate proximity of the prison. In 1835, 101 laborers identified as "craftsmen and apprentices of various trade" worked at the prison without clarification of their legal status, which suggests that this information was not important to the authorities in categorizing the workforce. But in 1849, when Eusébio de Queiroz became concerned with reforming the prison's labor force, he observed that salaried day workers "were almost all slaves, especially in the class of stonemasons".[82] He calculated that nineteen out of twenty stonemasons and sixteen out of twenty-seven ditch diggers were slaves.

Skilled workers also included liberated Africans as apprentices and as experienced craftsmen. It is possible that liberated Africans were already skilled artisans when they arrived in Brazil, and that they were transferring manual skillsets to the new environment. But the discourse of "apprentices of freedom" that regimented the lives of liberated Africans at the Casa de Correção shaped official perceptions of *emancipados* as unskilled workers who "showed more devotion and skills" than other laborers at the penitentiary.[83] Prison administrators highlighted the docility of liberated Africans and their eagerness to be trained as craftsmen to indicate the success of apprenticeship. By claiming that liberated Africans were dutifully learning

82. Brasil, *Relatório do anno 1849* 1A, p. 53.
83. Justice Minister Antonio Paulino de Abreu, *Relatório do anno 1836* (Rio de Janeiro, 1837), pp. 27–29.

a trade, the authorities could justify the benefits of utilizing them to build the prison while implicitly comparing them with the idle Brazilian vagrants.

Portuguese nationals were employed in managerial positions as foremen and overseers. Slave plantations routinely utilized Portuguese men as overseers, which allowed planters to deflect the violence of the slave regime to those who enforced the power of the whip. Portuguese overseers were known to be particularly violent. They often received the brunt of slaves' violence against enslavement.[84] By hiring Portuguese men as overseers, prison administrators recreated the racial and ethnic dynamic of the plantation at the Casa de Correção. Still, by having Portuguese supervisors and foremen work alongside other skilled workers, leased slaves, Brazilian nationals, convicts, and other Portuguese craftsmen, administrators deftly identified them as one undifferentiated group (Table 2). This strategy reinforced hierarchies of control through the manipulation of ethnic difference, legal status, and the infamous tensions between Brazilians and Portuguese subjects.

Tensions between Portuguese overseers and enslaved Africans exploded in the most famous case of resistance at the Casa de Correção, which involved a Congo-born liberated African, Bonifácio, who killed a Portuguese supervisor, Joaquim Lucas Ribeiro, in 1846. Ribeiro was scheduled to publicly chastise Bonifácio with a *palmatória*, a flat wooden instrument traditionally utilized to castigate domestic slaves. The authorities usually flogged Calabouço slaves between noon and 2.00 pm in the presence of their masters, who paid the government for the service. Bonifácio would have understood the lashing in the presence of slave owners as particularly degrading. When Ribeiro approached Bonifácio, the latter repeatedly struck the supervisor in the chest with a compass. At his trial, Bonifácio argued that "he had lost his mind" "because of the punishments that he had received and would still suffer" from Ribeiro. Surprisingly, Bonifácio was sentenced to only a year of "prison with labor", which suggests that the jurors did not really sympathize with Ribeiro. Despite the overseer's authority over the liberated African, he was still a disposable worker.[85]

Resistance at the prison took the form of grievances to improve treatment of workers and convicts but did not challenge its labor arrangement, as is apparent from an 1841 petition that legally free prisoners and liberated Africans wrote to the emperor.[86] The petition was divided into two sections that addressed the complaints of each group separately; this suggests that convicts and liberated Africans recognized their common experience as a

---

84. Bryan McCann, "The Whip and the Watch: Overseers in the Paraíba Valley, Brazil", *Slavery & Abolition*, 18:2 (1997), pp. 30–47.

85. *Gazeta dos Tribunaes (RJ)*, 30 June 1846.

86. Nelson, "Apprentices of Freedom", pp. 350–362, and Hawthorne, "'Being Now, as it Were, One Family'", pp. 53–77.

Table 2. *Casa de Correção's workforce by skills and status, March 1838.*

Stonemasons	54	Correctional and criminal inmates	103
Carpenters	15	Liberated Africans employed by the CC	104
Stonecutters/	17	Calabouço slaves	162
Cavouqueiros			
Foremen	7	Liberated Africans *in depósito*	18
Overseer/*Apontador*	1	Liberated African employees from other	–
		institutions	
Canteiro	52		
Cart pushers (*Carreiros*)	4		
Blacksmith (*Serralheiro*)	1		
Cook	1		
Cell keyholders	2		
Total	154		387

Sources: "Relação dos Trabalhadores e Operários Empregados nas Obras da Casa de Correção em o mez de Março 1838", in *Correio Official*, 6 June 1835. The administrative staff are not listed in this table. They included a surgeon, a nurse, a clerk, a *guarda de obra* (general supervisor), a chief administrator, a prison warden, a doorman at the main gate, and a supply collector or *arrecadador*.

confined population whose labor was vital for building the penitentiary despite their different legal status. Legally free prisoners pleaded with the emperor to "listen with compassion to their complaints and sufferings". They argued that the construction of the penitentiary, the navy arsenal, and "all other public works" in the city were important nation-building projects to which they contributed. They denounced the unequal treatment in the quality of food and clothing of convict workers at the Casa de Correção and at the navy arsenal. Their discussion of unjust treatment in the distribution and the quality of food and clothing articulated claims of citizenship that were based on the language of imperial paternalism. The letter denounced rampant corruption among prison administrators. Convicts criticized the administrative staff as primarily Portuguese and the prison population as mostly Brazilians. The petition reminded the emperor, who was born in Brazil, of the well-known "bitter rivalry between Portuguese and Brazilians" and argued that the predominance of Portuguese in the administrative staffs would eventually "lead to violence".[87] Bonifácio's killing of the overseer in 1846 dramatically fulfilled this prediction.

Liberated Africans took turns to beseech the emperor to look toward the "poor black Africans", who labored in public works in the city and sought "relief" from their sufferings at the Casa de Correção. They referred to

87. "Requerimento dos presos sentenciados a serviço da Casa de Correção a S.M.I. relatando a insuportável situação a que eram submetidos pelo administrador daquela casa e pedindo providências que lhes permitissem viver com dignidade", 2 March 1841, Manuscript, Biblioteca Nacional, RJ, II–34, 25, 011.

themselves as "slaves", but it was a strategic identification to gain the emperor's sympathy because slave detainees from the Calabouço were not included in the petition. The petitioners deployed the term to qualify their real lived experience and treatment at the prison and to alert the emperor to their plight. Liberated Africans also identified themselves as contributing members of society who supported the larger project of modernizing Brazil through their labor. They argued that prison administrators deprived them of some basic privileges – customary rights – that distinguished them from slave detainees at the Casa de Correção, such as the privilege to walk around the small garden plot at the prison on Sundays and saints' days. They were forced to live in the Calabouço with slave detainees and were kept in their cells on holy days. Even their *vintém* – partial wage – was withheld at times as punishment. The *emancipados* were therefore arguing that they were treated no better than slaves and convicts. They expected the emperor to know that they were neither slaves nor convicts but apprenticed laborers and freedmen. The petition also addressed the suffering of liberated African women – and one might imagine children – at the Casa de Correção. One liberated African woman was "castigated so vigorously" that her clothes ripped apart. She was subsequently sent to work in the chained water gang despite her wounds. The emancipated Africans asked the emperor to remove their "iron chains" and to relocate them to the navy arsenal. Their request is significant because in the 1840s naval officers began reforming the navy arsenal's workforce by replacing slave workers with free wage laborers, part of the politics to discipline the growing free black population in the city by impressing them into the navy, where corporal punishment was applied to sailors until the first decade of the twentieth century.[88] In November 1840, the administrator of the navy arsenal published a notice stating that the office would hire only "legally free craftsmen".[89] In September 1840, the armory "dismissed all slave craftsmen" and decided to "admit only free artisans", including those as sailors and operators of machinery.[90] Liberated Africans knew that the law had declared them free, and those who worked at the Casa de Correção were well cognizant of labor conditions at the arsenal. It is therefore possible that their request to be relocated to the navy arsenal was an attempt to claim "full freedom" as free blacks despite the precariousness of that position.[91]

88. Morgan, *Legacy of the Lash*, pp. 50–53.
89. *Diário do Rio de Janeiro*, 10 November 1840.
90. *Ibid.*, 23 September 1840.
91. Beatriz Gallotti Mamigonian, "Conflicts over the Meanings of Freedom: The Liberated Africans' Struggle for Final Emancipation in Brazil, 1840s–1860s", in R. Brana-Shute and R.J. Sparks (eds), *Paths to Freedom: Manumission in the Atlantic World* (Columbia, SC, 2009), pp. 235–264.

FROM SLAVERY TO FREE LABOR

On 7 July 1850, the Casa de Correção was inaugurated after sixteen years of construction under Eusébio de Queiroz's leadership. Queiroz hoped that inaugurating the penitentiary would finalize the process of sanitizing the city's prisons, especially following a devastating epidemic of yellow fever in 1849 that many linked to the city's crowded jails and the presence of slave vessels in its harbor. Queiroz observed that there was a "superabundance of labor" at the Casa de Correção and suggested discontinuing the utilization of enslaved workers and replacing the penitentiary's mixed slave and legally free workforce with free wage workers.[92] Effectively, in January 1849, Queiroz fired all wage-earning slaves and sent a call to hire only legally free workers to work at the penitentiary. He justified this decision by arguing that free workers "competed in more than sufficient numbers" for work in the city.[93] Queiroz concluded that the labor of leased slaves was inferior to that of legally free wage laborers and asserted that the difference between legally free workers and leased slaves was the "contrast between one who toiled for himself" and "one who labored for others". Queiroz's assessment was based on his knowledge that it was the masters of the leased slaves who pocketed their wages. Leased slaves therefore had no incentive to improve their performance and productivity.

Queiroz's opportunistically timely appreciation of free wage laborers was the result of his involvement in managing the "abolition crisis" that resulted from the cessation of the traffic between 1848 and 1850.[94] In 1845, the British Parliament passed the Aberdeen Act, which empowered cruisers to confiscate Brazilian ships to curtail the slave trade. The act challenged Brazilian sovereignty and culminated in the abolition of the traffic in 1850 with the passage of the Eusébio de Queiroz Law. The Brazilian government actively policed its coasts to enforce the law and a few slave ships were captured as late as 1856.[95] Reflecting on the events leading to the 1850 law, one justice minister argued that the illegal entry of millions of Africans into Brazil demonstrated that the country had failed to "execute effectively its laws" and "the imperial government" had to "bring about the complete extinction of the

---

92. Brasil, *Relatório do anno 1849*, 1A, p. 53.
93. *Ibid.*
94. Slaves continued to arrive in Rio until as late as 1854; for a revisionist perspective on abolition that attributes it to slave resistance, see Dale Graden, "An Act 'Even of Public Security': Slave Resistance, Social Tensions, and the End of the International Slave Trade to Brazil, 1835–1836", *Hispanic American Historical Review*, 76:2 (1996), pp. 249–282; Sidney Chalhoub, "The Politics of Disease Control: Yellow Fever and Race in Nineteenth-Century Rio de Janeiro", *Journal of Latin American Studies*, 25:3 (1993), pp. 441–443. Classic interpretations of the cessation of the traffic privilege the effects of British pressure on Brazil. See Leslie Bethell, *The Abolition of the Brazilian Slave Trade: Britain, Brazil and the Slave Trade Question* (Cambridge, 1970), and Conrad, *World of Sorrow*.
95. Bethell, *The Abolition of the Brazilian Slave Trade*, pp. 327–359.

traffic as a measure of social convenience, civilization, national honor, and even of public security".[96] The reference to public security was an allusion to the problem that the expansion of slavery represented in Brazil, while it was ideologically challenged in the aftermath of the Haitian Revolution.[97] Brazilian slave owners had fashioned the postcolonial state to protect the continuation of the traffic through draconian laws that inflicted severe punishment on slave rebels, including the death penalty.[98] Politicians continuously feared the implications of the predominance of Africans in the slave population, even as they asserted the necessity of slaves for national economic production. Seaports like Rio were under particular vigilance because, as one minister argued regarding the challenge of controlling urban slaves, "one does not guard this property, it walks through the streets".[99] Salvador's Police Chief established an 8.oo pm curfew to restrict the circulation of slaves and freed persons in the city after the 1835 Muslim uprising.[100] Powerful police forces were created in Rio, Salvador, and São Paulo to control their expanding urban slave population and acted as the "coercive power of the owner class" in these settings.[101] Queiroz oversaw the formation of Rio's police between 1833 and 1840. As Justice Minister in 1848, he administered the maintenance of public security in the empire and was at the heart of the diplomatic firestorm occasioned by the Aberdeen Act. On 4 September 1850, two months after the opening of the Casa de Correção, he promulgated the Eusébio de Queiroz Law, which authorized Brazilian authorities to apprehend all vessels caught with slaves aboard or with signs of involvement in the traffic.[102] The law stipulated that Africans freed from the traffic would be repatriated to their ports of origin on the African coast or "anywhere outside the Empire". The 1850 law closed a loophole in the 1831 regulation by specifying that liberated Africans who were not repatriated would be put to work under the "guardianship of the government" but not *consigned to private employers*. However, the utilization of liberated Africans as involuntary free laborers continued until their emancipation in 1864. By then, the

96. Minister of Justice José Idelfonso de Sousa Ramos to President of the Province of Rio de Janeiro Luis Pedreira do Couto Ferraz on the Eusébio de Queiroz Law, quoted in Graden, "An Act 'Even of Public Security'", p. 249.

97. Graden, "An Act 'Even of Public Security'", pp. 249–251; Ferrer, *Freedom's Mirror*, pp. 48–49.

98. Needell, *The Party of Order*, pp. 110–116 and 133–137; Brown, "'A Black Mark on our Legislation'", pp. 95–121; Ribeiro, *"No meio das galinhas as baratas não têm razão"*, pp. 43–67.

99. Justice Minister Diogo Feijó in *Relatório do anno 1833*, p. 24.

100. Graden, "An Act 'Even of Public Security'", p. 264.

101. Holloway, *Policing Rio de Janeiro*, pp. 114–115.

102. Law 581 of 4 September 1850, available at: http://www.planalto.gov.br/ccivil_03/leis/LIM/ LIM581.htm; last accessed 7 May 2016. On Eusébio de Queiroz's political biography and the Conservative Party, see Vainfas Ronaldo (ed.), *Dicionario do Brasil Imperial (1822–1889)* (Rio de Janeiro, 2002), pp. 245–246 and 166–168. On Queiroz's influence on policing Rio, see Holloway, *Policing Rio de Janeiro*, pp. 103–105.

government had already lost count of how many liberated Africans had been distributed, and to whom.

As the author of the 1850 law and the person in charge of public security in the empire, Queiroz had a keen understanding of the implications of the regulation for the continuation of slavery in Brazil. Without the continuous entry of African slaves, the production of coffee and sugar, the basis of national wealth, would decline. Queiroz, a slaveholder and a politician, contextualized his call to cease hiring leased slaves at the Casa de Correção as part of a policy to redirect slaves to plantation agriculture in rural zones for the preservation of slavery. He justified his forceful intervention in the Casa de Correção's workforce by arguing that "national interests called for the need to protect colonization and reduce the criminal introduction of slaves". Queiroz's reference to the traffic as "criminal" expressed the consensus among politicians in Brazil's important port cities, Rio, Salvador, São Paulo, that the significance of African slaves in the Brazilian population occasioned by the traffic posed a constant threat of violent slave uprisings. They were ever conscious of the reality that the slave vessel was the "material infrastructure" that renewed slave labor in Brazil while serving as the vehicle of "revolutionary antislavery".[103] In 1848, the provincial assembly of Bahia in the north-east passed a law which prohibited African slaves and freedmen from being employed as sailors, a recognition that the seaport was the seedbed for the entry of subversive ideas. The city's merchants went so far as to purchase 185 boats, which they offered to legally free Bahians to replace the African sailors.[104]

Queiroz understood that the abolition of the traffic necessitated a shift in the geography of slavery from coastal towns and busy port cities to the country's agrarian hinterland, where slave labor was most needed. He initiated that process at the Casa de Correção, not necessarily as a precursor of a foreordained abolition of slavery but as part of the politics of permutations of free and unfree labor from which Brazilian colonization and postcolonial state formation unfolded. Effectively after 1849, there were numerous calls to hire skilled artisans to work at the Casa de Correção, such as a call for ax carpenters, two master blacksmith, two shoemakers, and a tinsmith.[105] These new employees worked as instructors in the prison's workshops, initiating its transition into a reformatory penal institution to produce a disciplined citizenry. Liberated Africans continued to contribute to build the second pavilion of the penitentiary, which was completed in 1860. However, waged slaves disappeared from the prison's workforce, a fact which signified their exclusion from the city's labor market.

103. Ferrer, *Freedom's Mirror*, p. 58.
104. Graden, "An Act 'Even of Public Security'", p. 268.
105. *Diário do Rio de Janeiro*, 19 August 1852.

Slaves continued to shape Rio's economic life, but their numbers dwindled from thirty-eight per cent in 1849 to less than seventeen per cent of the city's residents by 1872. Most of the shift occurred among male slaves, the number of whom diminished by sixty-two per cent. The city's slaves, especially enslaved male workers, were being sold into Rio's hinterland to work in agriculture. The redistribution of the slave population from the north-east to the central-south region, and from coastal cities to the agrarian hinterlands, was a political process of managing the ripple effects of the cessation of the traffic to preserve slave labor for as long as possible in Brazil. The drop in Rio's male slaves corresponded with an upsurge of 113.3 per cent in the number of male Portuguese immigrants, an increase that started in 1849 and that facilitated the displacement of slaves as wage laborers from Rio's market to the countryside.[106] Portuguese immigration led to an expansion of free and foreign-born workers in the city and became associated with free wage labor. Lusophone immigrants eventually eclipsed slaves-for-hire in Rio's free-market economy.[107] Foreigners who joined the ranks of the free poor began taking occupations previously held by wage-earning slaves, such as carrying water in the city. The government modernized the business of carrying weights by encouraging immigrants to utilize wheeled carts, which were more efficient. The cessation of salaried slave labor at the Casa de Correção was, therefore, consistent with a broader process in which free wage workers began to substitute salaried slave laborers in Rio de Janeiro.

CONCLUSION

This story of the utilization of a mixed labor force to build the Casa de Correção between 1834 and 1850 demonstrates that port cities such as Rio were key nodal points from which to examine the relations between free and unfree labor in the Age of Abolitionism globally and postcolonial state formation in Latin America specifically. As Brazil's capital city and its most significant seaport, Rio became the experimenting ground for modernizing institutions of social control which were vital for securing the flow of people – slaves and immigrants – as labor commodities of the Atlantic to and from its hinterland. The government organized a labor force from the city's enslaved and legally free population to build the prison. Legally free individuals were also reduced to unfreedom through imprisonment and coerced labor, including navy and military labor, as Megan Thomas has argued, to erect the penitentiary and maintain order on the streets. The flexibility and opportunism that this labor practice evidenced highlights the underbelly of global capitalism and postcolonial state formation during a crucial period

106. *Ibid.*
107. Alencastro, "Prolétaires et Esclaves", pp. 133–136.

in which anti-slavery currents challenged chattel slavery in the Atlantic while convictism mobilized mass labor in the Indian Ocean.[108] The reorganization of the Casa de Correção's labor force after 1850 did not signify a termination of slave labor in Brazil, but rather its entrenchment in the coffee plantations of the hinterland until abolition in 1888. Slaves continued to inhabit the penitentiary's cells – notably at the Calabouço – for disobedience or for flight while legally free vagrants and criminals toiled in its workshops to inculcate in them the appreciation of work.

108. See Anderson in this Special Issue.

IRSH 64 (2019), pp. 205–227 doi:10.1017/S0020859019000129

Convicts, Commodities, and Connections in British Asia and the Indian Ocean, 1789–1866[*]

CLARE ANDERSON

School of History, Politics and International Relations
University of Leicester
University Road, Leicester LE1 7RH, UK

E-mail: ca26@le.ac.uk

ABSTRACT: This article explores the transportation of Indian convicts to the port cities of the Bay of Bengal and the Indian Ocean during the period 1789 to 1866. It considers the relationship between East India Company transportation and earlier and concurrent British Crown transportation to the Americas and Australia. It is concerned in particular with the interconnection between convictism and enslavement in the Atlantic and Indian Ocean worlds. Examining the roots of transportation in South Asia in the repressive policies of the East India Company, especially in relation to its occupation of land and expropriation of resources, it moves on to discuss aspects of convicts' lives in Moulmein, Singapore, Mauritius, and Aden. This includes their labour regime and their relationship to other workers. It argues that Indian convict transportation was part of a carceral circuit of repression and coerced labour extraction that was intertwined with the expansion of East India Company governance and trade. The Company used transportation as a means of removing resistant subjects from their homes, and of supplying an unfree labour force to develop commodity exports and to build the infrastructure necessary for the establishment, population, and connection of littoral nodes. However, the close confinement and association of convicts during transportation rendered the punishment a vector for the development of transregional political solidarities, centred in and around the Company's port cities.

[*] The research leading to these results has received funding from the European Research Council under the European Union's Seventh Framework Programme (FP/2007–2013)/ERC Grant Agreement 312542. It draws on statistical work funded by the Economic and Social Research Council (R000271268/RES-000-22-3484). I am grateful to the European Research Council, Economic and Social Research Council, editors and contributing authors of this Special Issue, and participants in the "port cities" conference held at the University of Pittsburgh in 2016.

INTRODUCTION

On 10 August 1851, in Moulmein, the capital of British Burma, a gang of one hundred Indian convicts was engaged in its routine monthly task of loading coal onto the East India Company's paddle steamer *HC Tenasserim*, at the docks of Mopoon. This ship was one of many that plied the Company's trading routes around the Bay of Bengal, connecting port cities in South and South East Asia.[1] Like other Company steamers, the *HC Tenasserim* carried a diverse cargo. This included men, women, and children – Company officials with their families and servants, merchants and traders, military officers and troops, and labourers – and trade goods like cotton, spices, pepper, opium, and betel nut. In common with other such vessels, the *Tenasserim* also routinely conveyed Indian transportation convicts into sentences of penal labour. Port cities like Moulmein, one such carceral site, were key locations through and in which the Company repressed and put to work colonized populations. They were places in which convicts joined other colonial workers in the formation of a remarkably cosmopolitan labour force.

The Moulmein convicts working in the docks of Mapoon had, in the early hours of the day, marched the three miles between their jail and the coal shed wharf. The deputy jailer, Mr Edwards, with twenty-six guards, had supervised their work, with a half dozen armed reserve stationed a short distance away. As usual, the convicts were close to finishing the task by the early afternoon. But this was no ordinary day in Moulmein. Just as they were finishing loading the boat, nineteen of the convicts grabbed three of the lascars (sailors) who were holding the ropes tethering the ship to the riverbank and threw them overboard. Their guards approached, but other convicts kept them back by pelting them with lumps of coal. The rest let go of the ropes and pushed the boat off. With Moulmein sitting at the southern confluence of the point at which the Salween River splits into four, they set sail north towards Martaban and got behind their oars, with both the wind and the flood tide in their favour. If port cities were places of convict repression and coerced labour, they were also always potential spaces of collective rebellion. Immediately, deputy jailer Edwards ordered a party to set off along the river in pursuit of the convicts. It quickly caught them up, for the coal boat was heavy, and managed to board the steamer and recapture the men. Despite the convicts' capitulation, the reaction of the guards was brutal. They killed

---

1. The port cities were: Akyab, Kyouk Phyoo, Bassein, Rangoon, Moulmein, Amherst Town, Tavoy, and Mergui (Burma); Georgetown (Penang), Malacca Town, and Singapore; Diamond Harbour and Saugor Roads (Bengal); Fort St George and Chingleput (Madras); and Fort George and Tannah (Bombay). Until their transfer to the Dutch in exchange for Malacca following the Anglo-Dutch Treaty of 1824, Amboyna and Bencoolen (Fort Marlborough) were also included in this circuit. Note that the capital of British Burma shifted to Rangoon following the Second Anglo-Burmese War of 1852.

three men, and wounded eleven, who suffered dreadful and multiple injuries, including sabre wounds, fractured skulls, and broken legs.[2]

The convicts' transportation to Burma, their work at the coal shed, their collective act of resistance, and the extreme violence countered against it raise key themes with respect to Asian convict workers. This article will explore the origins of Indian penal transportation in the context of earlier and concurrent metropolitan practice in Britain's Atlantic world and Australian colonies, the interconnection between convictism and enslavement, and the repressive policies enacted by the East India Company in response to subaltern resistance to its expropriation of land and other resources in the Indian subcontinent. It will trace convict journeys across the Bay of Bengal, and further afield in the Indian Ocean, and discuss aspects of convicts' lives in penal locations, notably the labour that they performed in port cities and their relationships with other workers. It argues that Indian convict transportation was one element of a connected imperial repertoire of repression, coerced labour extraction, and the expansion of East India Company governance and trade. The Company used transportation as a means of removing resistant subjects from their homes, and of supplying a malleable labour force to build the commodity chains and infrastructure necessary for the establishment, population, and connection of imperial port city nodes, with each other and their hinterlands. Depending on the availability of labour locally, as well as changing ideas about ideal forms of punishment and rehabilitation emanating from metropolitan Europe and Australia, convicts sometimes worked in parallel with other workers, including slaves, lascars, migrants, and locally convicted prisoners.

Paradoxically, though the Company deployed penal transportation as a means of quashing rebellion and resistance, the close confinement and association of convicts during their often long journeys to ports of departure and ports of arrival, over land, and by river steamers and sailing ships, rendered transportation a vector for their spread. Transportation thus enabled convicts to develop transregional political solidarities, and as such was productive of violent and collective anti-Company uprisings. It is now widely recognized that in the late nineteenth and early twentieth centuries, port cities in the Bay of Bengal and the Indian Ocean were places of cosmopolitan interaction, the economic and social meeting places of Asian sojourners and settlers, in which both friction could arise and syncretic cultural and political solidarities could form.[3] What is perhaps less appreciated is the extent and importance of

---

2. British Library, India Office records [hereafter, IOR] P/144/7: A. Bogle, commissioner Tenasserim provinces to J.P. Grant, secretary to government Bengal judicial department, 18 August 1851, enc. J.P. Briggs, magistrate of Moulmein, to Bogle, 18 August 1851.

3. Sunil S. Amrith, *Migration and Diaspora in Modern Asia* (Cambridge, 2011), especially the introduction and ch. 2; Mark Frost, "'Wider Opportunities': Religious Revival, Nationalist Awakening and the Global Dimension in Colombo, 1870–1920", *Modern Asian Studies*, 36:4

convict transportation for the cosmopolitanism of these sites. Refocusing on the turn of the nineteenth century and the decades up to the 1850s compels us not just to incorporate forced labour into the history of port cities and their cultural formations, but also to root the development of transregional anti-imperial solidarities to a much earlier period than has been previously recognized. This provides a new perspective not just on the history of port city workers and their solidarities, but on cosmopolitanism as an expression of the power of the colonial state during a crucial period in the globalization of capital. Following Britain's loss of the American colonies, metropolitan interests swung to the east, flinging unfree labour together and producing new forms of labour association, particularly in the often transitory and fluid context of port cities. These connections both cut across social hierarchies grounded in civil status, ethnicity, and race, and linked together the Company's regional hubs.[4]

CONVICTS, ENSLAVEMENT, AND EMPIRE

The East India Company instigated the transportation of Indian convicts in the late eighteenth century, in the context of a two-century-long history of British and Irish penal banishment, military impressment, and the selling of convicts into contracts of labour indenture in the Americas. Sixteenth-century destinations included Bermuda, Barbados, and Virginia, including for Scottish prisoners of war and Irish rebels. Gwenda Morgan and Peter Rushton have described other elements of this human cargo, partially constituted of vagrants and capital respites, as "the uncontainable poor".[5] Penal transportation became a more routine part of the criminal justice system after the passing of the 1717 Transportation Act, when the government extended the punishment beyond those offenders pardoned from execution. During the period up to the outbreak of the American War of Independence in 1775, Britain and Ireland shipped at least 50,000 convicts to Atlantic world plantation colonies, including Barbados, but also and in particular around the Chesapeake Bay. Hamish Maxwell-Stewart argues

(2002), pp. 937–967; Pamila Gupta, Isabel Hofmeyr, and Michael Pearson (eds), *Eyes Across the Water: Navigating the Indian Ocean* (Pretoria, 2010); Tim Harper and Sunil S. Amrith, "Sites of Asian Interaction: An Introduction", Special Issue, *Modern Asian Studies*, 46:2 (2012), pp. 249–257; Isabel Hofmeyr, Uma Dhupelia-Mesthrie, and Preben Kaarsholm, "Durban and Cape Town as Port Cities: Reconsidering Southern African Studies from the Indian Ocean", Special Issue, *Journal of Southern African Studies*, 42:3 (2016), pp. 375–387.
4. For a discussion of "subaltern cosmopolitanism" and the concept of "littoral Asia", see Sharmani P. Gabriel and Fernando Rosa, "Introduction: 'Lived Cosmopolitanisms' in Littoral Asia", Special Issue, *Cultural Dynamics*, 24:2–3 (2012), pp. 115–126.
5. Gwenda Morgan and Peter Rushton, *Banishment in the Early Atlantic World: Convicts, Rebels and Slaves* (London, 2013), p. 19.

that American planters' initial preference for a supply of expendable convict labour enabled the capital accumulation necessary for the development of industrial slavery, rendering convictism "the ideological precursor of plantation racism".[6] In 1775, the North American colonies refused to accept further transports. Subsequently, many convicts were incarcerated in prison hulks along the river Thames, and these quickly became overcrowded. The British sent a few batches of convicts to West African forts (including slave trading posts), but high death rates meant that this experiment did not last long. It was in the context of the failure of its African convict experiment that the government took the decision to use convicts to establish a new colony at Botany Bay, dispatching the first fleet to the southern Indian Ocean in 1787.[7]

A full twenty years before the abolition of the slave trade across Britain's Crown Colonies in 1807, and a year after the first fleet sailed to the Antipodes, across two oceans from the former American colonies Governor General of Bengal Charles Cornwallis prohibited the export of slaves from the presidency. Subsequent to the Bengal prohibition, both Indian and European elites continued to own slaves, but the East India Company no longer traded in them.[8] During this period, metropolitan abolitionists were arguing forcefully against the Atlantic slave trade, on the grounds of both humanitarianism and political economy. Many such abolitionists had political and economic interests connected to those of the East India Company.[9] Bengal's abolition of slave exports enabled them to claim India as a space of enlightened labour relations, and thus to seek advantage in global markets that were increasingly sensitive to the expropriation of slave labour.[10]

It would be another four decades before contemporaries compared convicts to slaves. This came in the aftermath of the abolition of slavery in parts of the British Empire (not including East India Company Asia), in

---

6. Hamish Maxwell-Stewart, "Transportation from Britain and Ireland 1615–1875", in Clare Anderson (ed.), *A Global History of Convicts and Penal Colonies* (London, 2018), pp. 183–210.

7. *Ibid.*, p. 191; Morgan and Rushton, *Banishment in the Early Atlantic World*; Emma Christopher, *A Merciless Place: The Lost Story of Britain's Convict Disaster in Africa and How it Led to the Settlement of Australia* (Sydney, 2010).

8. On the diversity of enslavement in pre-colonial and British Asia, see Indrani Chatterjee and Richard M. Eaton (eds), *Slavery and South Asian History* (Bloomington, IN, 2006). Note that Cornwallis had been a British general during the American War of Independence.

9. Eric Williams, *Capitalism and Slavery* (Chapel Hill, NC, 1944), pp. 137–138, 151.

10. Andrea Major, *Slavery, Abolitionism and Empire in India, 1772–1843* (Liverpool, 2012). The Company expressed a desire to abolish slavery altogether during the first decade of the nineteenth century but, as Richard B. Allen has argued, "foundered over concern about the potentially deleterious economic and socio-political consequences". See Richard B. Allen, "Slaves, Convicts, Abolitionism and the Global Origins of the Post-Emancipation Indentured Labor System", *Slavery & Abolition*, 35:2 (2014), p. 336.

1834, and in the context of a growing anti-penal transportation lobby, active in Britain and the Australian colonies. In the meantime, both the British state and the East India Company remained committed to transportation as a means of putting into motion an alternative unfree labour supply. Thus, in the dual context of Britain's first convict shipments to Australia in 1787 and Bengal's prohibition of slave trading in 1788, in 1789 the Company sent the first convoys of convicts to its trading factories. From the late eighteenth to the mid-nineteenth centuries the Company used Asian convict labour as a means to develop the infrastructure necessary to link port cities to each other, and then to build the roads and bridges vital for the connection of land, littoral, and sea. With very few exceptions, Asian convicts worked exclusively for the Company, and except during an early, experimental period they were not hired out to private individuals or used in private trading.

The trading factories were a distinct feature of East India Company Asia. From the start of the seventeenth century, the Company had sent merchants ("factors") from Britain to the east to strike deals with local rulers, and to establish trading posts (or "factories") as nodes of economic interest. The Company founded its first factory on the coast of western Java, at Bantam. It established others both in continental India and southward of the Bay of Bengal, in Sumatra, Borneo, the Molucca Islands, and, in common with the Dutch East India Company, Java (see Van Rossum in this Special Issue). The Indian factories ultimately developed into the three "presidencies" of Bengal, Madras, and Bombay, and this enabled the first Governor General of Bengal, Warren Hastings, and his successors, including Charles Cornwallis, to further expand the Company's sphere of influence. The Company defeated local rulers to extend its territories inwards over land and outwards over sea, and seized or acquired numerous rights of governance, including the power to collect revenue and to administer justice.[11]

Though the Company ceded its Indonesian territories to the Dutch following the 1814 Treaty of Paris, which concluded the Napoleonic Wars, its expansive ambitions continued. It had occupied Penang in 1786,[12] the Andaman Islands in 1793, Malacca in 1796, Singapore in 1819, and the Arakan and Tenasserim provinces of Burma in 1826. The Company abandoned the Andamans in 1796, due to extraordinarily high deaths rates, and

11. H.V. Bowen, *The Business of Empire: The East India Company and Imperial Britain, 1756–1833* (Cambridge, 2006); A. Farrington, *Trading Places: The East India Company and Asia 1600–1834* (London, 2002); Jörg Fisch, *Cheap Lives and Dear Limbs: The British Transformation of the Bengal Criminal Law, 1769–1817* (Wiesbaden, 1983); P.J. Marshall, "The British in Asia: Trade to Dominion, 1700–1765", in *idem* (ed.), *The Oxford History of the British Empire: Vol. 2, The Eighteenth Century* (Oxford, 1998), pp. 487–507; Radhika Singha, *A Despotism of Law: Crime and Justice in Early Colonial India* (New Delhi, 1998).
12. The British then named the island "Prince of Wales Island", which was also known as Pulo Penang, which means "betel nut island". It was briefly a fourth Indian presidency, during the period 1805–1830.

exchanged Bencoolen for Malacca, through a second Anglo-Dutch treaty in 1824. In the meantime, and subsequently, the Company shipped Indian convicts under sentences of transportation and hard labour to each of these locations. The Company lost its monopoly over trade in 1833, following pressure by the free trade lobby on the British parliament. However, it retained its administrative and revenue collecting functions until 1857, when, following the Indian rebellion, the British Crown assumed control of its territories. In the intervening period, penal transportation continued unabated, as the Company instituted this new form of mobile, coerced labour to underpin its expansive ambitions.[13]

During an early, experimental period the Company allowed a private merchant to take twenty dacoits (gang robbers) to Penang for a period of three years, and to employ them as he desired, on condition that he pay the cost of their passage, accommodation, rations, and return, and do everything in his power to prevent their escape. This was the first and last time that the Company organized the transportation of convicts in this way, and subsequently it took direct control of their shipment and labour.[14] Meantime, it justified transportation as a punishment by claiming that Indians lost caste during sea voyages, and so especially feared journeys over the *kala pani*, or black waters of the ocean. This rendered it ideal as both a penal sanction and as a deterrent.[15]

The Company never sold Asian convicts into contracts of indenture, as had been the case for the British and Irish convicts sent to the Americas. This was the result of a paradox: the Company's desire to position itself as the harbinger of enlightened labour relations, compared to the British Caribbean slave colonies, and its need for a labour force to facilitate the acquisition and development of maritime connections and territorial spheres of influence. Thus, penal transportation from British India followed Australian practice, where convicts were sentenced either for a term of seven or fourteen years, or for life, with hard labour, and the government

---

13. Clare Anderson, "After Emancipation: Empires and Imperial Formations", in Catherine Hall, Nicholas Draper, and Keith McClelland (eds), *Emancipation and the Remaking of the British Imperial World* (Manchester, 2014), pp. 113–127.

14. IOR G/34/3: E. Hay, secretary to government Bengal public department, to Francis Light, superintendent Penang, 21 January 1789. The short duration of the experiment may have been the result of the dire financial straits that the merchant in question found himself in the following year. A trading partner absconded with his investment of 50,000 rupees (more than £250,000 today). See IOR G/34/4: The humble petition of Julius Griffiths and Co. merchants of Prince of Wales Island on behalf of themselves and creditors, 14 May 1790.

15. This idea was most extensively discussed in IOR V/26/170/1 *Report of the Committee on Prison Discipline, 8 January 1838* (Calcutta, 1838), paper C. Though in subsequent years British administrators repeatedly invoked the idea of the horrors of the *kala pani*, there was dissent within the 1838 committee, which distinguished between the varying attitudes to crossing the ocean, held by country and city dwellers, seafarers, high and low caste Hindus, and Muslims.

determined how they should be employed.[16] If the British had used convicts as a means of colonizing the Australian continent, the appeal of the punishment in India at this time, though partially grounded in perceptions of "Indian" culture, was directly connected to the Company's need for labour in territories that it had already occupied, and in this port cities were hubs. Moreover, the Company's interests as a trading company intersected with those of the British Crown as an imperial power. Indeed, convicts flowed across the borders of Company and Crown lands, from India to Mauritius and from Ceylon to the Straits Settlements, with convict expulsion and exploitation of mutual political and economic benefit (Table 1).

Despite the late eighteenth-century Bengal prohibition against slave exports, slavery remained legal in areas under East India Company control until 1843, and in some of the early factories, convicts and enslaved people worked together. In the Moluccas, for instance, following a devastating smallpox epidemic that decimated both the free and the enslaved population, in 1801 the Company imported convicts to assist slaves and Malay labourers (then called "coolies") in salvaging the harvest on its nutmeg plantations. The Company's resident, R.T. Farquhar, lamented that since the British takeover, five years earlier, there had been no fresh importations of enslaved people, and this was causing unprecedented "universal distress".[17] During this period, the Company also transported convicts to Bencoolen, where many Malays had also died, for the harvesting of spices.[18] In 1818, the British governor of Bencoolen, T.S. Raffles, emancipated government slaves, an act of apparent benevolence that, in the context of the Company's desire for global labour advantage, was only possible because of the prospect of their replacement by convicts. Indeed, in the aftermath of emancipation, convict numbers in the factory increased fourfold.[19]

The close relationship between convictism and enslavement that was evident on the spice plantations of Company Asia during these early decades was also a feature of the Crown Colony of Mauritius. In 1814, shortly after Britain seized the island from France at the conclusion of the

16. Maxwell-Stewart argues that the origin of seven- and fourteen-year penal sentences lies in the competitive positioning of convicts, against the life value of slaves, in the eighteenth-century Americas. Maxwell-Stewart, "Transportation from Britain and Ireland", p. 187.
17. IOR P/5/25: Extract Bengal foreign department, 9 September 1801 – extract from a letter from R.T. Farquhar, Company resident at the Molucca Islands, 11 July 1801. The Moluccas comprised Amboyna and Bantam. Previously, Farquhar had served as lieutenant governor of convict-era Penang.
18. IOR P/5/13: Walter Ewer, commissioner of Bencoolen to H. Tucker, secretary to government Bengal public department, 19 April 1800; IOR P/5/30: Ewer to Wellesley, 21 October 1801.
19. IOR P/136/53: J.W. Rule, superintendent of convicts Bencoolen, to Edward Presgrave, officiating secretary to government Bengal judicial department, 7 January 1825.

Table 1. *East India Company convict transportation, 1789–1866.*

Convict destination		Dates of transportation	No. of convicts
Penang ⎫		1789–1860	⎫
Singapore ⎬ Straits Settlements		1826–1859	⎬ 13,023
Malacca ⎭		1826–1866	⎭
Andaman Islands		1793–1796	265
* Amboyna and Bencoolen		1797–1823	2,823
Mauritius		1815–1837	1,462
Burma		1830–1860	6,518
Aden		1841–1850	150
Labuan		1851–1858	130

* It is not always possible to distinguish these destinations in the records, though note that the Company occupied Amboyna only between 1796–1802 and 1810–1814. *Note*: Under-sentence convicts remained in these penal settlements after new importations of convicts ceased. The penal settlement in Mauritius remained open until 1853, Burma until 1862, and the Straits Settlements (as Penang, Malacca, and Singapore were known after 1826) until 1868, in the latter case after the India Office transferred their general administration to the Colonial Office.
Clare Anderson, *"Transnational Histories of Penal Transportation: Punishment, Labour and Governance in the British Imperial World, 1788-1939"*, Australian Historical Studies, *47:3 (2016), Table 1, p. 382.*

Napoleonic Wars, Governor R.T. Farquhar, who, as Company resident in the Molucca Islands, had overseen the introduction of convicts, requested a supply from Bengal.[20] The first transports arrived in 1815, and he allocated seventy-five of them to join enslaved men and women on the sugar plantation of Bel Ombre, in which his private secretary Charles Telfair had an economic interest.[21] In Mauritius as in Bencoolen and Amboyna, the British catapulted convicts into an economic system that had been established through conditions of labour unfreedom. Convicts joined slaves as foundational links in chains of commodity production and export that stretched from imperial hinterlands to imperial ports. In this, alongside other workers, convicts played a key role in the globalization of capital.

20. IOR F/4/534: R.T. Farquhar, governor of Mauritius, to the Earl of Moira, governor general of the Bengal Presidency, 20 September 1814.
21. In the aftermath of a convict uprising on the Bel Ombre estate, the Colonial Office criticized the allocation of convicts to a private interest. See Clare Anderson, "The Bel Ombre Rebellion: Indian Convicts in Mauritius, 1815–53", in Gwyn Campbell (ed.), *Abolition and its Aftermath in Indian Ocean Africa and Asia* (London, 2005), pp. 50–65. Charles Telfair died in 1833, at about which time, following the abolition of slavery, he and his heir received substantial compensation for their loss of property: over 200 enslaved persons. See the "Legacies of British Slave-Ownership" compensation database, available at: http://www.ucl.ac.uk/lbs/; last accessed 26 June 2017. Note that formerly enslaved persons never received compensation.

COMMODITY CHAINS, INFRASTRUCTURAL LABOUR, AND CONVICT WORKERS

If the transportation of convicts was a consequence of the Company's expropriation of land and resources in continental India, it enabled the appropriation of labour and the extension of commodity chains. As one Company merchant, R.S. Perreau, wrote in 1800, penal transportation to Bencoolen was "connected with the improvement of this settlement, and the opportunity […] of relieving [the] different zillahs (districts) from a number of subjects who are burthensome and expensive". He surveyed the trading factory's district of Benterin, reporting on its suitability for the cultivation of rice, cotton, mustard, hemp, Indian corn, sugar cane, sweet potatoes, and mulberries. Noting that many of the convicts in Bencoolen were weavers, he proposed their employment in the manufacture of cloth. They could cultivate rice, too, he added, obviating the need for imports and enabling ships "to be occupied by more valuable goods". Convicts' manufacture of gunny bags from hemp, meantime, could replace the 30,000 or so imported from Bengal each year, necessary for packing the pepper grown in the factory.[22]

Convicts were the human capital in a triangular trade that reached from the Company's interests in India and around the Bay of Bengal and the South China Sea, and across the southern Indian and South Atlantic Oceans to Britain. There were no special transportation vessels during the first half of the nineteenth century. Convicts travelled on "country" ships carrying cargo such as cotton, tea, indigo, and opium. They assisted in the labour of offloading that cargo in the Company's trading factories, and of loading up goods like nutmeg and pepper for export.[23] Dockside work occupied just a small number of convicts, however. The Company employed the majority of them in the infrastructural labour projects necessary for the extension of trade, or in other kinds of commodity production. The concept of "carceral circuits" – of people and objects – captures neatly the mobility and relationality between convicts and capital in the generation of value.[24]

---

22. IOR P/5/13: Ewer to Richard Wellesley, governor general of Bengal, 6 May 1800, enc. Mr Perreau's report, 4 May 1800.
23. See for example IOR L/MAR/B/210A, containing the log of the *Lord Duncan*, which sailed from Saugor Roads (Bengal) to Bencoolen on 11 September 1799, with 248 convicts on board. On Company trade more generally, see Bowen, *The Business of Empire*.
24. Nick Gill *et al.*, "Carceral Circuitry: New Directions in Carceral Geography", *Progress in Human Geography*, 42:2 (2018), pp. 183–204. They propose that a carceral circuit stretches regularly from place to place, is a "route along which things pass" (p. 189), is "a component of a larger system" (p. 190) and entails compulsory movement. Violence, on the other hand, is a key theme in Sven Beckert's exploration of the relationship between capital and labour in *Empire of Cotton: A Global History* (London, 2015).

The labour of convicts was important from the earliest years of transportation. From the 1790s, the Company was involved in numerous trials in sugar production in continental India, in the hope of both supplying the local market, and competing with Britain's West Indian export trade to lower prices for British consumers. Though ultimately unsuccessful, abolitionist sentiment greatly encouraged the Company, for it pointed to the east as an alternative source of non-slave-produced sugar.[25] During the first attempt to colonize the Andaman Islands, for example, convicts cleared land, planted fruit trees and vegetables from Bengal, and engaged in experiments in the cultivation of sugar cane, as well as rice, indigo, and other grains.[26] The employment of convicts in other forms of cultivation was common elsewhere too. As noted above, the Company used convicts on the spice plantations of Bencoolen and Penang. From the 1840s, Burma and the Straits Settlements did not only receive Indian convicts, they also transported their felons in the other direction, to the Madras Presidency. They were employed on the Company's coffee and cinchona plantations.[27] Convicts in Mauritius were used in experimental silk manufacture, during which time the governor specifically requested the transportation of Bengalis with knowledge of sericulture.[28] On a few occasions, the Company also conscripted convicts into its army, and used them in expansionary warfare, for instance in the 1800 march to Laboon, and during the Naning War in Malacca (1831–1832).[29]

The expansion of plantation production necessitated the development of road networks for the conveyance of produce to the coast for export, as well as to build infrastructure in the Company's ports. However, in early trading factories like Penang, the free population engaged in subsistence agriculture and did not have the means to pay tax to fund public works. In 1800, Lieutenant Governor George Leith wrote that in these circumstances only convicts could save the Company from "considerable expense", especially because roads were routinely damaged by heavy rains and thus under

25. Ulbe Bosma, *The Sugar Plantation in India and Indonesia: Industrial Production, 1770–2010* (Cambridge, 2013), ch. 2.

26. IOR G/34/1: Copy of the first part of a report from Major Kyd relative to the Settlements at Prince of Wales Island and the Andamans with its appendix, 4 March 1795.

27. Tamil Nadu State Archives [hereafter, TNSA] Madras judicial consultations, 19 October 1864, pp. 136–137: A.J. Arbuthnot, chief secretary to government Madras judicial department, to O. Cavenagh, governor of the Straits Settlements, 11 October 1864. Cinchona was used in the manufacture of quinine. The Company also transported South East Asian convicts to the Bombay Presidency, where they were employed on public works.

28. Clare Anderson, *Convicts in the Indian Ocean: Transportation from South Asia to Mauritius* (Basingstoke, 2000), pp. 46–48.

29. IOR P/5/19: Ewer to Wellesley, 18 December 1800, enc. statement of convicts hired by individuals from *primo* May to *ulto* October 1800; Emrys Chew, "The Naning War, 1831–1832: Colonial Authority and Malay Resistance in the Early Period of British Expansion", *Modern Asian Studies*, 32:2 (1998), p. 382.

constant repair. During that year, it employed convicts in Penang not just on road building, but also on the construction of a mile-long embankment between the sea and Fort Cornwallis, necessary to prevent encroachment from the water.[30]

In Mauritius, the expansion of road networks was spurred on in 1825, when the British Parliament removed preferential tariffs on Caribbean sugar, thus opening up competition in global trade. We have already seen that Governor Farquhar sent Indian convicts to work on the Bel Ombre sugar plantation; between 1814 and 1832 the proportion of land under sugar cane cultivation increased from fifteen to eighty-seven per cent. Convicts built fifty miles of brand-new road during 1823–1826 alone, and another twenty-six miles in 1835. These included routes from inland Moka to Port Louis, and a coastal route between the south-eastern ports of Grand Port and Mahebourg. Visiting the island during his global voyage on *The Beagle* in 1836, Charles Darwin surmised that the huge increase in sugar production was the direct result of the construction of "excellent roads" by convicts. Frequently, French plantation owners petitioned the British administration for the allocation of convicts to road and bridge building and repair in the districts.[31]

There was a high demand for cheap sugar to fuel the British workers employed in the mills and factories of the industrial revolution, and the abolition of slavery in the sugar colonies of the Caribbean and in Mauritius in 1834 buoyed the Company's efforts to compete globally.[32] In the mid-1840s, it engaged in the clearance of forest land for sugar production in the north of Province Wellesley in Malacca, on the mainland over the straits from Penang. This required an enhanced network of communications, and the governor of the Straits Settlements diverted an increased number of convicts to both areas for road building projects.[33] The convict-built roads connected the hinterlands to convict-built ports. Indeed, all over the Bay of Bengal convicts were engaged in the construction of bunds, docks, harbours, and lighthouses. Convict Bawajee Rajaram and his convict draughtsmen produced many of the architectural plans in the building of Singapore,

30. IOR P/5/13: Lieutenant Governor George Leith, Penang, to G.H. Barlow, vice president in council Bengal, 31 May 1800. Confusingly, the Company also called the first Andamans settlement Fort Cornwallis, though the two sites are entirely separate from each other.

31. Anderson, *Convicts in the Indian Ocean*, pp. 6–7, 44–45, 44 n. 87.

32. On the relationship between the Atlantic world and the industrial revolution, see the classic Williams, *Capitalism and Slavery*. On sugar cultivation in India, see Bosma, *The Sugar Plantation in India and Indonesia*, ch. 2.

33. IOR P/142/4: W.J. Butterworth, governor Straits Settlements, to A. Turnbull, secretary to government Bengal judicial department, 24 September 1845; IOR P/143/16: Butterworth to A.R. Young, undersecretary to government Bengal judicial department, 12 November 1847. Bosma estimates that India exported one third of its sugar to Britain in the late 1840s: *The Sugar Plantation in India and Indonesia*, p. 75.

for example, where convicts constructed St Andrew's Cathedral, Government House, and the Horsburgh lighthouse.[34]

The association between convict transportation and infrastructural development in British Asia and the Indian Ocean was part of a larger imperial pattern. Transportation convicts across the empire were routinely employed in urban development and the building of communication networks, linking port cities and their littorals to each other and to inland plantations. As Jennings shows in this volume, this was also the case in nineteenth-century Cuba. In Britain's Australian penal colonies, famous convict architect Francis Greenway designed some of the most enduring structures of the empire, including Hyde Park convict barracks in Sydney and the lighthouse at South Point. Indeed, in the 1820s, the aesthetic appeal of his elaborate designs formed part of the damning critique of transportation to New South Wales as a too soft and non-deterrent punishment.[35] From the 1820s, English and Irish convicts laboured on the construction of the great naval dockyards of the imperial Atlantic and Mediterranean outposts of Bermuda and Gibraltar.[36] Convicts in the isolated penal settlement of Mazaruni in British Guiana, set up along the Australian colonial model in 1843 but for locally convicted prisoners, worked in the extraction of granite from vast outcrops of rock. Prisoners in the penal settlement, some formerly enslaved, dispatched the slabs downriver to the capital of Georgetown, accompanied by batches of convicts, who used them to build and repair roads, pavements, and sea wall defences.[37]

The question arises: why did the East India Company rely so heavily on convicts as labour? In part, the answer lies in Perreau's summation of the function of transportation as a means of putting otherwise dependent and costly prisoners to work in colonial development – within the larger context of the metropolitan history of penal transportation and the striving for

---

34. Anoma Pieris, "On Dropping Bricks and Other Disconcerting Subjects: Unearthing Convict Histories in Singapore", *Fabrications*, 15:2 (2005), pp. 88–89. For a wonderful contemporary account of convict labour in the Straits Settlements, see also J.F.A. McNair, *Prisoners Their Own Warders: A Record of the Convict Prison at Singapore in the Straits Settlements established 1825, Discontinued 1873, together with a Cursory History of the Convict Establishments at Bencoolen, Penang and Malacca from the Year 1797* (Westminster, 1899). Government House is now the national museum of Singapore.

35. *The Evidence to the Bigge Reports: New South Wales under Governor Macquarie, Volume 2: the written evidence*, selected and edited by John Ritchie (Melbourne, 1971). See also the excellent resource available at: http://www.sl.nsw.gov.au/stories/francis-greenway-convict-architect; last accessed 27 June 2017.

36. C.F.E. Hollis Hallett, *Forty Years of Convict Labor: Bermuda 1823–1863* (Bermuda, 1999).

37. *Richard Schomburgk's Travels in British Guiana 1840–1844. Translated and Edited, with Geographical and General Indices, and Route Maps, by Walter E. Roth* [Stipendiary Magistrate of the Demerara River District], *Volume I* ("Daily Chronicle" Office, Georgetown, 1922); The National Archives, Kew CO111/270 7 November 1860, no. 160: inspection of the Mazaruni penal settlement.

competitive advantage described above. But the answer is also located in the
problem of the availability of alternative sources of labour following Bengal's
abolition of slave exports in 1788, which impacted on all of Company Asia,
and in regard to Mauritius specifically the Crown's abolition of the slave
trade in 1807. Places like Bencoolen were thinly populated, and with the
enslaved population in decline free labour was expensive. In the early nineteenth century, Company officials routinely claimed that convicts cost half
as much as local Malays and were far cheaper than other labour sources.[38]

Indeed, in Burma in the 1840s, the Company found it impossible to get
locals or migrants to accept the wages on offer. The commissioner of
Arakan wrote in 1845 that the former owned land, and so lacked skills in
public works, and would only hire themselves out at very high rates. The latter, largely Bengali labourers from Chittagong, moved south only during the
harvest and returned to India as soon as the monsoon arrived. They were
only available in very limited numbers. Though he had been able to employ
free labourers in parallel with convict gangs, the commissioner made observations in the following terms:

> I never met a Chittagong cooly who could […] line out a road properly, preserve
> an even surface, rand down and consolidate the earth, keep the proper slope, or
> excavate with neatness and regularity; in fact [,] the difference between the labour
> of a convict and cooly was all the difference between skilled and unskilled
> labour.[39]

The appeal of convict labour was also connected to the coercive means at the
Company's disposal in its management. A combination of confinement, surveillance, and restrictions on mobility deterred convicts from running away.
The Company paid local residents to return any who attempted to escape.
Otherwise, it compelled convicts to work, and overseers could punish
those who refused or resisted work: with confinement in the stocks,
enhanced labour tasks, reduced rations, flogging, or work in chain gangs.
This was not the case for free laborers, who if unhappy with their conditions
could simply desert their work. Threatened by the Company with the with-
drawal of transportation convicts, the second principal assistant commissioner of Arakan wrote in 1853: "We should not have the hold over
coolies that we have over the convicts".[40] In addition, convicts were highly
mobile, and could be sent out to labour wherever required, and moved
around the trading factories according to need. Indeed, the Company

38. For example, IOR P/6/2: Ewer to Wellesley, 22 June 1804.
39. IOR P/144/46: Henry Hopkinson, commissioner of Arakan, to Gordon Young, secretary to
government Bengal judicial department, 19 August 1853.
40. IOR P/144/46: W.J. Law, second principal assistant commissioner Arakan, to Hopkinson,
5 July 1853.

codified such mobility in one of its regulations on transportation, which passed into law in 1813.[41]

The supply of convicts was always limited to the outcome of judicial sentencing, however, and where local labour was either unavailable or in short supply the Company made efforts to induce free migration. Until the 1830s, these attempts met with only limited success. For instance, in the 1790s, the Company shipped free Bengali artificers (skilled craftsmen) and tradesmen to the Andamans, and artificers and cultivators to Penang.[42] At this time it could not persuade skilled laborers to go to a third site: Bencoolen.[43] This was part of a larger problem during the early settlement of trading posts, when potential labour migrants were unwilling to go to unknown locations.[44] Still, as Company factories developed into port cities during the first half of the nineteenth century they accommodated numerous kinds of mobile labour. This included Chinese workers in Bencoolen, the Moluccas, and Penang, who, during the eighteenth and early nineteenth centuries, the Company persuaded to migrate on the promise of land grants.[45] By the 1840s, Chinese labourers had also settled in Malacca.[46] More generally, the need to bring complementary skills together with raw labour power meant that transportation convicts were sometimes one element of a much larger workforce. This was the case in Mauritius, for instance, when Indian convicts laboured on the construction of the Port Louis citadel alongside government slaves, liberated Africans,[47] locally raised *corvée* (compulsory) workers, and locally convicted prisoners.[48] A strikingly similar mixed labour force, including the use of liberated Africans, was engaged in building the Rio de Janeiro penitentiary in the mid-nineteenth century (see Jean's article in this volume). In Burma, convicts and Chinese worked in mines following the discovery of tin in 1838, up the Tenasserim River

41. Regulation IX 1813, cited in Fisch, *Cheap Lives*, 78. Turnbull wrote Butterworth in 1846 that under this regulation "you may transfer transported convicts from settlement to settlement, in anticipation of sanction, wherever circumstances may render such a step advisable". See IOR P/142/42: Turnbull to Butterworth, 7 January 1846.
42. IOR G/34/4: Captain Light returns to Prince of Wales Island from Calcutta with "Bengali farmers", 25 February 1790; IOR P/4/24: Kyd to Hay, 30 November 1793; IOR P/4/40: Note from John Shore, governor general of Bengal, 7 March 1796.
43 IOR P/5/30: Proceedings of the vice president in council in the Bengal military department, 14 January 1802.
44. IOR P/136/31: Minute of W.E. Phillips, governor of Penang, 15 April 1824, detailing the 1796 report of former superintendent Major Forbes Ross McDonald.
45. Allen, "Slaves, Convicts, Abolitionism", pp. 332–335.
46. IOR P/143/16: Butterworth to Young, 12 November 1847.
47. The British sometimes referred to Liberated Africans as "prize negroes" or "apprentices". They were the illegally enslaved men, women, and children "liberated" into compulsory government service following their removal from slave ships, by the Royal Navy, after the abolition of the slave trade in 1807.
48. Anderson, *Convicts in the Indian Ocean*, p. 45.

from Mergui. Ultimately, the Chinese were willing to take low "coolie" wages, and so displaced the convicts.[49]

In the 1840s, the British employed Bombay convicts in Aden on the works necessary to carve a military post out of a vast outcrop of barren rock. Balancing the cost of shipment, accommodation, and the jail establishment against the value of convict labour, in 1842 the Bombay political agent in the port claimed that convicts did more work than free laborers, because he put them to task work, and that excepting the cost of their initial passage they cost him less.[50] Administrators elsewhere spent a great deal of time estimating convict labour value, and were frequently in dispute with each other about how best to construct their accounts – including how to divide over the years the cost of a convict's passage, and how to factor in the cost of employing overseers and guards. Clearly, convict labour was at a premium, where there was no alternative supply of workers (and thus labour was unattainable or wages were high). But administrators disputed the amount of work that they completed each day. Perhaps most importantly, however, and as administrators recognized, convicts performed work that would not otherwise have been completed, for the Company did not allocate sufficient resources for the hire of free workers. W.J. Butterworth, governor of the Straits Settlements, noted in 1847 that for this reason it was impossible to calculate the true value of convict labour. The port of Singapore, he wrote, "owes all and everything" to convicts, and Penang and Malacca were similarly indebted to them for the building of roads and canals, and the draining of swamps. Their value, he concluded, was always greater than statistical comparisons with free labourers implied.[51]

REPRESSION AND REBELLION

Most of the convicts involved in the 1851 outbreak in Moulmein, a description of which opened this article, were from the Punjab, which the Company

---

49. G.B. Tremenheere, executive engineer Tenasserim division, "Second Report on the Tin of Mergui", *Journal of the Asiatic Society of Bengal*, 11 (1842), pp. 839–852.
50. IOR P/403/9: J.B. Haynes, political agent Aden, to L.R. Reid, secretary to government Bombay judicial department., 11 April 1842. The calculations were as follows. Daily expense of maintaining one convict, 4 oz dhal, 18 oz flour, 4 oz vegetables, 32 oz firewood, 7/8 oz curry stuff, salt – 1 anna 11 pice. Yearly expense of one convict: 2 *cumlies* (blankets) 1 rupee, 1 *pugree* (turban) 8 annas, 1 *dhoti* (long waistcloth) 8 annas, soap 1 piece per month 6 annas, contingent for cooking pots 2 rupees. *1 convict's yearly expense = 47 rupees 13 annas + cost of passage, 90 rupees.* Free labour: daily expense paid by executive engineer 3 annas 6 pice. *1 free labourer's yearly expense = 68 rupees 7 annas 6 pice.* Excepting the one-off expense of the passage, Haynes noted the cost per year of each convict was 20 rupees 10 annas 6 pice less than the hire of a free labourer.
51. IOR P/142/60: Butterworth to Young, 9 December 1846; P/143/16: Butterworth to Young, 12 November 1847.

Figure 1. Arracan [Arakan] 14th February [1849] Kyook Phoo [Kyaukpyu] Ghat & Prisoners Carrying Water in Buckets, Isle of Ramree. Watercolour by Clementina Benthall.
Benthall Papers, Centre of South Asian Studies, University of Cambridge.

had annexed in 1849 following its victory in the first and second Anglo-Sikh Wars of 1845–1846 and 1848–1849 (Figure 1).[52] In the aftermath of these wars, the British convicted, jailed, and transported dozens of former soldiers to mainland prisons or penal settlements in South East Asia (Figure 2), many under charges of "treason". These military men were well trained, drilled, and experienced in handling weapons. In later years, particularly after remaining loyal to the East India Company during the Indian rebellion of 1857, the British came to favour men of this region for employment in both the Bengal army and the Indian police service. They constituted one of India's "martial castes", for their alleged physical superiority and military prowess.[53] During the intervening decade, however, they were certainly not preferred prisoners or transports. Defeated, demoralized, and dispossessed, Punjabi soldier convicts carried anti-imperial sentiment with them into transportation, and agitated continuously against their penal confinement, sometimes in concert with ordinary convicts.

In Burma, for instance, convicts organized mass escapes after a general tightening up of discipline, including the introduction of common messing. The new rules prescribed that convicts should cook and eat their rations

52. J.S. Grewal, *The Sikhs of the Punjab (revised edition)* (Cambridge, 2002), ch. 6.
53. Heather Streets, *Martial Races: The Military, Race and Masculinity in British Imperial Culture, 1857–1914* (Manchester, 2004).

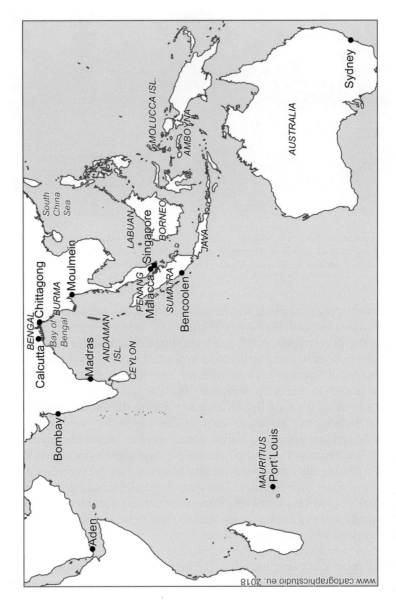

Figure 2. Indian Ocean Penal Settlements.

together, rather than in self-selecting groups, according to their own desires
or cultural and religious imperatives. In November 1846, convicts attempted
to break out, and when they failed instead burnt down their wards and guard
rooms.[54] A month later, a road gang of 120 mounted but did not succeed in
another mass escape attempt. Clearly pre-organized, the *jemadar* (head overseer) heard one convict say to another shortly before giving the signal to
attack the *tindals* (overseers), "Are you ready?" The commissioner of
Arakan claimed that the outbreak was at least partly the consequence of
the convicts' knowledge that he had no power to sanction them, for they
were already subject to the severe punishment of hard labour in chains for
life.[55] In 1849, there was a mutiny at the Moulmein coal depot in Mopoon
(which preceded the event that opened this chapter by two years). One hundred convicts employed in preparing coal for delivery to the Company
steamer rose against their guards. They, too, failed in their bid to escape,
with the Company guard killing three and severely wounding eight men in
an effort to prevent their flight. British commissioner Bogle reported: "the
Secks had [...] bound themselves by an Oath never to return to the prison
and to eat beef sooner than abandon their purpose [...] Bold men will ever
be found keen to emancipate themselves from thraldom, and when determined upon it, they are not to be restrained [...]".[56]

The following year, 1850, a military general named Narain Singh led a violent mutiny among thirty-nine convicts on board a river steamer on the way
to Alipur jail, in Calcutta, which was the holding depot for transportation to
Burma. After quelling the outbreak, and securing the convicts, they continued to plot their escape, including in prison stops along the way.[57] There
were significant logistical challenges both in moving convicts securely into
transportation, and in keeping them to labour in relatively open environments, which often bordered rivers or the sea. This was of course most notably the case in ports. Though convicts failed in their bid for freedom on that
occasion, there and in the other cases noted above, their penal mobility –
across land, along water, and in outdoor working gangs – put them into
close physical contact, which was necessary for the planning of collective
action. Paradoxically, whilst the Company effected transportation as a

---

54. IOR P/142/57: E. Money, executive officer Arakan division, to Major William Sage, super-
intending engineer south-eastern provinces, 11 November 1846.
55. IOR P/142/62: J.R. Colvin, commissioner Tenasserim provinces, to F.J. Halliday, secretary
to government of Bengal judicial department, 2 February 1847, enc. Inquiry into an outbreak of
convicts on the Nyoung Ben Zeik Road, 28 December 1846.
56. IOR P/143/40: Bogle to Grant, 16 November 1849.
57. For the extraordinary life history of Narain Singh, who eventually rose to the position of
chief warder of Moulmein jail, see Clare Anderson, *Subaltern Lives: Biographies of
Colonialism in the Indian Ocean World, 1790–1920* (Cambridge, 2012), ch. 4.

punishment, it also put into motion the spread of rebellious sentiments to the port cities of South East Asia.

The penal transportation of the soldiers of a defeated army following the Anglo-Sikh Wars was entirely consistent with Company justice, which can be dated in this regard to the turn of the nineteenth century. Following the loss of their kingdom during the wars of 1799–1801, Polygar chiefs, for instance, were shipped by the British from south India to both Fort William (Calcutta) and Penang.[58] Repressive penal transportations also followed the final crushing of the Chuar rebellion in 1816, the second and third Maratha Wars (1803–1805, 1816–1819), the Kol revolt of 1831, the 1835 Ghumsur war against the Konds in Orissa,[59] the 1844 anti-Company revolt in the princely state of Kolhapur,[60] and the Santal *hul* (rebellion) of 1855.[61] During this entire period, the East India Company also used transportation to expel peasant rebels, particularly low caste and tribal subjects resistant to the Company's occupation of land, extraction of natural resources (notably the timber used for railway sleepers), and taxation regime.[62]

The political convicts of Company Asia joined forces with ordinary, "criminal" convicts to resist their situation at every turn. In 1816, for instance, a dozen convicts rose up and escaped from the Bel Ombre plantation in Mauritius. Some of these men had been sepoys (soldiers), others were low-caste Kols or Chuars who had been convicted of offences relating to peasant rebellion in the Bengal Presidency. They had been confined together to await their transportation in Calcutta's Alipur jail, where a few of the men had been involved in serious riots and were transported in groups on three separate transportation ships. These men were religious rebels of sorts, protesting against the contravention of caste norms regarding the sharing of cooking and eating pots. They stole weapons and escaped into the mountains, allegedly joining a band of maroon (runaway) slaves. In the ensuing trial at the Court of Assizes, they called each other *camarade* (in French or

58. IOR P/321/95: R. Rickards, principal collector Malabar, to George Buchan, chief secretary to government Madras judicial department, 2 October 1803.

59. TNSA, Madras judicial proceedings, Vol. 304B: H.G.A. Taylor, commander Northern Division, to H. Chamier, secretary to government Madras judicial department, 26 January 1836. See also Felix Padel, *The Sacrifice of Human Being: British Rule and the Konds of Orissa* (New Delhi, 1995), ch. 2.

60. Richard Gott, *Britain's Empire: Resistance, Repression and Revolt* (London, 2011), pp. 343–344.

61. See the classic account, Ranajit Guha, *Elementary Aspects of Peasant Insurgency in Colonial India* (New Delhi, 1983).

62. IOR P/403/47: Political agent Aden to W. Escombe, secretary to government Bombay, 27 June 1845; governor's minute, n.d. On the history of Kolhapur in the nineteenth century, see *Imperial Gazetteer of India, Vol. XV* (Oxford, 1908), p. 383; Anderson, *Convicts in the Indian Ocean*, pp. 28–32.

Mauritian Kreol, comrade) or *bhai* (Hindustani for brother).[63] Kolhapur rebels transported to Aden in the mid-1840s likewise led repeated escape attempts, including one collective effort in which Company guards shot dead three convicts, whilst at least ten others drowned in their bid to escape.[64]

Though it succeeded in the expulsion of undesirable imperial subjects, transportation failed as a means of containing anti-imperial sentiment and action. Rather, it facilitated its spread, with subaltern action often turning on the same socio-political grievances that had underpinned convicts' initial transportation. As noted above, the close confinement of convicts' river journeys enabled them to plot collective action. The same was true of sea voyages, and there were over a dozen convict mutinies in the period to 1857. Many were both effected and repressed with spectacular levels of violence. The largest of all was the seizure of the *Clarissa* by more than one hundred convicts in 1854. This failed when the convicts ran aground off the coast of Burma and attempted to sign a treaty with a local ruler, in the false belief that he was holding out against the East India Company. In fact, he had already signed a treaty with the British.[65] In regard to the importance of often long journeys into transportation as spaces of rebellion, it is significant that the Company often referred to transportation convicts as transmarine, that is to say, from the other side of the sea. This connected together convicts' place of origin to their journeys and destinations in a way that suggested, implicitly at least, a close relationship between the three.

The 1857 revolt in India proved a turning point in the history of Indian convict transportation, as the British recognized and feared the consequence of the spread of transregional solidarities of resistance in their Asian settlements. One of the Punjabi convicts sent to Singapore following the Second Anglo-Sikh War, for example, Nihal Singh, had led anti-British forces and was widely regarded as a "saint-soldier", known by the honorific title Bhai Maharaj ("brother ruler") Singh. The British deputy commissioner wrote at the time: "He is to the Natives what Jesus Christ is to the most zealous of Christians. His miracles were seen by tens of thousands, and are more implicitly relied on, than those worked by the ancient prophets [...] This man who was a God, is in our hands". Afraid of his influence in the

---

63. Anderson, "The Bel Ombre Rebellion".
64. IOR P/403/47: S.B. Haines, political agent Aden, to W. Escombe, secretary to government Bombay judicial department, 27 June 1845.
65. IOR P/402/30: Deposition of Captain F.N. Pendygrass, 19 January 1839; J.A. Forbes, acting senior police magistrate, to J.P. Willoughby, secretary to government Bombay, 22 January 1839; IOR P/145/32: H. Fergusson, superintendent Alipur jail, to A.W. Russell, undersecretary to government Bengal, 24 January 1856. See also Clare Anderson, "The Age of Revolution in the Indian Ocean, Bay of Bengal, and South China Sea: A Maritime Perspective", *International Review of Social History*, 58 (2013), pp. 229–252.

cosmopolitan working environment of the port, the British did not put Nihal Singh to ordinary labour, and attempted to keep him away from both convicts and free workers. He had been transported to Singapore with Khurruck Singh, who the British described as his "disciple". By the time of the outbreak of rebellion in 1857 Nihal Singh had died, but the British expressed grave anxieties about Khurruck Singh's influence on the convicts and Indians then in Singapore. The British had formerly allowed him to live at large, under police surveillance, and he had gone to live with a free Parsee spice merchant. After the outbreak of revolt in the mainland, however, the governor of the Straits Settlements ordered his confinement in the civil jail, and no longer allowed him freedom of movement. Meantime, fearing revolutionary contamination, they evacuated all the "Sikh" convicts then in Singapore, some to the penal settlement of Penang.[66]

In the port city of Moulmein, too, the British feared the spread of rebellion. In July 1857, the superintendent of the jail reported that the convicts possessed "a most unsteady feeling". A shipload of fifty convicts had arrived on the *Fire Queen*, bringing, he claimed, "exaggerated stories" with them. The Company had put them in heavy chains, and in distinction to routine transportation practice they were guarded by Europeans, not Indians. The officiating commissioner refused to land them, however, directing them back to Calcutta. He wrote that, like the newly arrived convicts, the jail peons and town police were nearly all "up countrymen" (i.e. from northern India). Moreover, there were 250 ticket-of-leave convicts in the port. "From conversations which have been overheard", he reported, "it is not impossible that they and a portion of the Mahomedan population of the Town might form a collusion for a general outbreak of the Jail".[67] This fear was certainly not groundless, for one of the key features of the 1857 revolt was the breaking open of prisons. The consequence of this alliance between rebels and prisoners was the serious damage or destruction of over forty jails, and the escape of over 20,000 inmates.[68]

---

66. J. Cowper, assistant surgeon Singapore, to R. Church, secretary to governor Straits Settlements, 1 July 1856, and note of E.A. Blundell, governor Straits Settlements, 12 July 1856, cited in Nahar Singh (ed.), *Documents Relating to Bhai Maharaj Singh* (Ludhiana, 1968), pp. 200–202. See also Anderson, *Subaltern Lives*, pp. 110–114; Anoma Pieris, "The 'Other' Side of Labor Reform: Accounts of Incarceration and Resistance in the Straits Settlements Penal System, 1825–1873", *Journal of Social History*, 45:2 (2011), pp. 453–479; Rajesh Rai, "The 1857 Panic and the Fabrication of an Indian 'Menace' in Singapore", *Modern Asian Studies*, 47:2 (2013), pp. 365–405.

67. IOR P/146/12D: A. Fytche, officiating commissioner Tenasserim and Martaban provinces, to E. Lushington, officiating assistant secretary to government Bengal, 22 July 1857. "Ticket-of-leave" convicts were released on probation, with relative freedom of movement and employment subject to continuing good behaviour.

68. Clare Anderson, *The Indian Uprising of 1857–8: Prisons, Prisoners and Rebellion* (London, 2007).

CONCLUSION

During the period 1789 to 1866, transportation was linked to the repressive policies of the East India Company. Underpinned by representations of its peculiar appropriateness as a punishment in India, the Company used it as a means of removing rebels and undesirable criminal offenders from their home localities. Following their arrival in the Company's trading factories, Indian convicts played a vital role in building infrastructures of connection that linked port cities of the Bay of Bengal and the Indian Ocean to each other and to their hinterlands. Grounded in wider imperial practice, extending across Britain's empire in the Americas and Australia, convict transportation in this regard was connected to enslavement in the Atlantic and Indian Ocean worlds. However, Britain's Asian system was distinct from other imperial convict flows because the Company's trading factories were hubs in and through which the convict workforce was employed and distributed. The Company used convicts as a means of supplying the workforce necessary to create new circuits of connection to expand commodity production and export. Convicts were one element of the cosmopolitan port city labour force during this vital period in the development of imperial trade. One of the unintended consequences of penal transportation in British Asia was that the close confinement and association of convicts during transportation rendered the punishment a vector for the development of transregional political solidarities, centred in and around the Company's port cities. These created new kinds of unanticipated subaltern connections, in which the violence of penal transportation could be met with the violence of resistance against it.

IRSH 64 (2019), pp. 229–254 doi:10.1017/S0020859019000130
© 2019 Internationaal Instituut voor Sociale Geschiedenis

Street Food, Urban Space, and Gender: Working on the Streets of Nineteenth-Century Rio de Janeiro (1830–1870)*

MELINA TEUBNER

Universität zu Köln, a.r.t.e.s. Graduate School for the Humanities
Albertus-Magnus-Platz, 50923 Cologne, Germany

E-mail: mteubner@smail.uni-koeln.de

ABSTRACT: This article focuses on African women (*Quitandeiras*) who worked in the food sector of the fast-growing port city of Rio de Janeiro during the first half of the nineteenth century. The growing need to supply the harbour workers as well as the crews and captives on the slave ships stimulated the food economy in Rio de Janeiro. The absence of effective government food infrastructure offered opportunities for small businesses. The maritime world on a ship was, in many ways, male. However, there were a high number of female workers in the ports, especially in the informal food sector, frequently mentioned by contemporary authors. This article analyses the involvement of these women as part of a growing working class, who contributed to Rio de Janeiro's crucial role in global networks. The research also focuses on the formation of self-organized groups of female vendors. Thus, it provides further insights into strategies of local actors. By grouping together, the women gained some measure of protection, which empowered them to survive in a difficult and highly competitive market. Through their activities, they also changed the urban space of the port area, leaving their mark on it. They acted as crucial vectors for establishing different diaspora dishes, which met huge demand among many consumers. In doing so, they contributed to the formation of an African-American food culture on the streets of Rio de Janeiro.

INTRODUCTION

In March 1878, Emília Soares do Patrocinio and other food vendors published a petition in the Brazilian newspaper *Jornal do Commercio* opposing

---

* I would like to extend my gratitude to the participants in the two workshops on "Free and Unfree Labor in Atlantic and Indian Port Cities (c.1700–1850)" held at the University of Pittsburgh in May 2016 and May 2017 for their constructive comments. I would especially like to thank Pernille Røge, Niklas Frykman, and Pepijn Brandon for organizing this Special Issue. The research on which this article is based has received funding from the German Academic Exchange Service and the a.r.t.e.s. Graduate School for the Humanities, University of Cologne.

the exorbitant increase in rents at the local market.[1] For decades, Emília had been selling vegetables and poultry at many different stands at the port market (*Mercado da Candelária*), and, by doing so, had become relatively wealthy.[2] When she died in 1885 she bequeathed three houses, twenty slaves, jewellery, and money to her heirs.[3] It was a remarkable career for a West African woman shipped to Brazil in the first half of the nineteenth century and who had spent a great part of her life in slavery before buying her freedom in 1839. Emília Soares had hired a stand at the market, which meant a move to formalized areas of food selling. It required capital and was the mark of a relatively high social position for a woman like her. The case of Emília's upward mobility is indeed remarkable in its rarity, since most of the *Quitandeiras* had only a stand at the beach or worked as small ambulant traders under precarious living conditions. African women involved in the street-food sector were called *Quitandeiras*. At this point it is helpful to take a linguistic sidestep to clarify the origin of the word. *Quitanda* is a loan word adopted from Kimbundu, the second largest Bantu language, and means "to sell".[4]

Most of those who sold food with a permit (*licença municipal*) were male slaves.[5] There was a great variety among vendors. Some were slaves who went out to sell foodstuffs in their free time, on Sundays, or at night, while others worked on the streets with their masters' permission. Some free and unfree persons worked with an official licence (*licença municipal*), many as unlicensed vendors. As slaves, they had the opportunity to accumulate sufficient money to buy their freedom, often through activities in the food sector. Then, many of them continued with this business.

In recent decades, female street vendors have been studied by a number of Brazilian scholars, who have shed light on urban slavery, domestic slavery, and other forms of unfree labour. From a micro-historical perspective,

---

1. *Jornal do Commercio* (JC), 29 March 1878.
2. The market was located near the Baia da Guanabara. The idea was to construct a central and controlled place for the sale of varying commodities, modelled after European markets. See Samuel Gorberg and Sergio A. Fridman, *Mercados no Rio de Janeiro, 1834–1962* (Rio de Janeiro, 2003); Juliana Barreto Farias, "Mercados Minas: Africanos ocidentais na Praça do Mercado do Rio de Janeiro (1830–1890)" (Ph.D., University of São Paulo, 2012), p. 54. Juliana Barreto Farias, "De escrava a Dona: A trajetória da africana mina Emília Soares do Patrocínio no Rio de Janeiro do século XIX", *Locus. Revista de História*, 18:2 (2002), pp. 13–40, 14. See also Franklin W. Knight and Henry Louis Gates (eds), *Dictionary of Caribbean and Afro-Latin American Biography*, 6 vols (Oxford, 2016), V, pp. 90–91.
3. Farias, "De escrava a Dona", p. 14. See also Knight and Gates, *Dictionary of Caribbean and Afro-Latin American Biography*, V, pp. 90–91.
4. Flávio dos Santos Gomes and Carlos E.L. Soares, "'Dizem as quitandeiras...'. Ocupações urbanas e identidades étnicas em uma cidade escravista: Rio de Janeiro, século XIX", *Acervo*,15:2 (2002), pp. 3–16.
5. Luiz Carlos Soares, "Os Escravos de Ganho no Rio de Janeiro do Século XIX", *Revista Brasileira do História*, 8:16 (1988), pp. 107–142.

these studies incorporated labourers who were neglected by traditional historical studies and showed through both the study of particular cases and qualitative studies the agency of both enslaved and free/freed African women who took part in local trade, relying on their transatlantic experiences. These studies commonly focus on community building among urban slaves and the formation of a West African diaspora. The group of Mina vendors and their social mobility is the most studied group of these women.[6] The Mina came from the West African Coast, were sold in great numbers from Bahia to Rio de Janeiro, and "stood out from the rest of the slaves and freed persons for their strong ethnic links and ethnic-based organizations".[7]

There are, however, few studies that explore street-food vending in Rio de Janeiro as a social, everyday practice that was central for feeding the labouring population of the port city. Since cooking is not only one of the most time-consuming and widespread kinds of labour in history, it should not be underestimated how labour intensive the provisioning and feeding of a fast-growing port city probably was.[8] Furthermore, the focus on reproductive labour hints at another aspect often overseen in earlier studies of labour history, namely the fact that "not every kind of work aims at a market and not every kind of work is arranged on a market".[9] Especially in the food sector, different kinds of labour existed in parallel to one another (slaves, former slaves, wage-earning slaves, free and semi-free wage labourers, self-employed women, and women as unpaid reproductive workers within a household).[10] In general, according to Rockman, all of "these workers lived and worked within a broader system that treated human labor as commodity readily deployed in the service of private wealth and national economic

---

6. Sheila de Castro Faria, "Damas mercadoras: As pretas minas no Rio de Janeiro (século XVIII–1850)", in Mariza de Carvalho Soares (ed.), *Rotas atlânticas da diáspora africana: da Baía do Benim ao Rio de Janeiro* (Niterói, 2007), pp. 101–134; Carlos Eugénio Líbano Soares and Flávio dos Santos Gomes, "Negras Minas no Rio de Janeiro: gênero, nação e trabalho urbano no século XIX", in De Carvalho Soares, *Rotas atlânticas da diáspora africana*, pp. 191–221; Farias, "Mercados Minas".

7. João José Reis and Beatriz Gallotti Mamigonian, "Nagô and Mina: The Yoruba Diaspora in Brazil", in Toyin Falola and Matt D. Childs (eds), *The Yoruba Diaspora in the Atlantic World* (Bloomington, 2004), pp. 77–110, here p. 105.

8. Jürgen Osterhammel, *Die Verwandlung der Welt, Eine Geschichte des 19. Jahrhunderts* (Munich, 2009), p. 958: "Durch Arbeit wird etwas hergestellt – nichts häufiger als Mahlzeiten, so dass Kochen die am weitesten verbreitete und insgesamt zeitaufwändigste Verausgabung von Arbeitskraft in der gesamten Geschichte gewesen sein dürfte. Nicht alle Arbeit, das zeigt dieses Beispiel, zielt auf Märkte, und nicht alle Arbeitskraft wird über den Markt vermittelt".

9. *Ibid.*, p. 958.

10. Gisela Bock and Barbara Duden, "Arbeit aus Liebe – Liebe als Arbeit: Zur Entstehung der Hausarbeit im Kapitalismus", in *Frauen und Wissenschaft: Beiträge zur Berliner Sommeruniversität für Frauen, Juli 1976* (Berlin, 1977), pp. 118–199.

development".[11] Food sellers were not merely passive victims of slavery and marginalization, but a disparate group of capable actors, who created a gendered niche of economic opportunity, through the capitalization of their cooking and vending skills.[12]

Both the absence of an effective government food infrastructure and the inability of the police to control public spaces offered opportunities for small (informal) businesses, especially in the port area.[13] These businesses had a huge impact on the development of and change in the city's food culture. As in other port cities, European culinary customs were very influential in the nineteenth century, but through Rio de Janeiro's special role in the late transatlantic slave trade the *Quitandeiras* brought with them their own knowledge and culinary practices.[14] This article explores, in particular, the ways in which they not only introduced African cuisine, but also created city spaces for workers, despite the forces opposing them. The vending environment became an important space of sociability, for multi-ethnic inhabitants, port labourers, and foreign visitors.

This article argues that, despite all their efforts to modernize and control the city space, the city's authorities were unable to prevent the selling of food on the streets, since their intentions were undermined at a local level.[15] On the contrary, the street-food vendors became a highly visible part of the life of the city. The planning of Rio de Janeiro into a modern metropolis was forced to adapt to the *Quitandeiras*, who refused to relinquish their space in the city. Furthermore, since Rio de Janeiro was a globally connected port city, the reputation of the *Quitandeiras*, as a highly visible part of the city, reached distant parts of the world. The *Quitandeiras* can be regarded as part of a larger heterogeneous group of street working women who gained visibility and recognition in parts of contemporary popular culture, an aspect that until now has been completely overlooked.

In contrast to studies that focused on the ethnic diversity of workers, a perspective that highlights the differences between the vendors, this study concentrates on the similarities between very heterogeneous groups of free and unfree workers in their everyday struggles for survival on the streets, which was a result of their shared marginalized status.

11. Seth Rockman, *Scraping By: Wage Labor, Slavery, and Survival in Early Baltimore* (Baltimore, MD, 2009), p. 4.

12. Farias, "Mercados Minas".

13. Richard Graham, *Feeding the City: From Street Market to Liberal Reform in Salvador, Brazil 1780–1860* (Austin, TX, 2010), p. 4.

14. Selma Pantoja, "A dimensão atlântica das quitandeiras", in Júnia Ferreira Furtado (ed.), *Diálogos oceânicos: Minas Gerais e as novas abordagens para uma história do Império Ultramarino Português* (Belo Horizonte, 2001), pp. 45–67.

15. Patricia Acerbi, *Street Occupations: Urban Vending in Rio de Janeiro, 1850–1925* (Austin, TX, 2017).

The first part focuses on food, consumers, and the labour process of selling food on the streets. The second part centres on the urban space of Rio de Janeiro. Street vendors constantly had to fight for their spaces in the city against municipal authorities, the police, but also against other vendors, because public space then, as now, was an "indispensable resource of income".[16] The third part is focused on the gendered nature of street food, because the popularity of female hawkers was closely connected to their being women. I will combine recent approaches in research on aspects of street vending in urban contexts, case studies from Rio de Janeiro, and new sources mainly from contemporary Brazilian newspapers.

Rio de Janeiro, but also many other port cities, relied on the reproductive labour of women; this is often overshadowed by the much more studied male port labourers and sailors.[17]

STREET FOOD

The description given by a Parisian woman who travelled to Rio de Janeiro in the mid-1800s provides a closer view of the everyday business going on near the port. "There stand, under large linen umbrellas, negresses, who serve you, for two cents, [...] some *angú*".[18] A painting by Jean-Baptiste Debret (Figure 1) depicts a scene similar to what the Parisian women witnessed. Three vendors at a makeshift stand are preparing *angú* in cauldrons stabilized by large rocks over an open fire prepared in between them, constantly stirring with large wooden spoons and ladling the *angú* onto a plate, in order to serve it to the customer.

The sociocultural background and the place of residence were and still are decisive for where and how people take their meals. In the port area the habit of eating out, as a form of providing the highly mobile working class with food during their worktime and beyond, was very common. During the late eighteenth and the early nineteenth century, the city of Rio de Janeiro grew from a small village into the biggest city in South America and one of its most important commercial centres (Figure 2). The population expanded rapidly, nearly doubling in size from 50,000 to 100,000 inhabitants in the period 1808–1838 to 200,000 people in 1850.[19] The history of Rio de

16. Kristina Graaff and Noa Ha, "Introduction. Street Vending in the Neoliberal City: A Global Perspective on the Practices and Policies of a Marginalized Economy", in *idem* (eds), *Street Vending in the Neoliberal City: A Global Perspective on the Practices and Policies of a Marginalized Economy* (New York, 2015), pp. 1–15, 5.

17. For a similar highly gendered group of labourers and their social networks, see the article by Titas Chakraborty in this Special Issue. It examines the experiences of household workers and their agency in East Indian Company ports of precolonial Bengal.

18. Adèle Toussaint-Samson, *A Parisian in Brazil* (Boston, MA, 1891), p. 41.

19. Mary C. Karasch, *Slave Life in Rio de Janeiro, 1808–1850* (Princeton, NJ, 1987), p. 142.

Figure 1. Jean-Baptiste Debret, *Négresses marchandes d'angou* [Negress *angú* vendors]. *The Miriam and Ira D. Wallach Division of Art, Prints and Photographs, Print Collection, The New York Public Library, New York Public Library Digital Collections.*

Janeiro in the nineteenth century in many ways resembles the story of other fast-growing cities in different parts of the world.[20] What makes Rio de Janeiro special is the fact that its growth was largely interlinked with the history of the late transatlantic slave trade. Providing slave voyages to Africa with food was an important part of the infrastructure of the transatlantic slave trade. Food production and provision was one of "the labour-intensive ancillary activities" to the rise of which the slave trade contributed.[21] Even though Rio de Janeiro had been a slave society since the seventeenth century, fundamental changes were taking place regarding its political and economic importance at the end of the eighteenth and the beginning of the nineteenth century. Having been the capital of the Brazilian Empire since 1763, its political importance rose with the transfer of the Portuguese crown and administration as a consequence of the invasion of Portugal by Napoleon's army in

20. For more information on the development of cities in the nineteenth century, see Osterhammel, *Die Verwandlung der Welt*, pp. 355–412.
21. David Eltis, Paul E. Lovejoy, and David Richardson, "Slave-Trading Ports: Towards an Atlantic-Wide Perspective, 1676–1832", in Robin Law and Silke Strickrodt (eds), *Ports of the Slave Trade (Bights of Benin and Biafra): Papers from a Conference of Commonwealth Studies, University of Stirling, June 1998* (Stirling, 1999), pp. 12–34, 17.

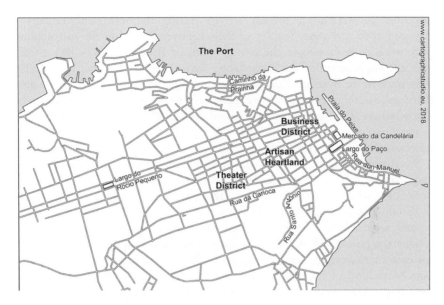

Figure 2. Rio de Janeiro in the nineteenth century.

1807. During the 1820s and even more so the 1830s, its economic importance relied on the extremely profitable coffee zones situated in central-south Brazil, and most of all in the Vale do Paraíba.[22] According to Dale Tomich and Michael Zeuske and their concept of the Second Slavery, central Brazil was one of the "highly productive new zones of slave commodity production" and became the biggest exporter of coffee in order to meet the demand from Europe and North America.[23] This demand also stimulated the import of new slaves, and Rio de Janeiro functioned as a link between the wider world and the Brazilian hinterland.[24] Even after the official prohibition of the transatlantic slave trade to Brazil in 1831, slaves were still entering the port up until at least 1850 (and some ships even arrived afterwards).[25] Of all the slaves

22. Rafael Marquese and Dale Tomich, "O Vale do Paraíba escravista e a formação do mercado mundial do café no século XIX", in Keila Grinberg and Ricardo Salles (eds), *O Brasil Império: Vol. II – 1831–1870* (Rio de Janeiro, 2009), pp. 341–383; João Luís Ribeiro Fragoso, *Homens de Grossa Aventura: Acumulação e Hierarquia na Praça Mercantil do Rio de Janeiro (1790–1830)* (Rio de Janeiro, 1998), p. 20; Ilmar Rohloff de Mattos, *O tempo saquarema* (São Paulo, 1987).
23. Dale Tomich and Michael Zeuske, "Introduction, The Second Slavery: Mass Slavery, World-Economy, and Comparative Microhistories", *Review (Fernand Braudel Center)*, 31:2 (2008), pp. 91–100, 91–92. Dale W. Tomich, *Through the Prism of Slavery: Labor, Capital, and World Economy* (Lanham, MD, 2004).
24. Manolo Garcia Florentino, *Em Costas Negras. Uma História do Tráfico Atlântico de Escravos entre a África e o Rio de Janeiro (séculos XVIII e XIX)* (Rio de Janeiro, 1995), p. 74.
25. The most famous cases were the Bracuhy (RJ) and the Sirinhaém (PE). Martha Abreu, "O caso do Bracuhy", in Hebe Maria Mattos de Castro and Eduardo Schnoor (eds), *Resgate:*

imported to Brazil, 2.1 million arrived during the nineteenth century.[26] Between 1820 and 1860, 803,815 of these captives arrived in the surrounding ports of Rio de Janeiro in the central-south of Brazil.[27] It was also mainly after the suppression of the transatlantic slave trade in 1850 that the internal slave trade in the Brazilian Empire gained new relevance.[28] Slaves from the northern and southern provinces were lucratively resold to the central-south provinces, where labourers were more needed than in other parts of Brazil. Brazil's economic development was possible only through the workers performing the necessary "hidden labour" in the port area, such as provisioning and feeding.[29]

Street vendors were able to do business because their customers, who lived and worked near the harbour, were very often mobile, staying in the city only for a while. For them and for the many other workers on the streets of Rio de Janeiro, eating out was practical or even necessary. The food-selling women were able to offer lower-priced meals especially for working and poor residents, who were often without access to a kitchen. Among the most important customers were seamen who stayed in the city for just a few days and did not always have a fixed address on land, which meant that they lived onboard their ships. After weeks at sea, with its monotonous diet, the crews often spent their wages on food and alcoholic drinks in the port areas. Other important customers were wage-earning (*ganhadores*) and fugitive slaves, who often shared a room with others, sometimes without access to a kitchen, or even slept on the streets, and in boats at the beach – like the forty-eight-year-old man from São Tomé known to sleep in a canoe at D. Manuel beach.[30] Another example of housing for slaves was inside the Rio de Janeiro market, where the market slaves could get permission from their masters, who rented the stand, to stay overnight.[31] As it was forbidden by law to sell pre-prepared dishes inside the market, these slaves had to find their meals elsewhere.[32]

Wage-earning slaves and former slaves were important consumers, and their preferences were observed by vendors.[33] They had specific expectations

Uma Janela para o Oitocentos (Rio de Janeiro, 1995), pp. 165–195; Gláucio Veiga, *O desembarque de Sirinhaém* (Recife, 1977).

26. www.slavevoyages.org; last accessed 3 December 2017.

27. *Ibid.*

28. Robert W. Slenes, "The Brazilian Internal Slave Trade, 1850–1888: Regional Economies, Slave Experience, and the Politics of a Peculiar Market", in Walter Johnson (ed.), *The Chattel Principle: Internal Slave Trades in the Americas* (New Haven, CT [etc.], 2004), pp. 325–371.

29. Cf. Rockman, *Scraping By*, pp. 101–102.

30. *JC*, 16 September 1845.

31. Farias, "Mercados Minas", p. 54.

32. *Diário do Rio de Janeiro* (DRJ), 7 December 1845 (Regulamento da Praça do Mercado Art. 29). For safety reasons, open fires were forbidden inside the market.

33. Manuel Schramm, *Konsumgeschichte*, available at: https://zeitgeschichte-digital.de/doks/frontdoor/deliver/index/docId/262/file/docupedia_schramm_konsumgeschichte_v2_de_2012.pdf; last accessed 6 October 2018.

regarding what buying food from *Quitandeiras* meant, which in return induced the *Quitandeiras* to adjust their behaviour in order to meet these expectations.[34] The marketing strategies were part of a performance and interaction with the consumer.[35] To attract the customer's attention, vendors would holler and sing.[36] Thomas Ewbank, who travelled around Brazil in the late nineteenth century, vividly described his impression of life on the streets of Rio de Janeiro: "The 'cries' of London are bagatelles to those of the Brazilian Capital. Slaves of both sexes cry wares through every street. Vegetables, flowers, fruits, edible roots, fowl, eggs, and every rural product; cakes, pies, rusks, *doces*, confectionery, 'heavenly bacon,' etc., pass your windows continually."[37] Through such immensely crowded streets the *Quitandeiras* walked; they were described as elegant, with a basket or a tray, and wearing characteristic clothing – such as a coloured dress, a turban, and a *pano da costa* over the shoulder.[38] The atmosphere surrounding the act of eating was also important for the overall experience, since dining is a multi-layered experience appealing to all senses.[39]

Toussaint-Samson and other travellers described *angú* as the slaves' staple food.[40] The labour-intensive dish *angú*, in other regions of the Atlantic world called *fufu*, is made by boiling either manioc or maize in water and then mashing it while stirring continuously until it is sticky. Its consistency is similar to, but thicker than, mashed potatoes. It is served with various ingredients.[41] *Angú* is still advertised as the ideal food for giving workers

---

34. Cf. Maren Möhring, *Fremdes Essen: Die Geschichte der ausländischen Gastronomie in der Bundesrepublik Deutschland* (Munich, 2012), pp. 29, 266.
35. Soares, "Os Escravos de Ganho", p. 112.
36. Recently, several studies have appeared that concentrate on soundscapes of cities and typical cries of street vendors in cities in France and Portugal. See especially Olivier Balay, "The Soundscape of a City in the Nineteenth Century", in Ian Biddle and Kirsten Gibson (eds), *Cultural Histories of Noise, Sound and Listening in Europe, 1300–1918* (London [etc.], 2017), pp. 221–234; João Silva, "Porosity and Modernity: Lisbon's Auditory Landscape from 1864 to 1908", in Biddle and Gibson, *Cultural Histories of Noise, Sound and Listening in Europe*, pp. 235–251. Studies of the soundscapes of nineteenth-century Rio de Janeiro are a desideratum.
37. Thomas Ewbank, *Life in Brazil; Or, A Journal of a Visit to the Land of the Cocoa and the Palm* (London, 1856), pp. 92–93.
38. Cf. Cristina F. Rosa, *Brazilian Bodies and Their Choreographies of Identification* (Basingstoke, 2015), p. 128; Toussaint-Samson, *A Parisian in Brazil*, p. 44.
39. Graham Campbell-Smith, *Marketing of the Meal Experience: A Fundamental Approach* (London, 1967). Quotation from Alan Warde and Lydia Martens, *Eating Out: Social Differentiation, Consumption and Pleasure* (New York, 2000), p. 5; Hasia R. Diner, *Hungering for America: Italian, Irish, and Jewish Foodways in the Age of Migration* (Cambridge, MA, 2003), p. 3.
40. Toussaint-Samson, *A Parisian in Brazil*, p. 41; Johann Baptist von Spix and Carl Friedrich Philipp von Martius, *Viagem pelo Brasil. Vol. 1* (Rio de Janeiro, 1938), p. 113.
41. Judith A. Carney and Richard Nicholas Rosomoff, *In the Shadow of Slavery: Africa's Botanical Legacy in the Atlantic World* (Berkeley, CA, 2009), p. 180.

energy in order to get through their day without hunger.[42] It was typically consumed in West Africa. Since *angú* was normally eaten without cutlery, as can be seen on the painting by Debret (Figure 1), the food had to be prepared in such a way that it did not stick to the fingers. The preparation of the dish varied considerably depending on the availability of ingredients.[43] Manioc or maize were the core ingredients in preparing *angú*, but to achieve a tasty meal a starchy sauce with the aforementioned ingredients would be served as well.[44] The preparation of the sauce, using palm oil (*azeite de dendê*) from West Africa and spices, was central to the specific taste of the dish. Toussaint-Samson notes that "the negroes, who are most dainty, even season everything with a sort of fat they call azeite de dindin".[45] Daily newspapers in Rio de Janeiro frequently advertised palm oil to *angú* sellers.[46] It was already being produced in Brazil, but it was also common to import it from West Africa.[47] Intermediaries, travellers, and ships' crews frequently crossed the Atlantic and through their access to various markets were able to engage in trade in the commodities requested.[48] Food could function as a strong "agent of memory", which is very important for diasporic groups in order to feel connected with their homeland.[49] As Pierre Bourdieu pointed

---

42. Available at: http://www.angudogomes.com.br/o-famoso-angu/; last accessed 3 December 2017. This is the website of a restaurant opened by a Portuguese in 1950. The text on the site emphasizes the long history of *angú*, its African origins, and its connection to a specific lifestyle led by the city's working class in the port area.

43. Hans Jürgen Teuteberg, *Die Revolution am Esstisch: Neue Studien zur Nahrungskultur im 19./20. Jahrhundert* (Stuttgart, 2004), p. 64.

44. Sidney Mintz developed the Core-Fringe-Legume hypothesis, which provides a model for the diet of most agrarian societies. According to this hypothesis, a "core" of seventy to eighty per cent of basic food is complemented by a "fringe", which adds taste, and fruits and vegetables, due to seasonal factors. See, for example, Sidney W. Mintz, "Die Zusammensetzung der Speise in frühen Agrargesellschaften. Versuch einer Konzeptualisierung", in Martin Schäffner (ed.), *Brot, Brei und was dazugehört: Über sozialen Sinn und physiologischen Wert der Nahrung* (Zurich, 1992), pp. 13–28, 17–18.

45. Toussaint-Samson, *A Parisian in Brazil*, p. 41.

46. *JC*, 10 July 1835; *JC*, 16 July 1830; *JC*, 27 September 1836.

47. Arquivo Histórico do Itamaraty, Rio de Janeiro, lata 13, maço 1 (Emilia). For example, the African mariner Jorge carried *azeite de dendê* on the slave ship *Emilia*. Robin Law, "Trade and Politics Behind the Slave Coast", *The Journal of African History*, 24:3 (1983), pp. 321–348. *JC*, 10 July 1835.

48. Arjun Appadurai, "Globale ethnische Räume: Bemerkungen und Fragen zur Entwicklung einer transnationalen Anthropologie", in Ulrich Beck (ed.), *Perspektiven der Weltgesellschaft* (Frankfurt am Main, 1998), pp. 11–40, 15. Gabriela dos Reis Sampaio, "Africanos em trânsito entre Salvador e Rio de Janeiro nas últimas décadas do século XIX", in George Evergton Sales Souza, Guida Marques, and Hugo Rubeiro da Silva (eds), *Salvador da Bahia: retratos de uma cidade atlântica* (Salvador da Bahia, 2016), pp. 325–352, 334, 338f.

49. Diner, *Hungering for America*, p. 8.

out, taste in food has an undeniably strong influence on our identities. "It is probably in tastes in food that one would find the strongest and most indelible mark of infant learning, the lessons which longest withstand the distancing or collapse of the native world and most durably maintain nostalgia for it."[50] Therefore, it was not surprising that the influx of thousands of forcibly immigrated people changed consumption habits in the cities.

In her description, Toussaint-Samson also specifies the customers, saying that the habit of eating out is above all a consumption behaviour maintained by those who are members of the lower classes: "[...] a negro's repast, and even that of the white people of the inferior classes".[51] As shown in Figure 3, a scene from the Largo do Paço (palace square), where seamen and officers are using their afternoon breaks to buy sweets and drinks from the *Quitandeiras*, street food was consumed not only by the lower classes. *Angú da Quitandeira* could be found not only on the streets but also on menus – "O bello e succulente almoço" – at a ball at the Casino Fluminense in 1886 and as part of a theatre piece alluding to the fact that the dish was very prominent.[52] In the play, social class differences in food consumption were used to produce an ironic effect.[53] In the Portuguese version the play was entitled *O angú da quitandeira*, which was clearly meant as an allusion to the exotic origin of the dish. In Brazil, however, *angú da Quitandeira* was far from extraordinary and, therefore, the play was called *O angú do barão*. The plot can be summarized as follows: An old baron, who is married to a beautiful young woman (a dualism), invites a colleague of his to his house for dinner. Instead of offering his guest a dish that would correspond to his social rank, he serves him *angú* (another dualism). Due to the palm oil, which is one of the typical ingredients of *angú*, the dish is apparently highly seasoned. Therefore, the baron drinks a considerable amount of alcohol, which inevitably makes him drunk. His guest, however, is more interested in his host's wife than in the taste of the meal. While the baron's body temperature is rising due to the spicy *angú*, his guest also feels the heat of his body because of the presence of the young woman, who is described as a dish too. Since the baron, who is clearly drunk, soon retires to his chambers his colleague is able to fulfil his emotional

---

50. Pierre Bourdieu, *Distinction: A Social Critique of the Judgement of Taste*, trans. Richard Nice (Cambridge, MA, 1984), p. 79.
51. Toussaint-Samson, *A Parisian in Brazil*, p. 41.
52. Francisco Lellis and André Boccato, *Os Banquetes do Imperador. Menus colecionados por Dom Pedro II. Receitas e Historiografia da Gastronomia no Brasil do século XIX* (São Paulo, 2013), p. 223.
53. The theatre piece was performed in Rio de Janeiro and advertised in *JC*, 24 December 1867 and 19 October 1867. It is unclear when it was performed in Portugal.

Figure 3. Jean-Baptiste Debret, *Les rafraîchissements de l'après-dîner sur la place du palais.*
[After-dinner refreshments on the palace square].
The Miriam and Ira D. Wallach Division of Art, Prints and Photographs, Print Collection, The New York Public Library, New York Public Library Digital Collections, 1834–1839, available at: http://digitalcollections.nypl.org/items/510d47df-7978-a3d9-e040-e00a18064a99; last accessed 8 October 2018.

and amorous desire, although the details are left to the spectator's imagination.[54]

For the middle and upper classes, eating at home was the most common way of taking their meals. Most well-off households had servants who prepared dishes for them.[55] In these social classes, eating at home – though frequently in the company of their kin, colleagues, or acquaintances – was a central element of domestic sociability.[56] However, the ingredients for these meals had to be bought at the local food markets or from vendors selling products door-to-door, in ways that effectively connected them with the street-food sector.

54. Arquivo Distrital de Leiria, J.F. Titulo, "O Angú da Quitandeira. Canção brasileira", in *Coleção: Coleção de monólogos e cançonetas n°29* (Lisbon, n.d.).
55. Sandra Lauderdale Graham, *House and Street: The Domestic World of Servants and Masters in Nineteenth-Century Rio de Janeiro* (Cambridge, 1992), pp. 17, 46.
56. Warde and Martens, *Eating Out*, p. 67.

To understand the street-food sector, it is important to look at the *Quitandeiras'* networks and to explain the local underground food distribution. The majority of foodstuffs arrived in the city from other parts of the province and other parts of Brazil.[57] A number of free blacks and slaves were part of this trade. Some worked on boats, others on small canoes, like João, a canoe man from Mozambique, who used to transport goods between Gamboa and Prainha.[58] Sometimes slaves would steal canoes in order to start a business.[59] In the port area, canoe men and street vendors came together, as in the case of a thirty-to-forty-year-old *Quitandeira*, who likely escaped with one of her seamen friends.[60] In another case, the grass-selling slave Antonio, well-known at D. Manuel beach, escaped. Sometimes, he could be seen with a little canoe near the food stall kept by his mother, a *Quitandeira*.[61] Sources that mention individual cases like these allow a glimpse of underground networks between street-food vendors and workers who supplied the city with food. The port area was a natural place to sell fish and shellfish, and for this reason slaves and free(d) men like the famous "pica peixe" went fishing in their canoes.[62] They could sell the fish they caught to vendors (at the market or outside of it). Through the implementation of high hygienic standards inside the market, any fish not sold the same day they were caught had to be thrown away.[63] It is conceivable that some of these leftovers could have been sold to ambulant vendors at a lower cost. Home-produced goods such as alcoholic drinks, jams, cakes and sweets, crops and fruits planted by slaves in small gardens, and chickens and other small farm animals raised on the same land were also sold on the streets. Fixed commercial establishments had their own vendors who sold the products in the streets.[64] João, for instance, a slave who escaped in 1824, had stolen from his master before and was selling the items on the streets.[65] A similar case was that of Cesario Coelho Paredes, who was convicted in 1855 for selling eleven stolen chickens and a rooster to a

---

57. Manioc flour was imported mostly from the south of the province of Bahia and from Santa Caterina; rice from the south of São Paulo; and dried meat and wheat from Rio Grande do Sul. Corcino Medeiros dos Santos, *O Rio de Janeiro e a conjuntura Atlântica* (Rio de Janeiro, 1993), p. 47.

58. *DRJ*, 22 December 1824; *DRJ*, 7 April 1824; Graham, *Feeding the City*, pp. 78, 81. Cf. also Nielson Rosa Bezerra, *As chaves da liberdade: confluências da escravidão no Recôncavo do Rio de Janeiro (1833–1888)* (Niterói, 2008).

59. *DRJ*, 19 February 1835.

60. *JC*, 24 January 1848.

61. *JC*, 6 November 1830.

62. *DRJ*, 7 November 1837.

63. *DRJ*, 7 December 1845 (Regulamento da Praça do Mercado, Art. 31, 33).

64. Acerbi, *Street Occupations*, p. 5. Cf. Karasch, *Slave Life*.

65. *DRJ*, 31 March 1824.

Quitandeira.[66] The atmosphere of the chaotic city with mule trains and other animal transports arriving from distant farms and women carrying large baskets of chickens on their heads made the city susceptible to missing animals, which could be taken by others.[67]

In addition to street-food vendors, over 1,000 taverns, small establishments where labourers could eat and drink, and over 700 corner stores could be found in the city around 1850.[68] Members of the economic and social elite consumed items imported from Europe, which were increasingly advertised in the daily newspapers.[69] French cuisine became the standard in the nineteenth century, and for this reason French chefs and the French restaurant concept were imported to Brazil after the middle of the century.[70] Most high-end restaurants would even announce in French "huitres fraiches, potage aux huitres frites, branlade de morue, et tout ce que l'on peut désirer dans un hôtel".[71] Portuguese and Italian restaurants also opened during this time, where it was commonly male chefs, recently emigrated from France, Portugal, and Italy, who ran the kitchen.[72] In comparison to street vendors and taverns that offered inexpensive foods and drinks, haute cuisine was not strongly represented in urban areas in the mid-nineteenth century.[73]

URBAN SPACE

Contemporary visitors to Rio de Janeiro left behind a narrative of the chaotic street commerce and narrow and highly frequented streets.[74] Although the

---

66. *DRJ*, 1 May 1855.
67. *DRJ*, 30 January 1841.
68. Zephyr L. Frank, *Dutra's World: Wealth and Family in Nineteenth-Century Rio de Janeiro* (Albuquerque, NM, 2004), p. 115; Leila Mezan Algranti, "Tabernas e Botequins Cotidiano e sociabilidades no Rio de Janeiro (1808–1821)", *Acervo*, 24:2 (2011), pp. 25–42, 28. For more on taverns in the Americas, see Sharon V. Salinger, *Taverns and Drinking in Early America* (Baltimore, MD, 2002).
69. Frank, *Dutra's World*, pp. 37–38. Frank defines the members of the economic and social elite as the "traditional land elite and the emergent mercantile families growing up in the hothouse of the Atlantic economy" (*ibid.*, p. 17).
70. For more on the concept of the modern restaurant, see Rebecca Spang, *The Invention of the Restaurant: Paris and Modern Gastronomic Culture* (Cambridge, MA, 2000); Osterhammel, *Die Verwandlung der Welt*, p. 343.
71. *JC*, 12 January 1851. Cf. Almir Chaiban El-Kareh and Héctor Hernán Bruit, "Cozinhar e comer; em casa e na rua: culinária e gastronomia na Corte do Império do Brasil", *Estudos Históricos*, 33 (2004), pp. 76–96, 84.
72. Tim Wätzold, *Vom kaiserlichen zum nationalen Koch: Ernährungsgeschichte des brasilianischen Kaiserreichs* (Mettingen, 2011), p. 78; Eva Barlösius, *Soziologie des Essens* (3rd edn., Weinheim, 2016), p. 147.
73. Wätzold, *Vom kaiserlichen zum nationalen Koch*, p. 78.
74. Among many others, travellers like Jean-Baptiste Debret (Jean-Baptiste Debret, *Viagem pitoresca e histórica ao Brasil: 1834–1839*, 2 vols (São Paulo, 1940)), John Luccock (John Luccock, *Notes on Rio de Janeiro, and the Southern Parts of Brazil: Taken during a*

provisioning of the city and its inhabitants relied, to a large degree, on a high number of food-selling women and the work they did, survival in the urban milieu was difficult. The study of contemporary newspapers sheds light on the everyday problems and struggles of the street sellers.

The authorities tried to regulate the city space and the places where vendors were allowed to sell foodstuffs because such spaces were intended as representative public spaces of the growing modern city. The food market was one of these projects – coined by a contemporary journalist as a place "capable of challenging the jealousy of Europe's important cities".[75] For this reason, enslaved purchasers were ordered to spend only a minimum of time at the market and to leave as quickly as possible.[76]

As in the case of Emília Soares, even vendors at the top of the food-selling hierarchy were not immune to the profit-maximizing interests of private investors or the state, both of which monopolized selling areas with the aim of increasing rents to make more money off the *Quitandeiras'* labour, hoping workers would accept the new conditions because there were no alternatives. The stallholders at the market formed a union and tried to combat the unequal power relationship by making their protest public in the local Rio newspapers.[77]

Hiring a stand on the market required more capital than most *Quitandeiras* could afford. Therefore, many of them sold their goods in other places, where they were the subject of regular complaints by city officials and/or citizens – oftentimes published in local newspapers.

The expulsion of food-selling women from certain parts of the city was justified by reference to those complaints, which related to noise, the accumulation of garbage and leftover foodstuffs from the vending sites, as well as criminal and immoral acts, such as prostitution.[78] These complaints show a typical perception of street-food vendors and poor people in general as a nuisance and a threat. Even today, such statements are used as justification for the treatment of people doing business on the streets.[79]

In 1863, for example, an anonymous citizen complained about a *Quitandeira* who worked at the Largo do Rocio in front of a building and sought to have her banned from the site because her numerous customers disturbed the neighbourhood regularly between five and ten o'clock in the

Residence of Ten Years in that Country, from 1808 to 1818 (London, 1820)); or Charles Ribeyrolles (Charles Ribeyrolles, *Brasil pitoresco*, vol. 1 (Belo Horizonte-São Paulo, 1980)) were fascinated with how street vendors – especially women – were deeply enmeshed in the daily life of the streets.

75. *DRJ*, 14 December 1836.
76. *DRJ*, 7 December 1845 (Regulamento da Praça do Mercado, Art. 31, 33).
77. *JC*, 29 March 1878.
78. Cf. Acerbi, *Street Occupations*, p. 52.
79. See, for example, Jonathan Shapiro Anjaria, *The Slow Boil: Street Food, Rights and Public Space in Mumbai* (Stanford, CA, 2016), p. 16.

evening by blocking both the front door and the sidewalk.[80] The complaint shows that the vending stalls were also places where people met, shared news, and grouped together. The vendors were deeply enmeshed in the everyday occurrences on the streets of their neighbourhood. Slaves who managed to escape had often begun building their networks before they escaped. This was a common occurrence on the streets, for example, when some of them visited *Quitandeiras*. Apparently, masters knew about their contacts, friendships, and visits, as in the case of the slave Benedicto, who had been in contact with the community of Mina slaves for some time before his escape.[81] Against the background of the Age of the Atlantic Revolutions and several slave rebellions such as the Malê revolt in Bahia in 1835, meetings of slaves and former slaves at places in the city could cause fear among the city's authorities.[82]

Another much-cited complaint from 1776 shows that the struggle for urban space had a long history in Rio de Janeiro. In this case, the complaint nearly caused the expulsion of the *Quitandeiras* from their selling point in front of the town hall.[83] The presiding judge of the town council (a Portuguese judge directly appointed by the Portuguese crown) had decreed the closing of the *Quitandeiras*' stands due to the constant noise the selling produced. Some *Quitandeiras* appealed to the town council attorney against their expulsion from their selling point, since they had been providing the inhabitants of the place with foodstuffs for years and – in contrast to other vendors – had an official licence. Their complaint convinced the town council attorney to support their claim to stay; he agreed to represent them and, in the end, was responsible for repealing the new law. He drew attention to the fact that the numerous illegal vendors probably would not be banished by a decree. The law would have ended up punishing the wrong vendors without solving the original problem. This incident sheds light not only on street vendors' struggles, but also on the chances that their voices would be heard, if they united. For vendors, to group together offered them protection. As a result of the street vendors' mobility and knowledge of narrow streets and alleys, as well as of hiding places, city authorities found it difficult to monitor their enterprises. They were also unable to stop the *Quitandeiras* from engaging in other commercial activities on the side, which in some cases were more profitable than the act of selling food. An article in the *Diário do Rio de Janeiro* mentions that a *Quitandeira* who worked as a fortune teller in the Rua da Carioca and earned 5,000 réis per customer continued with this

80. *DRJ*, 16 December 1863.
81. *JC*, 5 February 1844; *JC*, 4 July 1844; *JC*, 11 October 1845.
82. On the fear of the "urban mob" in London, see Osterhammel, *Die Verwandlung der Welt*, p. 392; João José Reis, *Slave Rebellion in Brazil: The Muslim Upspring of 1835 in Bahia* (Baltimore, MD, 1993).
83. For this case, see Gomes and Soares, "Ocupações urbanas".

work although she had been asked to end it.[84] The street-selling women were a visible part of society, but certain activities had to happen out of sight of the authorities. Clandestine meetings happened in taverns, specialized in providing drinks, or in the *casas de angú*, "small establishments where slaves and freed persons converged to eat".[85] Some of these rooms also functioned as hiding places. The authorities recognized their strength, considered them a threat to their power, and attempted to control them by invading their establishments.[86] They became important places of social interaction and also a place to practice African-Brazilian religions, which stressed female knowledge of the rituals of cooking and healing.[87] In these religions, preparing ritual dishes fed the different eating preferences of the spirits in order for them to release their energy into the world, and it was traditionally a space for women.[88] Members of the community would meet up at night to share meals, celebrate religious events, make music, gamble, or have their fortune told.[89]

Numerous newspaper articles contain reports of robbery, poverty, or violence. The bodies of many women showed marks of slavery and violence, like the one of "a black woman [...], who had a scar of a stab wound on her face and sold *angú* at *the Praia do Peixe*".[90]

Furthermore, many articles focus on acts of violence among poor people.[91] A certain Luiz Gonçalves was arrested because he had stolen money from a *Quitandeira* who was selling fruits. In another case, two people attempted to kidnap the son of Quiteria, a *Quitandeira* at the Prainha, and sell him into slavery even though he was a free person. Rodrigues, a forty-two-year-old coach driver from the province of Maranhão and a fifty-year-old *Quitandeira*, Maria Nacisado Espirito Santo, were sentenced to ten and eight years respectively in prison because the first raped a thirteen-year-old

---

84. *DRJ*, 12 March 1857.
85. Soares, "Os Escravos de Ganho", p. 123; Reis and Mamigonian, "The Yoruba Diaspora in Brazil", p. 103.
86. Carlos Eugênio Líbano Soares, *A capoeira escrava e outras tradições rebeldes no Rio de Janeiro (1808–1850)* (Campinas, 2008), pp. 86, 109.
87. Elizabeth Pérez, *Religion in the Kitchen: Cooking, Talking, and the Making of Black Atlantic Traditions* (New York, 2016), p. 94; Kelly E. Hayes, "Serving the Spirits, Healing the Person: Women in Afro-Brazilian Religions", in Lillian Ashcraft-Eason, Darnise C. Martin, and Oyeronke Olademo (eds), *Women and New and Africana Religions* (Santa Barbara, CA, 2010), pp. 101–122, 101.
88. Pérez, *Religion in the Kitchen*, p. 2.
89. Soares, *A capoeira escrava*, pp. 109–110; Robert W. Slenes, "'*Malungu, ngoma* vem!': África coberta e descoberta do Brasil", *Revista USP*, 12 (1992), pp. 48–67.
90. *DRJ*, 17 November 1835. On marks of violence on slave bodies, see Marcus Rediker, *Gesetzlose des Atlantiks: Piraten und rebellische Seeleute in der frühen Neuzeit* (Vienna, 2017), pp. 35–36; Michael Zeuske, *Sklaverei. Eine Menschheitsgeschichte von der Steinzeit bis heute* (Ditzingen, 2018), pp. 32, 37.
91. *JC*, 16 October 1873 or 15 December 1843.

girl, Leopoldina Carolina, the granddaughter of Maria, who sold him Leopoldina's virginity.[92] Although sexual abuse and violence were part of the everyday life of enslaved and freed women in the Atlantic world, the newspaper article about this specific case highlighted it as being from the lowest and most immoral parts of society.[93] In many instances, the alleged moral profligacy of these people served as an explanation for the violence among them, a global phenomenon. The poor were described in a way that contributed to an intense fear of these parts of the society and led to their further dissociation.[94]

Some dangers on the street are connected to their being women. Women could benefit from relationships with wealthy men who supported them financially.[95] Many of these relationships were formed through coercion, and numerous enslaved women resorted to prostitution to earn money for their master. Freed women prostituted themselves as a result of poverty and lack of other opportunities. In small-scale disputes, women developed strategies to defend themselves against some attacks. Camille de Meirelles, for instance, accused a twenty-year-old *Quitandeira* Mina, a slave woman owned by João de Oliveira Lima, of hitting him across the face as an insult. He claimed that the event took place in a tavern. The court found her not guilty, after she was able to prove that her accuser had made up the story after she had rejected his advances.[96] The reaction of the accuser is hardly surprising when put against a backdrop of a society that privileged white men. With regard to the European colonies and particularly to the plantations in nineteenth-century America, Jürgen Martschukat and Olaf Stieglitz have adapted Gilles Deleuze and Félix Guattari's concept of the "desire machine" (*machine désirante*), where they emphasize that

> the colonial expansion, as machine of conquest, subjugation, and government, was also a "machine désirante", a desire machine [...]. The colonies and especially the slave plantations in the Americas of the nineteenth century appeared as places in which everything was possible for the colonizers and specifically for the masters. Sex was an instrument and a technique of violent subjugation of the "other".[97]

92. *JC*, 18 August 1842.
93. Mariana Candido, "Strategies for Social Mobility: Liaisons between Foreign Men and Slave Women in Benguela, ca. 1770-1850", in Gwyn Campbell and Elizabeth Elbourne (eds), *Sex, Power, and Slavery* (Athens, OH, 2014), pp. 272–288, 272.
94. Osterhammel, *Die Verwandlung der Welt*, p. 891.
95. Toussaint-Samson, *A Parisian in Brazil*, p. 45.
96. *DRJ*, 28 February 1855.
97. Jürgen Martschukat and Olaf Stieglitz (eds), *Race & Sex: Eine Geschichte der Neuzeit: 49 Schlüsseltexte aus vier Jahrhunderten neu gelesen* (Berlin, 2016), p. 16.

The personal cases described by the newspaper illuminate the social problems in a slave society where manumission was not unusual but the marginalized status was very difficult to escape.[98]

GENDER

Several examples clearly illustrate that slaves preferred to work on the streets, and even tried to convince their masters to send them there to work. For example, a reward announcement for the capture of the runaway slave Dionizia, published in the *Diário do Rio de Janeiro* in 1825, shows that this slave woman begged her master to let her work as a *Quitandeira* on the streets. Dionizia's master refused her plea, whereupon she fled the confines of the household and tried to survive on her own.[99] Working in the food sector allowed women to combine domestic with productive labour in a job that offered them and their families a certain food security. In contemporary newspapers, slaveholders advertised female slaves mostly as general domestics with the addition of being very skilled at selling goods.[100] Female slaves were employed for general household duties, but these could easily be combined with occasional, or part-time, street vending.[101] For families or people with only one or a few slaves, it could be economical to buy one slave to keep the house clean and additionally make some money on the streets.

The work of men was more valued in Brazil. As a consequence, female slaves were easier to acquire and especially interesting for less wealthy groups. Investments in slaves indicated socio-economic mobility and were the easiest form of wealth to acquire.[102] In the 1840s, *Quitandeiras* were worth on average 300,000 réis according to the *Jornal do Commercio*. Comparing the cost with the potential income generated in the vending sector, it is obvious that purchasing a healthy female slave could be extremely profitable. In most newspaper announcements, being characterized as "Mina" was a positive description used to drive the price up and quicken the sale. Only in very few cases were Mina slaves not preferred but seen as

---

98. Many women, especially Mina women, had the opportunity to accumulate sufficient money to buy their freedom, often through activities in the food sector. See Manolo Florentino, "Alforria e etnicidade no Rio de Janeiro oitocentista", *Topoí. Revista de História*, 3 (2002), pp. 9–40, 27–28. For further information on how the state used penal discipline as a way of controlling the urban poor, who remained in a marginalized state even as free workers, see Martine Jean's article on different forms of work in the construction of Rio de Janeiro's prison (*Casa de Correção*) in the present volume.

99. *DRJ*, 14 January 1825; Soares, "Os Escravos de Ganho", p. 116.

100. Women were described in that way in nearly all the 380 announcements published in the *Jornal do Commercio* in 1840–1849.

101. Frank, *Dutra's World*, pp. 47–48.

102. *Ibid.*, p. 43.

rebellious.[103] Foreign visitors who came to the city in the nineteenth century highlighted the Mina's proficiency in trade and distinguished the food-vending women from the ordinary mass of the slave population.[104] Their reputation as good vendors was not only earned on the basis of skills acquired in their regions of origin in Africa, it was part of a discourse about the Mina's superiority known throughout many parts of the Atlantic world.[105] Food preparation, cooking, and selling were traditionally female enterprises in West and Central Africa.[106] In Luanda, *Quitandeiras* also sold their products in ways similar to those adopted by the women in Rio de Janeiro, but they did not enjoy the same reputation as the Mina women.[107] Certain advertisements boasted that the slaves were capable of paying their master up to 640 réis per day.[108] According to the paper, the average payment to the owner was 496 réis a day, i.e. around 150,000 réis a year.[109] Based on this calculation it was possible for a *Quitandeira* to earn her selling price within two years. It can therefore be assumed that owners bought women to use them as *Quitandeiras* because male slaves would have been more expensive, and not necessarily more successful as street vendors, while women could also carry out other, even more profitable tasks. The most successful vendors would have started their businesses as slaves, and self-employed people earned enough money to buy their freedom, hire a stand at the market, and eventually invest in slaves.[110] *Quitandeiras* also occasionally advertised slaves in local newspapers. A Mina woman who sold *angú* across the Santo Antonio Street invested in slaves and resold a slave woman called Thereza to another owner.[111]

---

103. *JC*, 18 June 1848.

104. Luíz Agassiz and Elizabeth Cary Agassiz, *Viagem ao Brasil: 1865–1866* (Belo Horizonte, 1975), pp. 68–69.

105. Reis and Mamigonian, "The Yoruba Diaspora in Brazil", p. 100; Stephen D. Behrendt, "Ecology, Seasonality, and the Transatlantic Slave Trade", in Bernard Bailyn and Patricia L. Denault (eds), *Soundings in Atlantic History: Latent Structures and Intellectual Currents, 1500–1830* (Cambridge, 2009), pp. 44–85, 84; John Adams, *Remarks on the Country Extending from Cape Palmas to the River Congo* (London, 1823), pp. 217–218.

106. Felix K. Ekechi, "Gender and Economic Power: The Case of Igbo Market Women of Eastern Nigeria", in Besse House-Midamba and Felix K. Ekechi (eds), *African Market Women and Economic Power: The Role of Women in African Economic Development* (London, 1995), pp. 41–58, 41–43.

107. Vanessa S. Oliveira, "Gender, Foodstuff Production and Trade in Late-Eighteenth Century Luanda", *African Economic History*, 43 (2015), pp. 57–81, 59.

108. Admittedly, one should note that the potential profit might have been exaggerated in an advertisement in which the *Quitandeira* was being offered for sale.

109. Assuming twenty-five working days per month. It is reasonable to assume that the *Quitandeiras* worked no more than six days per week.

110. Ribeyrolles, *Brasil pitoresco*, p. 203. *DRJ*, 30 August 1841.

111. *DRJ*, 30 August 1841.

These women created female spaces throughout the city, integrated their slaves into their communities, and were sometimes even regarded as part of the family (fictive kinship).[112] As Farias has pointed out in her study on Mina market women in Rio de Janeiro, this form of kinship could lead to the emergence of strong networks between women and the passing on of wealth from woman to woman (*Casamento de mulheres*).[113] However, it would be wrong to assume that these women always acted in solidarity with each other. On the contrary, one woman tried to sell her slave through a newspaper announcement, adding that the slave woman was behaving in a rebellious way and would not follow the orders of a "black" woman.[114] Sometimes, even poor "white" women could be part of the female spaces formed by the street-vending women. In the *Jornal do Commercio* an old white woman was advertised as a domestic servant. At the time, she was living in one of the *Quitandeira's* houses, which illustrates contacts between white women and *Quitandeiras* that go beyond the "normal" hierarchy with white women at the top.[115]

Through its interconnection as a port city, Rio de Janeiro was strongly linked with other parts of the world. A European reader interested in contemporary literature might have heard of the *Quitandeira* even though he or she had never been to Brazil. Because street vendors were typical figures of the nineteenth-century city landscape, they also appeared in these forms of entertainment. Natasha Korda shows that in early modern London both forms of entertainment, the performance of women selling on the streets and professional theatre plays, competed with each other.[116] A great number – but not all – of these novels and plays could trace their origins to France, more specifically to Paris, and were published in Brazilian newspapers or played at the theatres in Rio de Janeiro.[117] The highly successful social novel *Les mystères de Paris*, written by Eugène Sue and originally

112. Farias, "Mercados Minas", pp. 201–202. On fictive kinship, see Michael Zeuske, *Handbuch Geschichte der Sklaverei. Eine Globalgeschichte von den Anfängen bis zur Gegenwart* (Berlin [etc.], 2013), pp. 154, 170.

113. See again Farias, "Mercados Minas", pp. 201–202.

114. *DRJ*, 16 April 1825; *DRJ*, 21 August 1825.

115. *DRJ*, 23 September 1825.

116. Natasha Korda, "Gender at Work in the Cries of London", in Mary Ellen Lamb and Karen Bamford (eds), *Oral Traditions and Gender in Early Modern Literary Texts* (Hampshire, 2008), pp. 117–135, 118.

117. Serialized novels published in the *Jornal do Commercio* include *Les mystères de Paris*, by Eugène Sue (1844); *Soeur Suzanne*, by Xavier de Montépin (1855); *O Castello dos Phantasmas*, by Xavier de Montépin (1856); *A sombrinha do Conego II*, by Joaquim José Teixeira (1850); *Os Ciganos de Regencia*, by Xavier de Montépin (1857); *A miséria de Londres*, by Charles Dickens (1868); *O vampire*, by Leão Gozlan (1862). Plays staged in Rio: "A vendedora de Perus" (1852); "A cigana de Paris", by Emilio Doux (1856–1857); "O Pelotiqueiro" (1861); "La Bouquetière" (1854); "A Tia Bazú" (1855); O último dia de Pompeia" (1867).

published in the French newspaper *Le Journal des débats* between June 1842 and October 1843, was a description of nineteenth-century Paris, showing the social problems and the living and working conditions of the poor parts of the city's population.[118] Female workers, such as prostitutes and street vendors, are also featured in this novel. It was translated into Portuguese and published in the *Jornal do Commercio* in 1844. The novel was highly successful in Rio, attracting the interest of Brazilian readers.[119] Despite male vendors also existing, the plays and stories gave female characters a prominent role and a much higher degree of fame. The popularity of street-life representation in plays, with their diverse characters, ensured that the character of the *Quitandeira* appeared in theatre pieces like *The Boy and the Quitandeira* and in serialized novels published in the newspaper written by Brazilian authors.[120] The fictitious figure of the *Quitandeira* was created through these novels and plays but also through travel accounts, poems, and songs written in this period.

In Europe, the demand for travel accounts with stories about far-off lands and exotic characters was high, and, because of this, published accounts had a large number of readers. Contemporary descriptions by foreign visitors highlighted the beauty and seductiveness of the slave women. The announcements in contemporary newspapers confirm this view. In some of these announcements the beauty of the slave women is highlighted and gives an idea of "the quotidian monstrosity of the desire to which she was subjected".[121] This exoticism is reminiscent of the image of the women of colour in other parts of the Atlantic world in the nineteenth century.[122]

Eduard Duller, a contemporary Austro-German author, became so familiar with the *Quitandeira* through travel accounts that in 1834 he wrote a short story, "The *Quitandeira* from Rio Janeiro", without ever having visited

---

118. Antonio Hohlfeldt, *Deus escreve direito por linhas tortas. O romance-folhetim dos jornais de Porto Alegre entre 1850 e 1900* (Porto Alegre, 2003), pp. 64–65.

119. *JC*, 28 December 1844.

120. "O moleque e a Quitandeira", by Manoel Joaquim Teixeira Cardoso (August 1848, June 1857). Jürgen Kocka and others have pointed out the importance of social novels as one kind of bourgeois perspective on the "working class". According to Kocka, even before a working class emerged in the historical reality of nineteenth-century Germany, it existed in the imaginations of many citizens and in public discourse. See Jürgen Kocka, *Arbeiterleben und Arbeiterkultur. Die Entstehung einer sozialen Klasse* (Bonn, 2015), p. 343.

121. In twenty-seven of 380 announcements published in the *Jornal do Commercio* in 1840–1849, the beauty of the women is described with attributes such as "eye-catching", "beautiful", or "fine-figured". Lisa Ze Winters, *The Mulatta Concubine: Terror, Intimacy, Freedom and Desire in the Black Transatlantic* (Athens, GA, 2016), p. 6.

122. Dominique Rogers and Stewart King, "Housekeepers, Merchants, Rentières: Free Women of Color in the Port Cities of Colonial Saint-Domingue, 1750–1790", in Douglass Catterall and Jodi Campbell (eds), *Women in Port: Gendering Communities, Economies, and Social Networks in Atlantic Port Cities, 1500–1800* (Leiden, 2012), pp. 357–398, 395.

Brazil.[123] The main character, a *Quitandeira*, is defined by the love she has for a certain slave.[124] This love can never be, because the slave has already been promised to someone else in his home country. During his attempt to escape slavery and return to Africa, he trusts his former king, the father of his fiancée, to help him and ignores the advice of the *Quitandeira* not to trust the king. After the *Quitandeira* recognizes that the man she loves cannot be convinced of the king's false intentions, she accepts the advances of a rich white man. In this passage from the story, the power white men hold over the *Quitandeira* is clearly evident.[125] In the end, she saves the slave from slavery and drowns herself in the ocean. In the story, bourgeois virtues such as self-sacrifice, fidelity, and chastity are discussed.[126] The storyline is similar to that of the widely read novel *The Last Days of Pompeii*, also published in 1834 by Edward Bulwer-Lytton.[127] A female enslaved flower vendor plays a key role in the story. Even though she is blind, she leads her would-be lover and his lover through the streets of the city to the harbour where they escape before the volcano erupts, while thousands are killed. Because her would-be lover never loved her, Nydia the flower girl drowns herself just like the *Quitandeira*. This story presents Nydia not as a passive slave, but as a capable actor who, in spite of her blindness, knows the streets of the city better than anyone else. A sculpture of Nydia was made in 1859 and became very popular during the nineteenth century.[128] Since it is highly probable that Duller knew Bulwer-Lytton's novel, it does not seem far-fetched to assume that he constructed the character of the *Quitandeira* in allusion to Nydia and presents the Brazilian woman not as a helpless slave but as a capable actor.

Furthermore, during the World Exhibition in Vienna in 1857 the Brazilian commission decided to integrate the picture *Fruchtverkäuferin in Rio de Janeiro* into their exhibition (Figure 4).[129] The picture was taken by a well-known German photographer, Alberto Henschel, in his studio in Rio de

123. Eduard Duller, "Die Quitandeira von Rio Janeiro", in Eduard Duller (ed.), *Erzählungen und Phantasiestücke. Erster Band* (Frankfurt am Main, 1834), pp. 325–348.
124. On this literary motif, cf. B. Riesche, "Schöne Mohrinnen, edle Sklaven, schwarze Rächer. Schwarzendarstellung und Sklavereithematik im deutschen Unterhaltungstheater (1770–1814)" (Ph.D., Ludwig-Maximilians-Universität Munich, 2007), p. 141.
125. Duller, "Die Quitandeira von Rio Janeiro", p. 336.
126. Riesche, "Schwarzendarstellung und Sklavereithematik", p. 137.
127. Edward Bulwer-Lytton, *The Last Days of Pompeii* (London, 1834).
128. Available at: https://www.metmuseum.org/art/online-features/viewpoints/nydia; last accessed 20 January 2018.
129. See Sven Schuster and Alejandra Buenaventura, "Entre *blanqueamiento y paraíso racial*. El Imperio de Brasil y la legitimación visual de la esclavitud en las exposiciones universales", in Sven Schuster and Óscar Daniel Hernández (eds), *Imaginando América Latina. Historia y cultura visual, siglos XIX–XXI* (Bogota, 2017), pp. 59–91, here p. 82; Sven Schuster, *Die Inszenierung der Nation: Das Kaiserreich Brasilien im Zeitalter der Weltausstellungen* (Frankfurt, 2015).

Figure 4. Alberto Henschel, *Fruchtverkäuferin in Rio de Janeiro* [Fruit seller in Rio de Janeiro], c.1869. *Leibniz-Institut für Länderkunde, Leipzig (Germany).*

Janeiro. In the picture, a saleswoman, dressed in a clean white dress and a turban, smokes a pipe while she is sitting in front of her stall, which is decorated with exotic fruits. The background is that of a tropical landscape. Altogether, fruits, dress, stall, and background were designed to evoke "feelings of exotic authenticity and mysterious foreignness" among the visitors to the World

Exhibition.[130] In a companion volume to the World Exhibition, it was stated that, as a sign of progress, slavery in Brazil would soon be gone without rebellions or damage to the private property of the slave owners since the "release of slaves was common", which "confirmed the mild mind and the philanthropy of the Brazilian people".[131] As highly visible workers, the *Quitandeiras* would be a clear sign of this progress for visitors. Of course, her clean and perfect dress, as well as the absence of visual signs of violence or hunger, romanticized her life and work on the streets.[132]

Beginning in the 1880s, the women who were actually working as *Quitandeiras* on the streets were increasingly driven off the streets of Rio de Janeiro.[133] Paradoxically, the end of slavery also meant the end of the relatively autonomous branch of the economy in which these women had previously been able to work and live.

The *Quitandeiras* displayed a high degree of visibility during a period in which female vendors attained a public profile not only in Brazil but also abroad. This connects them to other poor working women in the urban milieus of nineteenth-century cities. As we can see from the serialized novels and theatre plays that appeared in Paris, London, Rio de Janeiro, and elsewhere, the figure of the female street vendor had entered popular culture. However ambivalent in their portrayal, and despite the sexual and exotic connotations that are frequent features of these stories, some of them also give their female characters a considerable degree of agency and power.

CONCLUSION

Research on street food has increased dramatically in recent years, with several case studies from different historical periods and cities around the world. These studies highlight street food as a typical source of income for women in urban areas. In the port city of Rio de Janeiro, many women of colour worked in a wide range of activities linked to the food sector in which free and different forms of unfree labour co-existed. These women created a niche of economic opportunity in a place dominated by men. The local

---

130. Nele Beck, "The Breathing Archive: Social Dynamics of Photographic Archives", available at: http://kjc-sv016.kjc.uni-heidelberg.de:8080/exist/apps/wiki/photocultures/beck/TheBreathingArchive; last accessed 3 July 2018.
131. Cf. Schuster and Buenaventura, "El Imperio de Brasil", here p. 82.
132. *Ibid.*
133. Henrique Espada Lima and Fabiane Popinigis, "Maids, Clerks, and the Shifting Landscape of Labor Relations in Rio de Janeiro, 1830s–1880s", *International Review of Social History*, 62: S25 (2017), pp. 45–73, especially p. 70. As the authors show, many of the *Quitandeiras* disappeared from the streets and began to work in private households because of growing competition in the street-food sector – the result of increasing immigration from Europe to Brazil in the late nineteenth century.

food markets were economically significant and inextricably linked to Rio de Janeiro's role in the late transatlantic slave trade. Despite their economic importance, they aided the development of urban cultures in Rio de Janeiro, which have to be seen in an Atlantic context. Street food not only helped to preserve the eating habits of the diaspora, it also gave rise to a consumer culture for the working class. Despite their different statuses, workers met up at taverns, *casas de angú*, or at meeting points on the streets to socialize.

Street vendors worked under conditions that were always hard, often dangerous, and financially precarious. To walk through the streets of the city for the whole day carrying a tray with several bottles of liquor, a large basket of fruits, and live chickens, for instance, was extremely exhausting; such work reflected absolute necessity rather than choice. The vendors engaged in different forms of protest and sometimes supported each other in order to find ways out of their marginalized status. Some of these struggles received public attention. Others were part of the everyday activities of the women and happened in the shadows of the port city. Despite all their efforts, the city's authorities were unable to prevent the selling of food on the street, since their intentions were undermined at a local level. The co-existence of different labour forms produced a very flexible labour market in Rio de Janeiro and resembles the "width of the forms of labour and exploitation in capitalism" in general.[134] Rather than banding together in a mutual struggle against these forces, women working in the food sector also fought against one another, in a competition for survival. Some women were themselves slaveholders.[135]

The *Quitandeiras* were highly visible and therefore defined the widespread image of the city. Their reputation extended to distant parts of the world due to the fact that Rio de Janeiro was a globally connected port city. This article has demonstrated that the *Quitandeiras* can be seen as part of a larger heterogeneous group of street working women who, in many parts of the world, gained visibility and recognition on the streets of growing cities and in popular culture in the first half of the nineteenth century.

134. Andrea Komlosy, "Arbeit und Werttransfer im Kapitalismus: Vielfalt der Erscheinungsformen und Operationalisierung", *Sozial. Geschichte Online*, 9 (2012), pp. 36–62, here p. 47.
135. Farias, "Mercados Minas".

IRSH 64 (2019), pp. 255–262 doi:10.1017/S0020859019000142

Afterword: Reflections on the Motley Crew as Port City Proletariat

MARCUS REDIKER

Department of History, University of Pittsburgh
3508 Posvar Hall, Pittsburgh, PA 15260, USA

E-mail: red1@pitt.edu

ABSTRACT: This essay reflects on the workers in Atlantic and Indian Ocean port cities who made possible the rapidly expanding system of global capitalism between 1650 and 1850. In all of the ports treated in this volume, a mixture of multi-ethnic, male and female, unskilled, often unwaged laborers collectively served as the linchpins that connected local hinterlands (and seas) to bustling waterfronts, tall ships, and finally the world market. Although the precise combination of workers varied from one port to the next, all had an occupational structure in which half or more of the population worked in trade or the defense of trade, for example in shipbuilding/repair, the hauling of commodities to and from ships, and the building of colonial infrastructure, the docks and roads instrumental to commerce. This "motley crew" – a working combination of enslaved Africans, European/Indian/Chinese indentured servants, sailors, soldiers, convicts, domestic workers, and artisans – were essential to the production and worldwide circulation of commodities and profits.

"They were a wild company; men of many climes – not at all precise in their toilet arrangements, but picturesque in their very tatters." So wrote Herman Melville in his novel *Omoo: A Narrative of Adventures in the South Seas* (1847) about the dirty, ragged, motley mutineers of the whale ship *Julia* as they were summoned to face a stern English consul in Tahiti. The sixteen sailors were indeed from "many climes": the names affixed on their round robin, the seamen's traditional instrument of protest, included "Black Dan", Antone the Portuguese, Wymootoo the Marquesan islander, Van the Finn, Pat the Irishman, and "Beauty", the ugly Englishman. Thirteen of them could not sign their names, each scrawling an "X" instead on the round robin. These workers of the world came together in a steadfast refusal to labor for their incompetent, contract-breaking captain.[1]

---

1. Herman Melville, *Omoo: A Narrative of Adventures in the South Seas*. Ed. by Harrison Hayford, Hershel Parker, and G. Thomas Tanselle (Evanston and Chicago, IL, 1968 [1847]), p. 78.

Neither the mutiny, nor the men were entirely fictional. Melville based the story in his novel on a defiant uprising that had actually taken place aboard the Australian whaler *Lucy Ann* in 1842. The writer knew whereof he spoke because he had participated in the mutiny. Like the literate narrator in *Omoo*, he may have drawn up a round robin. Melville the sailor also knew intimately the kind of men he wrote about: the motley crews that manned the ships and labored in port cities around the terraqueous globe, providing the labor that made possible a dynamic, throbbing, increasingly powerful system of global capitalism. Writing at the end of the period under study in this book, as steam ships brought the age of sail to an end, Melville penned what were probably the greatest portraits of the motley crew the world has ever known. He described precisely and vividly the social subject – and social force – at the heart of this volume.[2]

The mixture of peoples on board Melville's ship existed, on a larger scale, in port cities. Indeed, his shipmates had joined the whaler from places like New Bedford, Valparaíso, Honolulu, and Sydney. Brought together by global maritime capital and organized by their captain to labor in cooperative (and profitable) ways aboard the vessel, these workers had transformed their cooperation into something new, dangerous, and of their own choosing: they transcended their multi-ethnic origins, trusted each other, and developed a new kind of political cooperation as a band of mutineers. The workers' collective bonding and militant action bespoke a new kind of community based on class, on ship and ashore.

The essays in this volume treat motley crews in a far-flung collection of colonial and postcolonial port cities. In the Atlantic they range from Cape Town to Havana, Paramaribo, and Rio de Janeiro, while in the Indian Ocean they include Batavia, Hugli/Calcutta, and Manila. These ports had different origins, geographies, and chronologies, yet they rapidly developed common characteristics. All served as linchpins that connected local hinterlands (and seas) to the growing capitalist world market; all were essential to the production and worldwide circulation of commodities. Although the types and combination of workers varied from one city to the next, all had an occupational structure in which perhaps half or more of the population worked in trade or the defense of trade, for example in shipbuilding/repair, the hauling of commodities to and from ships, and the building of colonial infrastructure, the docks and roads instrumental to commerce.

---

2. Melville worked at sea, on merchant, whaling, and naval ships, from 1839 to 1844. On the mutiny of the *Lucy Ann*, see Wilson Hefflin, *Herman Melville's Whaling Years*. Ed. by Mary K. Bercaw Edwards and Thomas Farel Heffernan (Nashville, TN, 2004), ch. 17. The notion of the "motley crew" as a social subject and concept appeared in Peter Linebaugh and Marcus Rediker, *The Many-Headed Hydra: Sailors, Slaves, Commoners, and the Hidden History of the Revolutionary Atlantic* (Boston, MA, 2000).

Crucially, all had at their core a motley proletariat, composed of different kinds of workers of international origins.

This is not the working class we are accustomed to seeing in the pages of labor history books. Here, we have not white, male, skilled, waged, national industrial workers, but rather a mix of multi-ethnic, male and female, skilled and unskilled, waged and unwaged laborers who did not always produce commodities but definitely produced value and made possible the accumulation of capital on a global scale. The authors of the essays add breadth, depth, and texture to the portrait of this understudied group of worldwide workers. Matthias van Rossum finds that the "amphibious monster", the Dutch East India Company, mobilized 57,000 workers in the middle of the eighteenth century; they were European, south Asian, and east Asian contract and casual laborers, sailors, soldiers, dockworkers, slaves, *corvée* workers, and artisans. Kevin Dawson shows how highly skilled deep-sea divers came from West Africa to plumb the deep blue waters of the Caribbean. Titas Chakraborty discovers that the domestic workers in the settlements of the Dutch East India Company and the English East India Company in Hugli/Calcutta originated in global trade networks: they were Portuguese and Asian, from Indonesia, Ceylon, and various places in India. Pepijn Brandon explains how the Dutch rulers of Paramaribo in Suriname used racialization to divide and control the mobile African slaves and multinational sailors and soldiers who did the city's essential work. Some of the "British" soldiers who invaded and occupied Manila in 1762 were actually British, but many more, writes Megan C. Thomas, were Indian "sepoys", Indo-Portuguese "Topasses", African "Coffreys", Chinese "coolies", and French deserters. According to Evelyn P. Jennings, the road builders in and around the port city of Havana consisted of enslaved Africans, vagrants, recaptured runaways, indentured servants from three continents (Europe, North America, and Asia), as well as *irlandeses*, *yucatecos*, and *isleños* – contract workers from, respectively, Ireland, Mexico, and the Canary Islands off the coast of West Africa. Martine Jean describes the workers who built Rio de Janeiro's modern prison, the Casa de Correção: they were "a cosmopolitan working class that included African slaves, free people of color, and sailors of multinational origins, foreign immigrants, soldiers, and skilled artisans". Clare Anderson depicts the workers in the "carceral circuits" of the Indian Ocean, the slaves, convicts, lascars, migrants, and local laborers who cleared land and built roads, docks, harbors, and lighthouses. Melina Teubner draws a rich portrait of Rio's free and unfree multi-ethnic, mostly West African *quitandeiras*, who hollered, sang, and sold *angú* to hungry sailors, slaves, and other mobile workers within the city's proletarian micro-economy. These essays help to create a new, broader, more inclusive, more democratic labor history.

Gary B. Nash taught us long ago that colonial cities have been crucibles of class formation and dynamic sites for the development of capitalism. The two went hand in bloody hand as the rulers of Europe organized and disciplined workers to produce and transport commodities for the world market. Port cities were dynamic centers of "articulation" where producers in colonial hinterlands (slaves and farmers, for example) were linked to laborers in the port (porters and dockers), who were, in turn, connected to workers aboard ships and, after the voyage, to other port city workers and finally to consumers, in the metropoles, other parts of the empire, and beyond. Ports thus always faced two directions, inward toward productive hinterlands and outward toward the world market. Global capitalism, itself an "amphibious monster", was a differentiated set of subsystems articulated into new and highly profitable regimes of labor and accumulation.[3]

Port cities were defined by movement, just like the ever-churning seas that bordered them. People, ships, commodities, and ideas – all moved to the rhythmic labor of the motley crew. When tall ships sailed into port and docked, many "hands" rushed to the vessel to disgorge their precious global cargoes, then after a time many more refilled them with valuable local commodities before they set sail again. The work of the motley crew was shaped by both a colonial context of labor scarcity and the seasonal nature of labor, which was based on the timing of annual production in the hinterland (sugar, coffee, spices) and the synchronized arrival and departure of ships. Merchants, manufacturers, and military officers who organized port city workers needed huge quantities of labor power at certain times of the year and at the same time required flexibility in its usage because of seasonality, disruptions caused by nature, and the unpredictable ups and downs of global business and political cycles. They also required an extensive division of labor, from the artisanal labor required to repair ships to the mass labor needed to move heavy hogsheads to and from ships. Moreover, many if not most port city workers had to be mobile in order to link, for example, plantation to port. The port city itself, as a social formation, was something of a social factory that required careful coordination of many kinds of work, productive and reproductive. Because the slave trade out of Africa flowed into both the Atlantic and Indian Oceans, enslaved Africans could be found in practically all oceanic port cities between 1700 and 1850. They were joined by sailors, soldiers, indentured servants, convicts, domestic workers, *corvée* workers, and artisans. Rulers used the port cities as laboratories in which they experimented with various types and combinations of labor. As several of our essayists suggest, the flow of ruling-class experience in organizing labor systems is a critical theme in transoceanic history.

Controlling a mobile, many-headed urban proletariat was no easy matter. Port city ruling classes used the law as their greatest instrument of

---

3. Gary B. Nash, *The Urban Crucible: Social Change, Political Consciousness, and the Origins of the American Revolution* (Cambridge, MA, 1979).

disciplinary power, creating police powers and prescribing for urban "crimes" a range of violent punishments from whippings to incarceration to execution. Many port city governments criminalized unauthorized cooperation among members of the motley crew, creating differential punishments for white workers and those of color who ran away together. Only Brandon makes racialization a major theme in his essay, but the efforts by authorities both to create and manipulate social divisions were more or less universal across the port cities of the globe.

Cities by the sea were full of transient people, most of whom came to work, some willingly, some not. Many were fugitives, strangers, people trying to escape something or find something, like money. Almost all of them had a profound oceanic experience behind them, which could be a source of shared identity. As Steve Higginson and Tony Wailey wrote in their book *Edgy Cities*, the very word "port" derives from the Latin *portus*, which in ancient Rome had the dual meaning of harbor and haven. The port was a place of commerce based on the arrival and departure of ships, but it was potentially a place of freedom compared to the slavery and serfdom of the countryside. Cities by the sea have been "places of comers and goers, dodgers and drifters, grafters and grifters and anyone who prefers the cool welcoming fugitive night".[4]

The class structures of port cities reflected concentrated political, economic, and social power. Rulers were usually a combination of imperial and business authorities, the former representing the state, the latter the wealthiest men of the colony's leading enterprises – the lords of commercial agriculture, trade, and manufacture. Imperial representatives and local leaders of the economy never had identical interests, and rifts frequently emerged, making governance of those down below even more challenging. The middling classes of the port city consisted of professionals – lawyers, doctors, ministers – as well as master craftsmen, for example shipbuilders. These groups usually allied with the business elite as their economic fortunes depended on them. The social power of the port city lay in its workers of many skills, ethnic backgrounds, and relationships to authority. Although the specific economic activities of each port varied by place, climate, and commodities produced, most ports had roughly similar social compositions and class relations. Indeed, the port cities of the world often had more in common with each other than they did with their own national hinterlands – a distinctive sense of time shaped by the tides and the seasonal nature of work, which, in turn, made the imposition of discipline from above more difficult than it was in landed society. Shifting shorelines, from Naples to New Orleans to New York, produced what Higginson and Wailey call "edgy cities and 'edgy' people". The peoples of port cities

---

4. Steve Higginson and Tony Wailey, *Edgy Cities* (Liverpool, 2006).

"understand, better than most, change, flux and unpredictability" as these were central to their lives.[5]

Rulers implanted heavy architecture in port cities as bulwarks against the flux – and against their enemies, both imperial and indigenous. Many settlements featured massive, hulking European fortresses, and, of course, the motley crew had been the ones to set the stones. Havana had three: Castillo de la Real Fuerza (1555–1567), Castillo de los Tres Reyes del Morro (1589–1630), and Castillo de San Carlos de la Cabaña (1763–1774). Cape Town featured the Kasteel de Goede Hoop, while Paramaribo rested behind Fort Zeelandia, both built by global Dutch traders in the late seventeenth century. Other physical manifestations of European maritime power dotted seascapes from West Africa to South Asia. The very architecture of port cities reflected their origins in trade, war, colonialism, and capitalism.

Historically, the motley crew is, by definition, a work group above all else – a diverse assemblage of mobile workers who occupied a strategic position in the port city and indeed in larger regional, transoceanic, and world economies. It is an informal gang with a job to do; it is task-oriented and temporary in its existence. A crew might, for example, unload a ship or build a wharf, after which it would be disbanded. Enmeshed in a wider set of work groups, its collective power animated the entire port city economy. As the atom of class organization, the motley crew might also combine with other groups in resistance, in mob actions, strikes, or collective escapes from exploitation. The heterogeneous motley crew unified itself through the accomplishment of its tasks – in other words, through common cooperative work.

Port cities have long been female-centered. Because many men disappeared from port for long periods of time to work at sea, women played independent roles they might not have been permitted in other locations within the same colony or empire. Women worked as sellers of food on the waterfront; they worked in brothels; they cooked, washed clothes, and cleaned houses; they scavenged; they nursed and minded children. Independent economic activity was a must for the sake of survival. Just as sailors were said to have "a wife in every port", women might have multiple husbands who arrived in port at different times of the year. Because seafaring was dangerous and often resulted in premature death, port cities also had a larger than usual share of widows and female-headed households. As Titas Chakraborty makes clear, social and biological reproduction in port cities depended on unusual family formations – relationships that would often be denounced as sinful by middle-class moralizers and reformers.

---

5. *Ibid.* On the structure of port cities, see Jacob Price, "Economic Function and the Growth of American Port Towns in the Eighteenth Century", *Perspectives in American History*, 8 (1974), pp. 121–186; and Franklin W. Knight and Peggy K. Liss (eds), *Atlantic Port Cities: Economy, Culture, and Society in the Atlantic World, 1650–1850* (Knoxville, TN, 1991).

The motley crew was cosmopolitan and sophisticated. What Herman Melville said about sailors in the middle of the nineteenth century was to a large extent true of port city dwellers most anytime in the age of sail:

> No custom is strange; no creed is absurd; no foe, but who will in the end prove a friend. [...] Long companionship with seamen of all tribes: Manilla-men, Anglo-Saxons, Cholos, Lascars, and Danes, wear away in good time all mother-tongue stammerings. You sink your clan; down goes your nation; you speak a world's language, jovially jabbering in the Lingua-Franca of the forecastle.

Port workers not only had the experience of the world within them, they lived in a place where news of the world arrived with each and every ship.[6]

The motley crew had its own "proletarian public sphere" – the lower decks of the ships, the docks, the streets, and workplaces where people from various continents came together to spin their yarns and share their experience. Information circulated through these "cultural contact zones", about the pilfered goods of the shadow economy or the prospects of stowing away on a soon-to-depart vessel. During the 1790s, as Julius Scott has shown, the knowledge whispered on the "common wind" among Caribbean sailors, runaways, and market women concerned the abolition movement in Great Britain and revolution in France and Saint Domingue. Raucous waterfront taverns were an especially important setting for the motley crew: drink, music, dance, and sedition were born of desperation and extreme cultural variety. Ties of kinship – some real, some fictive – grew from such merry-making. Workers of all kinds called each other brother and sister, fostering the development of what Clare Anderson calls "transregional political solidarities".[7]

Because the motley crew was an important component of a larger global proletariat, it shared many of the characteristics Peter Linebaugh and I identified for the Atlantic portion of the class in *The Many-Headed Hydra: Sailors, Slaves, Commoners, and the Hidden History of the Revolutionary Atlantic*. The motley crew was *anonymous, nameless*. The port cities required the labor of millions of people to operate, but only a few of their names are now known to us: for example, the African deep-sea diver George Blacke and the runaway domestic worker Hanna of Calcutta. It was *expropriated*,

---

6. Herman Melville, *Mardi and A Voyage Thither*. Ed. by Harrison Hayford, Hershel Parker, and G. Thomas Tanselle (Evanston and Chicago, IL, 1970 [1849]), p. 13. On the cultural sophistication of early African workers, see Ira Berlin, "From Creole to African: Atlantic Creoles and the Origins of African-American Society in Mainland North America", *William and Mary Quarterly*, 53:2 (1996), pp. 251–288.

7. Julius S. Scott, *The Common Wind: Afro-American Currents in the Age of the Haitian Revolution* (London, 2018); Oskar Negt and Alexander Kluge, *Public Sphere and Experience: Analysis of the Bourgeois and Proletarian Public Sphere* (Minneapolis, MN, 1993); Marcus Rediker, *Outlaws of the Atlantic: Sailors, Pirates, and Motley Crews in the Age of Sail* (Boston, MA, 2015), ch. 1. The quotation by Anderson appears in her essay in this volume.

landless, and poor. Born in Africa, the Americas, or Asia, most members of the motley crew had lost their connection to the commons (although some, as maroons, reclaimed it). It was *terrorized, subject to coercion.* The redeployment of workers around the global empires required massive amounts of violence in the slave trades and the harsh disciplinary regimes that governed the lives of dispossessed workers. It was *mobile, transoceanic, planetary.* Global commodity chains required mobile workers. It was *cooperative and laboring.* Its power was based in its collective work. It was *motley,* often dressed in the "very tatters" Herman Melville noted and multi-ethnic in appearance. It was *vulgar.* On ship and shore the motley crew spoke in new ways in order to communicate – in pidgin and Creole languages, gestures and pantomime, story and song. It was *self-active, creative.* It resisted by flight and fight: the multi-ethnic enslaved Africans ran to the Suriname bush where they joined the Upper Saramacca maroons throughout the eighteenth century, and convicts aboard the steam ship *Tenasserim* rose up in mutiny at the docks of Mapoon in Moulmein (now Mawlamyine) in Burma (Myanmar) in 1851.[8]

Let us conclude with Herman Melville, sailor and fabled chronicler of the motley crew, who wrote in *Moby Dick*:

> If, then, to meanest mariners, and renegades and castaways, I shall hereafter ascribe high qualities, though dark; weave round them tragic graces; if even the most mournful, perchance the most abased, among them all, shall at times lift himself to the exalted mounts; if I shall touch that workman's arm with some ethereal light; if I shall spread a rainbow over his disastrous set of sun; then against all mortal critics bear me out in it, thou Just Spirit of Equality, which hast spread one royal mantle of humanity over all my kind!

The "meanest", most impoverished men and women, mournful and degraded by a violent system of global capitalism, survived and through the strength of their "tragic graces" helped to build not only the port cities but the entire modern world. They worked and resisted in many-sided, creative ways, fighting for their own autonomy and freedom against the subjection that was meant to be their fate. By raising the motley crew to the level of a knowing, acting, collective world historical subject, this collection of essays joins Melville in casting "ethereal light" on the history of common humanity.[9]

8. Linebaugh and Rediker, *The Many-Headed Hydra*, pp. 332–333.
9. Herman Melville, *Moby Dick, or The Whale.* Ed. by Harrison Hayford, Hershel Parker, and G. Thomas Tanselle (Evanston and Chicago, IL, 1988 [1851]), p. 117.